Elements of Probability and Statistics

McGRAW-HILL SERIES IN PROBABILITY AND STATISTICS

DAVID BLACKWELL, *Consulting Editor*

Elements of
Probability and Statistics

Frank L. Wolf

Associate Professor of Mathematics
Carleton College

1962

McGraw-Hill Book Company, Inc.

New York   San Francisco   Toronto   London

ELEMENTS OF PROBABILITY AND STATISTICS

THE MAPLE PRESS COMPANY, YORK, PA.

To my mother and father

Preface

This text was written for use in an introductory course in probability and statistics which presupposes only high school algebra. Such a course might be part of a mathematics sequence for general education, a basic one-semester statistics course for students in the social or physical sciences (perhaps to be followed by another semester of statistics applied to the student's particular field of interest), or a course in probability and statistics for students preparing to teach mathematics or science at the high school level. The first eight chapters cover essentially the same material as does the experimental probability text prepared by the Commission on Mathematics of the College Entrance Examination Board for a course recommended for the last year of high school.

The text is meant to be flexible enough to be suitable for students with various mathematical backgrounds. In a one-semester course in which the students have the minimum background, considerable time should be spent on the first three chapters, and several of the later chapters will have to be omitted. For a class with a stronger background, the first three chapters can be covered quickly and most of the later chapters taken up in the course of a semester. The text could also be used in a one-year course for students with no previous college mathematics, in which case the teacher will probably wish to supplement the material in the text. Some supplementary topics with references are suggested at the end of this introductory material.

The text emphasizes the logical structure of the subject and often follows the mathematical form of definition, theorem, proof. Many proofs are given in detail. It is the author's belief that the mathematical approach makes for easier and deeper understanding. Logical interconnections are emphasized so that the subject matter does not become simply a bag of disconnected tricks to be memorized by the student. However, it is not a primary purpose of the book to develop in the student the ability to create proofs. A proof is omitted whenever it requires mathematics above the assumed level or when it is so "messy" that it contributes little to the understanding of the results involved. Never-

vii

theless, some attempt is made to keep the number of "it-can-be-shown's" to a minimum, and several "messy" proofs are outlined in problems.

The elementary notions of set algebra are introduced early and used throughout subsequent presentations. A probability distribution is introduced as a mathematical model for an experimental situation, and the general notion of a mathematical model is discussed. Probability for discrete variables is thoroughly treated before statistical inference and continuous variables are considered. When continuous variables are considered, much use is made of (pictures of) "spinners" which generate the various continuous distributions. The notation of the definite integral is introduced and utilized. Many of the exercises make use of data to be collected by or in the class, rather than data from hypothetical situations.

Problems and sections with numbers preceded by asterisks are especially difficult or deal with a topic which is not in the main stream of the material covered in the text. Problems which require a knowledge of logarithms are also starred. The sequence of starred problems 3-6, 3-69, 3-70, and 7-87 through 7-92 constitutes a brief introduction to some of the notions of the mathematical theory of games.

I wish to express my thanks to David Blackwell and Kenneth O. May for their suggestions and encouragement while this book was being written. Thanks are also due to my elementary statistics classes at Carleton College, who used much of this material in preliminary form. The suggestions and reactions of these classes were very helpful to me in making final revisions. My thanks also to Judy Roth and Mrs. Julia Rubalcava, who did such excellent jobs of typing various stages of the manuscript.

I am indebted to Professor Sir Ronald A. Fisher, F.R.S., Cambridge, and to Oliver & Boyd, Ltd., Edinburgh, for permission to reprint Tables A-6 and A-8 in the appendix from their book *Statistical Methods for Research Workers*. I also wish to express my appreciation to W. J. Dixon, F. J. Massey, C. J. Clopper, E. S. Pearson, A. M. Mood, G. P. Wadsworth, and J. G. Bryan for the use of their tables.

Finally, I wish to express my appreciation to my wife for her patience, assistance, and encouragement while this book was being written.

Frank L. Wolf

To the Student

This book will introduce you to some of the basic ideas and results in probability and statistics. These ideas and results are involved in an amazing variety of scientific and practical endeavors. They appear in discussions about the clustering of galaxies in the universe and in discussions about the nature of the fundamental building blocks of matter, such as electrons. They are indispensable tools in attempts to predict the outcomes of national elections and in the study of individual behavior in situations of conflict. They have been used in planning advertising campaigns and in determining the effectiveness of certain medical treatments. They are very much a part of modern methods for estimating the age of the earth and for testing new agricultural methods. They are used in checking on the reliability of census data and in designing atomic reactors. They have been applied by businessmen in controlling the quality of industrial production and by scholars in attempts to settle disputes over the authorship of certain historical documents. They have been important aids in the construction of theories concerning genetics and in attempts to predict academic success at college.

Such a list could be continued for many pages, but the above perhaps succeeds in indicating the wide applicability of the notions of probability and statistics. The study of these notions will help you to read with understanding about such fields as those mentioned and, it is hoped, will equip you with concepts and techniques that you will find useful in scholarly and practical endeavors of your own.

As is the case with most mathematics books, this book should be read not only with the eyes but with a pencil. That is, a pencil and plenty of paper should be close at hand to use in checking details, making up examples and counterexamples, and jotting down questions to be brought up with your fellow students or instructor in class or out of it.

Be skeptical as you read. Important attributes of the mathematical sciences are the force and clarity of their arguments. Perhaps in no other field is it fair to be so demanding in getting clear and convincing answers to your questions as in mathematics. You can (and, indeed, should) insist on a rather thorough understanding of a topic before proceeding to new ideas. But such understanding is not something another person can hand you in some kind of neat package. It develops through careful reading, rereading, questioning of yourself and others, investigation of how new concepts are related to old, and the working of problems.

You should probably accumulate the problems you have worked in a loose-leaf notebook, since many of the exercises from different sections are interdependent.

Each important result, equation, and problem in the text is identified by a pair of numbers separated by a hyphen. The first number indicates the chapter in which the item occurs. The second shows its sequential position in that chapter. The numbers for important results and equations are enclosed in parentheses, while problem numbers are not so enclosed. Illustrations and tables are numbered similarly.

The appendix contains tables which you will find to be helpful. These tables are numbered in a separate sequence. Thus, Table A-5 is the fifth table in the appendix.

Contrary to what you might expect in view of common practice, it is not necessary in taking a mathematics course to restrict your reading to the textbook. Several helpful and interesting books, both popular and scholarly, are available in the library, and paperback versions of some of these can be purchased at very modest cost. The bibliography at the end of this section lists some of these. As you reach the later parts of the text, you will discover that you have an understanding of some of the statistical tools used in research in the various fields of the social and physical sciences. Hence, you will find it interesting, at that stage, to browse in the library among the various journals reporting research in these fields.

Some areas in which you may wish to do further reading are suggested below. The numbers given after each topic indicate books in the bibliography which will be helpful in the study of that topic. Further references will be found in the books listed. Supplementary topics: statistics and common sense (2, 5, 9, 18), the algebra of sets (14, 16), the probabilities involved in games of chance (6, 19), the mathematical theory of games (16, 21), statistical decision theory (11, 21), time series (15), further applications of the analysis of variance (13), index numbers (15), the foundations of probability theory (1, 3, 9, 10).

Bibliography

Paperback books

1. Braithwaite, R. B.: *Scientific Explanation*, Harper Torchbooks, Harper & Brothers, New York.

2. Bronowski, J.: *The Common Sense of Science*, Modern Library Paperbacks, Random House Inc., New York.

3. Cohen, J.: *Chance, Skill, and Luck*, Penguin Books, Inc., Baltimore, 1960.

4. Gamow, B.: *1-2-3 Infinity*, New American Library of World Literature, New York.

5. Huff, D., and I. Geis: *How to Lie with Statistics*, W. W. Norton & Company, Inc., New York.

6. Levinson, H. C.: *The Science of Chance*, Rinehart & Company Inc., New York, 1950.

7. Moroney, J. J.: *Facts from Figures*, Penguin Books, Inc., Baltimore, 1951.

8. Myers, J. H.: *Statistical Presentation*, Littlefield, Adams and Co., Paterson, N. J.

9. Newman, J. R.: *The World of Mathematics*, Simon and Schuster, Inc., New York.

10. Reichenbach, H.: *The Rise of Scientific Philosophy*, University of California Press, Berkeley, Calif., 1951.

Elementary Texts

11. Chernoff, H., and L. E. Moses: *Elementary Decision Theory*, John Wiley & Sons, Inc., New York, 1959.

12. Commission on Mathematics, *Introductory Probability and Statistical Inference for Secondary Schools*, College Entrance Examination Board, New York, 1957.

13. Dixon, W. J., and F. J. Massey, Jr.: *Introduction to Statistical Analysis*, 2d ed., McGraw-Hill Book Company, Inc., New York, 1957.

14. Goldberg, S.: *Probability, an Introduction*, Prentice-Hall, Inc., Englewood Cliffs, N. J., 1960.

15. Hoel, P. G.: *Elementary Statistics*, John Wiley & Sons, Inc., New York, 1960.

16. Kemeny, J. G., J. L. Snell, and G. L. Thompson: *Introduction to Finite Mathematics*, Prentice-Hall, Inc., Englewood Cliffs, N. J., 1957.

17. Mosteller, F., R. E. K. Rourke, and G. B. Thomas, Jr.: *Probability and Statistics*, Addison Wesley Publishing Company, Reading, Mass., 1961.

18. Wallis, W. A., and H. V. Roberts: *Statistics, a New Approach*, Free Press, Glencoe, Ill., 1955.

More advanced texts

19. Feller, W.: *An Introduction to Probability Theory and Its Applications*, 2d ed., John Wiley & Sons, Inc., New York, 1957.

20. Hoel, P. G.: *Introduction to Mathematical Statistics*, 2d ed., John Wiley & Sons, Inc., New York, 1954.

21. Luce, R. D., and H. Raiffa: *Games and Decisions*, John Wiley & Sons, Inc., New York, 1957.

22. Wadsworth, G. A., and J. G. Bryan: *Introduction to Probability and Random Variables*, McGraw-Hill Book Company, Inc., New York, 1960.

Contents

CHAPTER 1

Empirical Frequency Distributions

1-1. Summarization of data

A pair of dice was thrown 100 times. After each throw the total of the spots uppermost on the dice was recorded. The results are shown in Table 1-1. In this table we refer to each operation that yields a value for the total number of spots as a *trial*. In the table we have introduced the symbol X to stand for the result of an unspecified trial. We shall then call X the random variable for this experiment. Then we may make statements such as "X took on the value 4 at the 87th trial."

The results of this experiment are somewhat difficult to interpret from Table 1-1. A more compact way of presenting the results would be helpful. In Table 1-2 we have summarized the data in several ways.

We now proceed to discuss how this summary was made and what the various columns mean. However, the reader may find that even with the abbreviations used in the table he can now see what the various columns represent.

The first step in the construction of the table was to determine the values that X could possibly take on. In this experiment, this could be done either by consideration of the dice or by looking at the data. The collection of all possible values for the random variable associated with an experiment is called the *sample space* for that experiment (or for that random variable). Here, the sample space is the collection of values $\{2,3,4,5,6,7,8,9,10,11,12\}$. In most statistics problems the precise identification of the random variable and its sample space are crucial first steps.

Once the sample space was determined and the values in the space arranged in order of size, the values were entered in the first column in Table 1-2. This column was then given the heading "x." In the column headed $FR(x)$ there was then entered the *frequency* with which each value of x was taken on. The column headed "Tallies" (which is usually omitted in such tables) was included here to indicate the device used to obtain the values in the $FR(x)$ column. Note that the "x" over the first column is in lower case while the symbol used for our random variable is a capital letter. This distinction is intentional. Whenever we write "X," we are referring to a variable which gains its values by carrying out the experiment, whereas the "x" introduced in our table is a variable to which we assign values at will for purposes of discussion. Then we may

Table 1-1

(X = total spots uppermost on the two dice)

Trial no.	X	Trial no.	X	Trial no.	X
1	8	35	11	68	9
2	2	36	6	69	7
3	11	37	9	70	7
4	3	38	10	71	5
5	10	39	9	72	9
6	10	40	9	73	8
7	9	41	6	74	9
8	10	42	9	75	7
9	6	43	6	76	9
10	6	44	7	77	7
11	10	45	10	78	12
12	8	46	8	79	9
13	11	47	8	80	7
14	7	48	6	81	8
15	5	49	7	82	11
16	7	50	8	83	7
17	12	51	10	84	7
18	7	52	7	85	9
19	7	53	6	86	8
20	10	54	7	87	4
21	8	55	11	88	6
22	9	56	4	89	10
23	6	57	4	90	10
24	8	58	7	91	12
25	6	59	10	92	3
26	6	60	10	93	8
27	12	61	5	94	11
28	6	62	5	95	2
29	8	63	4	96	6
30	7	64	8	97	11
31	6	65	3	98	8
32	9	66	11	99	4
33	5	67	7	100	8
34	9				

make statements such as "$FR(x)$ is the number of times that X took on the value x in our experiment." If we were to use the same symbol "x" throughout this statement, it would not make sense.

We have used the "FR" in "$FR(x)$" to suggest "frequency." $FR(x)$ is the frequency associated with x. Thus, in Table 1-2 we see that

$FR(6) = 14$. That is, in our experiment, X took on the value 6 fourteen times.

In the next column in the table we used "$RF(x)$" to stand for the *relative frequency* associated with x. In other words, $RF(x)$ is the proportion (or fraction) of times that the value x was taken on. In our experiment this was obtained by dividing the frequency by 100—the

Table 1-2
Summary of Table 1-1
(X = total spots on the two dice)

x	Tallies	$FR(x)$	$RF(x)$	$CF(x)$	$RCF(x)$
2	//	2	.02	2	.02
3	////	4	.04	6	.06
4	ﾊﾊﾑ	5	.05	11	.11
5	ﾊﾊﾑ	5	.05	16	.16
6	ﾊﾊﾑ ﾊﾊﾑ ////	14	.14	30	.30
7	ﾊﾊﾑ ﾊﾊﾑ ﾊﾊﾑ ///	18	.18	48	.48
8	ﾊﾊﾑ ﾊﾊﾑ ////	14	.14	62	.62
9	ﾊﾊﾑ ﾊﾊﾑ ////	14	.14	76	.76
10	ﾊﾊﾑ ﾊﾊﾑ //	12	.12	88	.88
11	ﾊﾊﾑ ///	8	.08	96	.96
12	////	4	.04	100	1.00

total number of trials. In general, if n is the total number of trials, we define $RF(x)$ by

$$(1\text{-}1) \qquad RF(x) = \frac{FR(x)}{n}$$

In the column headed "$CF(x)$," we entered the number of times that X took on a value which did not exceed x. Thus, we see that $CF(4) = 11$ because X took on the value 2 two times, the value 3 four times, and the value 4 five times and, as a result, took on a value not exceeding 4 a total of eleven times. "CF" is meant to suggest "cumulative frequency," and we speak of $CF(x)$ as the *cumulative frequency* at x. We see that these cumulative frequencies can be obtained by adding successively the items in the $FR(x)$ column.

In the final column of Table 1-2 "$RCF(x)$" stands for the *relative cumulative frequency* associated with x. Thus, we may ask, what proportion of the time did our dice yield a result which was not larger than 4? We discover that that proportion was $^{11}/_{100}$, or .11. In other words, 11 per cent of the time we got a result no larger than 4. We can define $RCF(x)$ by

$$(1\text{-}2) \qquad RCF(x) = \frac{CF(x)}{n}$$

We also note that the values of $RCF(x)$ can be obtained by adding successive items in the $RF(x)$ column. This is in strict analogy with the relationship between $CF(x)$ and $FR(x)$.

If n, the total number of trials, is known and we are given any one of the columns in a table such as Table 1-2, we can find the other three. We then say that the "x column" with any other column gives an *empirical distribution* for the given experiment. In case $FR(x)$, $RF(x)$, $CF(x)$, or $RCF(x)$ alone is given, the distribution is referred to as an empirical *frequency distribution, relative frequency distribution, cumulative frequency distribution,* or *relative cumulative frequency distribution,* respectively.

In the following problems, the above notation should be used so that the reader becomes familiar with it. In a distribution the random variable should always be clearly specified.

PROBLEMS

1-3. Throw two dice together 100 times. After each throw record the total of the dots uppermost on the two dice.[1] Summarize your results as in Table 1-2.

1-4. Toss five coins together 100 times. After each toss record the number of heads obtained.[1] Summarize.

1-5. Remove all the face cards from an ordinary deck of cards. Shuffle the cards that remain, draw two cards from the deck, record the total of the spots on the two cards,[1] and replace the cards in the deck. Repeat this operation 100 times. Summarize.

1-6. Put 12 uniform thumbtacks in a cup, shake the cup, and throw the tacks onto a flat hard surface. Record the number of tacks that fall with the point up. Repeat the experiment 100 times.[1] Summarize.

1-7. In a five-place table of logarithms, record the fourth digit of a certain entry. Repeat for 100 consecutive entries. Summarize.

1-8. From a favorite novel of yours, record the number of words in the first complete sentence on 100 consecutive pages.[1] Summarize.

1-9. For a five- or seven-place table of logarithms (or sines or cosines) record the number of odd digits in 100 consecutive entries.[1] Summarize.

1-10. Two people A and B work together on this problem. A and B both have a 10-card deck containing five red and five black cards. They both shuffle their decks and then turn the cards face up one at a time together. It is called a "match" if A and B turn up cards of the same color at the same time. The number of matches is recorded after the last card is turned. The experiment is to be repeated 100 times,[1] and the result summarized.

1-11. The same as in Prob. 1-10 except that here B guesses the order in which A's cards will come up by writing down a sequence of five B's and five R's. (B may guess either before or after A looks at the cards, but one or the other of these two ways should be used consistently.)

1-12. Take a 10-card deck consisting of the ace, 2, 3, 4, 5, 6, 7, 8, 9, and 10 of spades. Shuffle the deck and then turn them face up one at a time. Before each card is

---

[1] Keep a list of your results in the order in which they were obtained so that you will know, for future reference, the result of the first trial, the result of the second trial, etc.

turned, guess what its denomination will be. Record the number of correct guesses. Repeat this 100 times.[1] Summarize.

1-13. Obtain a roll of 100 pennies. Record the dates on them.[1] Summarize.

1-14. From a baseball record book, determine the total number of runs scored in each of the first 100 games played by your favorite baseball team last season.[1] Summarize.

1-15. Throw two dice together and record the positive difference between the numbers that come up. Repeat 100 times.[1] Summarize.

1-16. Throw a red die and a green die together. Subtract the number of spots uppermost on the green die from that on the red. Record the result. Repeat 100 times.[1] Summarize.

1-17. Toss five coins together. Subtract the number of heads from the number of tails. Record the result. Repeat 100 times.[1] Summarize.

1-18. In general, what is the relationship between $RF(x)$ and the per cent of the time that X took on the value x?

1-19. Combine the results throughout the class for one of Probs. 1-3 through 1-17 and summarize.

1-20. What will be the total of the $FR(x)$ column in a frequency distribution?

1-21. Must the total of the $RF(x)$ column always be 1? Explain.

1-22. Given that $n = 50$ in the following relative cumulative frequency distribution, find $FR(x)$, $RF(x)$, and $CF(x)$.

x	$RCF(x)$
1	.08
2	.32
3	.60
4	.84
5	.92
6	1.00

1-23. As a class project, collect the following data on each student in the class and summarize the data in an appropriate way or ways:

(*a*) Number of siblings

(*b*) Number of living grandparents

(*c*) Number of living uncles and aunts (do not include aunts and uncles by marriage)

(*d*) Number of letters in full name

(*e*) Age in months

(*f*) Number of magazines and/or newspapers subscribed to

(*g*) Number of people living in the student's home

(*h*) Number of five-letter words the student can write down in one minute

(*i*) Number of names of states in the United States that the student can write down in one minute

1.2. Geometric representation of distributions

According to the old saying, one picture is worth a thousand words. There is often considerable truth in this in mathematics, as elsewhere.

---

[1] Keep a list of your results in the order in which they were obtained so that you will know, for future reference, the result of the first trial, the result of the second trial, etc.

To give a clear idea of the results of an experiment, graphical methods are often very valuable. In Fig. 1-1 we have graphed $FR(x)$ and $RF(x)$ from Table 1-2.

At each value for x we constructed a vertical line whose length was $FR(x)$ or $RF(x)$, depending on whether the left- or right-hand scale was used.

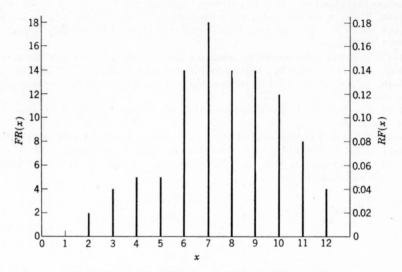

FIG. 1-1. Graph of $FR(x)$ and $RF(x)$ for Table 1-2.

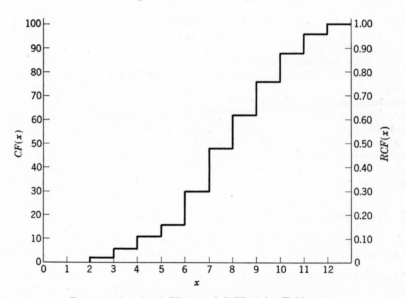

FIG. 1-2. Graph of $CF(x)$ and $RCF(x)$ for Table 1-2.

In Fig. 1-2 we have the graph of $CF(x)$ and $RCF(x)$ for the distribution of Table 1-2.

While the graph of $FR(x)$ or of $RF(x)$ consists only of some vertical line segments, the graph of $CF(x)$ or of $RCF(x)$ has been shown as a continuous stair-step curve. The agreement to do this is based on the following:

In our experiment with the dice, if we ask for the value of $FR(2.5)$, the only reasonable answer seems to be zero, since the value 2.5 was surely taken on zero times. Thus, we can think of the graph of $FR(x)$ as including many "vertical lines of zero length" between the values 2, 3, 4, etc. This agrees with our graph as shown in Fig. 1-1. If, on the other hand, we ask for the value $CF(2.5)$, we are evidently asking "How many times did X take on a value not exceeding 2.5?" The answer surely is not zero. In fact, we see that $CF(2.5)$ must be the same as $CF(2)$, since X cannot take on values between 2 and 2.5. If we draw a vertical line at 2.5 in Fig. 1-2, we see that it hits our graph at the same height as $CF(2)$, as it should.

PROBLEMS

1-24. Graph the distributions obtained in Probs. 1-3 through 1-17 that you worked.

1-25. Graph the distributions obtained in Prob. 1-23.

CHAPTER 2

Sets and Set Operations

2-1. Sets

In the previous chapter we were concerned with collections of results of trials, classes of possible values for a random variable, collections of frequencies, and groups of experiments. All these are examples of what we shall call a *set*. The notion of a set is a very fundamental and important one in logic and in mathematics. A set is simply a collection or class of objects.[1] A set may be a collection of numbers or of points on a line or of people or of experiments. One way to describe a particular set is to give a list of all the objects that belong in it. It is customary to enclose this list in braces. For example, in the experiment with the dice given in Chap. 1, the set of all possible values of the random variable (i.e., the set of all possible outcomes of the experiment) is the set $S = \{2,3,4,5,6,7,8,9,10,11,12\}$. The objects (in this case, numbers) that are in a set are called *elements* or *members* of that set and are said to *belong to* that set. Thus, we may say "2 is an element of the given set S" or else "2 belongs to S." On the other hand, we may say "1 is not an element of S" or else "1 does not belong to S." Since we often wish to consider assertions like these, we introduce a kind of shorthand for them. We write "$2 \in S$" as an abbreviation for the statement "2 belongs to S." In fact, we read "$2 \in S$" as "2 belongs to S" or as "2 is a member of S" or as "2 is an element of S." The symbol between "2" and "S" is a small Greek letter epsilon. We write the assertion "1 is not a member of S" more concisely as "$1 \notin S$."

We shall often be in a position where it will be helpful to have a brief and exact way to describe sets without listing elements. The device we shall use can best be introduced by an example. Suppose that we wish to speak of the set of all states in the United States. If we wish to call this set U, we may write

$$U = \{x : x \text{ is a state in the United States}\}$$

[1] We do not attempt to define the idea of a set but take it as being a "primitive" notion of which we all have an intuitive understanding.

We read this as "U is the set of all objects x which are states in the United States." Or else as "U is the set of all x such that x is a state in the United States." In general, if "$. . . x . . .$" is some statement form involving "x," we write

$$\{x: . . . x . . .\}$$

for the set of all x such that $. . . x . . . .$ We are not, of course, restricted to the use of x in this form but may use other letters such as t, y, or z in place of x throughout.

PROBLEMS

2-1. Let U be the set defined above. Are the following true?
(a) Missouri $\in U$ (b) Hawaii $\in U$ (c) Puerto Rico $\in U$
(d) Alaska $\in U$ (e) New England $\in U$ (f) New York $\in U$

2-2. Let $E = \{y: y$ is an even number$\}$
  $O = \{t: t$ is an odd number$\}$
  $H = \{z: z$ is a value for x which occurred with an even frequency in Table 1-2$\}$
  $F = \{x: x$ is a whole number and x is a multiple of 5$\}$
  $G = \{y: y$ is a frequency occurring in Table 1-2$\}$
  $A = \{x: x$ is a number and $x + 1 = x\}$
  $B = \{x: 5x + 1 = 7\}$

Write several true assertions about elements of each of these sets using the $\in$ notation. Similarly, using the $\notin$ notation.

2-3. Let $L = \{x: x$ is a literary work$\}$
  $M = \{y: y$ is a masterpiece$\}$
  $P = \{z: z$ is not prose$\}$
  $N = \{r: r$ is a novel$\}$
  $D = \{s: s$ is a play$\}$
  $T = \{t: t$ is a textbook$\}$

Make several true assertions about these sets using $\in$ and $\notin$.

2-4. Agreed that the only people under consideration will be the students in your class, let
  $F = \{x: x$ has four living grandparents$\}$
  $AT = \{x: x$ has at least three living grandparents$\}$
  $LT = \{x: x$ has fewer than three living grandparents$\}$
  $N = \{x: x$ has no living grandparents$\}$

From the results of Prob. 1-23b determine the number of people in each of these sets.

2-2. Unions and intersections

If two sets are involved in an argument, it is often important to consider the collection of elements which are members of both sets. This collection is a set itself. It is called the *intersection* of the two given sets. For example, the intersection of the sets $\{1,2,3,4,5\}$ and $\{3,5,7,9\}$ is the set $\{3,5\}$ since 3 and 5 (and only 3 and 5) are in both given sets. If A

and B are given sets, we write $A \cap B$ for their intersection. We read "$A \cap B$" as "A cap B" or as "A intersect B" or as "A intersection B." The intersection of two sets is sometimes also referred to as their logical product.

There is a convenient pictorial way to represent the intersection of two sets. In Fig. 2-1 we have drawn two intersecting circles. We think of

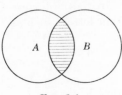

the circle on the left as being a fence inside which all the elements of A are trapped. The circle on the right is a fence trapping the elements of B. Evidently, the elements of $A \cap B$ must be in the shaded area. Formally, we can define the intersection of two sets by the equation[1]

Fig. 2-1

$$(2\text{-}5) \quad A \cap B = \{x : x \in A \quad \text{and} \quad x \in B\}$$

The intersection of two sets may not contain any elements. In this case, the two sets are said to be *disjoint*, and their intersection is called the *null set* or the *empty set*. That is, a null set is one which has no members. The notion of the null set is a useful one, and the letter ϕ (read as "fee") will be used to designate it. The set

$$A = \{x : x \text{ is a number and } x + 1 = x\}$$

of Prob. 2-2 is empty, that is, $A = \phi$.

The collection of objects which belong to one or the other or both of two given sets is called the *union* of the two given sets. For example, the union of $\{1,2,3,4,5\}$ and $\{3,5,7,9\}$ is the set $\{1,2,3,4,5,7,9\}$. If A and B are given sets, we write $A \cup B$ for their union. We read "$A \cup B$" as "A union B" or "A cup B." The union of two sets is also sometimes referred to as their logical sum. Using the same fence idea as in Fig. 2-1, the shaded portion of Fig. 2-2 represents $A \cup B$.

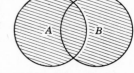

Formally, we have

$$(2\text{-}6) \quad A \cup B = \{x : x \in A \quad \text{or} \quad x \in B\}$$

Fig. 2-2

where, as is usual in mathematics, we use "or" in the sense of the "and/or" to be found in legal documents. This means that $A \cup B$ includes those objects which are in both A and B as well as all the objects which are in only one of them.

With the operations of intersection and union defined for sets we get an "algebra of sets," just as we get an "algebra of numbers" with the operations of multiplication and addition defined for numbers. Many of the

---

[1] Two sets are said to be equal if they contain exactly the same elements. Thus, we can use the sign "=" between names for sets to assert that they have the same elements.

basic laws for multiplication and addition in the algebra of real numbers have their analogues for intersection and union in the algebra of sets.

The details of this "set algebra" are not important for our work here, but the reader may find the following of interest.

If a and b are any real numbers, we know that $a + b = b + a$. Hence, we say that addition of real numbers is *commutative*. Similarly, we say that addition of real numbers is *associative* because, given any three real numbers a, b, and c, we know that, if we add a and b and then add c to the result, we get the same thing as when we add a to the result of adding b and c. That is, $(a + b) + c = a + (b + c)$. Multiplication of real numbers is also commutative and associative; that is, for any numbers a, b, and c, we have $ab = ba$ and $(ab)c = a(bc)$. An important joint property of the operations of addition and multiplication of real numbers is that multiplication *distributes* across addition. By this we mean that for any real numbers a, b, and c we have $a(b + c) = ab + ac$.

Intersections and unions for sets have similar properties. If A, B, and C are any sets, we have

(2-7) $\qquad A \cap B = B \cap A$ (commutative law for intersections)
(2-8) $(A \cap B) \cap C = A \cap (B \cap C)$
$\qquad\qquad\qquad\qquad\qquad\qquad$ (associative law for intersections)
(2-9) $\qquad A \cup B = B \cup A$ (commutative law for unions)
(2-10) $(A \cup B) \cup C = A \cup (B \cup C)$ (associative law for unions)
(2-11) $A \cap (B \cup C) = (A \cap B) \cup (A \cap C)$
(2-12) $A \cup (B \cap C) = (A \cup B) \cap (A \cup C)$

The last two laws here are called distributive laws. The fact that there are two of them contrasts with the situation for multiplication and addition of real numbers, since it is not true that addition distributes across multiplication.

Other important laws for unions and intersections are the following, which hold for any set A:

(2-13) $\qquad\qquad\qquad A \cup A = A$
(2-14) $\qquad\qquad\qquad A \cap A = A$
(2-15) $\qquad\qquad\qquad A \cap \phi = \phi$
(2-16) $\qquad\qquad\qquad A \cup \phi = A$

The reader may argue for each of the above laws in words, using the definitions of "$\cup$," "$\cap$," and ϕ, or he may verify them by means of pictures or by taking specific examples of sets.

PROBLEMS

2-17. Let $A = \{1,2,3,4,5,6,7,8\}$, $B = \{2,4,6,8\}$, $C = \{5\}$, $D = \{2,3,7\}$. Find
(a) $A \cup B$ $\qquad\qquad$ (b) $C \cup D$ $\qquad\qquad\qquad$ (c) $B \cup D$

(d) $A \cap C$ (e) $C \cap D$ (f) $B \cap A$
(g) $A \cap (C \cup D)$ (h) $A \cup (C \cap D)$ (i) $(B \cup C) \cap B$
(j) $(B \cup C) \cap D$ (k) $(\phi \cup A) \cap \phi$ (l) $(B \cup D) \cup A$

2-18. If the sets are those defined in Prob. 2-2, find

(a) $E \cap H$ (b) $H \cap E$ (c) $H \cap O$
(d) $F \cap E$ (e) $F \cap O$ (f) $F \cup E$
(g) $F \cup O$ (h) $E \cap O$ (i) $E \cap A$
(j) $A \cup E$ (k) $F \cap G$ (l) $B \cap F$
(m) $(E \cup O) \cup F$ (n) $E \cup (O \cup F)$ (o) $E \cap (F \cup O)$
(p) $O \cap (E \cup F)$ (q) $E \cup E$ (r) $E \cap E$
                          (s) $\phi \cup \phi$

2-19. Let A, B, and C designate collections of points inside the circles as shown in Fig. 2-3. In parts (a) through (e), make a sketch in which shading shows the given set.

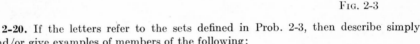

(a) $(A \cap B) \cap C$ (b) $(A \cap B) \cup C$
(c) $(A \cup B) \cup C$ (d) $(A \cap B) \cup B$
(e) $A \cap (B \cup C)$

FIG. 2-3

2-20. If the letters refer to the sets defined in Prob. 2-3, then describe simply and/or give examples of members of the following:

(a) $L \cup D$ (b) $L \cap D$ (c) $E \cap M$
(d) $P \cap D$ (e) $T \cap D$ (f) $N \cap P$
                          (g) $(M \cap P) \cap (N \cap L)$

2-21. For the sets given in Prob. 2-4 find the number of people in the following sets:

(a) $AT \cap LT$ (b) $AT \cup LT$ (c) $LT \cap N$
(d) $F \cup AT$ (e) $F \cap AT$ (f) $N \cup F$
                          (g) $F \cup (LT \cap LT)$

*2-22. By means of an appropriate argument or a picture, verify the following:

(a) (2-7)   (b) (2-8)   (c) (2-9)
(d) (2-10)   (e) (2-11)   (f) (2-12)
(g) (2-13)   (h) (2-14)   (i) (2-15)
                          (j) (2-16)

2-3. Complements

A set is usually thought of as being part of a large collection which contains all objects that might possibly be considered in a particular discussion. This large collection is then called the *universal set*. If A is a set which is part of a universal set I, we can talk about the set of objects which are not in A. This set is called the *complement* of A and is designated by A'. For example, if we are discussing positive whole numbers so that I is the set of all positive integers and if E is the set of even integers and O is the set of odd integers, then $O' = E$ and $E' = O$. Formally,

(2-23) $$A' = \{x : x \notin A\}$$

If A and B are sets, the following are true:

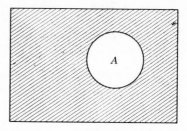

(2-24)	$(A')' = A$
(2-25)	$A \cup A' = I$
(2-26)	$A \cap A' = \phi$
(2-27)	$\phi' = I$
(2-28)	$(A \cap B)' = A' \cup B'$
(2-29)	$(A \cup B)' = A' \cap B'$

Fig. 2-4

Pictorially, if interiors of circles are used to represent sets as before and we wish to get the universal set into the picture, the circles are shown inside a box—the box representing a fence inside which is found the entire universal set.   In Fig. 2-4 A' is shaded.

PROBLEMS

2-30. Verify Eqs. (2-24) through (2-29) by pictures or argument.

2-31. With sets A, B, and C shown pictorially as in Fig. 2-5, make sketches with shaded areas representing the following sets:

(a) $A \cup B'$ (b) $A \cap B'$ (c) $(A \cup B)' \cap C'$
(d) $(A \cap B)' \cup C$ (e) $(A \cup C)' \cup C$ (f) $(A' \cap B)' \cup A$
(g) $(A \cup B \cup C)'$ (h) $(A \cap B \cap C)'$ (i) $(A \cup A)' \cap A$

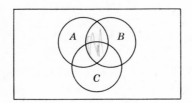

Fig. 2-5

2-32. With the sets as given in Prob. 2-4 determine the number of people in each of the following sets:

(a) F' (b) $(F \cup N)'$ (c) $(F \cap N)'$
(d) AT' (e) LT' (f) $(LT \cup F)'$
(g) H' (h) $(AT \cap LT)'$

2-33. With the universal set taken to be $\{2,3,4,5,6,7,8,9,10,11,12\}$, let

$$A = \{x : x < 3\} \qquad B = \{x : x \le 3\}$$
$$C = \{x : x \text{ is odd}\} \qquad D = \{x : x \text{ is even}\}$$

Describe each of the following sets by listing its elements:

(a) A (b) $A \cap B$ (c) $A \cap (B \cup D)$
(d) $A' \cap B$ (e) $A' \cap C$ (f) $(A \cup D)'$
(g) $(A \cup B \cup C)'$ (h) $(A \cap B \cap C)'$ (i) $(A \cup A) \cap (B \cup B)$

*2-34. Simplify the following:

(a) $(A \cap A) \cup (A \cap A)'$

(b) $(A \cap \phi) \cup (I \cap A)$

(c) $(A \cup I) \cap (A \cup \phi)$

(d) $A \cap (I \cup \phi)$

(e) $(A \cup I) \cap (B \cap \phi)$

(f) $(A \cup A \cup A) \cap I$

(g) $[(A \cap B) \cup C] \cap \phi$

(h) $(I \cup A) \cup (I \cap A) \cup A$

2-4. Subsets

In discussing the United States, we often speak of the Southern states, the New England states, the Western states, or the Midwestern states. Each of these collections of states is a part of the collection U of all the states. In mathematical language we should say that they are subsets of the set U. More generally, if every element of some set A is also an element of some set B, we say that A is a *subset* of B and write $A \subseteq B$ (which is read as "A is contained in B"). This relationship between sets is an important one and has many interesting properties. Among these are the following:

(2-35)   *For any set A, $\phi \subseteq A$.*

(2-36)   *For any set A, $A \subseteq A$.*

(2-37)   *For any sets A and B, $A = B$ if and only if $A \subseteq B$ and $B \subseteq A$.*

(2-38)   *For any sets A and B, $A \subseteq B$ if and only if $A \cap B = A$.*

PROBLEMS

2-39. If $A = \{a,b,c\}$, list all possible subsets of A.

2-40. Verify (2-35) through (2-38) by examples or argument.

2-41. If A contains n elements, how many subsets of A are there? *Hint:* Consider the cases $n = 1, 2, 3$ (see Prob. 2-39), and 4; in each case make a list of all the subsets.

2-42. If a set A contains n elements, how many subsets of A are there that contain exactly n elements? Exactly 0 elements? Exactly $n - 1$ elements?

2-43. Is it true that, given any two sets A and B, we must have either $A \subseteq B$ or $B \subseteq A$? Explain.

2-44. What further can be said about the sets A, B, and C if it is known that $A \subseteq B$ and $B \subseteq C$ and $C \subseteq A$? Explain.

*2-45. To say "All crows are black" is to say "$C \subseteq B$," where

$$C = \{x: x \text{ is a crow}\}$$

and

$$B = \{x: x \text{ is black}\}$$

By introducing the proper sets, state the following in set-inclusion language:

(a) All crows are birds.

(b) All even numbers less than 3 divide evenly into 6.

(c) All men are mortal.

(d) No birds are immortal.

(e) No birds are immoral.

(f) All examinations are imperfect.

(g) All typically neolithic sites in the old world have yielded bones of cattle, sheep, and/or goats.

(h) All rules have exceptions.

(i) Hopi nouns always have an individual sense.

CHAPTER 3

Notational and Computational Devices

3-1. Variables and subscripts

The notion of a random variable was introduced in Chap. 1. More generally, a symbol used to stand for an unspecified member of any set is said to be simply a *variable*. The set thus associated with the symbol is called the *domain* of the variable. In the reader's work in algebra, he has run across such expressions as "$x^2 + 2x$," where "x" stands for an unspecified real number. The expression yields a value when the name of a number is put in place of (i.e., substituted for) "x." In the expression "$x^2 + 2x$," the domain of x is evidently the set of all real numbers. Quite often when a variable is used, no specific mention is made of its domain and the domain must be inferred from the context in which the variable occurs. Thus, in much of elementary algebra a variable often has the set of all real numbers for its domain, even though this fact may not be mentioned explicitly.

The situation is especially simple if the domain of a variable is a finite set. This is often the case in the first part of this book. If x is a variable whose domain has N elements in it, it is often convenient to use subscripts (i.e., small-number names or letters written to the right and below) to designate these elements and write down the domain as $\{x_1, x_2, \ldots, x_N\}$. "$x_1$" is read "$x$ sub 1" or simply "x one." ". . ." is read as "and so forth until you reach." ". . ." is the mathematical symbol for "etc.," if you like. In the experiment with the dice the random variable had the domain $\{2,3,4,5,6,7,8,9,10,11,12\}$ (i.e., this was the sample space for X). Here, if the domain is written in subscript notation as $\{x_1, x_2, x_3, \ldots, x_N\}$, we could make the identifications $x_1 = 2$, $x_2 = 3$, $x_3 = 4$, $x_4 = 5$, $x_5 = 6$, $x_6 = 7$, $x_7 = 8$, $x_8 = 9$, $x_9 = 10$, $x_{10} = 11$, $x_{11} = 12$.

Subscripts may also be used to identify the values of a random variable which came up as results in the course of an experiment. Thus, with the dice, we had the result of our first throw, which we might call X_1.

The result of our second throw could be called X_2, and so forth. Referring to Table 1-1 and using subscripts in this sense, the reader may verify that in our example $X_1 = 8$, $X_2 = 2$, $X_3 = 11$, . . . , $X_{39} = 9$, . . . , $X_{100} = 8$. Using this notation, X_i (read as "capital X sub i") represents the result of the ith trial. (Note that here i is a variable whose domain is $\{1,2,3, \ . \ . \ . \ ,n\}$ if there were n trials.) This terminology will often be used in what follows.

The reader should remember that a random variable X gains a value as the outcome of an experiment. If the experiment is to be performed n times, we can let X_1, X_2, . . . , X_n denote the outcomes of these n trials. Then $(X_1, X_2, \ . \ . \ . \ , X_n)$ may be thought of as constituting the outcome of a larger experiment, namely, the experiment of carrying out the original experiment n times. When, however, we speak of the sample space for X, we are speaking of the set of values that could possibly be the outcome of the original experiment. We can usually discover the nature of this set by studying the experiment that is to be carried out without making even a single trial of the experiment. Thus when we say that the sample space for X is $\{x_1, x_2, \ . \ . \ . \ , x_N\}$, it is proper to use the lower-case x's, since we are not trying to represent results of actual trials of the experiment but only those outcomes which we judge to be possible. In an outcome $(X_1, X_2, \ . \ . \ . \ , X_n)$ of n trials some of the elements of $\{x_1, x_2, \ . \ . \ . \ , x_N\}$ may not even occur. The sample space for an experiment is a set, while the result of n trials of an experiment is not a set but an ordered sequence of n results. When a coin is flipped, for instance, the sample space is $\{H, T\}$ while the outcome of two trials might be (H, T) or (T, H), and these are two different results.

PROBLEMS

3-1. If $\{1,3,5,7,9\}$ is the domain of the variable x in the expression $(x - 3)(x - 5)$, find the value given by this expression for each possible value of x.

3-2. If $\{2,4,6,8,10\}$ is the domain of y, for what set of values of y is $y^2 - 8y = 0$ a true statement? For what set of values is it false?

3-3. In each of the experiments of Probs. 1-3 through 1-17 what is the domain of the random variable? That is, what is the sample space in each of these cases?

3-4. In a problem which you performed among Probs. 1-3 through 1-17, let X_i be the result of the ith trial. Find X_6, X_{19}, X_{44}, X_{99}.

*3-5. In algebra the set of all values of a variable which make an equation true is sometimes called the *solution set* for that equation. If the set of all real numbers is the domain of t, find the solution set for each of the following:

(a) $5t - 10 = 0$ (b) $4t + 8 = 0$ (c) $5t - 7 = 0$
(d) $t^2 = -4$ (e) $t^2 - t = 0$

*3-6. A rectangular array of numbers is called a *matrix*. We can use *double subscripts* to denote the number in a certain position in a matrix. "a_{ij}" (which is read as "a sub i, j" or simply "a-i-j") can be used, for example, to stand for the number in the ith row and the jth column.   For example, in

$$A = \begin{pmatrix} 5 & 1 \\ 3 & 5 \\ 2 & -2 \end{pmatrix} = (a_{ij})$$

we have $a_{11} = 5$, $a_{22} = 5$, $a_{31} = 2$, $a_{32} = -2$.   In

$$B = \begin{pmatrix} 3 & 0 & 1 \\ 2 & 0 & 3 \\ -1 & 1 & 1 \end{pmatrix} = (b_{ij})$$

and

$$C = \begin{pmatrix} 4 & 2 & 1 & 5 \\ -1 & 0 & 1 & 6 \end{pmatrix} = (c_{ij})$$

identify each number in each matrix by the proper expression involving subscripts. (We adopt the convention that the first subscript always indicates the row and the second the column.)

3-2. The Σ notation

Often the sum of a sequence of numbers is needed in statistical considerations.   For instance, in throwing a pair of dice 100 times as we did in our earlier experiment, the grand total of all the spots that showed up might (and will) be of interest.   If X_i is the result of the ith trial, we can represent the total of all the results of all the trials as $X_1 + X_2 + \cdots + X_{100}$. Since such expressions often arise, we introduce a concise notation for them.   In place of "$X_1 + X_2 + \cdots + X_{100}$," we write "$\sum_{i=1}^{100} X_i$."   We read this as "the sum of the X_i as i runs from 1 to 100" or sometimes, more briefly, "sigma from 1 to 100 of X_i."   The symbol "Σ" is the Greek letter "s," read as "sigma."   The "1" and "100" are called lower and upper limits for the sum, respectively.   The "i" that appears with the sigma is called a *dummy variable* (or, perhaps better, just a *dummy*). It is not a variable in the usual sense in that, if we replace it throughout by the name of a number, the expression becomes nonsense.   If, however, any other letter is substituted for i in both places where it occurs then the meaning of the expression is unchanged.   That is,

$$\sum_{i=1}^{100} X_i = \sum_{j=1}^{100} X_j = \sum_{k=1}^{100} X_k = \cdots$$

It should be clear that the upper and lower limits need not be 1 and 100. If, for example, we want the total of the "middle 50" trials, we can express it as $\displaystyle\sum_{i=26}^{75} X_i$.   Some important general properties of sums are

$$(3\text{-}7) \qquad \sum_{i=1}^{n} X_i + \sum_{i=n+1}^{m} X_i = \sum_{i=1}^{m} X_i$$

$$(3\text{-}8) \qquad \sum_{i=1}^{n} cX_i = c \sum_{i=1}^{n} X_i$$

$$(3\text{-}9) \qquad \sum_{i=1}^{n} c = nc$$

The last equation simply states that, if $X_i = c$ (c is a constant) for $i = 1, 2, \ldots, n$, then the sum of all the X_i's is nc.   Another important result is

$$(3\text{-}10) \qquad \sum_{i=1}^{n} (X_i + Y_i) = \sum_{i=1}^{n} X_i + \sum_{i=1}^{n} Y_i$$

The tedium and inaccuracies of adding up long columns of figures by hand are to be avoided if at all possible.   Hence, at this stage the reader should become familiar with the process of addition on a desk computer if such is available.   The manuals which come with these machines usually give instructions which are easy to follow, and in any event, learning how to add on a desk calculator is a simple process.   It is assumed that a desk calculator is available for the following problems and that it will be used in order to gain practice in its use.

PROBLEMS

3-11. In one of the problems from 1-3 to 1-17 which you have worked, let X_i be the result of the ith trial and find $\displaystyle\sum_{i=1}^{100} X_i$.

3-12. With X_i as in Prob. 3-11, find $\displaystyle\sum_{i=1}^{50} X_i$, $\displaystyle\sum_{i=51}^{100} X_i$, and $\displaystyle\sum_{i=1}^{50} X_i + \sum_{i=51}^{100} X_i$. Show how your results illustrate Eq. (3-7).

3-13. Find $\displaystyle\sum_{i=1}^{20} X_i$, $3 \displaystyle\sum_{i=1}^{20} X_i$, and $\displaystyle\sum_{i=1}^{20} 3X_i$, where X_i is as above.   Show how your results illustrate Eq. (3-8).

3-14. If $x_k = k^2$ (that is, $x_1 = 1$, $x_2 = 4$, $x_3 = 9$, $x_4 = 16$, ...), find $\displaystyle\sum_{k=1}^{12} x_k$.

3-15. If X_i is the result of the ith trial as in Prob. 3-11, find $\displaystyle\sum_{i=1}^{100} (X_i + 2)$ and $\displaystyle\sum_{i=1}^{100} X_i + 200.$ Show how your results illustrate Eqs. (3-9) and (3-10).

3-3. Standard notation and significant digits

a^2 means a times a. a^3 means a times a times a.   In general, a^n stands for the product of n factors equal to a. a^n is called the "nth power of a" or "a to the nth power."   On the other hand, a^{-2} means $1/a$ times $1/a$, a^{-3} means $1/a$ times $1/a$ times $1/a$, and, in general, a^{-n} means the product of n factors equal to $1/a$ if n is a positive integer. a^0 is defined to be 1 when a is different from zero. a^{-n} is read as "a to the minus n power."   Since we use the decimal system, the powers of 10 are of particular interest.   Consider the following table:

$$
\begin{array}{ll}
10^{-4} = .0001 & 10^1 = 10 \\
10^{-3} = .001 & 10^2 = 100 \\
10^{-2} = .01 & 10^3 = 1000 \\
10^{-1} = .1 & 10^4 = 10,000 \\
10^0 = 1 & 10^5 = 100,000
\end{array}
$$

Consider the number .00321.   This number is between 10^{-2} and 10^{-3}. It is the same as 3.21×10^{-3}.   On the other hand, the number 47,600 falls between 10^4 and 10^5 and is the same as 4.76×10^4.   A little thought convinces one that any number is a product of a power of 10 and a number between 1 and 10.   When a number is written as such a product, it is said to be written in *standard notation*.   This manner of expressing numbers is useful when either very small or very large numbers are involved.   For instance, giving the speed of light as 3×10^{10} cm/sec is much easier than giving it as 30,000,000,000 cm/sec, and the former expression is easier to comprehend.   Use of standard notation also has certain computational advantages.   Some of these we shall see as we proceed.

In the preceding section we have seen how a desk calculator greatly simplifies the task of adding several numbers together.   Since multiplication and division are basically processes of repeated addition and subtraction, respectively, these same computers can be used to multiply and divide.   In fact, some of the larger desk computers carry out these operations automatically.   The reader should learn how to multiply and divide on the calculator available to him.

There is, however, another device for multiplying and dividing which is very convenient and simple to use—the slide rule.   This device, while not indispensable, can be of considerable aid to the reader in problems which arise later in this text.   Thus, it would be helpful if the reader learned how to use a slide rule for multiplication and division.   (In understanding how a slide rule works or in using one, the reader will find standard notation very helpful.)

In applied statistics, as in all branches of applied mathematics, many of the numbers used are the result of measurements.   Any measuring device is, of necessity, limited in accuracy.   When a length is measured with a ruler, probably the utmost in accuracy we could expect would be to find the "true length" to the nearest $\frac{1}{32}$ in.   In weighing with a chemical balance we could expect to find the "true weight" perhaps to the nearest 0.0001 g.   If we are lucky, a drugstore scale will give us our "true weight" to the nearest pound.   Thus, when a young lady steps off a scale and says, "I weigh 115 lb," she does not mean that she weighs 115.0000 lb but rather that her "true weight" (assuming that she is truthful) is somewhere between 114.5 and 115.5 lb.

When it is known that a number is a result of a measurement, there is a conventional way of indicating its accuracy; namely, in stating the name of the number indicate all those digits and only those digits which are "significant."   Thus, if we say that a certain person weighs 115 lb, we understand that we mean that this is his weight to the nearest pound. If we know that his weight is 115 to the nearest tenth of a pound, then we should say that his weight is 115.0 lb.   If a more accurate scale is used which is accurate to the nearest hundredth of a pound, then his weight might be recorded as 115.00 lb.   We say that the expressions 115, 115.0, and 115.00 have three, four, and five *significant digits*, respectively.

Astronomers have estimated that our galaxy (the Milky Way) contains 200,000,000,000 stars.[1]   They do not, of course, mean that this figure is correct to the nearest unit.   In this case, probably the only significant digit is the 2.   In order to indicate this by the way in which the number is recorded, an astronomer uses standard notation and writes the number as 2×10^{11}.   If the estimate was known to be correct to the nearest 10 billion, then the number would be written with two *significant* digits as 2.0×10^{11}.   This illustrates the manner in which standard notation is used to indicate the significant digits in very large numbers.

In a physics book the mass of the electron is given as .000,000,000,000,-000,000,000,000,000,91 g.   Since all the "0's" before the 9 serve only to locate the decimal point, we say that this number has two significant digits and prefer (for obvious reasons) to write it as 9.1×10^{-28} g.   This automatically indicates that this measurement is correct to the nearest 0.1×10^{-28} or 1×10^{-29} g.   If a subsequent refinement of techniques leads to a measurement correct to the nearest 1×10^{-30} g, the mass of the

---

[1] It is of interest to note that the methods used to arrive at this estimate are statistical ones.

electron might turn out to be 9.10×10^{-28} or 9.11×10^{-28} or 9.14×10^{-28} g, etc.

In general, to determine the number of significant digits in the representation of a number, write the number in standard notation and count the digits appearing exclusive of the power of 10. Thus, $.00025 = 2.5 \times 10^{-4}$ has two significant digits. The number of significant digits in "25,000" is not well defined. It is not clear whether the number is supposed to be correct to the nearest 1000, to the nearest 100, to the nearest 10, or to the nearest unit. If, on the other hand, the person records the number as 2.50×10^4, then it is clear that the result is to be taken as correct to the nearest 100 and has three significant digits.

Even when we are not dealing with measurements, the numbers with which we shall become involved will often be only approximations to true values. When we use tables to find a square root (see Sec. 3-4) of a number, the table value is usually only an approximation to the true value.

Being involved with approximations to "true values" and computations with them, we should learn to compute sensibly with them. To this end we state the following rules for computation with approximate numbers.

(3-16)   *When adding or subtracting approximate numbers, always round off the result so that it contains the same number of digits to the right of the decimal point as found in the number given which has the smallest number of digits to the right of the decimal point.*

(3-17)   *In multiplying or dividing approximate numbers, always round off the result so that it contains the same number of significant digits as found in the number given which has the smallest number of significant digits.*

For example, if the numbers involved are approximate,

$$14.315 + 432.11 + 13.1 = 459.5 \qquad \text{and} \qquad 133.1 \times .0051 = .68$$

The addition rule in (3-16) must be modified if there are digits to the left of the decimal point which are not significant. This situation can be taken care of by putting all the numbers into units of some power of 10 (the same power for all numbers involved), so that all the nonsignificant digits occur to the right of the decimal point (and therefore will be omitted), and then applying (3-16). For example, if the numbers involved are approximate,

$$5.32 \times 10^5 + 5.1 \times 10^6 = 5.32 \times 10^5 + 51 \times 10^5$$
$$= 56 \times 10^5 = 5.6 \times 10^6$$

To illustrate the need for the rules for computing with approximate numbers let us suppose that we wish to find the perimeter and area of a rectangular field. Suppose further that we can measure the width with a surveyor's "chain" to the nearest tenth of a foot but must estimate the length by some rougher technique. Suppose that we find the width to be 500.1 ft and the length to be 1100 ft, where this last measurement is correct to the nearest 100 ft. (Using the above conventions, we would write these measurements as 5.001×10^2 ft and 1.1×10^3 ft.) If we compute the perimeter of the field as $2(500.1 + 1100) = 3200.2$ ft, we are certainly kidding ourselves. It appears that, even though we know the length only to the nearest 100 ft, we know the perimeter to the nearest tenth of a foot! The correct procedure is to round off the answer to the nearest 100 ft and write the answer as "3.2×10^3." The last is preferable to "3200," since this does not indicate the accuracy unambiguously. In computing the area, if we write simply $500.1 \times 1100 = 550,110.0$, we would again be misleading ourselves or someone who would read our results. Whereas we know the length only to about 9 per cent of the true value, we seem in these computations to come up with an area correct to about one part in 5 million $(.1/550,110)$! In order not to be misled, we round off the answer to two significant digits and write that the area is 5.5×10^4 sq ft.

PROBLEMS

3-18. Write each of the following in standard notation and state the number of significant digits:

(a) .013	(b) 1356	(c) 5100
(d) 3001	(e) .000401	(f) 555×10^6
(g) .4310	(h) 3.1416	(i) .00040

3-19. Assuming that the numbers involved are approximate, evaluate the following:

(a) $4.312 + 51.7 + 5.001 + .05 + 7.115$

(b) $3.01 \times .007111$

(c) $43(7.111 + 3.02)$

(d) $5.43 + 5.43 + 5.43 + 7.111 + 7.111 + 7.111 + 7.111 + 7.111$

(e) $(5.43 \times 10^6) \times (3.12 \times 10^4)$

(f) $(3.78 \times 10^{-3}) \times (1.15 \times 10^{-2})$

(g) $(4.31 \times 10^{-6}) \times (1 \times 10^3)$

(h) $(4.41 \times 10^{-4}) \times (7.1 \times 10^7)$

(i) $47(3.31 \times 10^5)$

3-4. Square roots

A square root of a number x is a number whose square is x. Thus, 2 is a square root of 4 because $2^2 = 4$. Also -2 is a square root of 4, since $(-2)^2 = 4$. We write $\sqrt{x}$ to denote the nonnegative square root of x.

That is, by definition,

(3-20) $$y = \sqrt{x} \text{ means } y^2 = x \quad and \quad y \geq 0$$

As we proceed, we shall often be faced with the problem of finding a decimal expression for the positive square root of a number. In some cases, such as $\sqrt{4}$, $\sqrt{81}$, $\sqrt{100}$, it is quite easy to find these expressions. In such cases as $\sqrt{6}$, $\sqrt{5.32}$, or $\sqrt{439}$ it is not so obvious how we can get our answer easily.

There are two easy methods for finding approximate values of square roots. The first is by means of the A and C scales on a slide rule. The details of this method will not be discussed here.

The other method involves having on hand a table of square roots for numbers between 1 and 100. Such a table is given as Table A-1 in the Appendix. Assuming that we wish to find the approximate value of $\sqrt{B}$, the method is as follows: Write B as a product of a number between 1 and 100 and an even (positive or negative) power of 10. That is, let $B = b \times 10^{2n}$. For example, if we wish to approximate $\sqrt{5300}$, we write $5300 = 53 \times 10^2$. Then, from the table, $\sqrt{53} = 7.280$ and $\sqrt{5300} = 72.80$. Similarly,

$$\sqrt{0.00530} = \sqrt{53.0 \times 10^{-4}} = \sqrt{53} \times 10^{-2} = 7.28 \times 10^{-2} = .0728$$

The accuracy of this method is, of course, limited by the accuracy of the tables. For our purposes, however, the method will almost always yield a result sufficiently close to the true value. It is assumed that the reader is familiar with the process of interpolation and will use it when it is needed.

A negative number does not have a real square root, since the square of any real number is nonnegative. If a and b are positive numbers, however, the following are important properties.

(3-21) $$\sqrt{ab} = \sqrt{a}\sqrt{b}$$

(3-22) $$\sqrt{\frac{a}{b}} = \frac{\sqrt{a}}{\sqrt{b}}$$

The first of these was used in our method of finding square roots from tables.

We shall often find it convenient to use the exponent $\frac{1}{2}$ instead of the radical sign. That is, for "$\sqrt{a}$" we can write "$a^{\frac{1}{2}}$" and mean the same thing. In taking the square root of an approximate number, the result should be rounded off to contain the same number of significant digits as the original number.

PROBLEMS

3-23. Find the approximate square root of each of the following numbers.

(a) 7   (b) 37   (c) 37.2

(d) 372   (e) 45,200   (f) 3000

(g) 4.62   (h) 0.0045   (i) 0.035

(j) 4.62×10^5 (k) 42,500   (l) 0.111

(m) 57,000,000   (n) 51×10^{-9} (o) 81×10^{-7}

3-24. Verify Eqs. (3-21) and (3-22) with various numerical examples.

3-25. Show that, in general, $\sqrt{a + b} \neq \sqrt{a} + \sqrt{b}$ even if a and b are positive.

3-5. Functions

One notion that will crop up repeatedly as we proceed is that of a function. Let us, as in a previous problem, consider the set U of all the states in the United States. Every state has a governor; i.e., with each state is paired a certain person called its governor. Also with each element of U we can connect the number of square miles of area that it contains or we can pair with each state its population or its capital city. In each of these cases some object (and only one object) is paired or associated with each element of U.

If we refer to Table 1-1, there we find paired with each number in the set $\{1,2,3, \ldots ,100\}$ a number in the result column. In Table 1-2 each element of $\{2,3,4,5,6,7,8,9,10,11,12\}$ is paired with a frequency.

Each of the above is an example of what is called a function. We say that we have a *function* defined on a set A if there is one and only one object paired with each element of A. The set on which a function is defined is said to be the *domain* of the function. The objects which are paired with elements of A are called *values of the function*, and the collection of all of them is called the *range* of the function.

Single letters such as g, f, h, F, G, H, etc., or double or triple letters such as FR, RF, CF, RCF, etc., can be used to designate functions. If x is in the domain of a function f, then "$f(x)$" stands for the object paired with x by this function. This notation is called *functional notation*. "$f(x)$" is read as "f of x" or "f at x" and is not to be confused with "f times x."

Functional notation has already been used in Secs. 1-1 and 1-2, where we wrote $FR(x)$ for the frequency of x, $CF(x)$ for the cumulative frequency of x, $RF(x)$ for the relative frequency of x, and $RCF(x)$ for the relative cumulative frequency of x.

In traditional elementary mathematics it is usually the case that one deals with functions defined on some set of real numbers and of such a nature that the object paired with a particular real number is also a real number. Such functions are called *real* (valued) *functions of a real variable*. Often these functions have the property that one can obtain the number paired with x by performing some algebraic operations on x.

In this case, the function can be defined by an algebraic formula.   For example, we can define a function s by the formula $s(x) = x^2$.   We understand that this formula tells us that to find the value that s pairs with x we simply take x and square it.   Then $s(2) = 2^2 = 4$, $s(3) = 9$, $s(-4) = 16$, $s(\frac{4}{3}) = {}^{16}\!/_9$, $s(h) = h^2$, $s(n) = n^2$,

$$s(1 + t) = (1 + t)^2 = 1 + 2t + t^2, \text{ etc.}$$

Having discussed functional notation, we can look at how the sigma notation for sums can be used with it.   If f is a function defined on the positive whole numbers, we make the following definition:

(3-26) $$\sum_{x=1}^{n} f(x) = f(1) + f(2) + f(3) + \cdots + f(n)$$

We can also use the sigma notation when the lower limit is not 1.   We define

(3-27) $$\sum_{x=m}^{n} f(x) = f(m) + f(m + 1) + f(m + 2) + \cdots + f(n)$$

In a more general fashion, if A is any finite set and f is a function defined on A, we write

$$\sum_{x \in A} f(x)$$

to stand for the sum of all the values $f(x)$ as x runs through all the elements of A.   For example, if $A = \{1,6,11,16\}$ and f is defined by $f(x) = 1/(x + 1)$, then

$$\sum_{x \in A} f(x) = \tfrac{1}{2} + \tfrac{1}{7} + \tfrac{1}{12} + \tfrac{1}{17}$$

In the case of a sequence of numbers $X_1, X_2, \ldots, X_n$ we can think of X_i as being the value of a function at i.   That is, such a sequence defines a function on the set $\{1,2, \ldots ,n\}$.   The function pairs X_i with i.   Then the above notation can also be used with subscripts.   If A is the set given above, for example,

$$\sum_{i \in A} X_i = X_1 + X_6 + X_{11} + X_{16}$$

Another way to think about functions is as follows.   If f is a function defined on a set A, then we can think of f as a kind of machine.   It is possible to "feed into" this machine any element x of A.   The machine then "operates" and puts out an object $f(x)$.   We illustrate this schemati-

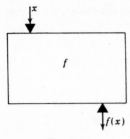

Fig. 3-1

cally in Fig. 3-1. If an element not in the domain of f is fed into the machine, then f simply fails to operate and gives no output. A real function of a real variable can be thought of as a machine which, when given a real number x in the domain, puts out a real number $f(x)$. For other types of functions the input might be a pair of real numbers (see Prob. 3-37) or a set. The outputs for most of the functions that we shall consider will be numbers, but for the most general notion of a function we allow the output to be any kind of object.

PROBLEMS

3-28. Let the function f be defined by $f(x) = x^2$ and find the following:

(a) $f(3)$ (b) $f(-1)$ (c) $f(0)$

(d) $f(-5)$ (e) $f(a)$ (f) $f(a + 1)$

3-29. If the function g is defined by $g(t) = (t + 1)/(t - 1)$ and f is as in Prob. 3-28, find

(a) $f(g(t))$ (b) $g(f(t))$

3-30. If C is the set of all students in your statistics class and $S(x)$ is defined to be the home state of student x in that class, show that S is a function. What is the domain of S? What is its range?

3-31. Let C be defined as in Prob. 3-30 and for x in C, let $W(x)$ stand for the weight of student x. Show that W is a function. What is the domain of W? What is its approximate range?

3-32. Let C be defined as in Prob. 3-30, and for x in C let $y = P(x)$ mean that y is a parent of x. Is P a function? Explain.

3-33. With C as before and for x in C, let $S(x)$ be zero if x is male and $S(x)$ be 1 if x is female. Is S a function? Explain. If we assume that there are n students in C and consider their names to be $x_1, x_2, x_3, \ldots, x_n$, interpret each of the following:

(a) $\sum_{i=1}^{n} S(x_i)$ (b) $\sum_{i=1}^{n} [1 - S(x_i)]$

*3-34. Let A be a set in a universal set I. Define a function f_A (read as "f sub A") on I by

$$f_A(x) = 1 \qquad \text{if } x \in A$$
$$f_A(x) = 0 \qquad \text{if } x \notin A$$

Then we call f the *characteristic function* for A. If $I = \{1,2,3, \ldots ,n\}$, interpret

(a) $\sum_{i=1}^{n} f_A(i)$ (b) $\sum_{i=1}^{n} [1 - f_A(i)]$

*3-35. Find a way to express $f_{A \cap B}$ in terms of f_A and f_B.

*3-36. Express $f_{A'}$ in terms of f_A.

3-37. If, to each pair of objects (x,y) in a given set of pairs D, there is made to correspond a single object from a set R, then this correspondence is said to be a function of two variables. If the function is called f, then the functional notation is used in a manner similar to that for functions of a single variable and we write $f(x,y)$ for the object made to correspond to (x,y). If x and y are real numbers and $x^2 + y^2$ is the real number made to correspond to (x,y) by the function f, find

(a) $f(0,0)$ (b) $f(1,2)$ (c) $f(2,1)$

(d) $f(0,y)$ (e) $f(a,b)$ (f) $f(t + 1, t - 1)$

3-38. More generally than in Prob. 3-37, we can define a function f of n variables $x_1, x_2, \ldots, x_n$ and write $f(x_1, x_2, \ldots, x_n)$ for the value corresponding to the n-tuple $(x_1, x_2, \ldots, x_n)$. Consider, for example, the functions defined by the following equations:

$$S(x_1, x_2, \ldots, x_n) = x_1 + x_2 + \cdots + x_n = \sum_{i=1}^{n} x_i$$

$$M(x_1, x_2, \ldots, x_n) = \frac{x_1 + x_2 + \cdots + x_n}{n}$$

$$s(x_1, x_2, \ldots, x_n) = x_1^2 + x_2^2 + \cdots + x_n^2$$

$$H(x_1, x_2, \ldots, x_n) = \frac{1}{1/x_1 + 1/x_2 + \cdots + 1/x_n}$$

(a) Find $S(x_1, x_2, \ldots, x_{10})$ if $x_i = 5$ for $i = 1, 2, \ldots, 10$.

(b) Find $S(x_1, x_2, \ldots, x_{10})$ if $x_i = i$ for $i = 1, 2, \ldots, 10$.

(c) Find $M(x_1, x_2, \ldots, x_{10})$ if $x_i = 5$ for $i = 1, 2, \ldots, 10$.

(d) Find $M(x_1, x_2, \ldots, x_{10})$ if $x_i = i$ for $i = 1, 2, \ldots, 10$.

(e) Find $s(x_1, x_2, \ldots, x_{15})$ if $x_i = 2$ for $i = 1, 2, \ldots, 15$.

(f) Find $H(x_1, x_2, \ldots, x_{10})$ for the values given in parts a and b.

3-39. If we define the function $\rho(x)$ ("ρ" is the Greek letter "rho" and is pronounced "row") by $\rho(x) = \sqrt{x}$, evaluate the following:

(a) $\rho(4)$ (b) $\rho(10)$ (c) $\rho(0)$

(d) $\rho(1)$ (e) $\rho(.0036)$ (f) $\rho(0.00001)$

3-40. Let $A = \{2,4,6,8,10\}$ and $B = \{3,5,8,10,13,15,18\}$. Write out the following in expanded form and simplify if possible.

(a) $\displaystyle\sum_{x \in A} \frac{1}{x}$ (b) $\displaystyle\sum_{x \in A} \frac{1}{x^2}$ (c) $\displaystyle\sum_{x \in B} \frac{1}{x - 1}$

(d) $\displaystyle\sum_{k \in B} X_k$ (e) $\displaystyle\sum_{j \in B} Z_j$ (f) $\displaystyle\sum_{k \in A \cup B} k$

(g) $\displaystyle\sum_{x \in A \cap B} x^2$ (h) $\displaystyle\sum_{i \in B \cap A'} X_i$

(i) $\displaystyle\sum_{k \in B} f(k)$ where $f(k) = 1$ if k is even and $f(k) = 0$ if k is odd

(j) $\displaystyle\sum_{i \in A} g(i)$ where $g(i) = 1$ if $i \in B$ and $g(i) = 0$ if $i \notin B$

3-41. Expand and simplify the following, if possible:

(a) $\displaystyle\sum_{k=2}^{5} k$ (b) $\displaystyle\sum_{k=3}^{5} \frac{1}{k^2}$ (c) $\displaystyle\sum_{i=2}^{9} y_i$

(d) $\displaystyle\sum_{k=0}^{4} \frac{1}{k + 1}$ (e) $\displaystyle\sum_{i=4}^{4} 6X_i$ (f) $\displaystyle\sum_{i=3}^{10} (X_i + Y_i)$

$(g) \displaystyle\sum_{i=2}^{5} (X_i + 6)$ $(h) \displaystyle\sum_{x=10}^{20} \frac{1}{x}$ $(i) \displaystyle\sum_{n=10}^{20} \left(1 + \frac{1}{n}\right)$

$(j) \displaystyle\sum_{x=0}^{5} f(x+1)$ $(k) \displaystyle\sum_{i=1}^{5} (i-r)^2$ $(l) \displaystyle\sum_{i=2}^{7} (i-t)^2$

3-6. Set functions

Let us return to the experiment with the two dice, where the random variable X represents the number of spots uppermost on the dice after they are thrown. The domain of this variable is the collection $S = \{2,3,4, \ldots ,12\}$. Recalling the experiment in which the dice were thrown 100 times and the results recorded, we note that, if A is any subset of S, we can associate with A the total frequency with which the values in A occurred as results in our 100 trials. For example, if $A = \{2,4\}$, we see from Table 1-2 that the frequency thus associated with A is 7, since the 2 occurred twice and the 4 five times. But if such a frequency is determined by each subset of S, some thought convinces us that this association is a function defined on the collection of all subsets of S. Such a function, i.e., one whose domain is a collection of sets, is called a *set function*.

If A is a finite nonempty set of numbers, the following are further examples of set functions:

(3-42)   max (A) = largest element in A
(3-43)   min (A) = smallest element in A
(3-44) $No\ (A)$ = number of distinct[1] elements in A

For example,[2] max $\{1,2,3,4,5\} = 5$, min $\{1,2,3,4,5\} = 1$, and

$$No\ \{1,2,3,4,5\} = 5$$

Each of these functions will be of use to us as we proceed. The reader should verify the following by considering some subsets of the set S described above:

(3-45)   max $(A \cup B)$ = max $\{$max (A), max $(B)\}$
(3-46)   max $(A \cup B) \geq$ max (A)
(3-47)   max $(A \cap B) \leq$ max (A)

---

[1] Two elements are said to be distinct if they are not the same; that is, x and y are distinct if $x \neq y$.

[2] In place of "max $(\{1,2,3,4,5\})$" we write more simply "max $\{1,2,3,4,5\}$," where the parentheses are omitted. In general, we allow the braces in a set description to play two roles when we indicate a value of a set function. They serve to indicate the beginning and end of the set description and, at the same time, serve as grouping symbols in the functional notation.

Some properties of the set function No will be of interest in what follows.

(3-48)   If $No\ (I) = n$, then, for all A, $No\ (A) \leq n$.
(3-49)   For all A, $No\ (A) \geq 0$.

Here, I is the universal set and (3-48) simply asserts that the number of elements in a set cannot exceed the number of elements in the universal set.   (3-49) is the assertion that any set has at least zero elements.

(3-50)   If $A \cap B = \phi$, then $No\ (A \cup B) = No\ (A) + No\ (B)$.
(3-51) $No\ (A \cup B) = No\ (A) + No\ (B) - No\ (A \cap B)$.

If A and B are disjoint, that is, if A and B have no elements in common, then the number of elements in the union of A and B is simply the sum of the number in A and the number in B.   Thus, (3-50).   If, on the other hand, A and B have elements in common and we consider $No\ (A) + No\ (B)$, we see that this sum counts each element in $A \cap B$ twice.   Hence, to get $No\ (A \cup B)$, we must subtract from $No\ (A) + No\ (B)$ the number of elements in $A \cap B$.   Hence Eq. (3-51).

The functions FR and RF introduced in Chap. 1 can now be generalized.   If $(X_1, X_2, \ldots, X_n)$ is the result of n trials for a random variable X, we defined $FR(x)$ to be the frequency with which the value x was taken on.   Using the notation of this section, this can be stated as

(3-52) $$FR(x) = No\ \{i: X_i = x\}$$

That is, $FR(x)$ is the number of subscripts i (number of trials) for which $X_i = x$.   More generally, if S is the sample space for X and A is any subset of S, we define the *empirical frequency function* for subsets of S by

(3-53) $$FR(A) = No\ \{i: X_i \in A\}$$

That is, $FR(A)$ is the number of results that were in the set A.   [This dual use of the notation "FR" should lead to no confusion since, for any $x \in S$, $FR(\{x\}) = FR(x)$, where on the left "FR" is used in the sense of (3-53) and on the right "FR" is used in the sense of (3-52).]   If, for instance, the result of five throws of a die is $(1,1,5,2,1)$ and $A = \{1,2,3\}$, then $FR(A) = 4$ for these data.

To generalize the empirical relative frequency function introduced earlier, we define

(3-54) $$RF(A) = \frac{FR(A)}{n}$$

for any A contained in S.   Then $RF(A)$ is the proportion of the results which are in A. $RF(A)$ is called the *empirical relative frequency* for A for the outcome $(X_1, X_2, \ldots, X_n)$.   For any A,

(3-55)
$$0 \leq RF(A) \leq 1$$

since we must have $0 \leq FR(A) \leq n$ [from (3-48) and (3-49)].   Also

(3-56)
$$RF(S) = 1$$

since every result must be in S, so that $FR(S) = n$.   If A and B are subsets of S and $A \cap B = \phi$, then the sets $\{i: X_i \in A\}$ and $\{i: X_i \in B\}$ must be disjoint.   Consequently,

$$No\ \{i: X_i \in A \cup B\} = No\ \{i: X_i \in A\} + No\ \{i: X_i \in B\}$$

and hence,

(3-57)   *If $A \cap B = \phi$, then $RF(A \cup B) = RF(A) + RF(B)$.*

If A and B are not necessarily disjoint, we have

(3-58)
$$RF(A \cup B) = RF(A) + RF(B) - RF(A \cap B)$$

If the results of 10 throws of a die are 6, 2, 6, 3, 1, 4, 5, 2, 1, 4 and $A = \{1,2\}$ and $B = \{2,4,6\}$, then $n = 10$ and $RF(A) = .4$, $RF(B) = .6$, $RF(A \cup B) = .6 + .4 - .2 = .8$.

In the general case, if A is any subset of S, then

(3-59)
$$RF(A) = \sum_{x \in A} RF(x)$$

[from (3-57), if you like] and

(3-60)
$$RF(A') = 1 - RF(A)$$

For instance, with the 10 throws of the die as given above,

$$RF\{1,2\} = RF(1) + RF(2) = .2 + .2 = .4$$

Also, $RF\{3,4,5,6\} = 1 - RF\{1,2\} = 1 - .4 = .6$.   If we wish to prove Eq. (3-60), we can do so as follows: $A' \cup A = S$ by (2-25) and $A' \cap A = \phi$ by (2-26).   Then $RF(A' \cup A) = RF(S) = 1$ by (3-56). But also $RF(A' \cup A) = RF(A') + RF(A)$ by (3-57).   Hence,

$$RF(A') = 1 - RF(A)$$

PROBLEMS

3-61. Let the universal set I be the collection of all students at your school or in your class.   Let M, W, F, S_1, J, S_2 be the set of all men, women, and freshman, sophomore, junior, and senior students, respectively.   Describe in words and ascertain or estimate the following:

(*a*) $No\ (M \cup W)$
(*c*) $No\ (W \cap F)$

(*b*) $No\ (M \cap S_1)$
(*d*) $No\ (W \cup S_2)$

(e) $No\,(F \cap S_1)$ (f) $No\,(F \cup S_1)$

(g) $No\,[(M \cap F) \cup (M \cap J)]$ (h) $No\,(M \cup S_2)$

(i) $No\,(M) + No\,(S_2) - No\,(M \cap S_2)$ (j) $No\,(F' \cap W)$

(k) $No\,(F' \cup W)$

3-62. State and argue for the validity of the analogues of (3-45), (3-46), and (3-47) for the function min (A).

3-63. Show that, if A is an infinite set of numbers, then min (A) may not exist.

3-64. For the data of Table 1-2 evaluate FR and RF for each of the following sets:

(a) $\{2,5\}$ (b) $\{2,4,6,8,10,12\}$

(c) $\{3,5,7,9,11\}$ (d) $\{2,11,12\}$

3-65. Using the data of Table 1-2 and appropriately chosen subsets, illustrate (3-57) through (3-60).

3-66. Verify by argument or examples that, if $A \subseteq B$, then $RF(A) \leqq RF(B)$.

3-67. Verify the following by examples or argument:

(a) If $A \subseteq B$, then max $(A) \leqq$ max (B).

(b) If $A \subseteq B$, then min $(A) \geqq$ min (B).

(c) If $A \subseteq B$, then $No\,(A) \leqq No\,(B)$.

(d) For any set A, min $(A) \leqq$ max (A).   (Does the equality ever hold?)

3-68. Prove Eq. (3-58).

*3-69. (Continuation of Prob. 3-6.) Suppose that a_{ij} is the number in the ith row and the jth column of a matrix A which has n rows and m columns. We let r_i be the smallest number in the ith row. That is,

$$r_i = \min\ \{a_{i1}, a_{i2}, \ldots, a_{im}\}$$

The largest of the numbers $r_1, r_2, \ldots, r_n$ is denoted by "$\max\limits_{i} \min\limits_{j} a_{ij}$." That is, by definition,

$$\max_{i} \min_{j} a_{ij} = \max\ \{r_1, r_2, \ldots, r_n\}$$

Similarly, if we let

$$c_j = \max\ \{a_{1j}, a_{2j}, \ldots, a_{nj}\}$$

then we make the definition

$$\min_{j} \max_{i} a_{ij} = \min\ \{c_1, c_2, \ldots, c_m\}$$

Determine for each of the following matrices whether or not $\min\limits_{j} \max\limits_{i} a_{ij} = \max\limits_{i} \min\limits_{j} a_{ij}$.

(a) $\begin{pmatrix} 3 & -4 \\ 2 & -2 \\ 1 & 1 \end{pmatrix}$ (b) $\begin{pmatrix} 3 & 2 & 1 \\ 4 & -5 & 3 \\ -4 & 2 & 1 \end{pmatrix}$

(c) $\begin{pmatrix} -1 & 1 \\ 1 & -1 \end{pmatrix}$ (d) $\begin{pmatrix} 1 & 2 & 3 & 4 & 5 \\ -5 & -4 & -3 & -2 & -1 \end{pmatrix}$

*3-70. (See preceding problem.) If $a_{i_0 j_0}$ is an element in a matrix A for which

$$a_{i_0 j_0} = \max_{i} \min_{j} a_{ij} = \min_{j} \max_{i} a_{ij}$$

then $a_{i_0 j_0}$ is called a *saddle point* for A.

Interpret the entries in the matrix as altitudes (above and below sea level) at the intersection of north-south and east-west lines on a map and explain the source of the name "saddle point." Find the saddle points, if any, for the matrices of Prob. 3-69.

3-7. Inequalities and absolute values

In the preceding material we have often used the symbols "$<$" and "$\leq$". For those readers not familiar with inequalities and their properties we now discuss briefly the use of these symbols.

If a and b are real numbers, $a < b$ means that $b - a$ is positive. $a > b$ means that $b - a$ is negative. $a \leq b$ means that $a < b$ or $a = b$. $a \geq b$ means that $a > b$ or $a = b$. Inequalities share many properties with equalities, but there are occasional marked differences. If a, b, and c are any real numbers, the following are true:

(3-71)   *Either $a < b$ or $b < a$ or $a = b$.*
(3-72)   *If $a < b$ and $b < c$, then $a < c$.*
(3-73)   *If $a < b$, then $a + c < b + c$.*
(3-74)   *If $a < b$ and $c > 0$, then $ac < bc$.*
(3-75)   *If $a < b$ and $c < 0$, then $ac > bc$.*

If "$<$" is replaced by "$\leq$" in (3-72) through (3-75), we obtain the analogous laws for "$\leq$." With these laws we can "solve" simple inequalities in a manner similar to that used with equalities. For example, from

$$\frac{x - 4}{3} < 10$$

we obtain $x - 4 < 30$, by (3-74), and then $x < 34$, by (3-73). As another example, from

$$\frac{x + 3}{-2} < .4$$

we get $x + 3 > -.8$ and then $x > -3.8$. The *continued inequality* $a < x < b$ means that $a < x$ *and* $x < b$. For example, $3 < x < 5$ means that $3 < x$ and $x < 5$; that is, x lies between 3 and 5.

Another notion which will be useful to us is that of the absolute value of a number. The *absolute value* of a number x is denoted by $|x|$ and is defined by

(3-76) $\qquad\qquad \begin{aligned} |x| &= x \qquad \text{if } x \geq 0 \\ |x| &= -x \qquad \text{if } x < 0 \end{aligned}$

Thus, $|4| = |-4| = 4$ and $|-1.7| = |1.7| = 1.7$. If x is any number,

(3-77) $|x| < a$ *if and only if* $-a < x < a$.

For example, $|x| < 2$ is equivalent to $-2 < x < 2$; that is, x is between -2 and 2. If we wish to find the values of x for which $|x - 3| < 2$, we write $-2 < x - 3 < 2$, by (3-77), and then $1 < x < 5$, by (3-73). Then, for example, $\{x : |x - 3| < 2\} = \{x : 1 < x < 5\}$.

Sets such as this last one arise so often that there is a special terminology for them.   The set $\{x: a < x < b\}$ is called an *interval* from a to b.   It is also called an interval from a to b if "$\leq$" occurs in place of either or both of the "$<$" symbols.   The set $\{t: -3 \leq t < 6\}$ is, for instance, called an interval from -3 to 6.   We may also speak of the set $\{x: x > a\}$ as an *interval* or an *infinite interval*.   Such a set consists of all those numbers greater than a.   Similarly, $\{x: x < a\}$ is said to be an *interval* or an *infinite interval*.

PROBLEMS

3-78. Express each of the following sets as intervals or unions of intervals:

(a) $\{x: 5x > 7\}$ (b) $\{x: 3 < 4x < 8\}$ (c) $\left\{x: 5 \leq \dfrac{4-x}{3}\right\}$

(d) $\left\{x: \left|\dfrac{x-3}{10}\right| < 1\right\}$ (e) $\left\{x: \left|\dfrac{x-10}{2}\right| < 2\right\}$ (f) $\{x: |x| \geq 2\}$

(g) $\left\{x: \left|\dfrac{x+2}{2}\right| > 2\right\}$ (h) $\left\{x: \left|\dfrac{x-2}{10}\right| \geq 1\right\}$ (i) $\left\{x: \left|\dfrac{x-4}{2}\right| \geq 3\right\}$

3-79. Prove that, for all x, $|x^2| = x^2$.

3-80. Verify by example that $\sqrt{x^2} = |x|$ for all x.

3-81. Make up examples to illustrate the fact that, for all numbers x and y, $|x + y| \leq |x| + |y|$.

3-82. Simplify

(a) $\{x: 1 \leq x < 3\} \cup \{x: 3 \leq x < 5\}$ (b) $\{x: 1 \leq x < 3\} \cap \{x: 2 \leq x < 4\}$
(c) $\{x: x > 5\} \cap \{x: x \leq 7\}$ (d) $\{x: x \geq 5\} \cap \{x: 0 \leq x \leq 7\}$

3-83. Describe the following sets as intervals or unions of intervals:

(a) $\{x: x^2 < 1\}$ (b) $\{y: y^2 \geq 4\}$ (c) $\{z: z^2 + 1 \leq 0\}$

*3-84. If A is any (finite or infinite) set of numbers, the *least upper bound* of A [denoted by "lub (A)"] is defined to be a number x_0 with the properties that (1) if $x \in A$, then $x \leq x_0$ and (2) if $x \leq x_1$, for all $x \in A$, then $x_1 \geq x_0$.   Find lub (A) if A is

(a) $\{x: 0 < x < 1\}$ (b) $\{x: 0 < x \leq 1\}$ (c) $\{x: x^2 < 2\}$
(d) $\{\frac{1}{2}, \frac{2}{3}, \frac{3}{4}, \frac{4}{5}, \ldots\}$ (e) $\{1, \frac{1}{2}, \frac{1}{3}, \frac{1}{4}, \ldots\}$

*3-85. In analogy with lub (A) as defined in Prob. 3-84 define the greatest lower bound of A [glb (A)].   Find the glb for the sets of Prob. 3-84.

*3-86. Prove that, if lub (A) exists, then it is unique (so that lub is a set function).

*3-87. Prove that, if A is finite, then lub $(A) = \max (A)$.

3-88. Prove that $a - e < b < a + e$ if and only if $b - e < a < b + e$.

*3-89.   Prove that, if $0 \leq p \leq 1$, then $0 \leq p(1 - p) \leq \frac{1}{4}$.

3-90. If $Y = aX + b$, where $a > 0$, show that $x_1 < X < x_2$ if and only if $ax_1 + b < Y < ax_2 + b$.

3-91. Show that

$$\left|\frac{x-b}{a}\right| \leq K$$

if and only if $aK - b \leq x \leq aK + b$. $(a > 0.)$

3-8. Graphs

In a town in which the streets meet at right angles it is easy to instruct a stranger how to get from the corner we are on to some other intersec-

tion. "Go this way (pointing) three blocks and then four blocks to the
left."   In a similar fashion, it is easy to describe how to go from one point
on a plane to another if certain directions in the plane are established.
In Fig. 3-2 a plane is indicated on which we find horizontal and vertical
lines intersecting at right angles at a point O.

We can locate the point P shown in the plane by saying that it is three
units to the right of and four units above the point O.   The point Q is two
units to the left of and three units below O.   In general, a point in the

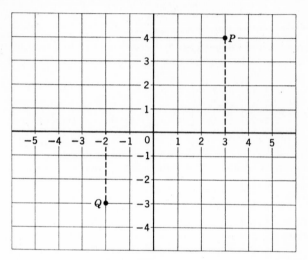

Fig. 3-2

plane can be located by giving two "directed numbers" which tell us how
far to go right or left and how far to go up or down in order to reach the
point from O.   If we adopt the (standard) convention that to the right is
"positive" and upward is "positive" while the opposite directions are
"negative," then we can locate (i.e., identify) a point by simply giving
an ordered pair of real numbers.   With this convention we would say that
P *is* the point $(3,4)$ while Q *is* the point $(-2,-3)$.   The point $(5,-4)$
would be the one we reach by going five to the right from O and then
down four.   The point $(-3,3)$ would be reached by going three to the left
from O and then up three.   The numbers used to identify a point are
called *coordinates* of the point, and we speak of the points as being in a
rectangular coordinate system.   The point O is called the *origin*, and the
horizontal and vertical lines through O are called the *coordinate axes*.

Often we introduce variables to stand for the coordinates of points.
Thus, we may speak of the point P with coordinates (x,y).   Using "x" to
refer to the first coordinate of the point and "y" to refer to the second, we
then speak of the horizontal axis in Fig. 3-2 as the x axis and the vertical

one as the y axis. The x coordinate of P is then its (directed) distance from the y axis, and the y coordinate of P is its (directed) distance from the x axis.

If A is a set of points in the plane, by the term *graph of A* we mean a pictorial representation of the set. For example, the set $\{(x,y): x \geqq 1$

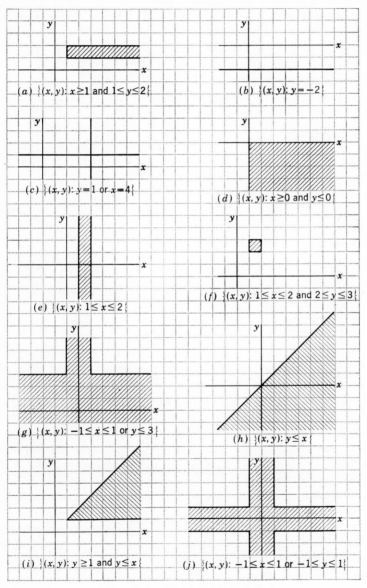

(a) $\{(x, y): x \geq 1$ and $1 \leq y \leq 2\}$

(b) $\{(x, y): y = -2\}$

(c) $\{(x, y): y = 1$ or $x = 4\}$

(d) $\{(x, y): x \geq 0$ and $y \leq 0\}$

(e) $\{(x, y): 1 \leq x \leq 2\}$

(f) $\{(x, y): 1 \leq x \leq 2$ and $2 \leq y \leq 3\}$

(g) $\{(x, y): -1 \leq x \leq 1$ or $y \leq 3\}$

(h) $\{(x, y): y \leq x\}$

(i) $\{(x, y): y \geq 1$ and $y \leq x\}$

(j) $\{(x, y): -1 \leq x \leq 1$ or $-1 \leq y \leq 1\}$

FIG. 3-3. Graphs of several sets.

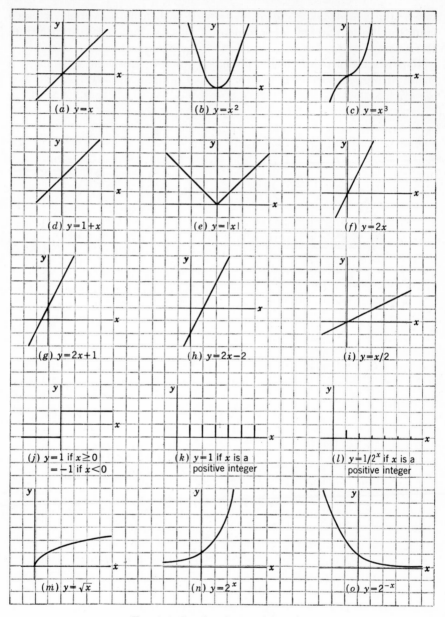

Fig. 3-4. Graphs of several functions.

and $1 \leqq y \leqq 2$} is the set of those points whose x coordinates are greater than or equal to 1 and whose y coordinates are between 1 and 2, inclusive. The graph of this set is shown in Fig. 3-3a.   The graphs of several other sets are also shown in Fig. 3-3.

If f is a real function whose domain is a set of real numbers, a graph of $\{(x,y): y = f(x)\}$ is called a *graph of the function*.   That is, a graph of f is a graph of those points whose coordinates satisfy $y = f(x)$, where x is the first coordinate and y is the second. f, being a function, pairs at most one y value with each real x.   This means geometrically that any vertical line in the plane intersects the graph in at most one point.   The graph of a function f is also spoken of as the *graph of the equation* $y = f(x)$.   In Fig. 3-4 the graphs of several functions are shown.

In many cases the graph of a function is an unbroken smooth curve. In other cases, the graph is a straight line or a broken curve.   In any case, however, when a function is defined for all real numbers, we speak of its graph as being a "curve," although it may not be a curve in the usual sense.   In the case of functions such as that shown in Fig. 3-4k we make a convention to aid the eye in reading the graph.   Actually for that function the only points that should appear are the points $(1,1)$, $(2,1)$, $(3,1)$, $(4,1)$, ...   However, when we draw the graph, we also draw the vertical lines running between these points and the x axis.   The points on these segments that we add do not belong to the graph of the function, but their existence makes the graph easier to read.   We already made use of this convention in Sec. 1-2 when we graphed the functions RF and FR (see Fig. 1-1).

A natural question to ask is: "What functions have graphs which are straight lines?"   The answer is given by the following result.

(3-92)   *A real function f whose domain is the set of all real numbers has a straight line for its graph if and only if, for some constants m and b, $f(x) = mx + b$.*

Hence, if we are asked to graph the function $f(x) = x + 2$, we recognize immediately that its graph will be a straight line (with $m = 1$ and $b = 2$). Once we realize that the graph of a certain function is a straight line, it is easy to draw the graph, since two points determine a line.   To graph $f(x) = x + 2$, we note that $(0,2)$ and $(1,3)$ are points whose coordinates satisfy the defining equation, graph these points, and then draw the straight line through these points (see Fig. 3-5).

As a consequence of (3-92), a function f given by $f(x) = mx + b$ is called a *linear function*.   The constant m is called the *slope* of the line determined by f. m is the number of units that y increases as we move along the line and let x increase one unit.   A slope of 10 means that we must go up 10 units to stay on the line as we move to the right one unit. A slope of -5 means that we must move down five units to stay on the line as we move to the right one unit.

If a certain line is the graph of $f(x) = mx + b$, then we say that $y = mx + b$ is the *equation of the line*. We also then speak of the line as *being* the line $y = mx + b$. The constant b is called the y *intercept* of the line. This is so because the line "intercepts" the y axis at the point $(0,b)$.

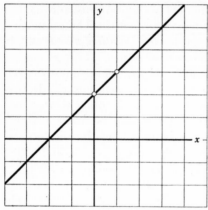

FIG. 3-5. Graph of $y = x + 2$.

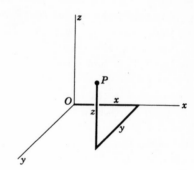

FIG. 3-6

If a line passes through the points (x_1,y_1) and (x_2,y_2), then its slope is given by

$$(3\text{-}93) \qquad\qquad m = \frac{y_2 - y_1}{x_2 - x_1}$$

as we might expect, since the slope m is the change in y per unit change in x (see Prob. 3-100). If a line passes through the point (x_1,y_1) and has slope m, then the equation of the line is

$$(3\text{-}94) \qquad\qquad y = y_1 + m(x - x_1)$$

This is so because if (x,y) is any point on the line different from (x_1,y_1), we must have $m = (y - y_1)/(x - x_1)$, from (3-93), and solving this equation for y yields (3-94).

A great deal of time could be spent graphing different kinds of functions, but for our purposes we need primarily (1) to know what the graph of a function is, (2) to be able to graph a linear function, and (3) to be able to find the equation of a line if we know its slope and a point on it.

If we expand our horizons and consider a three-dimensional space instead of simply a plane, we get the situation shown in Fig. 3-6.

In this picture we have represented a point O (called the *origin*) through which three mutually perpendicular lines (the axes) are drawn. We are to think of the lines Ox and Oz as lying in the plane of the paper while the line Oy "comes out of the paper" perpendicular to both the other axes.   To locate the point P in this *three-dimensional rectangular coordinate system* we say that to reach P from O one should go x units to the right, then y units out from the plane of the paper (toward the observer), and then z units up.   The point P is then identified by giving three directed numbers if we adopt the conventions that "to the right," "toward the observer" (or "in front of"), and "up" are the positive directions.   We call these three directed numbers the *coordinates* of P. The plane determined by the lines Ox and Oy is called the xy plane.

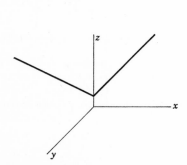

Fig. 3-7. Graph of $z = x + y + 1$.

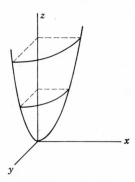

Fig. 3-8. Graph of $z = x^2 + y^2$.

Similarly for the yz plane and xz plane.   The point P with coordinates x, y, and z is denoted by "(x,y,z)" and lies x units to the right of the yz plane, y units in front of the xz plane, and z units above the xy plane. Most of the details of the three-dimensional case need not concern us, but we do wish to discuss briefly the nature of a graph of a "function of two variables."   Suppose that f is a real function whose domain is a set of points in the xy plane.   That is, f pairs with each point in a certain region in the xy plane a real number z.   If a point P in this region has coordinates (x,y) in the xy plane and f pairs the number z with P, then we write $z = f(x,y)$.   We call f a *function of two* (real) *variables*.   The *graph* of f is the set of points $\{(x,y,z): z = f(x,y)\}$.   Whereas the graph of a function in two dimensions is, in general, a curve, the graph of a function of two variables is, in general, a surface.

An example is shown in Fig. 3-7, where we have graphed the function defined by $f(x,y) = x + y + 1$.   The surface which is the graph of this function is a plane intersecting the coordinate planes in the lines shown. The graph of $f(x,y) = x^2 + y^2$ is shown in Fig. 3-8.   (Actually Fig. 3-8 shows only one-quarter of the surface, the other parts being hidden behind the coordinate planes.)

PROBLEMS

3-95. Graph the following sets in the plane:
$A = \{(x,y): x \leq 0\}$, $B = \{(x,y): x > 0 \text{ and } y > 0\}$
$C = \{(x,y): |x| > 1\}$, $D = \{(x,y): -1 < y < 1\}$
$E = \{(x,y): x < 2 \text{ and } y > 1\}$, $F = \{(x,y): x < 2 \text{ or } y > 1\}$
3-96. For the sets of Prob. 3-95, graph $A \cap C$, $C \cap D$, $F \cap D$, $C \cup D$, $D \cup B$, $F \cap C$.

3-97. Graph the straight lines

(a) $y = -4$ (b) $y = x$ (c) $y = 2x + 5$
(d) $y = 7 - x$ (e) $y = -2x - 2$ (f) $y = 2x$
(g) $y = -2x$ (h) $y = 3 + 2(x - 4)$ (i) $y = 10(x - 1)$
(j) $y = \frac{1}{2}x + 1$ (k) $10y = x - 20$ (l) $10y + x = 20$
                  (m) $4y = x$

3-98. Sketch the line and find its equation for the following (m is the slope and b is the y intercept):

(a) $m = 1$ and $b = -4$ (b) $m = -1$ and $b = -4$
(c) $m = 3$ and $b = 0$ (d) $m = 0$ and $b = 0$
(e) $m = -2$ and $b = 4$

3-99. Sketch the line and find its equation if it has slope m and passes through (x_1, y_1), where

(a) $m = 1$, $x_1 = 0$, $y_1 = 0$ (b) $m = 2$, $x_1 = 10$, $y_1 = 5$
(c) $m = -4$, $x_1 = 3$, $y_1 = 3$ (d) $m = -4$, $x_1 = -3$, $y_1 = 3$
(e) $m = -4$, $x_1 = -3$, $y_1 = -3$ (f) $m = -\frac{1}{2}$, $x_1 = 1$, $y_1 = 1$
(g) $m = -3$, $x_1 = 0$, $y_1 = 3$ (h) $m = -1$, $x_1 = -10$, $y_1 = 10$

3-100. Prove Eq. (3-93).

3-101. Graph the following functions:

(a) $f(x) = 0$ if $x < 0$ (b) $F(x) = 0$ if $x < 0$
     $f(x) = 1$ if $0 \leq x \leq 1$ $F(x) = x$ if $0 \leq x \leq 1$
     $f(x) = 0$ if $x > 0$ $F(x) = 1$ if $x > 0$

(c) $g(x) = 1$ if $|x| < 1$ (d) $h(x) = x + 1$ if $-1 \leq x \leq 0$
     $g(x) = 0$ otherwise $h(x) = -x + 1$ if $0 < x \leq 1$
                               $h(x) = 0$ otherwise

(e) $f(x) = \frac{1}{10}$ if $x = 1, 2, 3, 4, 5, 6, 7, 8, 9,$ or 10
     $f(x) = 0$ otherwise
*(f) $f(x) = (\frac{1}{2})^x$ if $x = 0, 1, 2, \ldots$
     $f(x) = 0$ otherwise
*(g) $f(x) = 0$ if $x < 0$
     $f(x) = x^2$ if $0 \leq x \leq 1$
     $f(x) = x$ if $x > 1$

*(h) $f(x) = \dfrac{1}{1 + x^2}$

3-102. Graph the function $f(p) = \sqrt{p(1 - p)}$.

3-103. In a three-dimensional rectangular coordinate system graph the following points: $(0,0,1)$, $(1,1,1)$, $(2,0,3)$, $(0,1,3)$, $(2,1,0)$, $(1,2,3)$, $(2,1,2)$.

3-104. Graph the following sets in three space: $\{(x,y,z): x > 1\}$, $\{(x,y,z): z \geq 1\}$, $\{(x,y,z): 1 \leq z \leq 2\}$, $\{(x,y,z): 1 \leq x \leq 2 \text{ and } 1 \leq y \leq 2\}$.

3-105. Graph the functions of two variables defined by

(a) $f(x,y) = 2$

(b) $f(x,y) = x + 1$ (a plane)

(c) $f(x,y) = 2x$ (a plane)

*(d) $f(x,y) = \dfrac{1}{x^2 + y^2}$

*(e) $f(x,y) = \dfrac{1}{1 + x^2 + y^2}$

*(f) $f(x,y) = 2^{-(x^2+y^2)}$

*3-106. f is called a *linear function* of two variables if $f(x,y) = ax + by + c$ for some constants a, b, and c. The graph of such a function is always a plane. Explain how a and b play a role similar to the "slope of a straight line." What is the geometric interpretation of c?

CHAPTER 4

Averages

4-1. The arithmetic mean

No doubt each of you is somewhat familiar with the term "average." Such terms as "the average man," "average value," and "average rainfall" occur frequently in everyday discourse. An "average" is often thought of as being somehow a "typical" or "representative" element for a set, but in some cases this idea may be a trifle misleading.

There are many kinds of averages, although it is common practice in nontechnical discussions to assume that "average" refers to the "mean" or "arithmetic mean," which we now define. If Y_1, Y_2, Y_3, $\ldots$, Y_n are numbers, the *mean* or *arithmetic mean* of these numbers is defined to be the sum of all of them divided by the number of them. Symbolically, we have

$$(4\text{-}1) \qquad \bar{Y} = \frac{\sum_{i=1}^{n} Y_i}{n}$$

where we have written "$\bar{Y}$" (read as "Y bar") for the arithmetic mean of the Y's. This last notation will be used throughout the text. That is, for the arithmetic mean of the numbers X_1, X_2, $\ldots$, X_n we shall write "$\bar{X}$," and similarly when other letters are used.

For example, the mean of the numbers 2, 3, 4, 5, 6, 7, 8, 9, 10, 11, 12 is

$$\frac{2 + 3 + 4 + 5 + 6 + 7 + 8 + 9 + 10 + 11 + 12}{11} = 7$$

PROBLEMS

4-2. Find the mean of the results in each of Probs. 1-3 to 1-17 which you worked. (Use the desk calculator and/or your results of Prob. 3-11.)

4-3. Argue for the fact that min $\{y_1, y_2, \ldots, y_n\} \leqq \bar{y} \leqq$ max $\{y_1, y_2, \ldots, y_n\}$.

4-4. If y_1, y_2, $\ldots$, y_n consist of k values equal to y' and m values equal to y'' and $k + m = n$, then

$$\bar{y} = \frac{ky' + my''}{k + m}$$

Verify that this is so with various numerical examples, or prove it by algebra.

4-5. The reader should note that $\bar{y}$ is determined by the numbers y_1, y_2, . . . , y_n. That is, we can think of $\bar{y}$ as the value of a function M which is a function of the n variables y_1, y_2, . . . , y_n (see Prob. 3-38). In other words, we can write

$$\bar{y} = M(y_1, y_2, \ldots, y_n)$$

to define the function M. Verify the following properties of M by numerical examples or prove them by algebra:

(a) $M(y, y, y, \ldots, y) = y$
(b) If $y_1' > y_1$, then $M(y_1', y_2, y_3, \ldots, y_n) > M(y_1, y_2, y_3, \ldots, y_n)$
(c) $M(cy_1, cy_2, \ldots, cy_n) = cM(y_1, y_2, \ldots, y_n)$
(d) $M(y_1 + d, y_2 + d, \ldots, y_n + d) = M(y_1, y_2, \ldots, y_n) + d$

4-2. Computation of the arithmetic mean from a frequency distribution

In Prob. 4-2 in the previous section, the mean of a set of 100 results was of interest. Direct application of the definition of the mean leads to the process of adding up the 100 individual results (Table 1-1) and then dividing by 100. Since these 100 results may be collected in a frequency distribution (Table 1-2), we ask if we could not simply get the mean from the frequency distribution without considering 100 individual results. This we can do, and in fact, the calculation of the mean from the frequency distribution usually involves less labor than does calculation from the original list of results.

Considering the data of Table 1-2, we see that, in the experiment with the two dice, two results were equal to 2 (i.e., 2 occurred with the frequency 2), four results were equal to 3, five results were equal to 4, etc. If we wish to find the sum of all the results, we may take the individual items in the order suggested by the frequency distribution rather than in the order in which they came up. Then, as we start to add, our sum starts out like this: $2 + 2 + 3 + 3 + 3 + 3 + 4 + 4 + 4 + 4 + 4 + 5 + \cdots$. But this suggests an easier way to get the sum. Instead of writing down the individual items, we should start out $2 \times 2 + 4 \times 3 + 5 \times 4 + \cdots$. Evidently, then, we shall get the grand total of all the results if we multiply each possible result by the frequency with which it occurred and then add all these products. That is, if $X_1, X_2, \ldots, X_{100}$ are the results of the individual trials,

$$\sum_{i=1}^{100} X_i = \sum_{x=2}^{12} xFR(x)$$

The right side of this equation is easier to compute by hand than the left. With a desk calculator which multiplies automatically and accumulates the results of successive multiplications, the right side is much less tedious to work out.

Considering now the general case, suppose that X is a random variable with domain $\{x_1, x_2, \ldots, x_N\}$ and n trials are made which yield the results $X_1, X_2, \ldots, X_n$. If $FR(x_j)$ is the frequency with which x_j occurs in these n trials, then

$$(4\text{-}6) \qquad \sum_{i=1}^{n} X_i = \sum_{j=1}^{N} x_j FR(x_j)$$

and hence,

$$(4\text{-}7) \qquad \bar{X} = \frac{1}{n} \sum_{j=1}^{N} x_j FR(x_j)$$

since there were n trials and to get the mean of the results we divide their sum by n. If we remember that a constant multiplier can be taken inside the "Σ" sign [see Eq. (3-8)] and if we recall the definition of relative frequency [see Eq. (1-1)], we deduce from Eq. (4-7) that also

$$(4\text{-}8) \qquad \bar{X} = \sum_{j=1}^{N} x_j RF(x_j)$$

where $RF(x_j)$ is the relative frequency of x_j.

A good part of the trick of making a long computation less tedious (*and* more accurate!) is to have a clear-cut plan of the step-by-step process you will follow and to display the results of each step in a systematic fashion. Such a plan and systematic display often amounts to the construction of a helpful table.[1] The computation of the mean of the dice experiment is shown in Table 4-1.

Note that in the table and in the sum at the bottom of the table it is possible to omit the subscripts on the x's without confusion. In fact, in this case, since x takes on successive whole numbers as values, the sum below the table could be taken to be

$$\sum_{x=2}^{12} x FR(x)$$

However, a random variable need not, in general, assume only whole numbers as values, and hence we need the more general formulation of Eq. (4-7).

The mean can also be computed directly from the relative frequency distribution and Eq. (4-8). This fact is illustrated in Table 4-2.

---

[1] The construction of such a table is often the core idea in "programming" an electronic computer to do a large problem for you.

Table 4-1
Computation of the Mean for the Data of Table 1-1
$[X$ = total on the two dice; $FR(x)$ = frequency]

x	$FR(x)$	$xFR(x)$
2	2	4
3	4	12
4	5	20
5	5	25
6	14	84
7	18	126
8	14	112
9	14	126
10	12	120
11	8	88
12	4	48
Totals......	100	765

$$n = 100 \qquad \Sigma\, xFR(x) = 765$$
$$\bar{X} = {}^{765}\!/_{100} = 7.65$$

Table 4-2
Computation of the Mean from $RF(x)$ for the Data of Table 1-1
$[X$ = total on the two dice; $RF(x)$ = relative frequency]

x	$RF(x)$	$xRF(x)$
2	.02	.04
3	.04	.12
4	.05	.20
5	.05	.25
6	.14	.84
7	.18	1.26
8	.14	1.12
9	.14	1.26
10	.12	1.20
11	.08	.88
12	.04	.48
Totals......	1.00	7.65

$$\bar{X} = \Sigma\, xRF(x) = 7.65$$

PROBLEMS

4-9. Compute the mean for the data of Probs. 1-3 through 1-17 which you worked. Work directly from the frequency distributions and/or the relative frequency distributions.

4-10. Find the mean for each set of data obtained in Prob. 1-23.

4-11. Find the mean for the data of Prob. 1-19.

4-12. Collect the following data on each person in the class:

(a) Hair color   (b) Eye color   (c) Sex

Determine the frequency with which each hair color, each eye color, and each sex occurs in the class. Does it make sense to ask for the mean hair color, the mean eye color, or the mean sex? Explain.

4-13. Show that in the notation used in this section

$$\sum_{i=1}^{n} X_i^2 = \sum_{j=1}^{N} x_j^2 FR(x_j)$$

4-3. Other averages

Loosely, an average should somehow indicate the "center" of a set of numbers. Hence, averages are sometimes referred to as "measures of central tendency." To show the need for different measures of central tendency, we shall consider various examples.

Suppose that you are interested in family incomes in a certain small town and you make inquiries among the town's citizens. Suppose, further, that Mr. A tells you, "The average annual family income in this town is $1999" and that later Mr. B informs you, "Essentially all the families in this town have annual incomes below $1100." Is it possible that both of these men told you the truth? If by "average" Mr. A meant the arithmetic mean, it is possible! A distribution of incomes which makes both statements true is the following: The town has 999 families with incomes of $1000 and one family with an income of $1,000,000. Then the mean family income is $1999, and yet 99.9 per cent of the families have incomes below $1100.

This example points to the fact that the arithmetic mean is very sensitive to the existence of a few large numbers among a set of many smaller numbers. In some instances such sensitivity is desirable, and in others it is not. If you lived in the above town, had a family income of $1000, and wanted to know how your income "stacked up" with those of your neighbors, it would not be very helpful to you to be told that the mean income was $1999.

The kind of average that probably would be most useful in this situation would be the median. If $Y_1, Y_2, \ldots, Y_n$ are numbers, the *median* of these numbers is the number that occurs in the middle of the list obtained by arranging the Y's in order of increasing magnitude. If there is no middle number, then the mean of the two middle numbers is taken to be the median. (Often any number between the two middle numbers is called a median. However, we shall use the preceding definition so that there is only one median.) In the above example of 999 incomes of $1000 and 1 income of $1,000,000, the median income is evidently \$1000.[1]   In the list of numbers 2, 5, 9, 12, 50, the median is 9. In the list of numbers 2, 5, 9, 10, 12, 50, the median is 9.5.

If, as in Prob. 4-12, we determine the number of people in a class with each different eye color, it does not make sense to speak of the mean eye color or of the median eye color unless different colors are assigned numerical values or (at least) ranked in some fashion.   Even without such assignment of numerical values or such ranking, it does make sense, however, to ask which eye color occurred most often, if any.   This eye color we would call the *modal* color.   To be more general, if as a result of observation each of several classes is assigned a frequency, then the class with the highest frequency is called the *modal class*.   In the case of a frequency distribution similar to that obtained in the experiment with the dice, the classes to which frequencies are assigned are identified by unique numbers.   In this case, the unique number identifying the modal class is called the *mode*[2] (rhymes with "load") of the distribution.   More simply, in a frequency distribution the *mode* is that value of the random variable which is taken on most often—if any such exists.   For example, the mode of the distribution of Table 1-2 is 7.   If in a frequency distribution the highest frequency occurs for two or more classes, then we say that the distribution has no mode.   In the graph of a frequency distribution the value of the variable corresponding to the tallest vertical line is the mode.

Let us restate the definitions of the median and mode in our technical notation.   Suppose that $\{x_1, x_2, \ldots, x_N\}$ is the domain for X and that n trials yield the results $X_1, X_2, \ldots, X_n$.   Let FR be the frequency function for these results.   If we renumber the results so that they are arranged in order of magnitude and call these results $X_1', X_2', \ldots, X_n'$ (where $X_i' \leq X_j'$ if and only if $i \leq j$), then the median is defined as follows: If n is odd, the median is $X_{(n+1)/2}'$.   If n is even, the median is

$$\tfrac{1}{2}[X_{n/2}' + X_{(n+2)/2}']$$

The mode is that unique value x_j with the property that

(4-14) $FR(x_j) = \max \{FR(x_1), FR(x_2), \ldots, FR(x_N)\}$

if such a unique value exists.

---

[1] Although the above example of distribution of incomes is oversimplified and artificial, the discrepancy between mean income and median income is not unusual. For example, in 1954, lawyers in the United States had a median income of \$7833 and a mean income of \$10,218 (*Statistical Abstracts of the United States*, p. 148, 1957).

[2] The reader may well have seen "mode" used to mean fashion or custom.   This usage tends to agree with the technical meaning given here.

In a frequency distribution if x_k is the smallest number in the sample space for which $RCF(x_k)$ is at least C per cent, then we call x_k a Cth *percentile*. For example, the 90th percentile is the smallest number in the sample space for which $RCF(x_k) \geqq .90$. We shall use "P_C" to refer to the Cth percentile. P_{25}, the 25th percentile, is also called the *lower quartile*. P_{75}, the 75th percentile, is called the *upper quartile*. For the data of Table 1-2, $P_{10} = 4$, $P_{25} = 6$, $P_{75} = 9$, and $P_{90} = 11$. Percentiles are handy measures in many applications—especially so in psychological testing, where, if a person made a score equal to, say, P_{90}, this means that 90 per cent of the scores were lower than his.

In this last connection it should be remarked that in discussing scores on tests one often hears such a phrase as "His grade was *in* the 90th percentile." That is, the 90th percentile is often thought of as an interval, namely, the interval between the numbers that we have called P_{90} and P_{91}.

PROBLEMS

4-15. Find the median and mode of the results that you obtained in the experiments in Probs. 1-3 through 1-17.

4-16. Find the median and the mode for each set of data in Prob. 1-23.

4-17. Find the modal hair color, modal eye color, and modal sex for your class from the data of Prob. 4-12.

4-18. Find the median and mode for each distribution obtained in Prob. 1-19.

4-19. Characterize the median in terms of the cumulative frequency function $CF(x)$ and/or the relative cumulative frequency function $RCF(x)$.

4-20. Find P_{10}, P_{25}, P_{50}, P_{75}, and P_{90} for the data that you collected in one of Probs. 1-3 through 1-17.

4-21. On an examination in a mathematics course, the following grades were made: 96, 68, 86, 89, 83, 79, 75, 78, 86, 72, 86, 85, 94, 50, 72, 98, 90, 78, 86, 98. Find the mean, median, and mode of these grades. Find P_{25} and P_{75} for these grades.

*4-22. Given the numbers $y_1, y_2, \ldots, y_n$, their *geometric mean* is defined to be
$G(y_1, y_2, \ldots, y_n) = \sqrt[n]{y_1 y_2 y_3 \cdots y_n}$.
Their *harmonic mean* is defined to be

$$H(y_1, y_2, \ldots, y_n) = \frac{n}{1/y_1 + 1/y_2 + \cdots + 1/y_n}$$

Find the harmonic and geometric means for the following data:

(a) 3, 3, 3, 3 (b) 3, 4, 5, 6, 7, 8 (c) 2, 4, 8
(d) 10, 100, 1000 (e) 10, 100, 100, 1000 (f) 5, 5, 5, 10, 10, 10

*4-23. If you are familiar with logarithms, prove that the log of the geometric mean is the arithmetic mean of the logs of the results.

4-4. Properties of the mean

Looking again at the graph of the results of the experiment with the dice in Chap. 1, we might ask if the mean has any special geometric significance. It has. In the graph of the frequency distribution let us think of the horizontal axis as a weightless rod and the vertical segments as uniform rods with weight. We then ask at what single point we could put a support under the horizontal axis so that the graph would balance. This point of support is exactly at the mean of the distribution! Thus, we can say that $\bar{X}$ is the horizontal distance from the zero point of the x axis to the center of gravity of the graph. That this is so can easily be proved in terms of the notions of moments in physics. We do not give the proof here but simply comment that the arithmetic mean is sometimes referred to as the *first moment* of the relative frequency distribution $RF(x)$. If the reader is familiar with moments, he will see that this is consistent with the fact that $\bar{X} = \Sigma\, xRF(x)$ [see (4-8)].

Intimately involved with the above interpretation of $\bar{X}$ is the fact that

$$(4\text{-}24) \qquad \sum_{i=1}^{n} (X_i - \bar{X}) = 0$$

The proof of this is easy to follow.

$$(4\text{-}25) \qquad \sum_{i=1}^{n} (X_i - \bar{X}) = \sum_{i=1}^{n} X_i - \sum_{i=1}^{n} \bar{X} \qquad \text{by (3-10)}$$

$$= \sum_{i=1}^{n} X_i - n\bar{X} \qquad \text{by (3-9)}$$

$$= n\bar{X} - n\bar{X} \qquad \text{by (4-1)}$$

$$= 0$$

If we speak of $X_i - \bar{X}$ as the deviation of X_i from the mean, this result can be stated in words as follows: The sum of the deviations from the mean is zero.

Restating (4-24) in terms of $FR(x)$ and $RF(x)$, we have

$$(4\text{-}26) \qquad \sum_{j=1}^{N} (x_j - \bar{X})FR(x_j) = 0$$

and

$$(4\text{-}27) \qquad \sum_{j=1}^{N} (x_j - \bar{X})RF(x_j) = 0$$

where the sample space for X is taken to be $\{x_1, x_2, \ldots, x_N\}$.

If $X_1, X_2, \ldots, X_n$ and $Y_1, Y_2, \ldots, Y_n$ are results from two different experiments and we let $Z_i = X_i + Y_i$, how are the means

$\bar{Z}$, $\bar{X}$, and $\bar{Y}$ related?   We have

$$\bar{Z} = \frac{1}{n} \sum_{i=1}^{n} Z_i = \frac{1}{n} \sum_{i=1}^{n} (X_i + Y_i)$$

$$= \frac{1}{n} \left(\sum_{i=1}^{n} X_i + \sum_{i=1}^{n} Y_i \right)$$

$$= \frac{1}{n} \sum_{i=1}^{n} X_i + \frac{1}{n} \sum_{i=1}^{n} Y_i$$

$$= \bar{X} + \bar{Y}$$

That is, the mean of the sums is the sum of the means.   This can be stated as follows:

(4-28)   *If $Z_i = X_i + Y_i$, then $\bar{Z} = \bar{X} + \bar{Y}$.*

Similarly,

(4-29)   *If $Z_i = X_i - Y_i$, then $\bar{Z} = \bar{X} - \bar{Y}$.*

If every number in a sequence of results is multiplied by a constant c, the mean of these new results is simply c times the mean of the originals. This is easily proved and can be stated as follows:

(4-30)   *If $Z_i = cX_i$, then $\bar{Z} = c\bar{X}$.*

If the same number b is added to each result, the mean is simply increased by the amount b.   That is,

(4-31)   *If $Z_i = X_i + b$, then $\bar{Z} = \bar{X} + b$.*

The proof of this fact is left as a problem.
Combining the results of (4-30) and (4-31), we obtain

(4-32)   *If $Z_i = aX_i + b$, then $\bar{Z} = a\bar{X} + b$.*

This result can be interpreted as saying that the mean is preserved under a linear change of scale.   (This idea will be discussed more fully in Sec. 5-3.)   It is an important result which will be referred to quite often.

PROBLEMS

4-33. Verify Eq. (4-24) by direct computation for $X_i = i + 1$ for $i = 1, 2, 3, 4, 5$.
4-34. Prove (4-29).
4-35. Prove (4-30).
4-36. Prove (4-31).
4-37. Prove (4-32).
4-38. Verify (4-27) by direct computation with the data of Table 1-2.

*4-39. If we ask what value of b makes $\sum\limits_{i=1}^{n} (X_i - b)^2$ as small as possible, the answer is the value $b = \bar{X}$. Verify this by computing $\sum\limits_{i=1}^{n} (X_i - b)^2$ for the X_i values given in Prob. 4-33 for $b = 0, -1, 2, 3, 5, 6$, and $\bar{X}$.

*4-40. Prove by an algebraic argument that the value of b that makes $\sum\limits_{i=1}^{n} (X_i - b)^2$ as small as possible is $b = \bar{X}$.

CHAPTER 5

Measures of Dispersion

5-1. The range

Table 1-1 shows the results of 100 throws of a pair of dice. We now consider the results there as intermediate results in a different experiment. In this new experiment we throw a pair of dice four times, note the total spots uppermost on each throw, and find the mean of these four totals. Let Y represent this mean; i.e., let Y be the random variable for this new experiment. The domain of Y is evidently $\{2,2.25,2.50,2.75,3,3.25, \ldots ,11.75,12\}$. We take the first four results in Table 1-1 as our first trial in this new experiment. The resultant value of Y, which we call Y_1, is

$$\frac{8 + 2 + 11 + 3}{4} = 6$$

We take the next four values in Table 1-1 to get $Y_2 = {}^{39}\!/_4 = 9.75$. We continue in this fashion, getting values Y_3, Y_4, $\ldots$, Y_{25} for 25 trials of the new experiment. The frequency distribution for these values is shown in Table 5-1.

As usual, a little thought ahead of time leads to less trouble when handling data. We have added a column headed $4y$ to the usual columns for a frequency table. Then we go through Table 1-1, noting totals of groups of four and tallying these. Then each division by 4 is performed only once for each value of y given in the table.

Table 5-1 also shows a computation of the mean $\bar{Y}$. Note that the mean here agrees with the $\bar{X}$ found in Table 4-1. That is, the mean of the means of four trials is the same as the mean of the individual trials.

Figure 5-2 shows the graph of the distribution of Table 5-1. In Fig. 5-1 we find the graph of the distribution given in Table 1-2 with the same scale on the horizontal axis. The pictured distributions have the same mean, but there is a striking difference in their spread. The amount of spread or dispersion of a distribution is a very important characteristic of that distribution. The mean, as we have seen, is a useful measure of the "center" of a distribution. What shall we use to measure the spread of a distribution?

One convenient measure of spread is the *range*, which is the difference between the largest and smallest values occurring in the data. For the

Table 5-1

(Y = mean of totals on four throws of a pair of dice)

$4y$	y	$FR(y)$	$yFR(y)$
20	5.00	0	0
21	5.25	0	0
22	5.50	1	5.50
23	5.75	0	0
24	6.00	1	6.00
25	6.25	1	6.25
26	6.50	0	0
27	6.75	2	13.50
28	7.00	3	21.00
29	7.25	0	0
30	7.50	4	30.00
31	7.75	4	31.00
32	8.00	2	16.00
33	8.25	2	16.50
34	8.50	0	0
35	8.75	2	17.50
36	9.00	1	9.00
37	9.25	1	9.25
38	9.50	0	0
39	9.75	1	9.75
40	10.00	0	0
Totals.........		25	191.25

$$\bar{Y} = \frac{\Sigma\, yFR(y)}{n} = \frac{191.25}{25} = 7.65$$

data of Table 5-1 the range is $9.75 - 5.50 = 4.25$. For the original data with the dice (Table 1-1) the range is 10.

In the general case, where $X_1, X_2, \ldots, X_n$ are the results of n trials of an experiment with random variable X, the range is given by

(5-1) $RNG(X_1, X_2, \ldots, X_n)$
$$= \max \{X_1, X_2, \ldots, X_n\} - \min \{X_1, X_2, \ldots, X_n\}$$

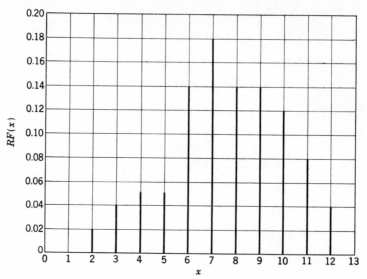

FIG. 5-1. Graph of $RF(x)$ for Table 1-2.

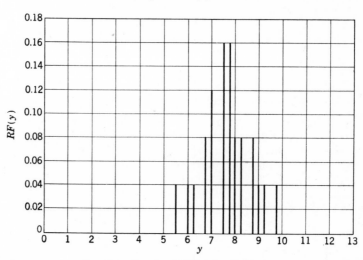

FIG. 5-2. Graph of $RF(y)$ for Table 5-1.

PROBLEMS

5-2. Treat your data for one of Probs. 1-3 through 1-17 as we did the data of Table 1-1 (i.e., let Y be the mean of four successive results). Find the frequency distribution, mean, and range for the resulting values of Y.

5-3. Combine the similar results from the entire class in Prob. 5-2 into single distributions. Find the mean and range.

5-4. Argue for the fact that

$$RNG(X_1, X_2, \ldots, X_n) = \max \{y \colon y = X_i - X_j\}$$

5-5. Under what conditions would we have

$$RNG(X_1, X_2, \ldots, X_n) = 0$$

5-6. Show that

$$RNG(|X_1|, |X_2|, \ldots, |X_n|) \leqq RNG(X_1, X_2, \ldots, X_n)$$

5-2. The standard deviation

A measure of dispersion which is not so easy to compute as the range but which is in many ways more useful is the *standard deviation*. If a set of results $X_1, X_2, \ldots, X_n$ has mean $\bar{X}$, the *standard deviation* of these results is defined to be

$$(5\text{-}7) \qquad s = \sqrt{\frac{\sum\limits_{i=1}^{n} (X_i - \bar{X})^2}{n}}$$

If we refer (as seems natural) to $X_i - \bar{X}$ as the *deviation* of X_i from the mean, then we can say that the standard deviation s is the square root of the mean of the squares of the deviations from the mean or (more briefly) the *root mean square* of these deviations.

To the beginner in statistics the standard deviation always seems a cumbersome and unnatural measure of dispersion. It is true that its evaluation is often tedious, but we shall discover as we proceed that, if any measure of dispersion is a "natural" for most of our purposes, it is the standard deviation. Its many uses will become clear as we proceed, and the reader's tolerance and patience are requested until he becomes convinced of its usefulness.

To illustrate the computation of s, suppose that we have the results 3, 4, 5, 6, 7. The mean is 5. The sum of the squares of the deviations from the mean is

$$(3 - 5)^2 + (4 - 5)^2 + (5 - 5)^2 + (6 - 5)^2 + (7 - 5)^2$$
$$= 4 + 1 + 0 + 1 + 4 = 10$$

Hence

$$s = \sqrt{10/5} = \sqrt{2} = 1.41$$

In the case of a large number of results, it is convenient to compute the standard deviation from the frequency distribution. The method of computation depends on the following important equation:

$$(5\text{-}8) \qquad \sum_{i=1}^{n} (X_i - \bar{X})^2 = \sum_{i=1}^{n} X_i^2 - n(\bar{X})^2$$

The reader interested in the proof of (5-8) may check the steps in the following:

$$(5\text{-}9) \qquad \sum_{i=1}^{n} (X_i - \bar{X})^2 = \sum_{i=1}^{n} (X_i^2 - 2X_i\bar{X} + \bar{X}^2)$$

$$= \sum_{i=1}^{n} X_i^2 - 2\bar{X} \sum_{i=1}^{n} X_i + n\bar{X}^2$$

$$= \sum_{i=1}^{n} X_i^2 - 2n\bar{X}^2 + n\bar{X}^2$$

$$= \sum_{i=1}^{n} X_i^2 - n\bar{X}^2$$

If we put Eq. (5-8) in a form suitable for use with a frequency distribution function, we have (see Prob. 4-13)

$$(5\text{-}10) \qquad \sum_{i=1}^{n} (X_i - \bar{X})^2 = \sum_{j=1}^{N} x_j^2 FR(x_j) - n\bar{X}^2$$

or

$$(5\text{-}11) \qquad \sum_{i=1}^{n} (X_i - \bar{X})^2 = \sum_{j=1}^{N} x_j^2 FR(x_j) - \frac{\left[\sum_{j=1}^{N} x_j FR(x_j)\right]^2}{n}$$

From (5-11) we get the formula generally used to compute s from a frequency distribution:

$$(5\text{-}12) \qquad s = \left\{ \frac{\sum_{j=1}^{N} x_j^2 FR(x_j) - \left[\sum_{j=1}^{N} x_j FR(x_j)\right]^2 / n}{n} \right\}^{1/2}$$

This equation appears quite formidable, but its application is straightforward. We see that, to use it to compute s, we need find only n, $\Sigma\, xFR(x)$, and $\Sigma\, x^2FR(x)$. This can be done in a systematic fashion as shown in Table 5-2, where we compute the standard deviation for the data of Table 1-2.

The items in the column headed $\Sigma\, x^2FR(x)$ are found by multiplying corresponding items in the columns headed x and $xFR(x)$. Note that the totals of the last three columns are the only numbers needed to apply (5-12) to find s.

Since the square of the standard deviation often occurs in discussions, it is given a special name. It is called the *variance* of the results.

Table 5-2
Computation of s for the Data of Table 1-2

x	$FR(x)$	$xFR(x)$	$x^2FR(x)$
2	2	4	8
3	4	12	36
4	5	20	80
5	5	25	125
6	14	84	504
7	18	126	882
8	14	112	896
9	14	126	1134
10	12	120	1200
11	8	88	968
12	4	48	576
Totals.......	100	765	6409

$$\bar{X} = \frac{\Sigma \, xFR(x)}{n} = \frac{765}{100} = 7.65$$

$$s = \left\{ \frac{\Sigma \, x^2FR(x) - [\Sigma \, xFR(x)]^2/n}{n} \right\}^{1/2}$$

$$= \left[\frac{6409 - (765)^2/100}{100} \right]^{1/2} = 2.36$$

If we write Eq. (5-12) in terms of relative frequencies, we have for the variance

(5-13)
$$s^2 = \sum_{i=1}^{N} x_i^2 RF(x_i) - \bar{X}^2$$

PROBLEMS

5-14. Directly from the definition of s, find s for the results 3, 7, 4, 4, 6, 9, 7, 5, 4, 1.

5-15. Find the standard deviation for your data in one of Probs. 1-3 through 1-17.

5-16. Find the standard deviation for the data of Prob. 5-2.

5-17. Find the standard deviation for each distribution in Prob. 1-23.   Also find the range for the distributions.

5-18. Directly from the definition for s find s for the following results:

(a) -1, 3, 0, 0, 2, 5, 3, 1, 0, -3 (b) 12, 28, 16, 16, 24, 36, 28, 20, 16, 4

5-19. Note that the data in Prob. 5-18a are obtained by subtracting 4 from each item of data in Prob. 5-14.   Also note that the data in Prob. 5-18b are obtained by multiplying each item in Prob. 5-14 by 4.   Compare the standard deviations found for these three sets of data.   Make general conjectures suggested by our results.

5-20. Find the standard deviation for the data of Prob. 1-19.

5-3. The coding of data

Suppose that we wish to find the standard deviation for the data of Table 5-1.   It is clear that we could use the procedure illustrated in

Table 5-2, but in doing the necessary computations by hand we would find ourselves with squares of numbers such as 6.25 and the calculations would begin to get a bit cumbersome.   By going through a process called *coding* the data, we can simplify the needed calculations.   This process depends on algebraic properties of the mean and standard deviation.

Suppose that $Y_1, Y_2, \ldots, Y_n$ are n values of the random variable Y. Suppose further that we introduce a new random variable Z related to Y by the equation

(5-21) $$Z = a(Y - b)$$

where a and b are constants.   That is, the random variable Z gets its values by performing the experiment which gives a value to Y and then

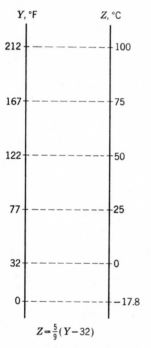

computing Z from Eq. (5-21).   This may be thought of as simply a change of the units in which the results of the experiment are recorded, and we say that Z is obtained from Y by a *linear change of scale*.   If, for example, the original Y's were temperatures in Fahrenheit degrees and we let $Z_i = \frac{5}{9}(Y_i - 32)$, then the Z's would simply be the same temperatures in centigrade degrees.   With this interpretation in mind, we can speak of a as the "change of scale factor" and b as the "zero correction."   The latter term is suggested by the fact that what used to be b (in the units used for Y) is now zero (in the units used for Z) (see Fig. 5-3).

Letting $Z_i = a(Y_i - b)$ for $i = 1, 2, \ldots, n$ the question is: How are the means and standard deviations of the Z's and Y's related? The answer is given by

(5-22) $$\bar{Z} = a(\bar{Y} - b)$$

and

(5-23) $$s_Z = a s_Y$$

Fɪɢ. 5-3. Comparison of centigrade and Fahrenheit temperature scales.

where s_Z and s_Y are the standard deviations of the Z's and Y's, respectively [see (4-32) and Prob. 5-19].

These results show that the means are related in exactly the same way as the Z_i and Y_i values while the new standard deviation is not affected by b at all but is affected by the change of scale factor a.   That is, the standard deviation is changed by the same scale factor as is Y, while to get the new mean we simply change the units of the old mean as we did for each measurement. Equation (5-22) is a special case of Eq. (4-32). For the readers who may be interested in the proof of (5-23) we display the following:

$$(5\text{-}24) \qquad \begin{aligned} s_Z{}^2 &= \frac{1}{n} \sum (Z_i - \bar{Z})^2 \\ &= \frac{1}{n} \sum [a(Y_i - b) - a(\bar{Y} - b)]^2 \\ &= \frac{1}{n} \sum (aY_i - a\bar{Y})^2 \\ &= \frac{a^2}{n} \sum (Y_i - \bar{Y})^2 \\ &= a^2 s_Y{}^2 \end{aligned}$$

Since Eqs. (5-22) and (5-23) hold for any values of a and b as long as a is positive, we can change the scale of our measurements at will and use these equations to get the corresponding changes in the mean and standard deviation.

Given data such as those in Table 5-1, then, we might ask if we could find values for a and b so that the transformation $Z = a(Y - b)$ gives us values for Z which are easy to handle in computation. If so, we could perform the transformation, find the mean and standard deviation for the Z values, and then use Eqs. (5-22) and (5-23) to find the mean and standard deviation of the original Y values.

Since small (positive or negative) whole numbers are easy to handle in computation, we should try to choose a and b so that the Z values are small whole numbers. In Fig. 5-4 we have displayed the Y scale for the average number of spots on four throws of a pair of dice (of Table 5-1) and the Z scale that we have chosen (rather arbitrarily) to use. We chose the zero for the Z scale first, at $Y = 7.50$, locating it near the center of the Y values for which we have frequencies. Then, since consecutive Y values in the table differ by one-fourth, we chose the scale for Z so that a change of $\frac{1}{4}$ in Y makes a change of one unit in Z. The equation connecting Y and Z is then $Z = 4(Y - 7.50)$.

In Table 5-3, $\bar{Z}$ and s_Z were computed by the methods that we have used before. We then have from Eqs. (5-22) and (5-23) that $\bar{Z} = 4(\bar{Y} - 7.50)$ and $s_Z = 4s_Y$. Solving these equations, we have $\bar{Y} = \bar{Z}/4 + 7.50$ and $s_Y = s_Z/4$. These results were used in Table 5-3 to find $\bar{Y}$ and s_Y.

In Fig. 5-4 we have shown the locations of $\bar{Z}$, $\bar{Y}$, $\bar{Z} \pm s_Z$, $\bar{Y} \pm s_Y$, $\bar{Z} \pm 2s_Z$, and $\bar{Y} \pm 2s_Y$. Note that the various points correspond as they should.

Consider now the general case of n measurements $Y_1, Y_2, Y_3, \ldots, Y_n$, where the random variable Y has the sample space $S = \{y_1, y_2, \ldots, y_N\}$.

Table 5-3
Computation of the Mean and Standard Deviation for the Data of Table 5-1 by Coding

y	z	$FR(z)$	$zFR(z)$	$z^2FR(z)$
5.50	-8	1	-8	64
5.75	-7	0	0	0
6.00	-6	1	-6	36
6.25	-5	1	-5	25
6.50	-4	0	0	0
6.75	-3	2	-6	18
7.00	-2	3	-6	12
7.25	-1	0	0	0
7.50	0	4	0	0
7.75	1	4	4	4
8.00	2	2	4	8
8.25	3	2	6	18
8.50	4	0	0	0
8.75	5	2	10	50
9.00	6	1	6	36
9.25	7	1	7	49
9.50	8	0	0	0
9.75	9	1	9	81
Totals.........		25	15	401

$$\bar{Z} = \frac{\Sigma\, zFR(z)}{n} = \frac{15}{25} = .60$$

$$\bar{Y} = \frac{\bar{Z}}{4} + 7.50 = 7.65$$

$$s_Z{}^2 = \frac{1}{n}\left[\sum z^2FR(z) - \frac{[\Sigma\, zFR(z)]^2}{n}\right]$$

$$= \frac{1}{25}\left(401 - \frac{15^2}{25}\right) = 15.68$$

$$s_Z = 3.96 \qquad\qquad s_Y = \frac{s_Z}{4} = .99$$

If the values in S are equally spaced so that $y_{i+1} - y_i = d$ for

$$i = 1, 2, \ldots, N - 1$$

we can use a coding procedure if it is convenient to do so. We choose a particular y value, call it y_0, near the center of the frequency distribution. Then we let $Z = (1/d)(Y - y_0)$. All the Z values will be whole numbers, so that computation with them will be quite easy. Having found s_Z and $\bar{Z}$, we have

(5-25) $$\bar{Y} = d\bar{Z} + y_0$$

and

(5-26) $$s_Y = ds_Z$$

by taking $a = 1/d$ and $b = y_0$ in (5-22) and (5-23) and solving for $\bar{Y}$ and s_Y. The *method of coding* for finding the mean and standard deviation

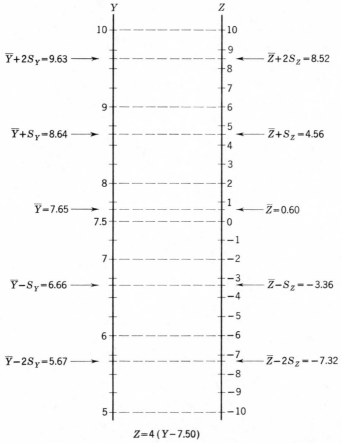

$$Z = 4(Y - 7.50)$$

FIG. 5-4. Comparison of scales for Y and Z in Table 5-3.

uses the usual formulas for finding $\bar{Z}$ and s_Z and then (5-25) and (5-26) to get $\bar{Y}$ and s_Y.

PROBLEMS

5-27. Find the standard deviation of the data of Prob. 5-2. (Use coding.)

5-28. Find the standard deviation of the data of Prob. 5-3. (Code the data.)

5-29. Verify Eqs. (5-25) and (5-26).

5-30. Under what conditions is the standard deviation equal to zero?

5-31. In Prob. 5-2 what proportion of the measurements lies within one standard deviation of the mean (that is, what proportion of the numbers lies between $\bar{Y} - s_Y$ and $\bar{Y} + s_Y$)? What proportion of the measurements lies within two standard deviations of the mean? Within three standard deviations of the mean?

5-32. Answer the questions of Prob. 5-31 for the data of Prob. 5-3.

5-4. Properties of the standard deviation

In an earlier section we discovered that the mean of a frequency distribution could be interpreted as the location of the center of gravity of the graph of the distribution. We may well ask if the standard deviation has a physical interpretation. It has.

If the reader has ever watched a figure skater doing a spin, and if the reader has been observant, he will have noticed that, while the skater has his arms out from his sides, he revolves rather slowly but, as he pulls his arms in, he begins to revolve more rapidly.[1] A physicist would say that this is owing to the fact that, as he brings in his arms, his "moment of inertia" decreases. The physicist would go on to explain that angular momentum—which is the product of the moment of inertia and the angular velocity—must be conserved. Thus, if the moment of inertia decreases, the rate of rotation must increase.

The moment of inertia of a body is a measure of its resistance to angular (i.e., rotational) acceleration about a certain axis. A high moment of inertia indicates that it would be difficult (i.e., require high torque) to start the body revolving or to stop it once it is revolving. A flywheel is designed to have a high moment of inertia so that, once it is spinning, it is difficult to change its angular velocity, with the result that the motor to which the flywheel is attached "runs smoothly."

If we consider the graph of a relative frequency distribution as consisting of uniform vertical rods resting on a weightless axis and ask for the moment of inertia of the "graph" about the vertical axis through the mean, we discover that this desired moment of inertia is the square of the standard deviation of the distribution (i.e., the variance). If your experience with physical objects has given you some "feel" for the fact that the more "spread out" a body is, the more difficult it is to start it spinning, you will have some intuitive understanding of the "naturalness"

---

[1] There is also a famous physics "experiment" that the reader may have seen where a person stands on a small table set on a bearing so it can revolve. Someone starts him spinning, and he changes his rate of rotation by raising and lowering his arms. The phenomenon can also be observed on a carousel, where the rate of rotation increases as the riders move from the edge to the center.

of using the standard deviation as a measure of spread (measure of dispersion).

To get at another important property of the standard deviation, we again consider the data of Table 5-1. For these data the mean was found to be $\bar{Y} = 7.65$ and the standard deviation was $s_Y = .99$. What proportion of all the measurements in the distribution lies within one standard deviation of the mean? That is, what proportion of the data lies between $7.65 - .99$ and $7.65 + .99$ (i.e., between 6.66 and 8.64)? Inspection of Table 5-1 shows that, of the 25 values of Y, 17 of them are between 6.66 and 8.64. Thus $17\!/\!25 = 68$ per cent of the values of Y are within one standard deviation of $\bar{Y}$. How many of the Y values are within $2s_Y$ of $\bar{Y}$, that is, between $7.65 - 1.98 = 5.67$ and

$$7.65 + 1.98 = 9.63$$

Inspection shows that 23 of the 25 values (or 92 per cent) of the Y values lie in this interval. We also observe from the table that all (100 per cent) of the results lie within $3s_Y$ of $\bar{Y}$.

Is there a general statement that can be made about the proportion of values that must fall within k standard deviations of the mean? There is such a statement which applies to all frequency distributions. It is called Chebyshev's theorem and is as follows:

(5-33)   *In an empirical frequency distribution, the proportion of the results lying within k standard deviations of the mean is at least as large as*

$$1 - \frac{1}{k^2}$$

Thus, in *any* frequency distribution at least

$$1 - \tfrac{1}{4} = \tfrac{3}{4} = 75 \text{ per cent}$$

of the items must fall within two standard deviations of the mean. At least

$$1 - \tfrac{1}{9} = \tfrac{8}{9} = 89 \text{ per cent}$$

of the items must fall within three standard deviations of the mean. We note that the data of Table 5-1 conform to these predictions.

We shall not prove Chebyshev's theorem here but give an outline of its proof in a problem.

We previously discussed the fact that, if $(X_1, X_2, \ldots, X_n)$ and $(Y_1, Y_2, \ldots, Y_n)$ are two sequences of results, then the mean for $Z_i = X_i + Y_i$ is $\bar{X} + \bar{Y}$. It is natural to ask about s_{X+Y}. Is it by any chance true that, if $Z_i = X_i + Y_i$, then $s_Z = s_X + s_Y$? The answer, in general, is "no." We have

$$(5\text{-}34) \quad s_Z{}^2 = \frac{1}{n} \sum_{i=1}^{n} (Z_i - \bar{Z})^2 \qquad\qquad \text{by (5-7)}$$

$$= \frac{1}{n} \sum_{i=1}^{n} [(X_i + Y_i) - (\bar{X} + \bar{Y})]^2 \qquad \text{by (4-28)}$$

$$= \frac{1}{n} \sum_{i=1}^{n} [(X_i - \bar{X}) + (Y_i - \bar{Y})]^2$$

$$= \frac{1}{n} \sum [(X_i - \bar{X})^2 + 2(X_i - \bar{X})(Y_i - \bar{Y}) + (Y_i - \bar{Y})^2]$$

$$= \frac{1}{n} \sum (X_i - \bar{X})^2 + \frac{1}{n} \sum (Y_i - \bar{Y})^2$$

$$+ \frac{2}{n} \sum_{i=1}^{n} (X_i - \bar{X})(Y_i - \bar{Y})$$

$$= s_X{}^2 + s_Y{}^2 + \frac{2}{n} \sum_{i=1}^{n} (X_i - \bar{X})(Y_i - \bar{Y})$$

That is, to get the variance for $X + Y$ we "almost" add the variance for X and that for Y, but there is another term entering in. This is a result which will be of interest later. We state it briefly as

$$(5\text{-}35) \quad s_{X+Y}^2 = s_X{}^2 + s_Y{}^2 + \frac{2}{n} \sum_{i=1}^{n} (X_i - \bar{X})(Y_i - \bar{Y})$$

PROBLEMS

5-36. Proof of Chebyshev's theorem. Let X have sample space $\{x_1, x_2, \ldots, x_N\}$, and let the results $X_1, X_2, \ldots, X_n$ have mean $\bar{X}$ and standard deviation s. If k is any positive number and we let

$$A = \{x_i : |x_i - \bar{X}| > ks\}$$

then

$$ns^2 = \sum_{i=1}^{n} (X_i - \bar{X})^2$$

$$= \sum_{j=1}^{N} (x_j - \bar{X})^2 FR(x_j)$$

$$\geq \sum_{x_j \in A} (x_j - \bar{X})^2 FR(x_j)$$

$$\geq k^2 s^2 \sum_{x_j \in A} FR(x_j)$$

$$= k^2 s^2 FR(A)$$

Hence,

$$\frac{FR(A)}{n} \leq \frac{1}{k^2}$$

Then

$$RF(A') = 1 - RF(A) \geq 1 - \frac{1}{k^2}$$

and the proof is complete. Justify each step in the proof by appropriate reference or argument.

5-37. Fill in the blanks (the notation is that of Prob. 5-36):

(a) In any frequency distribution at least _____ per cent of the observations must fall within 4 standard deviations of the mean.

(b) At least _____ per cent of the X_i values must satisfy $|X_i - \bar{X}| \leq 2s$.

(c) At least _____ per cent of the X_i values must satisfy $-\frac{3}{2}s \leq X_i - \bar{X} \leq \frac{3}{2}s$.

(d) At most, _____ per cent of the X_i values will be in the set $\{X: |X - \bar{X}| \geq 2s\}$.

(e) At most, _____ per cent of the X_i values will be in the set $\{X: X \geq \bar{X} + 2s$ or $X \leq \bar{X} - 2s\}$.

(f) At most, _____ per cent of the X_i values will differ from $\bar{X}$ by more than $3s$.

(g) At least 84 per cent of the X_i values will fall within _____ standard deviations of the mean.

(h) At most 1 per cent of the X_i values will fall more than _____ standard deviations away from the mean.

5-38. In the notation used in this section is there any simple relationship between the range for $X + Y$ and the range for X and Y?

5-39. What can be said about the range of $X + b$ in terms of the range for X?

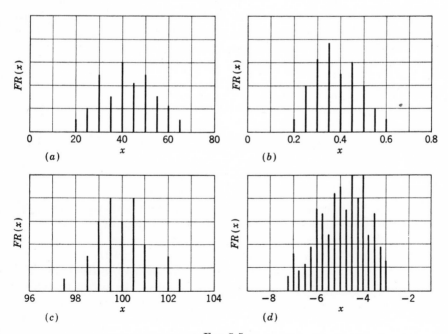

Fig. 5-5

5-40. What can be said about the range for $aX + b$ in terms of the range for X?

5-41. In view of Chebyshev's theorem and our experience with earlier problems, roughly, how would you expect the size of the range to compare with the size of the standard deviation?

5-42. With an understanding of Chebyshev's theorem it is easy to make a rough estimate of the standard deviation when given the graph of a relative frequency distribution. Estimate the standard deviation for each distribution shown in Fig. 5-5. Also estimate the mean of each distribution.

*5-5. Least-squares line and the correlation coefficient

Many experiments yield as a result a pair of numbers rather than just a single number. For example, a person may be chosen from a certain group and both his height and weight determined, or for a student chosen from a certain college class we may determine his score on a certain college entrance examination and the average grade he made in his college courses, or we may analyze a sample of a certain chemical by each of two different methods and record the two results. If such an experiment is carried through n times, the result is a set of ordered pairs of numbers (X_1, Y_1), (X_2, Y_2), . . . , (X_n, Y_n).

Each of these ordered pairs can be thought of as giving the coordinates of a point in a rectangular coordinate system. A graph showing these points is called a *scatter diagram* for the data. In Fig. 5-6 we find the scatter diagram for the data given in Table 5-4.

Table 5-4
Heights and Weights for the Five Members of a Certain Family
(X = height, in inches; Y = weight, in pounds)

i	X_i	Y_i
1	41	35
2	48	48
3	61	87
4	64	125
5	70	135

In many cases, as in Fig. 5-6, we find that the points in a scatter diagram tend to cluster together and to lie near a straight line. In fact, in many cases, without even observing the scatter diagram but simply from our knowledge of the nature of the variables, we expect the two variables involved to depend approximately in a linear fashion on each other. That is, as one variable increases one unit, we expect the other to tend to increase (or decrease) by a fixed amount. In such cases, we may take the scatter diagram and attempt to "fit" a straight line to the data. In the case where the points already fall along a straight line, this is, of course, easy, but we shall usually find that this is not the case. There is need then for some criterion by which to measure how well a certain line fits the data.

Given a scatter diagram, suppose that we draw on it a line through the point (x_0, y_0) with slope m. Then the equation of the line will be $y = y_0 + m(x - x_0)$. The y coordinate at the point on this line which has x coordinate X_i is $y_0 + m(X_i - x_0)$, and a measure of how far the observed point (X_i, Y_i) is from the line is the difference, $Y_i - [y_0 + m(X_i - x_0)]$ (see Fig. 5-6). If we wish the line somehow to "fit" the

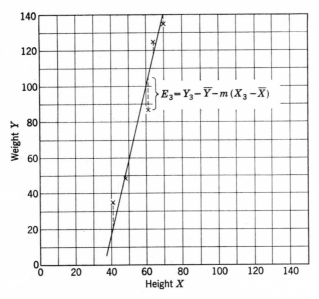

$$E_3 = Y_3 - \overline{Y} - m(X_3 - \overline{X})$$

FIG. 5-6. Scatter diagram for Table 5-4.

points, we would like all such deviations of the observed points from the line to be small. We might consider the sum of the absolute values of all these deviations and try to choose the line to make this small, but this turns out to be unsatisfactory. In many ways, the best measure for "goodness of fit" turns out to be the sum of the squares of these deviations:

$$\sum_{i=1}^{n} [Y_i - y_0 - m(X_i - x_0)]^2$$

The smaller this quantity, the better the line fits the data. The line that makes this sum of squares as small as possible is called the *least-squares line* for the data. It is also called the *regression line for Y on X*. (The reason for the qualifying phrase "Y on X" is that the line minimizes the sum of squares of the deviations in the Y direction. If we find the line that minimizes the sum of squares of the deviations in the X direction, we obtain the regression line for X on Y.)

Given the coordinates of the points in a scatter diagram the least-squares line turns out to have the equation

(5-43) $$y = \bar{Y} + m(x - \bar{X})$$

with

(5-44) $$m = \frac{\sum\limits_{i=1}^{n} (X_i - \bar{X})(Y_i - \bar{Y})}{n s_X{}^2}$$

where $\bar{X} = \Sigma X_i/n$ is the mean of the X_i values, $\bar{Y} = \Sigma Y_i/n$ is the mean of the Y_i values, and $s_X{}^2 = \Sigma (X_i - \bar{X})^2/n$ is the variance of the X_i values. The proof of the above result need not concern us.

We see from (5-43) that the least-squares line passes through the point $(\bar{X}, \bar{Y})$.

The quantity involved with $s_X{}^2$ on the right of Eq. (5-44) occurs often enough to be given a special name. It is called the *covariance* and is denoted by cov (X,Y); that is, the *covariance* is defined to be

(5-45) $$\text{cov } (X,Y) = \frac{\sum\limits_{i=1}^{n} (X_i - \bar{X})(Y_i - \bar{Y})}{n}$$

With the use of this notation, the slope of the regression line for Y on X is given by

(5-46) $$m = \frac{\text{cov } (X,Y)}{s_X{}^2}$$

"Covariance" seems a natural name for $(1/n)\Sigma (X_i - \bar{X})(Y_i - \bar{Y})$, since it has a form similar to a variance except that, instead of both factors after the summation sign involving the same variable, one factor involves X and the other Y. The form given in Eq. (5-45) is not an easy one to use for computation. It is not difficult to show that

(5-47) $$\text{cov } (X,Y) = \frac{\Sigma X_i Y_i}{n} - \bar{X}\bar{Y} = \frac{\Sigma X_i Y_i - (\Sigma X_i)(\Sigma Y_i)/n}{n}$$

[See (5-8) for the similar equation for the variance.] Both of these forms are convenient to use in computation. In a table for finding the least-squares line we need columns for X_i, Y_i, $X_i{}^2$, and $X_i Y_i$. A column for $Y_i{}^2$ is usually included so that the variance for Y can be computed (and so that we can make some of the computations discussed below). In the case of a large number of points, it is sometimes helpful to introduce something like a frequency distribution and code the data, but we shall not discuss this matter here.   The computations for the least-squares line for the data of Table 5-4 are shown in Table 5-5.   The line in Fig. 5-6 is close to the least-squares line for this set of data.

Table 5-5
Computation of the Least-squares Line and Correlation Coefficient for the Data of Table 5-4

X	Y	X^2	Y^2	XY
41	35	1,681	1,225	1,435
48	48	2,304	2,304	2,304
61	87	3,721	7,569	5,307
64	125	4,096	15,625	8,000
70	135	4,900	18,225	9,450
Totals...284	430	16,702	44,948	26,496

$$\bar{X} = {}^{284}\!/_5 = 56.8 \qquad \bar{Y} = {}^{430}\!/_5 = 86$$

$$s_X{}^2 = \frac{16,702}{5} - (56.8)^2 = 114.2$$

$$\text{cov}\,(X,Y) = \frac{26,496}{5} - (56.8)(86) = 414.4$$

$$m = \frac{414.4}{114.2} = 3.63$$

Least-squares line: $y = 86 + 3.63(x - 56.8)$

$$s_Y{}^2 = \frac{44,948}{5} - (86)^2 = 1593.6$$

$$r = \frac{414.4}{\sqrt{114.2}\,\sqrt{1593.6}} = .97$$

When the least-squares line has been found for a set of data, it is of interest to investigate the value of the sum of the squares of the deviations from this line.   It was this value which we made as small as possible by choosing the line as we did.   Let

$$(5\text{-}48) \qquad E_i = Y_i - \bar{Y} - m(X_i - \bar{X})$$

Then E_i is the deviation of the ith point from the line.   We can think of E_i as the "error" made if we tried to estimate the value of Y_i by the y coordinate at the point on the line with $x = X_i$.   Substituting the value of m as given in (5-44) and wading through considerable algebraic manipulation, we find (Prob. 5-56)

$$(5\text{-}49) \qquad \sum_{i=1}^{n} E_i{}^2 = n s_Y{}^2 - \frac{n[\text{cov}\,(X,Y)]^2}{s_X{}^2}$$

The mean of the numbers $E_1, E_2, \ldots, E_n$ is zero, since

$$\Sigma\, E_i = \Sigma\, (Y_i - \bar{Y}) - m\, \Sigma\, (X_i - \bar{X}) = 0$$

by Eq. (4-24).

Since $\bar{E} = 0$, the variance of the numbers $E_1, E_2, \ldots, E_n$ is

$$(5\text{-}50) \qquad s_E{}^2 = \frac{\Sigma\, E_i{}^2}{n} = s_Y{}^2 \left\{ 1 - \left[\frac{\text{cov}\,(X,Y)}{s_X s_Y} \right]^2 \right\}$$

from Eq. (5-49).   The quantity $\text{cov}\,(X,Y)/s_X s_Y$ is called the *correlation coefficient* for the data and is denoted by r.   That is, by definition, the *correlation coefficient* is

$$(5\text{-}51) \qquad r = \frac{\text{cov}\,(X,Y)}{s_X s_Y}$$

Using this notation, (5-50) becomes

$$(5\text{-}52) \qquad s_E{}^2 = s_Y{}^2(1 - r^2)$$

Since $s_E{}^2$ must be nonnegative, we see from (5-52) that

$$(5\text{-}53) \qquad -1 \leqq r \leqq 1$$

From (5-46) we see that the slope of the least-squares line is given by

$$(5\text{-}54) \qquad m = \frac{s_Y}{s_X}\, r$$

Hence, m will have the same algebraic sign as r.

If $r = 1$, then from Eq. (5-52) $s_E{}^2 = 0$.   But this can be the case only if all the E_i's are zero.   Hence, when $r = 1$, all the points fall exactly on a line with positive slope.   Similarly, if $r = -1$, then all the points fall exactly on a line with negative slope.

If r is very close to 1, then from Eq. (5-52) we see that $s_E{}^2$ is very small in comparison with $s_Y{}^2$.   This means that the errors E_i are very closely packed about their mean zero; that is, all the points are very close to the least-squares line (which must in this case have a positive slope).   In this case we say that Y *is highly positively correlated with* X.   Similarly, if r is close to -1, the points are very close to the least-squares line and this line has a negative slope.   In this case, we say that Y *is highly negatively correlated with* X.

How are we to interpret intermediate values of r which are not close to 1 or to -1?   Consider that $r = \frac{1}{2}$.   In this case we see that the least-squares line has a positive slope.   Also

$$s_E{}^2 = s_Y{}^2(1 - \tfrac{1}{4}) = \tfrac{3}{4}s_Y{}^2$$

so that the errors made in using the least-squares line to estimate the Y_i values have a somewhat smaller variance than does Y, but not by much. This means that using the line to estimate Y_i is somewhat better than simply estimating Y_i to be $\bar{Y}$ (no matter which X_i we are given).

If X and Y are highly correlated, it does not necessarily follow that there is any causal connection between X and Y. A classic example is the case of a very high positive correlation coefficient between teachers' salaries and the consumption of liquor over a period of years. It does not follow that increasing teachers' salaries will increase liquor consumption *or* that an increase in liquor consumption will increase teachers' salaries. Nevertheless, the correlation coefficient is in many cases a convenient measure of the linear interrelatedness of two variables.

Fig. 5-7

Note that, if a correlation coefficient is zero, it does not follow that there is no relationship among the variables. For example, the scatter diagram in Fig. 5-7 would have $r = 0$.

The correlation coefficient for the data of Table 5-4 is computed in Table 5-5.

Helpful to a correct interpretation of a correlation coefficient is the realization that r is unitless and does not depend on the units used to measure X and Y. That r is unitless follows from the fact that s_X and $X_i - \bar{X}$ are in the same units, s_Y and $Y_i - \bar{Y}$ are in the same units, and

$$r = \frac{1}{n} \sum \left[\frac{(X_i - \bar{X})}{s_X} \frac{(Y_i - \bar{Y})}{s_Y} \right]$$

It is not difficult to do the algebra to show that, if $Z_i = aX_i + b$ and $W_i = cY_i + d$, then the correlation coefficient for Z and W is precisely the same as that for X and Y. Thus, r does not change for any linear change of scale of the variables. (Here we assume that a and c are both positive.)

PROBLEMS

5-55. The following are some suggestions for data that might be collected for members of your class or certain subsets thereof. After the data are collected in each case, construct a scatter diagram, find the least-squares line, and find the correlation coefficient. You may well think of some other data that you would like to collect and treat similarly.

(a) Height in inches, weight in pounds

(b) Circumference of waist in inches, weight in pounds

(c) Grade on the first hour exam in this course, grade on second hour exam in this course

(d) Number of siblings, number of aunts and uncles (aunts and uncles by marriage not included)

(e) Age in months, grade on last hour exam in this course

(f) Number of meals last week at which a dessert was eaten, weight in pounds

(g) Hours per week spent in watching television, grade index

(h) Number of books checked out from a library during the last month, grade index

(i) Number of books read last summer, grade on last hour exam in this course

(j) Number of hour exams taken during the week of the last hour exam in this course, grade on last hour exam in this course

(k) Number of semester courses in mathematics taken in high school, grade on last hour exam in this course

(l) Number of times last week that time was spent reading the editorial page of a newspaper, grade on last hour exam

(m) Number of movies seen last month, number of hours spent watching television last week

(n) Length of right arm, height

(o) Shoe size, height

(p) Hat size, height

(q) Number of hours of sleep the night before last hour exam, grade on last hour exam

(r) Number of siblings, grade on last hour exam

(s) Average grade on daily work, grade on last hour exam

5-56. Prove Eq. (5-47).

5-57. Prove that $s_{X+Y}^2 = s_X{}^2 + s_Y{}^2$ if and only if $r = 0$ [see Eq. (5-35)].

5-58. Roll a red and a green die together 10 times and each time record X, the number of spots on the red, and Y, the number of spots on the green. Plot a scatter diagram for the points (X,Y). Find the least-squares line and the correlation coefficient.

5-59. Toss five coins and a die together, and let X be the number of heads and Y be the number of spots obtained. Plot the scatter diagram for the points (X,Y), and find the correlation coefficient for 10 trials.

5-60. Have someone write down a sequence of 20 "random" digits. If X_i is the ith digit, plot the scatter diagram for the points (X_i, X_{i+1}). Find the least-squares line and the correlation coefficient.

5-61. Choose a city of interest to you, and let $X_1, X_2, \ldots, X_{20}$ be the population of the city during each of the last 20 years. Plot a scatter diagram for the points (X_i, X_{i+1}). Find the least-squares line and the correlation coefficient.

5-62. Do Prob. 5-61 if $X_1, X_2, \ldots, X_{20}$ are the list prices of the lowest priced Ford automobile during the last 20 years.

5-63. For the data in Table 1-1 let $Y_i = X_{2i}$ and $Z_i = X_{2i-1}$ for $i = 1, 2, 3, \ldots, 15$. Plot the scatter diagram for the points (Z_i, Y_i); find the least-squares line and the correlation coefficient.

5-64. Treat one of your sets of data for Probs. 1-3 through 1-17 as indicated in Prob. 5-63.

5-65. Prove that, if $Z_i = aX_i + b$ and $W_i = cY_i + d$, then the correlation coefficient for Z and W is the same as that for X and Y.

5-66. To show that if we assume that the least-squares line must pass through $(\bar{X}, \bar{Y})$ then (5-44) gives the correct slope, we first let $u_i = X_i - \bar{X}$ and $v_i = Y_i - \bar{Y}$. Then $E_i = v_i - mu_i$ and

$$\Sigma E_i{}^2 = \Sigma (v_i - mu_i)^2$$
$$= \Sigma v_i{}^2 - 2m\Sigma u_i v_i + m^2\Sigma u_i{}^2$$
$$= \Sigma u_i{}^2 \left[m^2 - \frac{2\Sigma u_i v_i}{\Sigma u_i{}^2} m + \left(\frac{\Sigma u_i v_i}{\Sigma u_i{}^2}\right)^2 + \frac{\Sigma v_i{}^2}{\Sigma u_i{}^2} - \left(\frac{\Sigma u_i v_i}{\Sigma u_i{}^2}\right)^2 \right]$$
$$= \Sigma u_i{}^2 \left[\left(m - \frac{\Sigma u_i v_i}{\Sigma u_i{}^2}\right)^2 + \frac{\Sigma v_i{}^2}{\Sigma u_i{}^2} - \left(\frac{\Sigma u_i v_i}{\Sigma u_i{}^2}\right)^2 \right]$$

Then if we wish to choose m to make this as small as possible, we must take

$$m = \frac{\Sigma u_i v_i}{\Sigma u_i{}^2}$$

Check the details of this argument and show that the last equation here is equivalent to (5-44).

5-67. Show that

$$r = \pm \sqrt{1 - \frac{s_E{}^2}{s_Y{}^2}}$$

5-68. Sometimes a least-squares line is useful in *time series* analysis. Such a line can be used to indicate the over-all trend, ignoring chance fluctuations. Find the least-squares line for the following data:

Production of Pig Iron and Ferroalloys in the United States for 1932 to 1951*

(In millions of metric tons)

Year	Production	Year	Production
1932	8.9	1942	55.3
1933	13.6	1943	57.0
1934	16.4	1944	57.0
1935	21.7	1945	49.9
1936	31.6	1946	42.0
1937	37.8	1947	54.6
1938	19.5	1948	56.2
1939	32.3	1949	49.8
1940	43.0	1950	60.2
1941	51.5	1951	64.7

* Data from *United Nations Statistical Yearbook*, p. 222, 1952.

5-69. Fit the following time series with a least-squares line.

Production of Pig Iron and Ferroalloys in Brazil for 1941 to 1951*

(In thousands of metric tons)

Year	Production	Year	Production
1941	209	1947	481
1942	214	1948	552
1943	248	1949	512
1944	292	1950	729
1945	260	1951	759
1946	371		

* Data from *United Nations Statistical Yearbook*, p. 222, 1952.

5-70. Let X_i be the production of pig iron and ferroalloys in the United States in the ith year. Let Y_i be the production in Brazil of the same material during the ith year. Plot the scatter diagram for the points (X_i, Y_i) for $i = 1941, 1942, \ldots, 1951$ (see Probs. 5-68 and 5-69). Find the least-squares line and the correlation coefficient for this data.

5-6. Review

One of the real dangers in the study of any subject is that the student will miss the forest for the trees. It is only too easy to bog down in details and miss the over-all structure of a topic. To counteract this tendency, outlines are very helpful. Therefore, we shall now collect the important definitions and results as we have discussed them. Having them all in a relatively small space should be helpful. Logical patterns which will arise again will be more evident. The definitions and theorems are numbered here in a natural order. After each item is found a reference to the body of the text.

We let X be a random variable with sample space

$$S = \{x_1, x_2, \ldots, x_N\}$$

$X_1, X_2, \ldots, X_n$ are the results of n trials for X.

DEFINITION 1

(a) $FR(x) = No\{i: X_i = x\}$ = empirical frequency for x.
(b) $RF(x) = FR(x)/n$ = empirical relative frequency for x.   (1-1)
(c) $CF(x) = No\{i: X_i \leq x\}$ = empirical cumulative frequency for x.
(d) $RCF(x) = CF(x)/n$ = empirical relative cumulative frequency for x.   (1-2)

DEFINITION 2

(a) If $A \subseteq S$ then the empirical frequency for A is

$$FR(A) = No\{i: X_i \in A\}   (3\text{-}53)$$

(b) The empirical relative frequency for A is $RF(A) = FR(A)/n$. (3-54)

THEOREM 1
$$0 \leq RF(A) \leq 1   (3\text{-}55)$$
THEOREM 2
$$RF(S) = 1   (3\text{-}56)$$
THEOREM 3

If $A \cap B = \phi$, then $RF(A \cup B) = RF(A) + RF(B)$

THEOREM 4

$$RF(A \cup B) = RF(A) + RF(B) - RF(A \cap B) \qquad (3\text{-}57)$$

THEOREM 5

$$RF(A) = \sum_{x \in A} RF(x) \qquad (3\text{-}59)$$

THEOREM 6

$$RF(A') = 1 - RF(A) \qquad (3\text{-}60)$$

DEFINITION 3

$$\bar{X} = \frac{\sum_{i=1}^{n} X_i}{n} = \text{arithmetic mean} \qquad (4\text{-}1)$$

THEOREM 7

$$\bar{X} = \frac{1}{n} \sum_{j=1}^{N} x_j FR(x_j) \qquad (4\text{-}7)$$

THEOREM 8

$$\bar{X} = \sum_{j=1}^{N} x_j RF(x_j) \qquad (4\text{-}8)$$

THEOREM 9

$$\sum_{i=1}^{n} (X_i - \bar{X}) = 0 \qquad (4\text{-}24)$$

THEOREM 10

$$\text{If } Z_i = X_i + Y_i, \text{ then } \bar{Z} = \bar{X} + \bar{Y} \qquad (4\text{-}28)$$

THEOREM 11

$$\text{If } Z_i = X_i - Y_i, \text{ then } \bar{Z} = \bar{X} - \bar{Y} \qquad (4\text{-}29)$$

THEOREM 12

$$\text{If } Z_i = aX_i + b, \text{ then } \bar{Z} = a\bar{X} + b \qquad (4\text{-}32)$$

DEFINITION 4

(a) The *median* of the results is the "middle value" when the results are ranked.

(b) The *mode* is the value taken on most often.   (4-14)

DEFINITION 5

The *range* is

$$\max \{X, X_2, \ldots, X_n\} - \min \{X_1, X_2, \ldots, X_n\} \qquad (5\text{-}1)$$

DEFINITION 6

$$(a) \quad s = \left[\frac{\sum_{i=1}^{n} (X_i - \bar{X})^2}{n} \right]^{1/2} = standard\ deviation \qquad (5\text{-}7)$$

$(b) \quad s^2 = variance$

THEOREM 13

$$s = \left\{ \frac{\sum_{j=1}^{N} x_j^2 FR(x_j) - \left[\sum_{j=1}^{N} x_j FR(x_j) \right]^2 / n}{n} \right\}^{1/2} \qquad (5\text{-}12)$$

THEOREM 14

$$s^2 = \sum_{j=1}^{N} x_j^2 RF(x_j) - \bar{X}^2 \qquad (5\text{-}13)$$

THEOREM 15

$$s_{aX+b} = a s_X \qquad (a > 0) \qquad (5\text{-}23)$$

THEOREM 16 (Chebyshev)

In an empirical frequency distribution, the proportion of the data lying within K standard deviations of the mean is at least as large as $1 - 1/K^2$. (5-33)

THEOREM 17

$$s_{X+Y}^2 = s_X^2 + s_Y^2 + \frac{2}{n} \sum_{i=1}^{n} (X_i - \bar{X})(Y_i - \bar{Y}) \qquad (5\text{-}35)$$

DEFINITION 7

The *least-squares line* for the points (X_1, Y_1), (X_2, Y_2), $\ldots$, (X_n, Y_n) is the line $y = y_0 + m(x - x_0)$ which minimizes $\sum_{i=1}^{n} \{Y_i - [y_0 + m(X_i - x_0)]\}^2$.

DEFINITION 8

$$\text{cov } (X,Y) = \frac{\sum\limits_{i=1}^{n} (X_i - \bar{X})(Y_i - \bar{Y})}{n} = \text{\textit{covariance} of } X \text{ and } Y \qquad (5\text{-}45)$$

THEOREM 18

The least-squares line for a set of points is given by $y = \bar{Y} + m(x - \bar{X})$, where

$$m = \frac{\text{cov } (X,Y)}{s_X{}^2} \qquad (5\text{-}43), \ (5\text{-}46)$$

THEOREM 19

$$\text{cov } (X,Y) = \frac{\Sigma X_i Y_i}{n} - \bar{X}\bar{Y} \qquad (5\text{-}47)$$

DEFINITION 9

$$r = \frac{\text{cov } (X,Y)}{s_X s_Y} = \text{correlation coefficient for } X \text{ and } Y \qquad (5\text{-}51)$$

THEOREM 20

If $E_i = Y_i - \bar{Y} - m(X_i - \bar{X})$, then $s_E{}^2 = s_Y{}^2(1 - r^2)$ \qquad (5\text{-}52)

THEOREM 21

The slope of the least-squares line is

$$m = \frac{s_Y}{s_X} r \qquad (5\text{-}54)$$

THEOREM 22

The slope of the least-squares line has the same sign as r and all the points are on this line if and only if $r = 1$ or $r = -1$.

CHAPTER 6

Probability

6.1. Mathematical models

A scientist fresh from Decatur
Said, "Now that we've got all this data,
We'll have to devise
A pithy surmise
From which we deduce what comes later."

A basic phase of any scientific investigation is the collection of data. Thus astronomers from ancient times have observed the planets and stars in their heavenly paths. Newton observed the apple, today's anthropologist observes the behavior of members of an isolated community, an agronomist observes the effect of various fertilizers on crop yield, and pollsters observe people's reactions to questions about political candidates or about color preferences for the living-room walls. Faced with a large mass of data about a particular phenomenon, the scientist finds it necessary to be able to organize and summarize these data so that they are comprehensible to himself and his colleagues. If the data are quantitative, many of the devices that we have discussed may be useful at this stage. The various forms of frequency distributions and their graphs are convenient organizational devices. Measures of central tendency (such as the mean, mode, and median) and measures of dispersion (such as the range and standard deviation) are useful for summarizing data. The problem of organization and summarization of data is the central problem in what is called *descriptive statistics*. Up to this point in this book, we have been, in large measure, studying descriptive statistics. But in most instances, the collection, organization, and summarization of data are hardly the culmination of a scientific investigation. The scientist would like, in some sense, to "explain" the data. The "explanation" being sought is a *theory*. This theory consists of a relatively small body of comprehensive statements about the subject matter being studied. How the scientist discovers the statements that make up his theory need not concern us here, but we can say that he attempts to characterize as simply as possible the interrelationships between the observed variables. If the theory is to be satisfactory, the

78

observed data must, at the least, be compatible with the theory and, preferably, it should be possible to derive logically from the statements of the theory the statements which assert the facts already observed and statements which *predict* the outcome of future observations.

Thus, from Newton's laws of motion (the theory) it is possible to deduce statements about the behavior of moving bodies which express the observed facts about such motion.   Thus, the (observed) existence of variation among types of finches may be compatible with (and to a certain extent deducible from) Darwin's theory of evolution.   Thus, the observed behavior of adults in a particular society may be compatible with (and to a certain extent deducible from) the observed treatment of infants in that society and a certain theory about the effect of infant experiences on later adult behavior.

In many cases the theory that the scientist develops will be a *mathematical model*.   The reader is somewhat familiar with euclidean geometry.   This geometry may be thought of as a mathematical model for the space in which we live.   It consists of a series of statements called axioms.   From these axioms we derive the theorems of this geometry. Involved in the axioms are technical terms such as "point' and "line." In order to check the truth of the axioms or to apply the theorems, a scientist must have in mind some way of tying these technical terms up with the observed space in which we live.   That is, he must have operational definitions for these technical terms.   Thus, for a surveyor, "point" means the intersection of two cross hairs and "line" means the path followed by a ray of light.

To illustrate the above points we present the following dialogue:

JOE: If you take a large piece of paper, make three dots on it with your pencil, take a ruler, connect the dots with straight lines, and then measure the interior angles of the resulting triangle, what will be the sum of the three angles you find?

MOE: Easy—180°.

JOE: Exactly 180°?

MOE: Well, probably not.   If I simply measured my angles with a protractor I suppose I would be lucky if I got 180°, even to the nearest degree.   Also, my lines might be off some.   If I was very careful in drawing my triangle and measuring the angles, though, the sum would be very close to 180°.

JOE: You would say then that you are sure you will get approximately 180°?

MOE: Yes.

JOE: But how do you know this before you even draw the triangle?

MOE: Oh, come now!   Everybody knows that it is a geometric fact that the sum of the angles of any triangle is 180°.

JOE: You mean that it is a theorem of plane geometry?

MOE: Yes.

JOE: By "theorem" you mean a statement which follows logically from the axioms? In other words, it can be proved from the axioms for plane geometry?

MOE: Of course. And I expect the sum of the angles of a triangle to be 180° because it can be proved from the axioms and the axioms are true.

JOE: Do you happen to remember any of the axioms of plane geometry?

MOE: Let's see. I think there is one that says something like, "Through any two points you may draw one and only one line."

JOE: Good. But wait! Is this axiom true of the points and lines on your paper? A minute ago you spoke of drawing the triangles more carefully. I suppose you meant with better lines. But then it seems that you can draw more than one line through two points.

MOE: Wait a minute. You're right, of course. But the lines the axiom is talking about are lines with no thickness. I could never draw a line with no thickness—and if I could you couldn't see it.

JOE: Then the axiom isn't talking about the "lines" you draw on the paper? What "lines" and "points" is it talking about?

MOE: It's talking about what we might call "ideal" points and lines—abstractions which kind of ignore some of the properties of the lines we draw and emphasize and retain others.

JOE: Now I begin to see. These "lines" of the axiom are a kind of convenient fiction which to a certain degree of approximation have the same properties that lines drawn on paper have?

MOE: Yes. But now look here! This is supposed to be a book on statistics—not a book on geometry. Why all this fuss about points and lines?

JOE: Well, in my original question about points and lines I asked you to draw a triangle and measure the angles and find the sum of the angles. *Without even drawing the triangle*, you told me the sum would be approximately 180°. My next question has the same form as the question about the triangle. Suppose you were to throw 1000 pennies in the air and let them fall. How many "heads" would you get?

MOE: I certainly don't know exactly, but I would expect to get somewhere in the neighborhood of 500.

JOE: Now, as before, I would like to ask you how you know this before you have even done the experiment.

MOE: Well, I don't really know, I guess. I've had some experience tossing coins and that has something to do with it, certainly. But I would like to emphasize that my answer was nowhere near as definite to your "coin question" as to your "triangle question." I, for one, would not be too surprised to get as few as 470 heads in tossing 1000 coins and I certainly would not be surprised to get as few as 490.   The answer I can give seems to be much more indefinite than the one I can give to the question about the sum of the angles in a triangle.

JOE: Would you be surprised if the coins all came up tails?

MOE: Yes.   Wait a minute!   I anticipate that your next question will be, "Why?" and that then you will probably ask me exactly how few heads I must get before I will be surprised.   I confess, I don't know.

Well, let us leave Joe and Moe to finish their discussion on their own time.   The discussion seems to imply that it would be helpful if we had some kind of mathematical model to help us answer questions about tosses of coins (and similar experiments), as Euclid's model helps us to answer questions about triangles.   The theory that does this for us is called probability theory.

Following the pattern for the construction of theories, we start with observations.   A coin was tossed 10,000 times with the results indicated in Table 6-1.

Table 6-1

n	100	500	1000	5000	10,000
Relative frequency of heads	.540	.480	.475	.504	.5035
Relative frequency of tails	.460	.520	.525	.496	.4965

In the table, n is the number of tosses completed at a given stage.   In the first 100 tosses heads came up 54 times.   That is, in the first 100 tosses heads occurred with a relative frequency of 0.54 (or 54 per cent). In the first 500 tosses, heads occurred with a relative frequency of .480. In the first 5000 tosses the relative frequency of heads was .504.   In the 10,000 tosses it was .5035.   The striking fact about the results is that, as the number of tosses increases, the relative frequency seems to settle down.   To get our "theory" then, it does not take much of a leap of the imagination to postulate the existence of a real number which this relative frequency must approach as the number of trials gets larger and larger.   This simple (?!) leap then leads us to our mathematical model for the coin.   We let X be the random variable for the experiment of tossing the coin and claim that the sample space for X is the set {heads, tails}.   A model is obtained by assigning to "heads" a certain real number which is to be the "long-run relative frequency" with which heads occurs.   We then call this number the *probability of* getting a head on a single toss.   Evidently, if we assign a probability p to heads, the probability we assign to tails (and interpret similarly) must be $1 - p$. With a given model in mind (i.e., a specific value of p such as $p = \frac{1}{2}$) we can deduce theorems about the behavior of the coin.   Whether or not the model is a good one for a given coin under given conditions can then be ckecked by comparing the results observed with those predicted from the model.

The technical term used in the model is "probability." Just as a surveyor can approximate the "ideal point" of euclidean geometry by using finer cross hairs, we can approximate the "probability of getting a head" more closely by taking more and more tosses of the coin and observing the relative frequency of heads.

Let us now consider a more general situation. We assume that we have a certain experiment E and that there are a finite number of possible outcomes for E. If we use X to represent the result of a single trial of E, then X is called the random variable for the experiment. If there are N possible values of X, the set of all of them is called the sample space and is designated by $S = \{x_1, x_2, \ldots, x_N\}$. We now associate with each point x_i in S a number called the probability at x_i and designated by $P(x_i)$. Intuitively, $P(x_i)$ is the quantity that the relative frequency $RF(x_i)$ of x_i approaches as more and more trials of E are made. In other words, $P(x_i)$ is the proportion of times x_i occurs "in the long run." We say that $P(x_i)$ is the probability that X will take on the value x_i. That is, we say that $P(x_i)$ is the probability that $X = x_i$.

If these probabilities are to represent long-run relative frequencies, they must have certain properties regardless of their specific values. Two of these properties we take as axioms.

(6-1) $$0 \leqq P(x_i) \leqq 1$$

(6-2) $$\sum_{i=1}^{N} P(x_i) = 1$$

From these two axioms we can develop probability theory for finite sample spaces. We consider the assignment of different values to the probabilities as yielding different models for the experiment. A particular model is called a *probability distribution* for the experiment. We notice that, once the model is given, the value $P(x_i)$ can be thought of as the value of a function P defined on the sample space S. The range of P is some set of real numbers between zero and 1, inclusive. We call P the *probability function* for the model.

What we must ultimately do is find the theorems which follow from the above axioms so that, for proposed values of the probabilities, we can compare these consequences with observed results. Before we do this, however, we shall look at an example and state precisely how we are going to use certain technical language. Suppose that we throw a cubical die whose sides are numbered from 1 to 6 and note the number of the side uppermost when the die stops moving. If X represents the number obtained, the sample space is $S = \{1,2,3,4,5,6\}$ for the random variable X.   By this we simply mean that the outcome of a single trial must be one of the numbers in S.   It is often convenient to speak of the elements of S (or any sample space) as points, and in the experiment we are considering we can actually draw a geometric representation of S. S is pictured in Fig. 6-1, where we have simply taken a line of numbers (an axis) and circled the points (numbers) which belong to S.   With this picture in mind the outcome of a single throw of the die must be one of the circled points.   It is because a geometric representation is so helpful that we call S a sample *space*.

In throwing the die we might well be interested in whether or not the number obtained was even.   Certain points in the sample space correspond to the numbers which are even.   If, then, we speak of the *event* of

Fig. 6-1   Fig. 6-2

getting an even number when we throw the die, we can say that this means ending up at one of the points corresponding to an even number. This kind of thinking leads us to define "*event*" to mean a subset of the sample space.   To say that an *event A happens* is to say that the result of the experiment is a point in A.

The event of getting a number greater than 3 is the subset $\{4,5,6\}$, since the points in this subset are exactly those which satisfy the given condition.   The event of getting a number divisible by 3 is the subset $\{3,6\}$.

A certain subset of a sample space can be shown pictorially by using colored circles, by putting crosses in the circles, or by blacking in the circles.   For example, the event of getting an even result with the die is shown in Fig. 6-2.

If A and B are events, $A \cup B$ is also an event (i.e., a subset of the sample space).   A point is in $A \cup B$ if and only if it is in A or in B. Thus to say that an event $A \cup B$ happens is to say that either A happens or B happens.   Similarly, the event $A \cap B$ happens if and only if A happens and B happens.   Also, the event A' happens if and only if A fails to happen.

PROBLEMS

6-3. A special deck of cards contains 10 cards numbered 1, 2, 3, 4, 5, 6, 7, 8, 9, 10. The deck is shuffled, a card is drawn, and the number on the card is noted.   If X is the number so obtained, what is the sample space for X?   Draw a geometric representation of this sample space.   Use pictures to show the following events: (*a*) getting an even number, (*b*) getting a multiple of 3, (*c*) getting a prime number, (*d*) getting an even number or a 7, (e) getting a number between 6 and 9, (f) getting an even number and a number more than 4, (g) getting an even number divisible by 5.

6-4. Suppose that 100 coins are tossed together. If X is the number of heads obtained, what is the sample space for X? What sets constitute the following events: (a) getting more than half heads, (b) getting more than 30 heads, (c) getting a number of heads which differs from 50 by less than 10, (d) getting fewer than 11 heads or more than 89?

6-5. Fifty people are asked if they approve a certain presidential candidate. X people answer "yes." What is the sample space for X? What sets constitute the following events: (a) more than 20 per cent answer "yes," (b) fewer than 60 per cent answer "yes," (c) more than 90 per cent answer "yes," (d) the number of "yes" answers is at least twice as great as all the other responses?

6-2. Theorems about probabilities

The mathematician Laplace
Thought gambling problems first class:
"To figure the odds
Is not just for gods
(But never shoot dice in the grass)."

Let $S = \{x_1, x_2, \ldots, x_N\}$ be the sample space for a random variable X, and let $P(x_i)$ be the probability that $X = x_i$. Then $P(x_i)$ satisfies Eqs. (6-1) and (6-2). If A is a possible event for our experiment (that is, $A \subseteq S$), we wish to associate with A a certain probability—the probability that $X \in A$.

In view of the fact that we are thinking of $P(x_i)$ as the value approached by $RF(x_i)$ and that

$$RF(A) = \sum_{x \in A} RF(x) \qquad (3\text{-}59)$$

it seems natural to define $P(A)$ (a set function) to be the sum of the values of $P(x_i)$ for all the $x_i \in A$. In other words, for any $A \subseteq S$ we make the definition

(6-6) $$P(A) = \sum_{x_i \in A} P(x_i) \qquad P(\phi) = 0$$

where the summation is to extend over all the values of x_i which are members of A. For example, if $S = \{1,2,3,4,5,6,\}$ and $A = \{2,3,5\}$, then $P(A) = P(2) + P(3) + P(5)$.

We now proceed to establish a sequence of theorems about this set function $P(A)$ which is evidently defined for all subsets of S (i.e., for all possible events).

(6-7) $$P(S) = 1$$

This follows from (6-2), since

$$P(S) = \sum_{x_i \in S} P(x_i) = \sum_{i=1}^{N} P(x_i) = 1$$

(6-8)   *If $A \subseteq B$, then $P(A) \leq P(B)$.*

This follows from the fact that $P(x_i) \geq 0$ for all x_i's (6-1) and from the definition of $A \subseteq B$.

(6-9)   *If $A \subseteq S$, then $0 \leq P(A) \leq 1$.*

This is a consequence of (6-1), (6-7), and (6-8).

(6-10)   *If $A \cap B = \phi$, then $P(A \cup B) = P(A) + P(B)$.*

It is not difficult to see that if $A \cap B = \phi$,

$$\sum_{x_i \in A \cup B} P(x_i) = \sum_{x_i \in A} P(x_i) + \sum_{x_i \in B} P(x_i) = P(A) + P(B)$$

If A and B are events and $A \cap B = \phi$, this means that it is impossible to end up at a point in the sample space which is in the set A and the set B. That is, if $A \cap B = \phi$, then the events A and B cannot both happen. Two such events are said to be *mutually exclusive*. In set terminology, two events are mutually exclusive if they are disjoint. If we wish to apply (6-10), we must be sure the events involved are mutually exclusive. Equation (6-10) is called the *addition theorem for mutually exclusive events*.

(6-11) $$P(A) = 1 - P(A')$$

Here A' is the complement of A with S as the universal set. Since $A \cap A' = \phi$ and $A \cup A' = S$, we have

$$1 = P(S) = P(A \cup A') = P(A) + P(A')$$

Equation (6-11) follows from this.

A more general *addition theorem* than the one for mutually exclusive events is as follows:

(6-12) $$P(A \cup B) = P(A) + P(B) - P(A \cap B)$$

This follows from the fact that

$$\sum_{x_i \in A} P(x_i) + \sum_{x_i \in B} P(x_i)$$

contains two terms for each x_i in $A \cap B$. Hence, to get the correct sum of the probabilities over $A \cup B$ we must subtract $P(x_i)$ for each $x_i \in A \cap B$. That is, we must subtract $P(A \cap B)$ from $P(A) + P(B)$ to get $P(A \cup B)$.

The reader has no doubt noticed that these theorems for probabilities are direct analogues of results for the empirical relative frequencies [see Eqs. (3-54) through (3-60)]. This is to be expected, since the probabilities are supposed to be long-run relative frequencies. If we wish, we can think of a probability for an event as a "theoretical relative frequency" obtained from the model (theory) we are using, whereas an empirical relative frequency for an event is obtained from actual observations of values of the random variable.

To illustrate some of the above theorems let X be the number of spots uppermost on a die after it is thrown. Then the sample space is $S = \{1,2,3,4,5,6\}$. Suppose that the die is perfectly balanced. That is, suppose that the model which fits is the one where each point is assigned a probability $\frac{1}{6}$. In other words, assume that

$$P(1) = P(2) = P(3) = P(4) = P(5) = P(6) = \tfrac{1}{6}$$

Let A be the event of getting an even number. Then

$$A = \{2,4,6\} \quad \text{and} \quad P(A) = P(2) + P(4) + P(6) = \tfrac{3}{6} = \tfrac{1}{2}$$

Note that we could have written this result as

$$P(\{X : X \text{ is even}\}) = \tfrac{1}{2}$$

We adopt the convention that we could have written this more briefly as $P(X \text{ is even}) = \frac{1}{2}$. In general, in place of $P(\{X : \ldots X \ldots\})$ we may write $P(\ldots X \ldots)$, where "$\ldots X \ldots$" is any statement form involving X. We then read "$P(\ldots X \ldots)$" as "the probability that $\ldots X \ldots$." Note that then

$$P(\{X : X = x_i\}) = P(X = x_i) = P(x_i)$$

Continuing with the die problem, we have the following:

$$P(S) = P(1) + P(2) + P(3) + P(4) + P(5) + P(6) = 1 \qquad (6\text{-}7)$$

$$\begin{aligned} P(X \text{ is even or } 5) &= P(\{X : X \text{ is even}\} \cup \{X : X = 5\}) \\ &= P(X \text{ is even}) + P(X = 5) = \tfrac{1}{2} + \tfrac{1}{6} = \tfrac{2}{3} \end{aligned}$$
$$(6\text{-}10)$$

$$\begin{aligned} P(X \text{ is odd or } 5) &= P(X \text{ is odd}) + P(X = 5) \\ &- P(X \text{ is odd and } 5) = \tfrac{1}{2} + \tfrac{1}{6} - \tfrac{1}{6} = \tfrac{1}{2} \qquad (6\text{-}12) \end{aligned}$$

$$P(X \text{ is odd}) = 1 - P(X \text{ is even}) = 1 - \tfrac{1}{2} = \tfrac{1}{2} \qquad (6\text{-}11)$$

$$\begin{aligned} P(X \text{ is odd or exceeds } 4) &= P(X \text{ is odd}) + P(X \text{ exceeds } 4) \\ &- P(X \text{ is odd } and \text{ exceeds } 4) = \tfrac{1}{2} + \tfrac{1}{3} - \tfrac{1}{6} = \tfrac{2}{3} \qquad (6\text{-}12) \end{aligned}$$

PROBLEMS

6-13. Let X be a random variable with sample space $S = \{0,1,2,3,4,5,6,7,8,9\}$. Let $P(i) = \frac{1}{10}$ for all i in S. Find

(a) $P(X$ is even$)$

(b) $P(X \geq 8)$

(c) $P(X + 3 = 7)$

(d) $P(X^2 \geq 4)$

(e) $P(X$ is even or 5$)$

(f) $P(X$ is even or divisible by 3$)$

(g) $P(X$ is not 6$)$

(h) $P(X$ is not 6 and is greater than 4$)$

6-14. Let X be a random variable with sample space $S = \{0,1,2,3,4,5\}$. Let $P(0) = P(5) = \frac{1}{32}$, $P(1) = P(4) = \frac{5}{32}$, and $P(2) = P(3) = \frac{5}{16}$. Verify that $P(S) = 1$. Find

(a) $P(X \geq 4)$

(b) $P(X < 4)$

(c) $P(X$ is odd$)$

(d) $P(X$ is not odd and not 4$)$

(e) $P(X$ is 7 or 9$)$

(f) $P(X < 4$ or even$)$

(g) $P(X \geq 4$ and even$)$

(h) $P(X + 1 < 3)$

(i) $P(|X - 2| < 3)$

(j) $P(1 < |X - 1| < 4)$

6-15. Let Y be a random variable with sample space $\{1,2,3, \ldots ,1000\}$. Let $P(i) = \frac{1}{1000}$ for all i in the space. Find

(a) $P(Y \neq 5)$

(b) $P(Y$ is even$)$

(c) $P(Y$ is even or different from 5$)$

(d) $P(Y$ is a multiple of 3$)$

(e) $P(Y$ is not a multiple of 3$)$

(f) $P(Y$ is not a multiple of 3 or not even$)$

6-3. Uniform probability distributions and independent events

The probability model where each point in the sample space is assigned the same probability often arises. A probability distribution which assigns the same value to each point is called a *uniform distribution*. For such a distribution we have the following important theorem. As usual, we assume that the random variable X has sample space

$$S = \{x_1, x_2, \ldots , x_N\}$$

(6-16)   *If $P(x_i) = P(x_j)$ for all x_i's and x_j's in S, then $P(x_i) = \dfrac{1}{N}$ for $i = 1, 2, \ldots , N$ and for $A \subseteq S$, $P(A) = \dfrac{No\ (A)}{N}$*

Given that the probability assigned to each of the N points in S is the same, it follows that the probability must be $1/N$, since the sum of all the probabilities must equal 1. Then $P(A)$ is the sum of $No\ (A)$ values equal to $1/N$ and we must have $P(A) = No\ (A)/N$. [Here $No\ (A)$ is the number of elements in A, the set function introduced in Sec. 3-6.] This completes the proof of (6-16).

Suppose that a special deck of cards contains 10 cards marked 1, 2, 3, 4, 5, 6, 7, 8, 9, and 10. We "shuffle" the deck, draw a card, and note its number, X. If the deck is "well shuffled," the natural model to assign is the uniform one which assigns a probability of $\frac{1}{10}$ to each point. It is easy to work out various probabilities for this example, but we wish to consider a more complex experiment with this deck of cards. Suppose that we draw a card. Let its denomination be X. We then replace this card, shuffle the deck, and draw another card. Let the denomination of this card be Y. We now have an experiment whose outcome is an *ordered pair* of numbers (X,Y). The sample space for the experiment is $S = \{(1,1), (1,2), (1,3), \ldots, (1,10), (2,1), (2,2), \ldots, (10,9), (10,10)\}$. Here again, however, we may get a geometric representation for S. This representation is shown in Fig. 6-3.

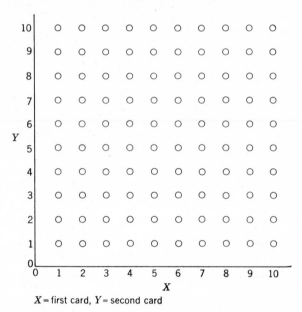

$X =$ first card, $Y =$ second card

FIG. 6-3. Graph of the sample space for two draws with replacement from a 10-card deck.

If the deck is "well shuffled" before each draw, the natural distribution to assume is the uniform one which assigns the same probability to each point in S. Since there are 100 points in S, the probability assigned to each point is $\frac{1}{100}$. Then, for example, $P(X = 3 \text{ and } Y = 3) = \frac{1}{100}$. If we wish the value of $P(X = 3)$, we should evidently find the points in S for which $X = 3$, count them, and multiply their number by $\frac{1}{100}$. Inspection of Fig. 6-3 shows there are 10 points where $X = 3$. Hence, $P(X = 3) = \frac{1}{10}$. Similarly, $P(Y = 3) = \frac{1}{10}$.

Again from Fig. 6-3, there are 50 points where X is even, so that $P(X \text{ is even}) = \frac{1}{2}$. Similarly, $P(Y \text{ is even}) = \frac{1}{2}$. How many points are there where X and Y are both even? (At this point the student will find it convenient to graph S on squared paper and use crosses or colored dots to indicate the desired points or else to draw boundaries around the desired sets.)   There are 25 such points.   Then

$$P(X \text{ even and } Y \text{ even}) = \frac{1}{4}$$

$P(X \geq 3) = \frac{8}{10}$ by inspection of Fig. 6-3.   Also $P(Y \leq 2) = \frac{2}{10}$. The number of points where $X \geq 3$ *and* $Y \leq 2$ (these are points in a rectangle at the lower right corner of the graph) is 16.   Hence

$$P(X \geq 3 \text{ and } Y \leq 2) = \frac{16}{100}$$

If we collect results from the above computations, we find that

$$P(X = 3 \text{ and } Y = 3) = P(X = 3)P(Y = 3)$$

$$P(X \text{ even and } Y \text{ even}) = P(X \text{ even})P(Y \text{ even}), \text{ and}$$

$$P(X \geq 3 \text{ and } Y \leq 2) = P(X \geq 3)P(Y \leq 2)$$

This suggests the following conjecture: $P(A \cap B) = P(A)P(B)$ for any events A and B.   This equality, however, does not always hold.   The reason for its validity in the above examples is that X and Y are *independent* random variables and the events considered are *independent* events.   Intuitively, X and Y are independent random variables if the value taken on by X does not in any way affect the probability that Y will take on a certain value, and vice versa.   This evidently should be so in our card experiment because the cards are well shuffled between draws and "the deck cannot remember" what the result of the first draw was. Suppose that $P(X = a) = p$ and $P(Y = b) = q$ when X and Y are independent (in the intuitive sense given).   Then in n trials of the experiment with n very large we should have $X = a$ with a relative frequency of about p.   In other words, we should find $X = a$ about np times.   But *among these* (approximately) *np trials* of the experiment about what proportion of the results will have $Y = b$?   Since what happens to X is not supposed to affect the probability of $Y = b$, we would expect approximately a proportion q of these (approximately) np trials to have $Y = b$.   But then the number of results with $X = a$ *and* $Y = b$ will be about npq and the relative frequency with which the event ($X = a$ *and* $Y = b$) will occur will be about pq.   This kind of thinking leads us to *define* X and Y to be *independent* random variables if for all a and b

(6-17) $$P(X = a \text{ and } Y = b) = P(X = a)P(Y = b)$$

This, then, is the meaning that we shall attach to "independent random variables."   We shall, however, in many problems be able to see that two variables are independent on the basis of our intuitive understanding of independence and the nature of the experiment.   In such cases, we can then use (6-17) to compute the probability that $X = a$ and $Y = b$ when we know $P(X = a)$ and $P(x = b)$.   For example, if a well-balanced coin is flipped twice, the outcomes of the two tosses are evidently independent and

$$P(2 \text{ heads}) = P(\text{first is a head } and \text{ second is a head})$$
$$= P(\text{first is a head})P(\text{second is a head}) = (\tfrac{1}{2})(\tfrac{1}{2}) = \tfrac{1}{4}$$

Following the lead of (6-17), if A and B are events, we say that they are *independent events* if

(6-18) $$P(A \cap B) = P(A)P(B)$$

An argument similar to that following (6-17) will show that this definition agrees with the intuitive interpretation of "independence" in the sense that, whether A happens or fails to happen, the probability for B is unaffected.

Equation (6-18) is sometimes referred to as the multiplication theorem for independent events. In our presentation it is not a theorem but a definition. We shall, though, often use it to find probabilities, being able to see from the nature of the experiment that two events are independent.

PROBLEMS

6-19. For the above experiment where two cards are drawn (with replacement of the first) from a 10-card deck, find the following:

(a) $P(X > 2)$
(b) $P(Y > 2)$
(c) $P(X > 2 \text{ and } Y > 2)$
(d) $P(X < 2 \text{ or } Y < 2)$
(e) $P(X \leq 2)$
(f) $P(X = Y)$
(g) $P(X + Y < 7)$
(h) $P(X > Y + 1)$
(i) $P(X \neq 5)$
(j) $P(X \neq 5 \text{ or } Y = 5)$
(k) $P(\text{at least one of the cards is a 5})$
(l) $P(\text{at most one of the cards is a 5})$
(m) $P(\text{both cards exceed 9})$
(n) $P(\text{at least one card exceeds 9})$
(o) $P(\text{neither of the cards exceeds 9})$

6-20. In an ordinary deck of cards there are 52 cards of 4 suits and 13 denominations. The suits are clubs (C), diamonds (D), hearts (H), and spades (S). The denominations are 1, 2, 3, . . . , 10, jack (J), queen (Q), and king (K). Thus, the 52 cards are C1, C2, C3, . . . , C10, CJ, CQ, CK, D1, . . . , DK, H1, . . . , HK, S1, . . . , SQ, SK. Suppose that we shuffle an ordinary deck, draw a card X, replace the card, shuffle, and draw a card Y. The outcome of the experiment is then an ordered pair (X,Y). Indicate how the graph of the sample space would look (do not show all the points, only enough to grasp the picture). Assign the uniform distribution and find the following:

(a) $P(X = \text{S2 and } Y = \text{H3})$
(b) $P(X \text{ is a C})$
(c) $P(Y \text{ is a C})$
(d) $P(X \text{ is a C and } Y \text{ is a C})$
(e) $P(X \text{ is a C or } Y \text{ is a C})$
(f) $P(X \text{ is a face card or } Y \text{ is a C})$
(g) $P(\text{at least one card is a C})$
(h) $P(\text{neither card is a C})$
(i) $P(\text{both cards are kings})$
(j) $P(\text{either } X \text{ is not a king or } Y \text{ is not a king})$

6-21. Five coins of five different denominations are tossed. Heads (H) or tails (T) is then noted for each one. The outcome is then a 5-tuple of H's and T's. For example, (H,T,H,H,H) and (T,T,T,H,H) are different possible outcomes. Assuming "perfectly balanced" coins and that the outcomes for the various coins are independent, find the following:

    (a) P(all heads)   (b) P(all tails)
    (c) P(at least one head)   (d) P(at least one tail)

6-22. A person X is chosen from a town in such a way that the probability that he is a college graduate is .10.   A person Y is chosen from a different town in such a way that the probability that he is a college graduate is .30.   Find the following:

    (a) P(both are college graduates)   (b) P(X is not a college graduate)
    (c) P(X is not a college graduate but Y is)
    (d) P(at most one of them is a college graduate)

6-23. Since a town contains only a finite number of people, what are likely interpretations for the probabilities of .10 and .30 given in Prob. 6-22?

6-24. If the probability of a baby being born a boy is .5, what is the probability that a family of three children will contain all boys?   All girls?   At least one of each sex?   (What are the assumptions you are making?)

6-25. In a box there are four white and two black balls.   A ball X is drawn and replaced.   Then a ball Y is drawn.   Designating the white balls by W_1, W_2, W_3, W_4 and the black ones by B_1, B_2, graph the sample space.   Assuming the uniform distribution, find the following:

    (a) P(X is white)   (b) P(X is either white or black)
    (c) P(exactly one of the balls is black)   (d) P(both balls are black)
    (e) P(neither ball is black)
    (f) P(the first ball is black or both balls are black)
    (g) P(at least one of the balls is black)

6-26. In 1955 the number of people in the United States surviving to a specified age per 100,000 born live is given in the *Statistical Abstract of the United States, 1957,* as follows:

Age	20	45	65
Male	95,743	90,183	65,704
Female	97,013	93,969	79,982

We can use these figures to estimate the probability that a newly born child will live to a specified age.   For example, P(boy baby will live to be 20) $\cong$ .957.   If Joe and Mary are newly born, find the following:

    (a) P(Mary lives to 45)   (b) P(Joe and Mary live to 45)
    (c) P(Joe lives to 45 and Mary lives to 65)
    (d) P(Joe dies before he is 45)   (e) P(Joe and Mary both die before 45)
    (f) P(Joe dies before 45 while Mary survives to 65)
    (g) P(neither survives to 65)

6-27. A red and a green die are thrown together.   Let X be the number of spots uppermost on the red die and Y be the number of spots uppermost on the green.   Graph the sample space.   Assume "perfect" dice, so that we take the uniform distribution.   Find

$$P(X + Y = K) \qquad \text{for } K = 2, 3, 4, \ldots, 12$$

Compare your results with the relative frequencies found in Prob. 1-19 for the class data on Prob. 1-3 (or with the results of Table 1-2).   Would you say that the data indicate that the dice used were "perfect"?

6-28. All the face cards are removed from an ordinary deck. Two cards (X and then Y) are drawn without replacement. Assume "perfect shuffling," so that we take the uniform distribution. Indicate the nature of the graph of the sample space. Find

$$P(X + Y = K) \qquad \text{for } K = 2, 3, 4, \ldots, 20$$

Compare these probabilities with the relative frequencies obtained in Prob. 1-19 for the class data of Prob. 1-5 or with your data for Prob. 1-5.

6-29. Develop a probability model for the experiment and compare with your empirical results in the following problems:

(*a*) 1-7	(*b*) 1-9	*(c)* 1-10
(d) 1-11	*(e)* 1-12	(*f*) 1-15
(*g*) 1-16	(*h*) 1-17	

6.4. Dependent events and conditional probabilities

In the preceding section it was pointed out that events A and B are independent if and only if $P(A \cap B) = P(A)P(B)$. If events A and B are not independent, then (naturally enough) they are said to be *dependent*. Evidently, A and B are dependent if and only if

$$P(A \cap B) \neq P(A)P(B)$$

Intuitively, this means that whether A happens or not will affect the probability of B happening. To get some grasp of this we look at a new experiment.

We take again a 10-card deck. We shuffle, draw a card X, and then draw a card Y before we replace the first card. The sample space is again a set of ordered pairs,

$$S = \{(1,2),(1,3),(1,4), \ldots ,(1,10),(2,1),(2,3),(2,4), \ldots ,(10,8),(10,9)\}$$

It is the same set as for the previous experiment of drawing two cards except that all the pairs $(1,1)$, $(2,2)$, $\ldots$, $(10,10)$ are omitted. (Clearly, we cannot get the 1 on the second draw if we already got it on the first and did not replace the first card.) S is shown geometrically in Fig. 6-4. We again assume the uniform distribution.

Here it seems clear intuitively that X and Y are not independent, since the value that X takes on seems to affect the possibilities for Y. To check this, we see from the graph that $P(X = 2 \text{ and } Y = 3) = \frac{1}{90}$, $P(X = 2) = \frac{1}{10}$, and $P(Y = 3) = \frac{1}{10}$, so that

$$P(X = 2 \text{ and } Y = 3) \neq P(X = 2)P(Y = 3)$$

Suppose that we think of performing the above experiment n times with n very large. Then we expect about $n/10$ of these results to have $X = 2$. Of these results where $X = 2$, about what proportion will have $Y = 3$? Looking at the graph of S we see that there are nine points where $X = 2$

and of these there is exactly one where $Y = 3$. Since these points all have the same probability, we would expect that about $\frac{1}{9}$ of the results with $X = 2$ would also have $Y = 3$. That is, in the technical language we wish to introduce, the *conditional probability* that $Y = 3$, given that $X = 2$, is $\frac{1}{9}$. We see that this value of $\frac{1}{9}$ was obtained by dividing the number of points where $X = 2$ into the number of points where $X = 2$ and $Y = 3$.

In the general case of two events A and B with a uniform distribution, the *conditional probability* that B happens, given that A has happened,

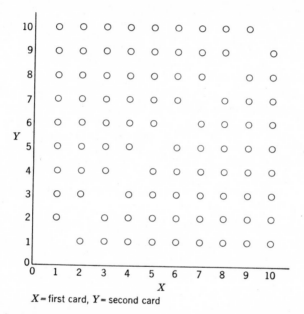

$X =$ first card, $Y =$ second card

FIG. 6-4. Graph of the sample space for two draws without replacement from a 10-card deck.

would evidently be $No\ (A \cap B)/No\ (A)$. But if we wish to express the ratio in terms of the original probabilities we note that

$$\frac{No\ (A \cap B)}{No\ (A)} = \frac{No\ (A \cap B)/No\ (S)}{No\ (A)/No\ (S)} = \frac{P(A \cap B)}{P(A)}$$

This leads us to make the following definition: The *conditional probability* for B, given A (that is, the probability that B will happen after A has happened), is given by

(6-30)
$$P(B|A) = \frac{P(A \cap B)}{P(A)}$$

Although we were led to make this definition by considering a uniform distribution, we take it to apply to any probability model. Doing so, we shall always find that the intuitive interpretation is correct.

Often for a given experiment it is easy to see the value of the probability that B will happen, given that A has already happened. Then we can use (6-30) to find $P(A \cap B)$, since it gives

(6-31) $$P(A \cap B) = P(A)P(B|A)$$

This result is sometimes called the *multiplication theorem for dependent events* (or else the general multiplication theorem). We note that, if A and B are independent, we have $P(A \cap B) = P(A)P(B)$ and hence

$$P(B|A) = \frac{P(A \cap B)}{P(A)} = P(B)$$

Thus, for A and B independent, the probability that B will happen is not affected by the occurrence of A. This agrees with our previous intuitive interpretation of "independent."

We now give an example of the application of (6-31). When two cards (X and then Y) are drawn without replacement from our 10-card deck, what is $P(X = 3 \text{ and } Y \text{ is odd})$? Evidently, $P(X = 3) = \frac{1}{10}$. After the 3 is drawn, there are nine cards remaining of which four are odd. Hence, $P(Y \text{ is odd}|X = 3) = \frac{4}{9}$. Then, by (6-31),

$$P(X = 3 \text{ and } Y \text{ is odd}) = \frac{1}{10} \times \frac{4}{9} = \frac{2}{45}$$

We can check this by noting that there are 4 points among the 90 in S where $X = 3$ and Y is odd and $\frac{4}{90} = \frac{2}{45}$.

PROBLEMS

6-32. Two cards (X and then Y) are drawn without replacement from the 10-card deck. Find the following:

(a) $P(X \text{ and } Y \text{ are both odd})$

(b) $P(X \text{ is odd and } Y \text{ is even})$

(c) $P(X = 3 \text{ and } Y \text{ is even})$

(d) $P(X \geq 8 \text{ and } Y \geq 8)$

(e) $P(X \geq 8 \text{ or } Y \geq 8)$

(f) $P(X \text{ is odd or } Y \text{ is odd})$

(g) $P(X \geq 3 \text{ and } X \text{ or } Y \text{ is odd})$

(h) The probabilities a through o of Prob. 6-19 with X and Y taken to refer to the experiment given here.

6-33. Do Prob. 6-20, assuming that the two cards are drawn without replacement.

6-34. Do Prob. 6-25, assuming that the draws are made without replacement.

6-35. Using the data given in Prob. 6-26, find the following:

(a) $P(\text{a man of 20 will survive until he is 45})$

(b) $P(\text{a woman of 20 will survive until she is 45})$

(c) $P(\text{a man and a woman both 20 will both survive until 45})$

(d) $P(\text{a man and a woman both 20 will both survive until 65})$

(e) $P(\text{for a man and a woman both 20, the man will not survive to 65 while the woman will})$

(*f*) P(a 20-year-old person will survive until 65) (assume the same number of men and women of age 20)

(*g*) P(of a man and a woman both 20, neither will survive to 65)

6-36. Four draws without replacement are made from an ordinary deck of cards. Find the following:

(*a*) P(all four cards are hearts)   (*b*) P(all four cards are aces)

(*c*) P(all four cards are red)   (*d*) P(all four cards are face cards)

(*e*) P(at least one of the cards is not a face card)

6-37. If A and B are independent events, then A' and B' are independent events. Prove this or illustrate with an example.

6-38. Let X_1 and X_2 both have the uniform distribution on the set $\{0,1,2,3,4,5, 6,7,8,9\}$. If X_1 and X_2 are independent, find the following:

(*a*) $P(X_1 = 3 | X_2 = 3)$ (*b*) $P(X_1 + X_2 = 1 | X_1 = 1)$

(*c*) $P(X_1 + X_2 = 3 | X_1 \leq 1)$ (*d*) $P(X_1 + X_2 \geq 1 | X_1 = 1)$

(*e*) $P(X_1 + X_2 \geq 3 | X_1 = 1)$ (*f*) $P(X_1 + X_2 \geq 3 | X_1 \geq 2)$

(*g*) $P(X_1 + X_2 = 10 | X_1 > 5)$ (*h*) $P(X_1 = 3 | X_1 + X_2 < 5)$

6-39. If X and then Y are the results of two draws without replacement from a 10-card deck as in Fig. 6-4, find the following:

(*a*) $P(Y = 3 | X \leq 2)$ (*b*) $P(Y < 3 | X \leq 2)$

(*c*) $P(Y \geq 3 | X \leq 2)$ (*d*) $P(Y \neq 2 | X = 2)$

(*e*) $P(X + Y = 5 | X \neq 2)$ (*f*) $P(X + Y < 5 | X = 5)$

(*g*) $P(X + Y < 5 | X = 1)$ (*h*) $P(X < Y | X = 3)$

(*i*) $P(2X < Y | X + Y = 5)$ (*j*) $P(X^2 \leq Y | X = Y)$

(*k*) $P(X^2 \leq Y | X + Y > 5)$

6-40. If A and B are events, then $P(A \cap B) = P(A)P(B|A)$ and also $P(A \cap B) = P(B)P(A|B)$. Therefore,

$$P(B|A) = \frac{P(B)P(A|B)}{P(A)}$$

Suppose that box I contains five white and four black balls while box II contains two white and seven black balls. If a box is chosen at random[1] and a ball chosen from that box at random turns out to be white, what is the probability that box I was the one chosen? (Let A be the event of choosing a white ball and B be the event of choosing box I.) Interpret your answer as a long-run relative frequency.

6-41. Work Prob. 6-40 for the case where a die was thrown and box I was chosen only if a 1 or a 6 was obtained.

6-42. Let $A_1, A_2, \ldots, A_k$ be disjoint events whose union is the sample space. Show that for any event B

$$P(B) = \sum_{i=1}^{k} P(B|A_i)P(A_i)$$

6-43. Show that, if $A_1, A_2, \ldots, A_k$ are disjoint events whose union is the sample space, then for any event B and any i

$$P(A_i|B) = \frac{P(B|A_i)P(A_i)}{\displaystyle\sum_{i=1}^{k} P(B|A_i)P(A_i)}$$

This result is called *Bayes' formula.*

[1] To say that a choice is made "at random" from among several possibilities is to say that each of the possibilities is to be assigned the same probability.

6.5. Permutations

It was noted in an earlier section that, if A is an event in a sample space S and S has a uniform probability distribution, then

$$P(A) = No\ (A)/No\ (S)$$

Thus, in many problems we are interested in finding how many members there are in a set.   Results which will help us in counting certain collections will be the major concern of this section and the next.

Suppose that we wish to go from town A to town B and then from B to town C.   Suppose that to get from A to B we can drive (D), fly (F), or go by train (T).   Suppose further that town C has no air service and to go from B to C we must either drive (D) or go by train (T).   In how many ways can we go from A to B to C?   Since we can choose either of three methods in going from A to B and for each of these choices two methods from B to C, there are $(3)(2) = 6$ ways of going from A to B to C.

To make this clear we list all possible ways of going from A to B to C in a table as:

$$(D,D),\ (D,T)$$
$$(F,D),\ (F,T)$$
$$(T,D),\ (T,T)$$

Each of the first choices gives a row in this table, and each of the second choices gives a column.   There are thus $3 \times 2 = 6$ possible ways to travel.

The above illustration is a special case of a general principle which we call the *fundamental counting lemma*.

(6-44)   *If an act A_1 can be performed in n_1 ways and if after A_1 has been performed another act A_2 can be performed in n_2 ways, then the act A_1 followed by A_2 can be performed in $n_1 n_2$ ways.*

In how many ways can two coins fall?   The first can fall two ways and the second can then fall two ways, so (by our lemma) the two coins can fall $2 \times 2 = 4$ ways.   [These four ways are (H,H), (H,T), (T,H), (T,T).]

How many different two-card draws from an ordinary deck of cards are there if the draws are made without replacement?   There are 52 different ways of choosing the first card.   After the first draw there are 51 ways of choosing the second card.   Hence, there are $51 \times 52 = 2652$ different two-card draws without replacement.   Notice that here we have considered the result[1] (S2,H3) as a different draw from (H3,S2).   The case where we do not wish to consider these as different results (as is the case in most card games) will be considered later.

[1] For the notation used here see Prob. 6-20.

In set terminology, the fundamental counting lemma may be restated as follows:

(6-45) $No \ \{(x,y): x \in A \text{ and } y \in B\} = No \ (A) \ No \ (B)$

The set $\{(x,y): x \in A \text{ and } y \in B\}$ is the set of all ordered pairs (x,y), where $x \in A$ and $y \in B$. For example, if $A = \{D,F,T\}$ and $B = \{D,T\}$, then

$$\{(x,y): x \in A \text{ and } y \in B\} = \{(D,D),(D,T),(F,D),(F,T),(T,D),(T,T)\}$$

In general, as in our travel example, if A is the collection of possible ways of performing the first act and B is the collection of possible ways of performing the second act after the first has been performed, then $\{(x,y): x \in A \text{ and } y \in B\}$ is the collection of ways of performing the first act and then the second. Hence (6-45) may be thought of as a restatement of (6-44). [Actually, (6-45) is a very fundamental notion about sets. In a sophisticated mathematical approach to the nature of numbers and operations with them, (6-45) might well be taken as the definition of multiplication for positive whole numbers and even for so-called transfinite numbers.]

If there is a sequence of more than two acts to perform, we can apply the fundamental counting lemma to successive pairs and get the following:

(6-46)   *If act A_1 can be performed in n_1 ways, then act A_2 in n_2 ways, . . . , and then A_k in n_k ways, the act A_1 followed by A_2 . . . followed by A_k can be performed in $n_1 n_2$ . . . n_k ways.*

For instance, there are $52 \times 51 \times 50 = 132{,}600$ different draws of three cards from an ordinary deck of cards if the draws are made without replacement. [Again we are considering the order to be important, so that (S2,H3,D5) is a different draw from (H3,D5,S2).]

Consider the set $A = \{a_1, a_2, . . . , a_n\}$. Suppose that we are to choose k elements from A, choosing them one at a time and keeping them in the order in which they are drawn. In how many ways can this be done? There are evidently n ways to make the first draw, then $n - 1$ ways to make the second, . . . , and then $n - k + 1$ ways to make the last draw. Then there are $n(n - 1)$ . . . $(n - k + 1)$ ways to make all k draws.

For example, if $A = \{a,b,c\}$ and $k = 2$, there should be $3 \times 2 = 6$ such draws. We can check by listing all these draws. They are (a,b), (a,c), (b,a), (b,c), (c,a), and (c,b).

An ordered arrangement of k objects is called a *permutation* of those objects.   With the use of this terminology the above result may be stated as follows:

(6-47)   *If No (A) = n, there are n(n − 1)(n − 2) . . . (n − k + 1) permutations of the elements of A taken k at a time.*

A handy device for working with counting problems is the *factorial function* defined by

(6-48) $0! = 1, \; n! = n(n − 1)(n − 2) \ldots 3 \times 2 \times 1$

"*n*!" is read as "*n* factorial."   The domain of the factorial function is the set of all nonnegative whole numbers.   We have $0! = 1$, $1! = 1$, $2! = 2$, $3! = 6$, $4! = 24$, $5! = 120$, ...   Using the factorial notation, we may say that

(6-49)   *If No (A) = n, the number of permutations of the elements of A taken k at a time is n!/(n − k)!.*

Thus, if $A = \{a,b,c\}$ the number of permutations of objects in A taken two at a time is $3!/1! = 6$.

From a group of 20 people a nominating committee is to nominate a president, a vice-president, and a secretary.   How many different choices are possible for the committee?   We may recognize this to be a "permutation problem" in disguise and write immediately that there are

$$20!/17! = 20 \times 19 \times 18 = 6840$$

different possible slates for the committee to choose from.   We may also, of course, solve the problem by use of the counting lemma and say, "There are 20 choices for the president, then 19 choices for the vice-president, and then 18 choices for the secretary."   Hence, there are $20 \times 19 \times 18 = 6840$ different possible slates for the committee to choose from.

PROBLEMS

   6-50. Verify (6-49) by showing that

$$n(n − 1)(n − 2) \ldots (n − k + 1) = \frac{n!}{(n − k)!}$$

   6-51. Let $A = \{a,b,c,d\}$.   How many permutations of the elements of A taken two at a time are there?   List all of them.
   6-52. Do Prob. 6-51 with $A = \{x_1,x_2,x_3,x_4,x_5\}$.
   6-53. If by "a word" we mean any ordered set of letters from our alphabet, how many two-letter words are there?   How many three-letter words?   How many two-letter words which do not contain repeated letters?   How many three-letter words if no letter may be used more than once?

6-54. Using "word" as in Prob. 6-53, how many three-letter words are there if no letter may appear more than twice?

6-55. A basketball team (with each person assigned to a particular position) is to be chosen from a class of 20 men. How many different teams are possible? If two teams are to be chosen from this group to play each other, in how many ways can this be done?

6-56. In a certain game with 10 players there is always a winner and a runner-up. How many different possible outcomes are there?

6-57. In how many ways can six dice fall?

6-58. On a preferential ballot listing five names the numbers 1, 2, 3, 4, 5 are to be assigned to the names. In how many ways can this be done?

6-59. A baseball league contains eight teams. In how many different orders can the teams finish the season? How many different possible outcomes are there for the first division (i.e., the top four)?

6-60. In how many different ways can five coins fall? Ten coins?

6-61. Five numbered balls are to be put into four boxes. In how many ways can this be done? How about n balls and k boxes? (More than one ball may be put in a box.)

6-62. In how many ways can five balls be put in six boxes if at most one ball may be put in each box? How about n balls and k boxes?

6-63. Five coins are tossed together and how each falls is noted. How many points in the sample space? What probability is assigned to each point if the coins are perfectly balanced?

6-64. How many three-card draws are there if the draws are made from a 10-card deck with replacement? Without replacement? Consider different orders as constituting different draws, so that (1,2,3) is different from (3,2,1). The cards are numbered 1, 2, 3, 4, 5, 6, 7, 8, 9, 10.

6-65. A box contains seven balls marked a, b, c, d, e, f, g. Two balls are drawn without replacement from the box. How many different possible outcomes are there (i.e., how many points are in the sample space for this experiment)? Consider the order to be important in discerning differences among draws. Assuming the uniform distribution, find the probability that

(a) Ball a is drawn and then ball b is drawn.

(b) Ball a and ball b are drawn (in any order).

(c) Ball a is one of the ones drawn.

(d) Either ball a or ball b is drawn.

*6-66. For large values of n, $n!$ is difficult to evaluate. Rather extensive tables of the factorial are available, but a means of approximating $n!$ for large n is *Stirling's formula:*

$$n! \cong \sqrt{2\pi} \ \sqrt{n} \ n^n e^{-n}$$

where $\pi \cong 3.142$ and $e \cong 2.718$. For example, $10! = 3,628,800$ while

$$\sqrt{2\pi} \ \sqrt{10} \ 10^{10} e^{-10} = 3.60 \times 10^6$$

so that the approximation is already fairly good for n as small as 10. Use Stirling's formula and logs to estimate

(a) 25!   (b) 50!   (c) 100!

6-6. Combinations

If $A = \{1,2,3, \ldots ,n\}$, there is clearly only one subset of A containing n elements, namely, A itself. There is also exactly one subset of A with zero elements, namely, ϕ. How many subsets of A are there that contain exactly one element? Evidently, there are n of them, namely, $\{1\}, \{2\}, \ldots, \{n\}$. More generally, how many subsets of A are there that contain exactly k elements? The answer is given by the following theorem.

(6-67)   *If No $(A) = n$, then there are $n!/k!(n - k)!$ different subsets of A that contain k elements.*

For example, if $A = \{a,b,c,d\}$, then $No\ (A) = 4$ and there should be $4!/2!2! = 6$ subsets of A which contain two elements. We check this by actually listing the subsets: $\{a,b\}, \{a,c\}, \{a,d\}, \{b,c\}, \{b,d\}, \{c,d\}$. In order to prove (6-67) we let $A = \{a_1, a_2, a_3, \ldots, a_n\}$. We know from the preceding section that there are $n!/(n - k)!$ permutations of the elements of A taken k at a time. How many of these permutations involve the particular k elements $a_1, a_2, \ldots, a_k$? Since there are $k!$ permutations of these particular elements, $k!$ of the $n!/(n - k)!$ permutations must involve these particular elements. But the same must hold for any subset of k elements. Then, since each subset of k elements leads to $k!$ of the permutations, there must be $n!/k!(n - k)!$ such subsets. This proves the theorem.

A set of k elements is sometimes called a *combination* of k elements. Using this terminology, we can restate (6-67) as follows:

(6-68)   *The number of different combinations of n things taken k at a time is given by $n!/k!(n - k)!$.*

The fraction involved in this theorem occurs so often that we introduce a special notation for it. By definition,

(6-69)
$$\binom{n}{k} = \frac{n!}{k!(n - k)!}$$

We read "$\binom{n}{k}$" as "n choose k" or "the number of combinations of n things taken k at a time." The numbers $\binom{n}{k}$ are often called binomial coefficients.[1] They have many interesting properties and arise in many different connections.

We now have the tools that we need to solve "counting problems" where we make successive draws from a collection and do not wish to consider the outcomes as different because of difference in the order in which the elements are selected. For example, how many different five-card poker hands can be dealt from an ordinary deck of cards? In a

---

[1] In some other books you will also find $\binom{n}{k}$ denoted by $_nC_k$ or C_k^n.

(draw) poker hand, the order in which the cards are dealt into a particular hand is of no importance. Hence, we would consider the hands (SK,HK, SQ,CQ,S2) and (SQ,HK,CQ,SK,S2) to be the same. Then the number of different poker hands is simply the number of subsets of the deck which contain five cards. This is given by

$$\frac{52!}{5!47!} = \frac{52 \times 51 \times 49 \times 48}{5 \times 4 \times 3 \times 2 \times 1} = 2,598,960$$

The formulas that we have developed which give the number of combinations of n things taken k at a time and the number of permutations of n things taken k at a time are not magic formulas for solving counting problems. Such problems are notoriously tricky. Each such problem must be considered on its own merits. The fundamental counting lemmas, the permutations and combinations formulas, precise language, and ingenuity will all be useful tools in attacking such problems.

Suppose that two cards are drawn without replacement from an ordinary deck of cards. In most instances, we would not consider the order in which the cards are drawn to be of importance. If we ignore the order in which the cards are drawn, there are

$$\binom{52}{2} = \frac{52 \times 51}{2} = 1326$$

different possible outcomes (that is, 1326 different possible two-card hands). If we consider each of these outcomes as equally likely (i.e., we assume the uniform distribution), it is easy to find the probability that both cards are spades. There are $\binom{13}{2} = 78$ draws containing two spades. Hence, the probability of getting two spades is $78/1326 = 3/51$. We note that this is the second of two easy ways to work this problem. The other way was:

$P(2 \text{ spades}) = P(\text{first a spade and second a spade})$
$\quad = P(\text{first a spade})P(\text{second a spade}|\text{first a spade}) = \frac{1}{4} \cdot \frac{12}{51} = \frac{3}{51}$

by the multiplication theorem.

PROBLEMS

6-70. A committee with three members is to be appointed in a club with 20 members. In how many ways can this be done?

6-71. Find an expression giving the number of different bridge hands. Do the computations involved if time permits. How many different deals are there in bridge? (There are two ways to interpret the last question.)

6-72. An elementary class contains 20 girls and 10 boys. In how many different ways can the "class monitors" be chosen if there are to be three of them? In how many ways if there are to be one girl and two boy monitors?

6-73. Among the 32 ways that five coins may fall, how many contain exactly k heads ($k = 0,1,2,3,4,5$)?

6-74. In a group of 10 voters there are four Republicans and six Democrats. Three election judges are to be chosen from these 10. In how many ways can this be done? In how many ways if both parties must be represented among the judges? In how many ways if four judges are to be selected, two from each party?

6-75. Eleven dice are thrown together. What is the probability of getting a total of 11? Of 12? Of 13? Of 66? Of 65? Of 64?

6-76. Eleven dice are thrown. What is the probability of getting 5 threes and 6 twos? Of getting exactly 5 threes?

6-77. Two draws without replacement are made from an ordinary deck of cards. What is the probability of getting two hearts? Two face cards? Two aces?

6-78. Prove that

$$\binom{n}{k} + \binom{n}{k+1} = \binom{n+1}{k+1}$$

This is the "rule of formation" for Pascal's triangle, with which you may be familiar.

6-79. Verify that $\displaystyle\sum_{k=0}^{n} \binom{n}{k} = 2^n$ for $n = 0, 1, 2, 3, 4, 5$. Argue that the equality must hold for all n (see Prob. 2-41).

6-80. If $No\,(A) = n$ and an experiment chooses a subset of A in such a way that each subset is equally likely, what is the probability that an n = element subset will be chosen? What is the probability that the subset contains two elements, three elements, k elements (see Prob. 2-41)?

6-81. In Prob. 6-80 what is the probability that the subset contains an odd number of elements?

6-82. In Prob. 6-80 assume that a second draw is made after the first has been replaced. What is the probability that both subsets drawn are empty? That at least one is nonempty?

6-83. Two subsets of size 3 are drawn with replacement from a set A (containing n elements) in such a way that on each draw every subset of size 3 is equally likely to be drawn. What is the probability that the subsets drawn are disjoint?

6-84. In a group of n people what is the probability that no two people have the same birthday? (*Hint:* See Probs. 6-61 and 6-62 and assume 365 boxes.) If you are familiar with logarithms or can use a slide rule, estimate the probability for $n = 20$.

*6-85. Use the results of Prob. 6-66 to evaluate $\binom{50}{25}$ and $\binom{100}{50}$.

CHAPTER 7

Discrete Probability Distributions

7-1. Populations and samples

What proportion of the students at your school regularly read newspapers? We could obtain an answer to this question by asking each student in school some such question as "Do you read a newspaper at least once a week?" and recording the answers. But talking with every student in the school would be time-consuming and probably quite difficult to arrange. We might then try our question on just a portion of the student body and try to infer something about the whole student body from what we find out about this portion.

This is an example of a typical situation in statistics: We wish to make inferences about a large set when we know something about a (small) subset of that set. There are certain technical terms used for the things involved. Any set of objects that we wish to study will be called a *population*. In the above example, the student body at your school would be the population. Any subset of a population is called a *sample* from that population. With the use of these terms, the above problem is to infer something about the population on the basis of information about the sample.

In most of the problems with which we shall be concerned, there is a certain value of a variable associated with each item in the population. For instance, in the above study of newspaper-reading habits, we might agree to associate with each student a value of the variable X with $X = 1$ if that student answered "yes" and $X = 0$ otherwise. If a sample of size n from that population yields the values $X_1, X_2, \ldots, X_n$, then we speak of $(X_1, X_2, \ldots, X_n)$ as a *sample of n values of X*. X_i is 1 or zero according to whether the ith person in the sample answers "yes" or not.

There are many ways to select a sample from a given population. In our study of student reading habits, suppose that we have decided to select a sample of size 20. To select the 20 students we could (1) pick the first 20 students we happen to run into in the halls; (2) pick the first 20 students who enter the campus malt shop; (3) pick the first 20 students we see sit down at a certain table in the library near the newspaper racks; (4) select every fifth name in the student directory until we get 20; (5) choose 20 students who sit toward the front in a course in modern history; (6) put each student's name on a slip of paper, put the slips in a hat, mix them, and draw 20 slips with replacement; (7) the same as in (6) but make the draws without replacement, etc.   What we wish to do, however, is have a method of selecting the sample which enables us to make inferences about the population from information about the sample.   We shall be able to make such inferences if we can apply our probability models to the situation.   To discuss the applicability of our probability models we distinguish between the cases of finite populations and infinite populations.

Finite Populations.   If the population involved is finite, our experience with uniform distributions suggests one method of selection: When we choose a student to be in our sample, he should be chosen in such a way that each student in the population has the same chance of being chosen. This method seems to be approximated by method 6 above.   If all the students' names are on slips of paper, these are mixed up, and then 20 slips are drawn with replacement, it seems true that each person has the same chance of being drawn on each draw.   A sample drawn from a finite population by this method is said to be a *random sample.*   Using this method of drawing individuals and thinking in terms of the values of the variable X associated with each item in the population, we say that X is a random variable which obtains its value by performing the following experiment: Draw an item from the population by the indicated method, and note the value of X associated with the item drawn.   If, then, we know the distribution of the X values in the population, we can find the probability distribution for X.   Suppose, for example, that 65 per cent of the student body answered "yes" to our question about newspaper reading.   Then if X is 1 when the student chosen answers "yes" and zero otherwise, we would have $P(X = 1) = .65$ and $P(X = 0) = .35$.   This is so because each of the items in the population has the same probability of being drawn and 65 per cent of the items have $X = 1$.   More generally, if a proportion p answered "yes," we would have $P(X = 1) = p$ and $P(X = 0) = q = 1 - p$.

When the n draws to obtain the sample are made with replacement, the variables $X_1, X_2, \ldots , X_n$ are evidently independent and we have

$$(7\text{-}1) \quad P(X_1 = a_1 \text{ and } X_2 = a_2 \text{ and } \cdots X_n = a_n)$$
$$= P(X_1 = a_1)P(X_2 = a_2) \cdots P(X_n = a_n)$$

for all values of the a's.   This result is a most important characteristic for random samples drawn from a finite population.   We shall take it as our definition for randomness of samples drawn from an infinite population.

The reader was probably annoyed by the above method allowing the same item to be drawn twice. If we are going to ask 20 students our question, it would seem that we are being wasteful of time and energy if we ask the same student the question twice. Nevertheless, we shall often use random samples in the above sense because it makes our theoretical work much simpler.

The commonly used method for obtaining a sample in which no item of the population can appear twice we shall call *random sampling without replacement.* By this method, a sample of size n is drawn in such a way that each possible sample of size n has the same chance of being drawn. This method is essentially method 7 described above, where the slips are drawn without replacement. In this case, if X_1 is the result on the first draw and $P(X_1 = 1) = p$, then $P(X_2 = 1)$ will depend on X_1, so that X_1 and X_2 are not independent. If, however, the population is *very* large compared with the sample size, $P(X_2 = 1)$ will not be very much affected by the outcome X_1, and in the case of very large populations and relatively small samples, we have (7-1) holding approximately. Hence, in the case of very large populations, a random sample without replacement will be approximately a random sample.

Infinite Populations. If the population is infinite and with each item in the population is associated a value of the variable X, let us suppose that we have some specific method for selecting an item from the population. Then X can be thought of as the random variable determined by the following experiment: Select an item from the population by the given method and note its value of X. If the probability distribution for X is known and a sample $(X_1, X_2, \ldots, X_n)$ is drawn, we say that it is a *random sample* if

$$P(X_1 = a_1 \text{ and } X_2 = a_2 \text{ and } \cdots \text{ and } X_n = a_n)$$
$$= P(X_1 = a_1)P(X_2 = a_2) \cdots P(X_n = a_n)$$

for all values of the a's. That is, *the sample is random if the successive results are independent random variables.*

For example, consider our dice-throwing experiment of Chap. 1. There the population is best thought of as all possible throws of the pair of dice (under essentially fixed conditions). It is most convenient to consider this population to be infinite. In Table 1-1 we find a sample of 100 values of the random variable X = total spots uppermost on the two dice. Our method of selection of items from the population is evidently dictated by the physical situation. We simply throw the dice 100 times and note the outcomes. The method seems to yield random samples because the outcomes on the successive throws seem to be independent.

Note that in either the finite or the infinite case a sample is random because of the *method of obtaining it, not* because of the values that happen to be in it. The reason we want random samples is that, if the sample is random, we can use *probability theory.* If a sample is random, we can use this theory to tell us to what degree we can have confidence that the sample is "representative" or "typical" of the population. This matter will be discussed more fully later.

Since such a device as putting names in a hat and drawing from the hat is hardly practical for large populations, we must eventually face the question "What is a practical procedure for drawing random samples from a finite population?" We shall return to this question in Sec. 7-3.

PROBLEMS

7-2. Each of the following is supposedly the title of a research report. What population is implied in each case, and what variable or variables might be pertinent?
(*a*) Car Ownership in New York City
(*b*) Dating Practices of the American Teen-ager in 1958
(*c*) The Distribution of Prime Numbers
(*d*) The Distribution of Polio Cases in the United States, 1959
(*e*) Distribution of Grades at Graduation at the University of Minnesota in 1959
(*f*) Variation of Stock Prices on the New York Exchange in 1959
(*g*) Illiteracy Rates among Draftees
(*h*) Smoking and Lung Cancer in American Males
(*i*) Airline Accident Rates in 1959
(*j*) Hereditary Factors in Diabetes
(*k*) Anatomical Data on the African Pygmy

7-3. Suppose that 60 per cent of the student body at your school either work part time or are on scholarships. In a random sample of three students let $X_i = 1$ if the *i*th student in the sample works part time or is on a scholarship and let $X_i = 0$ otherwise ($i = 1,2,3$). What is the probability that
(*a*) $X_1 + X_2 + X_3 = 3$ (*b*) $X_1 + X_2 + X_3 = 0$

7-2. Binomial distributions

A broad class of experiments requires one of the simplest kinds of models—one in which the sample space contains only two points. If, for example, a person is chosen from a town and he is asked whether or not he is married, there seem to be only two possible outcomes: "yes" and "no." If a box contains red and black balls and a ball is drawn, there are only two possible outcomes: "red" and "black." In a study of unemployment, each person is either "employed" or "unemployed."[1] The model which is applicable to these cases and many others has a two-point sample space. For convenience, we let the space be $S = \{0,1\}$, where

---

[1] We should remark that some clear-cut definition of "unemployed" must, of course, be on hand.

in a given case the "1" may correspond to "yes" or "black" or "unemployed." We let the probability assigned to the point 1 be p. Then that assigned to the point 0 will be $q = 1 - p$. The model is summarized by the table

(7-4)

x	$P(x)$
0	$q = 1 - p$
1	p

Such a model we call a *two-point probability model.*

Suppose now that a random sample of n values of X is drawn from a population having a two-point model. Denote the result by $(X_1, X_2, \ldots, X_n)$. We consider the new random variable $Y = \sum_{i=1}^{n} X_i$. What is Y? It is simply the number of 1's in our sample. In the study of marital status above it would be the number of "yes" answers if "1" denotes "yes." That is, Y would be the number of people in the sample who said they were married. In the case of balls drawn from a box, where 1 denotes "black," Y is the number of black balls in the sample.

The sample space for Y is $T = \{0, 1, 2, \ldots, n\}$. We now ask what must be the distribution for Y.[1] Some values of $P(Y = y)$ are easy to get.

$$
\begin{aligned}
P(Y = 0) &= P(X_1 = 0 \text{ and } X_2 = 0 \text{ and } \cdots \text{ and } X_n = 0) \\
&= P(X_1 = 0)P(X_2 = 0) \cdots P(X_n = 0) \\
&= qq \cdots q = q^n \\
&= (1 - p)^n
\end{aligned}
$$

Here the first equality holds because the only way by which Y would be zero would be to have each of the X_i values equal to zero. The equality in the second line holds because we are told that the sample is random. In a similar manner, we have

$$
\begin{aligned}
P(Y = n) &= P(X_1 = 1 \text{ and } X_2 = 1 \text{ and } \cdots \text{ and } X_n = 1) \\
&= P(X_1 = 1)P(X_2 = 1) \cdots P(X_n = 1) \\
&= p^n
\end{aligned}
$$

How about the value of $P(Y = 1)$? We get $Y = 1$ if $X_1 = 1$ and all the other X's are zero, or if $X_2 = 1$ and all the other X's are zero, or if $X_3 = 1$ and all the other X's are zero, etc. Hence,

[1] This is an instance of a broad class of problems in mathematical statistics where we know the distribution for X, have a random sample of n values of X, introduce a new variable $Y = f(X_1, X_2, \ldots, X_n)$ as some function of the sample values, and wish to find the distribution for Y. In most cases such problems require mathematics above the level assumed here, but the derivation in the above instance is elementary.

$$
\begin{aligned}
P(Y = 1) &= P[(X_1 = 1 \text{ and } X_2 = 0 \text{ and } X_3 = 0 \text{ and } \cdots \text{ and } X_n = 0) \\
&\quad \text{or } (X_1 = 0 \text{ and } X_2 = 1 \text{ and } X_3 = 0 \text{ and } \cdots \text{ and } X_n = 0) \\
&\quad \text{or } \cdots \text{ or } (X_1 = 0 \text{ and } X_2 = 0 \text{ and } \cdots \text{ and } X_{n-1} = 0 \\
&\quad\quad\quad\quad\quad\quad\quad\quad\quad\quad\quad\quad\quad\quad\quad\quad\quad\quad \text{and } X_n = 1)] \\
&= P(X_1 = 1 \text{ and } X_2 = 0 \text{ and } X_3 = 0 \text{ and } \cdots \text{ and } X_n = 0) \\
&\quad + P(X_1 = 0 \text{ and } X_2 = 1 \text{ and } X_3 = 0 \text{ and } \cdots \text{ and } \\
&\quad\quad X_n = 0) + \cdots + P(X_1 = 0 \text{ and } X_2 = 0 \text{ and } \cdots \text{ and } \\
&\quad\quad\quad\quad\quad\quad\quad\quad\quad\quad\quad\quad X_{n-1} = 0 \text{ and } X_n = 1) \\
&= P(X_1 = 1)P(X_2 = 0)P(X_3 = 0) \cdots P(X_n = 0) \\
&\quad + P(X_1 = 0)P(X_2 = 1)P(X_3 = 0) \cdots P(X_n = 0) + \cdots \\
&\quad + P(X_1 = 0)P(X_2 = 0) \cdots P(X_{n-1} = 0)P(X_n = 1) \\
&= pqq \cdots q + qpq \cdots q + \cdots + qq \cdots qp \\
&= npq^{n-1}
\end{aligned}
$$

The second equality is justified by noting that the events involved are mutually exclusive and by applying the addition theorem for mutually exclusive events. The third equality holds because the sample is random.

Now we shall generalize the above argument to find the value of $P(Y = y)$ for any y. One way to get $Y = y$ would be to have $X_1 = 1$, $X_2 = 1, \ldots, X_y = 1$, $X_{y+1} = 0$, $X_{y+2} = 0, \ldots,$ and $X_n = 0$. But because of the randomness of the sample the probability for this is $p^k q^{n-k}$. Any other values of the X's which give $Y = y$ will have y 1's among them and $n - y$ 0's. How many arrangements of 0's and 1's have this property? This seems to be simply the question: How many ways can we choose the y places to put the 1's? The answer to this is $\binom{n}{y}$. Thus, there are $\binom{n}{y}$ arrangements of 0's and 1's which yield $Y = y$. But the probability of a particular one of these arrangements being the outcome is $p^y q^{n-y}$. Hence, $P(Y = y) = \binom{n}{y} p^y q^{n-y}$. This proves the following:

(7-5) *If X has the sample space $\{0,1\}$ and $P(X = 1) = p$ and $Y = \sum_{i=1}^{n} X_i$,*

where $(X_1, X_2, \ldots, X_n)$ is a random sample of n values of X, then

$$P(Y = y) = \binom{n}{y} p^y q^{n-y} \text{ for } y = 0, 1, 2, \ldots, n \text{ and } q = 1 - p.$$

This theorem can be restated in different language if we consider getting a 1 to be a "success."

(7-6) *If the probability of a success on a single trial is p and Y is the number of successes in n random trials, then $P(Y = y) = \binom{n}{y} p^y q^{n-y}$ where $q = 1 - p$.*

What is the probability of getting exactly three heads in five tosses of a perfect coin? Since on each toss the probability of getting a head is $\frac{1}{2}$, we have, by the theorem, $P(3 \text{ heads}) = \binom{5}{3}\left(\frac{1}{2}\right)^3\left(\frac{1}{2}\right)^2 = \frac{5}{16}$.

If in a certain town 60 per cent of the adult males are homeowners, what is the probability that a random sample of 10 adult males will contain 6 homeowners? Here we would take the probability to be .60 that, when a single adult male is chosen, he will be a homeowner. Then the desired probability is $\binom{10}{6}(.6)^6(.4)^4 = .251$.

For large values of n and k the numerical evaluation of $\binom{n}{k}p^kq^{n-k}$ becomes tedious. Large tables of the values of this distribution for various values of n, k, and p have been worked out and published.[1] A small table of such values is given in the Appendix as Table A-2. The reader should use this table but not lose sight of the meaning given by (7-5) and its derivation.

The distribution that was derived for Y in (7-5) is called the *binomial distribution*. In general, if Y is a random variable with sample space $\{0,1,2, \ldots ,n\}$, we say that Y is a *binomial variable* and has a *binomial distribution* if, for each y, $P(y) = P(Y = y) = \binom{n}{y}p^yq^{n-y}$ for some real number p between zero and 1 and for $q = 1 - p$. The numbers n and p are called *parameters* of the distribution. When we think of the collection of all binomial distributions, it is the values of n and of p which tell us which one of them we have. n and p, the *parameters*, are numerical properties of the distribution. If Y has the binomial distribution with parameters n and p, we say more concisely that "Y has the distribution $B(n,p)$" or even "Y is $B(n,p)$."

If we ask for the value of $P(Y \leq y)$, we see that

$$P(Y \leq y) = P(Y = 0 \text{ or } Y = 1 \text{ or } \cdots \text{ or } Y = y)$$
$$= P(Y = 0) + P(Y = 1) + \cdots + P(Y = y)$$
$$= \sum_{k=0}^{y} \binom{n}{k}p^kq^{n-k}$$

If we were told the value of $P(Y \leq y)$ for each value of y, we would be able to find $P(Y = y)$, since $P(Y = y) = P(Y \leq y) - P(Y \leq y - 1)$. Then the values of $P(Y \leq y)$ completely determine the distribution. But $P(Y \leq y)$ will be some function of y. We call it the *cumulative*

---

[1] See *Tables of the Binomial Probability Distribution*, Department of Commerce, National Bureau of Standards, 1949.

probability function and denote it by $CP(y)$.[1]   Values of $CP(y)$ for some binomial distributions are given in Table A-3 in the Appendix.

In general (and not simply for the binomial distribution), when the sample space is a finite set of real numbers, the distribution is completely determined by giving either the probability function P or the *cumulative probability function* CP defined by $CP(y) = P(Y \leq y)$.   We can use either to specify the distribution, depending on which is more convenient.

A probability function or a cumulative probability function can be graphed in much the same way that empirical relative frequency functions

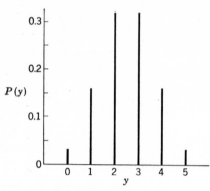

FIG. 7-1. Graph of

$$P(y) = \binom{5}{y} (\tfrac{1}{2})^y (\tfrac{1}{2})^{5-y}$$

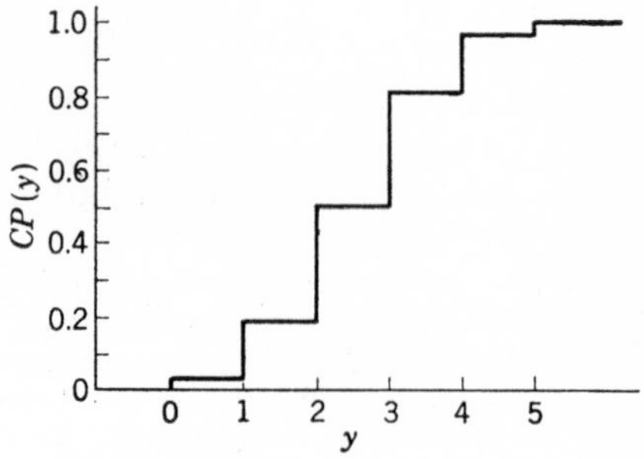

FIG. 7-2. Graph of

$$CP(y) = \sum_{k=0}^{y} \binom{5}{k} (\tfrac{1}{2})^k (\tfrac{1}{2})^{5-k}$$

and empirical cumulative relative frequency functions were graphed in Chap. 1.   This is not surprising, since $P(x)$ and $CP(x)$ are, if you like, the "theoretical counterparts" of $RF(x)$ and $RCF(x)$.   For a large sample we expect $RF(x)$ to be almost the same as $P(x)$ and similarly for $RCF(x)$ and $CP(x)$.   In Figs. 7-1 and 7-2 we have graphed these functions for Y, the number of heads obtained in five tosses of a perfect coin.

As a final example for this section we ask for the probability of getting at least 10 sixes in tossing a perfect die 30 times.   On a single toss the probability of getting a 6 is $\tfrac{1}{6}$.   Hence, the probability of getting y sixes would be

$$\binom{30}{y} (\tfrac{1}{6})^y (\tfrac{5}{6})^{30-y}$$

Then the probability of getting at least 10 sixes would be

$$\sum_{y=10}^{30} \binom{30}{y} (\tfrac{1}{6})^y (\tfrac{5}{6})^{30-y}$$

---

[1] Many texts use $f(y)$ for the probability function and $F(y)$ for the cumulative probability function.   We prefer the suggestive notation used here.

[by (6-10), since to get at least 10 sixes we must get 10 sixes or 11 sixes or 12 sixes . . . or 30 sixes]. The term-by-term evaluation of this sum would be laborious. We can use Table A-3 in the Appendix instead. We first note that the desired probability is $1 - CP(9)$ for $B(30, \frac{1}{6})$. Interpolating between the values of $CP(9)$ given for $B(30, .1)$ and $B(30, .2)$ we find that the desired probability is approximately $1 - .98 = .02$.

PROBLEMS

7-7. A "perfect coin" is tossed five times. List all possible outcomes [for example, one possible outcome would be (H,T,H,H,H)]. Put these outcomes into groups according to the number of heads obtained. Find the probability of $Y = y$ for $y = 0, 1, 2, 3, 4, 5$ if Y is the number of heads obtained. Do this two ways: by counting points in the sample space and by applying (7-5).

7-8. Ten students are chosen at random from a college at which 10 per cent of the students are married. What is the probability that exactly two married students will be chosen? That at least one married student will be chosen?

7-9. In a certain town 40 per cent of the school children have had measles. In a random sample of five children what is the probability that exactly two have had measles? That at least two have had measles?

7-10. In a certain community 50 per cent of the voters are registered Republicans. What is the probability that a random sample of 30 voters will contain 15 registered Republicans? A majority of registered Republicans?

7-11. If a perfect coin is tossed 100 times, find an expression for the probability of getting exactly 50 heads. For getting between 45 and 55 heads inclusive. (Do not evaluate.)

7-12. In a random sample of 30 students from a school where 20 per cent of the students are taking mathematics, what is the probability that fewer than four are taking mathematics?

7-13. In a certain hospital five patients are to undergo an operation for which there is an 80 per cent survival rate. What is the probability that all survive? That exactly three survive? That more than half survive?

7-14. Graph $P(x) = \binom{10}{x} p^x q^{10-x}$ for $p = .1, .5,$ and $.9$. Graph the corresponding cumulative probability functions.

7-15. Graph $P(x) = \binom{20}{x} p^x q^{20-x}$ for $p = .1$ and $p = .9$. Explain the similarity in these two graphs.

7-16. On a single sheet, graph $P(x) = \binom{n}{x} (.3)^x (.7)^{n-x}$ for $n = 5, 10, 20$.

7-17. Graph the corresponding cumulative probability functions for Prob. 7-15.

7-18. Graph the corresponding cumulative probability functions for Prob. 7-16.

7-19. A "perfect" coin is tossed 100 times. If X is the number of heads obtained, find expressions for the following probabilities. (Do not evaluate.)

(a) $P(X \leq 40)$ (b) $P(45 \leq X < 55)$ (c) $P(45 < X \leq 55)$
(d) $P(x - 50 < 3)$ (e) $P(|X - 50| > 3)$ (f) $P(|X - 50| > 5)$
                       (g) $P(|X - 50| \geq 5)$

7-20. If X is the number of heads obtained in tossing a perfect coin 30 times, what is the probability that $X < 20$?

7-21. If you are familiar with the binomial theorem of algebra, show that the terms in the expansion of $(p + q)^n$ are precisely the probabilities for a binomial distribution with parameters n and p $(q = 1 - p)$.

7-22. In a random sample of 10 balls from a box containing 80 per cent white balls, what is the probability that between 25 and 55 per cent of the balls will be white?

7-23. If a coin is perfectly balanced, should we be surprised to obtain five or fewer heads in 20 tosses?

7-24. Suppose that X has sample space $S = \{0,1,2,3,4,5,6,7,8,9\}$ and a uniform distribution. Let Y be the number of times the event A occurs in 10 independent trials, and find $P(Y = 3)$ for the following events:

(a) $A = \{X: X \leq 5\}$ (b) $A = \{X: X \text{ is odd}\}$ (c) $A = \{X: X < 3\}$
(d) $A = \{X: X \leq 4\}$ (e) $A = \{X: |X - 5| \leq 2\}$

7-25. If X is $B(30,.2)$, find

(a) $P(X = 5)$ (b) $P(4 \leq X \leq 6)$ (c) $P(5 \leq X \leq 8)$
(d) $P(X \leq 2)$ (e) $P(X > 2)$ (f) $P(|X - 5| < 2)$
(g) $P(|X - 5| \geq 2)$ (h) $P(|X - 5| < 3)$ (i) $P(|X - 5| \geq 3)$

7-26. Do Prob. 7-25 with $n = 30$ and $p = .6$.

7-27. Do Prob. 7-25 with $n = 20$ and $p = .4$.

7-28. Do Prob. 7-25 with $n = 10$ and $p = .4$.

7-29. Table A-2 in the Appendix gives values of $\binom{n}{y} p^y q^{n-y}$ for $n = 5, 10, 20,$ and 30 and for $p = .1, .2, .3, .4, .5, .6, .7, .8, .9$. It can be used with interpolation to estimate probabilities for other values of n and p. Estimate in this fashion the following probabilities if X is a binomial variable with the indicated parameters:

(a) $P(X = 5), n = 20, p = .25$ (b) $P(X = 3), n = 20, p = .25$
(c) $P(X = 18), n = 20, p = .85$ (d) $P(X = 4), n = 30, p = .15$
(e) $P(X = 7), n = 30, p = .57$ (f) $P(X = 5), n = 25, p = .2$
(g) $P(X = 7), n = 28, p = .4$ (h) $P(X = 20), n = 25, p = .85$

7-30. A perfect coin is tossed until a head is obtained. Let X be the number of tosses required to produce the first head. What is the sample space for X? Find the distribution for X. Graph the probability function.

7-31. If X is $B(n_1,p)$ and Y is $B(n_2,p)$, what is the distribution of $Z = X + Y$?

7-32. If X has a binomial distribution with parameters n, p and we let $Y = X/n$, then Y is the proportion of successes in the sample. What is the sample space for Y? What is the probability function for Y?

7-33. If 50 per cent of the families in a certain town have savings exceeding $1000, approximately how large a random sample must we take to make the probability at least .50 that the sample will contain at least five families who have savings exceeding $1000?

7-3. Random digits

The problem of finding a practical means of choosing a random sample from a finite population was posed in Sec. 7-1. Suppose that a population contains N objects. If we had some means for making random choices from the set of numbers $A = \{1,2,3, \ldots ,N\}$, we could number the items in the population, draw a random sample from A, and then take the items with the corresponding numbers from our population as our sample. Such a sample would be random. It would seem that what we should like would be something like an "N-sided die." Since the construction of such a die is usually impractical, we need another approach.

One such is the use of a table of random digits.   A table of random digits is supposed to represent a large random sample of values of a random variable X with sample space $S = \{0,1,2,3,4,5,6,7,8,9\}$ and the uniform distribution.   (Given such a table, there are many tests that can be made to see if it is reasonable to assume that it is a random sample for such a variable.   We shall see some of these later.)   Table A-4 in the Appendix is a small table of random digits.   Much larger tables are available.

Suppose that a population contains 850 items to which we have assigned the numbers 1, 2, 3, . . . , 850.   We can use Table A-4 to draw a random sample of size 20 from this population as follows: Start at any position in the table and write down successive groups of three digits as found in the table until we have found 20 numbers between 1 and 850, inclusive.   Use these numbers to identify your sample.   We shall here take "001" as being "1," "002" as being "2," etc.   If we find a set of three digits such as "951," we simply skip it and move on to the next group of three because we have no item numbered 951.   If the table is random, the resulting sample will be random, since each number from 1 to 850 has the same chance of occurring at each place in our list.

Random digits could be generated by a 10-sided die.   Electronic computers can also be programmed to produce (apparently) random digits.

The underlying distribution from which a table of random digits is supposed to be a sample is displayed in (7-34).   This distribution we call the *uniform distribution on the decimal digits*.

(7-34)

x........	0	1	2	3	4	5	6	7	8	9
$P(x)$......	.1	.1	.1	.1	.1	.1	.1	.1	.1	.1

Another method for choosing a sample of 20 from a student body of 850 would be to take a student directory which lists all students in the school, choose a random number k between 1 and 40, inclusive, from the table of random digits, take the kth student listed in the directory as the first member of your sample, then count down 40 names and take the name 40 after the kth one, then count down 40 names, etc., until you have a sample of 20 names.   For many purposes, the sample resulting by such a method is very close to being a random sample without replacement, and if the population is large, it may be treated as a random sample.   For some purposes the method would not be satisfactory, however.   Suppose, for example, that the directory is alphabetical and we are interested in studying how many students have the same last name as some other student in school!

In using a table of random digits, you should have some method decided on ahead of time for choosing your place to start. You must be careful, since you may have an unconscious preference for certain digits (see Prob. 7-36). If you have a table of random digits which you do not mind marking up, you may simply start at the beginning, make a mark after the last digit you use, and, next time you wish to use the table, start at the first unused digit. If in your class you all did this with the table in the Appendix, however, you would almost all be getting the same samples of digits at the same time, and this is undesirable. Another method is to jab your finger arbitrarily at the first page in the table and use the first two digits it falls on to tell you the line in which to start and the next two digits to tell you where to start in that line.

PROBLEMS

7-35. Starting at an arbitrary position in a table of random digits, draw 100 consecutive digits. Find the mean and standard deviation for these results.

7-36. Have each person in the class write down a "random sequence" of 20 decimal digits without the use of any tables or any chance devices. Collect the class results in a frequency distribution showing the number of times each digit occurred. Does the distribution suggest that the choices were random or otherwise? Suggest other tests for randomness which we might apply here.

7-37. Describe in some detail how you would choose a random sample of size 20 from the populations of

(a) Students at your school
(b) High school teachers in Minnesota
(c) Automobiles in your state
(d) Pages of this book
(e) Outcomes on a roulette wheel
(f) Families in a small town
(g) Families with telephones in a small town
(h) Registered voters in a small town
(i) Stocks listed in the Sunday *Times* financial section
(j) Inmates in a prison
(k) Faculty at your school
(l) Female students at your school

7-38. Draw 20 samples of five digits each from a table of random digits. Find the mean of each sample. Rank the results. Find the mean of these 20 sample means.

7-39. Combine the results for samples of size 5 obtained by various members of the class in Prob. 7-38 into a single relative frequency distribution. Find its mean and standard deviation. Graph the relative frequency distribution.

7-40. If the random variable X has the infinite sample space $\{0,1,2,3,4, \ldots\}$, and if

$$P(x) = e^{-m} \frac{m^x}{x!} \qquad \text{where } e \cong 2.72$$

and m is any positive constant, then X is said to have a *Poisson distribution* and to be a *Poisson variable*. Many observed variables seem to have approximately a Poisson distribution, for example, the number of telephone calls per minute at a switchboard, the number of atoms that decay per millionth of a second in a radio-active compound, the number of accidents per week in a large factory, etc. A binomial distribution for which n is very large and p is very small will be approximately a Poisson distribution with $m = np$. Compare $P(x)$ as given by the Poisson distribution for $x = 0$, 1, and 2 with $m = 3$ with the corresponding binomial probabilities when $n = 30$ and $p = .1$. As an aid to computation we give a table of some powers of e.

m.......	.1	.5	1	2	3	.5
e^{-m}......	.904	.606	.368	.135	.0498	.00674

7-41. Compare $P(X = 0)$, $P(X = 1)$, $P(X = 2)$, and $P(X = 3)$ for the case when X is $B(20,.1)$ and when X is a Poisson variable with $m = 2$.

7-42. Find the following probabilities if X is a Poisson variable (see Prob. 7-40) with the indicated value of m:

(a) $P(X = 0)$, $m = 2$ (b) $P(X = 1)$, $m = 2$ (c) $P(X = 2)$, $m = 2$
(d) $P(X < 4)$, $m = 2$ (e) $P(X > 4)$, $m = 2$ (f) $P(4 \leqq X \leqq 6)$, $m = 5$

7-4. Properties of discrete probability distributions

In Chaps. 4 and 5 we discussed measures of central tendency and measures of dispersion for empirical frequency distributions. We now introduce their theoretical counterparts for probability distributions.

The n values of a random variable X which give rise to an empirical frequency distribution can always be thought of as a sample of n values of X. If n is very large, we expect $RF(x)$ to approximate $P(x)$ for each value of x in the sample space. For the sample, we found that the mean and standard deviation were given by $\bar{X} = \Sigma \, xRF(x)$ and

$$s = \sqrt{\Sigma \, (x - \bar{X})^2 RF(x)}$$

where the sums ranged over the entire sample space. By analogy, we then define the *mean* μ (read as "mew") and the *standard deviation* σ (read as "sigma") of the probability distribution for X by

(7-43) $\mu = \Sigma \, xP(x)$
(7-44) $\sigma = [\Sigma \, (x - \mu)^2 P(x)]^{\frac{1}{2}}$

where again the sums range over the entire sample space. The square of the standard deviation is called the *variance*. We also speak of μ as the *mean* of X and σ as the *standard deviation* of X. Notice, then, that the terms "mean" and "standard deviation" now refer either to a probability distribution or to a sample (i.e., to an empirical frequency distribution). It will be important always to understand which meaning is intended. From this point in this book the mean and standard deviation of a sample will always be referred to as the *sample mean* and *sample standard deviation*. When the terms are used without the qualifying adjective "sample," we understand that the probability distribution is referred to and not a sample. The notation attempts also to make the above distinction clear. μ (the small Greek m) and σ (the small Greek s) refer to the probability distribution, while $\bar{X}$ and s refer to the sample. In general, Greek letters will be used to refer to numerical properties of the probability distribution and roman letters to numerical properties of the sample.

To emphasize further the distinction: If X has a certain probability distribution, then μ and σ are fixed numbers while $\bar{X}$ and s are random variables which vary from sample to sample as various samples are drawn.

The mean and standard deviations will be referred to as *parameters*. They are numerical properties of the distribution just as n and p are numerical properties (and, hence, parameters) of the binomial distribution as discussed in Sec. 7-2. In contrast to this, a sample mean or a sample standard deviation will be called a *statistic*. In general, a *statistic* is a numerical property of a sample.

What are the intuitive interpretations of μ and σ? If we take larger and larger random samples, we expect the sample mean $\bar{X}$ to approximate μ more and more closely and we expect the sample standard deviation s to approximate σ more and more closely. In terms of the graph of the probability function $y = P(x)$, μ and σ^2 play the same role as $\bar{X}$ and s^2 for the graph of $y = RF(x)$ for a sample. μ is the position on the x axis where the graph of $y = P(x)$ could be balanced on a knife-edge. σ^2 is the moment of inertia of this graph about the vertical line through μ.

If we are involved with more than one variable, subscripts will be used to distinguish between various means and variances. μ_X and $\sigma_X{}^2$ will be the mean and variance for X, while μ_Y and $\sigma_Y{}^2$ will be the mean and variance for Y.

Before computing the mean and standard deviation for some particular distributions, we shall find it helpful to have the following result:

$$(7\text{-}45) \qquad\qquad \sigma^2 = \Sigma \, x^2 P(x) - \mu^2$$

The proof of this equation is as follows:

$$
\begin{aligned}
\sigma^2 &= \Sigma \, (x - \mu)^2 P(x) & \text{by } (7\text{-}44)\\
&= \Sigma \, (x^2 - 2\mu x + \mu^2) P(x)\\
&= \Sigma \, x^2 P(x) - 2\mu\Sigma \, xP(x) + \mu^2\Sigma \, P(x)\\
&= \Sigma \, x^2 P(x) - 2\mu^2 + \mu^2 & \text{by } (7\text{-}43) \text{ and } (6\text{-}2)\\
&= \Sigma \, x^2 P(x) - \mu^2
\end{aligned}
$$

Equation (7-45) is the analogue for the probability distribution of Eq. (5-13) for a sample. The variance σ^2 is often computed by means of (7-45) rather than by the original definition.

In the case of the two-point probability model, we have the sample space $\{0,1\}$ with $P(1) = p$ and $P(0) = q = 1 - p$. In Table 7-1 we have computed the mean and standard deviation for this distribution.

Note the similarity with the computation of the mean and standard deviation of a sample.

Table 7-1
Computation of the Mean and Standard Deviation
for the Two-point Probability Model

x	$P(x)$	$xP(x)$	$x^2P(x)$
0	q	0	0
1	p	p	p
Totals........	1	p	p

$$\mu = \Sigma \, xP(x) = p$$
$$\sigma^2 = \Sigma \, x^2P(x) - \mu^2 = p - p^2$$
$$= p(1 - p) = pq$$
$$\sigma = \sqrt{pq}$$

In Table 7-2 we have computed the mean and standard deviation for the uniform distribution on the decimal digits. Again the pattern is similar to what was done for samples. Since a table of random digits is intended to be a sample from this distribution, we should expect the mean and variance of the entries in a large table of random digits to be very close to 4.5 and 8.25, respectively, as given by our computations in the table.

In case X has the binomial distribution $B(n,p)$, the mean and stand-

Table 7-2
Computation of the Mean and Standard Deviation for the
Uniform Distribution on the Decimal Digits

x	$P(x)$	$xP(x)$	$x^2P(x)$
0	.1	0	0
1	.1	.1	.1
2	.1	.2	.4
3	.1	.3	.9
4	.1	.4	1.6
5	.1	.5	2.5
6	.1	.6	3.6
7	.1	.7	4.9
8	.1	.8	6.4
9	.1	.9	8.1
Totals.......	1	4.5	28.5

$$\mu = \Sigma \, xP(x) = 4.5$$
$$\sigma^2 = \Sigma \, x^2P(x) - \mu^2 = 28.5 - (4.5)^2$$
$$= 8.25$$
$$\sigma = \sqrt{8.25}$$

ard deviation for X can be computed in a similar manner. The computations are somewhat messy, however, for the general case and will be omitted here and discussed, in part, in a problem. The outcome of these computations is very important, however.

(7-46)   *If X is $B(n,p)$, then $\mu_X = np$ and $\sigma_X = \sqrt{npq}$ where $q = 1 - p$.*

This result should be memorized by the reader. As an example, consider X to be the number of heads obtained in 100 tosses of a perfect coin. Then X is $B(100,\frac{1}{2})$ and $\mu_X = 50$ and $\sigma_X = \sqrt{100(\frac{1}{2})(\frac{1}{2})} = 5$. In a sample of a very large number of trials for X we would expect the mean to be close to 50 (which is, perhaps, not a surprise) and the standard deviation to be close to 5.

The mean and standard deviation are probably the most useful parameters of a distribution, but others are defined in a manner analogous to the corresponding statistics for samples.

The *mode* of a probability distribution for a random variable X with sample space $\{x_1, x_2, \ldots, x_N\}$ is that value x_k in the sample space at which $P(x)$ is a maximum, if exactly one such x_k exists. Formally, the mode is the unique value x_k such that

(7-47) $P(x_k) = \max \{P(x_1), P(x_2), \ldots, P(x_N)\}$

if exactly one such x_k exists.

A *median* for a probability distribution is the smallest value x_0 in the sample space for which $P(X \leq x_0) \geq .5$. That is, the median is the smallest value x_0 for which $CP(x_0) \geq .5$.

We note that, as was the case with samples, the definition of the mode makes sense when the sample space is any set of objects while the definition of the median requires that the sample space be a set of numbers (or, at least, have its points ranked in some manner).

The median and mode of a probability distribution are again *parameters*, while a sample median or sample mode is a *statistic*.

Another parameter of a probability distribution is the *range* defined by max (S) − min (S), where S is the sample space for the variable.

PROBLEMS

7-48. Let Y be the number of homeowners in a random sample of nine families drawn from a town where 50 per cent of the families are homeowners. Find the mean and standard deviation for Y.

7-49. Let Y be the number of heads obtained in 30 tosses of a perfect coin. Find the mean and standard deviation for Y. What is a median for Y? What is the mode for Y?

7-50. If X is the number of "yes" answers to a certain question in a random sample of 30 people drawn from a population in which $\frac{1}{6}$ of the people would answer "yes," find the mean and standard deviation for X.

7-51. Find μ and σ for the uniform distribution on the sample space $\{0,1,2,3,4\}$.

7-52. Find $P(x)$ for each x if X has a binomial distribution with $n = 10$ and $p = .3$. Using these values, compute μ and σ from (7-43) and (7-45). Do your computations in tabular form. Find the median and mode.

7-53. If X is the number of spots uppermost after a throw of a pair of perfect dice, find the mean and standard deviation for X. Compare these results with those found for the dice in Probs. 4-11 and 5-20 if you did those problems.

7-54. In a certain town 10 per cent of the people refuse to answer any question about their political affiliation. If Y is the number of people who refuse to answer such a question in a random sample of 100, find the mean and standard deviation for Y.

7-55. If Y has probability function $P(y) = \binom{n}{y} p^y q^{n-y}$, where $q = 1 - p$, the mean of Y is given by

$$
\begin{aligned}
\mu &= \sum_{y=0}^{n} y \binom{n}{y} p^y q^{n-y} \\
&= \sum_{y=1}^{n} y \binom{n}{y} p^y q^{n-y} \\
&= \sum_{y=1}^{n} y \frac{n!}{y!(n-y)!} p^y q^{n-y} \\
&= np \sum_{y=1}^{n} \frac{(n-1)!}{(y-1)!(n-y)!} p^{y-1} q^{n-y} \\
&= np \sum_{k=0}^{n-1} \frac{(n-1)!}{k!(n-1-k)!} p^k q^{n-1-k} \\
&= np \sum_{k=0}^{n-1} \binom{n-1}{k} p^k q^{n-1-k} \\
&= np
\end{aligned}
$$

This proves that the mean of the binomial distribution is np. Justify each step in the proof.

7-56. For each distribution graphed in Prob. 7-14 find μ and σ. Find for each of these distributions $P(\mu - \sigma < X < y + \sigma)$, $P(\mu - 2\sigma < X < \mu + 2\sigma)$, and $P(\mu - 3\sigma < X < \mu + 3\sigma)$.

7-57. Do Prob. 7-56 for the distributions graphed in Prob. 7-16.

7-58. If X has a binomial distribution with $n = 30$ and $p = .6$, find μ and σ and
(a) $P(\mu - \sigma < X < \mu + \sigma)$ (b) $P(\mu - 2\sigma < X < \mu + 2\sigma)$
(c) $P(|X - \mu| < 3\sigma)$ (d) $P(|X - \mu| \geq 3\sigma)$
(e) $P(|X - \mu| < 4\sigma)$ (f) $P(|X - \mu| > 2\sigma)$

7-59. Do Prob. 7-58 with $n = 30$ and $p = .2$.

*7-60. If X has a uniform distribution on $\{1,2,3, \ldots ,N\}$, find μ and σ.

7-61. Find an expression for the mean of the distribution of Y in each case in Prob. 7-24.

7-62. It can be shown that the mean and standard deviation of the Poisson distribution are given by $\mu = m$, $\sigma = \sqrt{m}$. Argue for these results in terms of the information given in Prob. 7-40.

7-63. The average number of calls per minute at a certain switchboard in the late afternoon is 3. In a given minute (say 4:50 to 4:51) what is the probability of 0 calls? One call? Two calls? Three calls? (See Prob. 7-62.)

7-64. Over the past several years a certain large factory has had an average of 52 accidents per year. What is the probability of having two or more accidents during the next full working week? (See Prob. 7-62.)

7-65. What are the mean and the standard deviation of Y as defined in Prob. 7-32?

7-66. What are the mean and standard deviation of Z as defined in Prob. 7-31?

7-5. Expected values

Suppose that someone offers to let us play the following game: We are to toss five coins and note the number of heads obtained. We shall then be paid a number of dollars equal to this number of heads. How much should we pay to play the game if it is to be "fair"? We can answer this question if we think of playing the game a very large number of times and find out how much we expect to win per trial in the long run. Evidently, if we pay this long-run average winning per trial to play the game, it will be "fair." Suppose that we play the game n times where n is very large. Then, since the probability of getting zero heads is $\frac{1}{32}$, we expect to get zero heads about $n/32$ times. Similarly, we expect to get one head about $5n/32$ times, two heads about $10n/32$ times, three heads about $10n/32$ times, four heads about $5n/32$ times, and five heads about $n/32$ times. Then the total amount we win will be approximately

$$0 \times \frac{n}{32} + 1 \times \frac{5n}{32} + 2 \times \frac{10n}{32} + 3 \times \frac{10n}{32} + 4 \times \frac{5n}{32} + 5 \times \frac{n}{32}$$

$$= n\left(0 \times \frac{1}{32} + 1 \times \frac{5}{32} + 2 \times \frac{10}{32} + 3 \times \frac{10}{32} + 4 \times \frac{5}{32} + 5 \times \frac{1}{32}\right)$$

This simplifies to $2.5n$. But if we expect to win about $2.5n$ in n trials, we expect to win about 2.5 dollars per trial and we should be willing to pay 2.5 dollars to play the game.

Let us now generalize the above argument. Suppose that a game (or an experiment) has N possible outcomes. Let X be the outcome and $S = \{x_1, x_2, \ldots, x_N\}$ be the sample space for X. Suppose further that, when the outcome is x_i, we are paid the amount $f(x_i)$ dollars, where f is some function defined on S. If the probability that $X = x_i$ is given by $P(x_i)$ and we play the game n times where n is large, we expect to get the outcome x_i about $nP(x_i)$ times. From this outcome, then, we expect to get about $nf(x_i)P(x_i)$ dollars during the n trials. The total amount we expect to get in the n trials is about

$$\sum_{i=1}^{N} nf(x_i)P(x_i) = n \sum_{i=1}^{N} f(x_i)P(x_i)$$

It follows that we expect our long-run winnings per play of the game to be $\sum_{i=1}^{N} f(x_i)P(x_i)$. This leads us to make the following definition: If f is a function defined on a sample space $S = \{x_1, x_2, \ldots, x_N\}$ which has probability function P, we call

(7-67) $$E(f(X)) = \sum_{i=1}^{N} f(x_i)P(x_i)$$

the *expected value* of $f(X)$ (for the given probability distribution). We read "$E(f(X))$" as "E of f of X" or "the expected value of f of X."

Consider, for example, the space $S = \{1,2,3,4,5,6\}$ with the uniform distribution. If $f(X) = X^2$, we have

$$E(f(X)) = E(X^2) = \sum_{x=1}^{6} x^2 \times \tfrac{1}{6}$$
$$= \tfrac{1}{6}(1 + 4 + 9 + 16 + 25 + 36) = {}^{91}\!/_6 = 15.17$$

Thus if you were to throw a single die and then get paid a number of dollars equal to the square of the number of spots uppermost, you should be willing to pay \$15.17 to play the game because this would be your long-run winnings per throw.

If the random variable X has sample space $\{x_1, x_2, \ldots, x_N\}$ and we consider the function $f(X) = X$, we have

(7-68) $$E(f(X)) = E(X) = \Sigma\, x_iP(x_i) = \mu$$

That is, the expected value of a random variable is its mean.

We can then speak of "the mean of X" or "the expected value of X" and be referring to the same thing in either case. If, for example, a perfect die is tossed and X is the number of spots uppermost when it stops, we can say equivalently that "the mean of X is 3.5" or "the expected value of X is 3.5" or even "the expected number of spots is 3.5." It should be clear that, when we use this last terminology, we do not mean that we expect to get 3.5 spots each time we throw the die. It is, in fact, impossible to get 3.5 spots on one throw. We *do* mean that the long-run average number of spots per throw will be 3.5.

If X is $B(n,p)$, then its mean—and, hence, its expected value—is np. For instance, if a town contains 60 per cent Democrats, the expected number of Democrats in a random sample of 20 residents from the town is 12.   This is so because X, the number of Democrats in the sample, is $B(20,.6)$ and, therefore, its mean is $(.6)(20) = 12$.

In general, when f is any function defined on a sample space, we can speak of the expected value of the function.   Some particular functions are of interest.   If f always has the value c, then its expected value is c. That is,

(7-69) $$E(c) = c$$

This follows immediately from the fact that $\Sigma\, P(x) = 1$, since

$$E(c) = \Sigma\, cP(x) = c \Sigma\, P(x)$$

In the case of a linear function we have

(7-70) $$E(aX + b) = aE(X) + b$$

This is proved as follows:

$$\Sigma\, (ax + b)P(x) = \Sigma\, [axP(x) + bP(x)]$$
$$= a \Sigma\, xP(x) + b \Sigma\, P(x) = aE(X) + b$$

If X and Y are both random variables, we can consider the random variable $X + Y$, which gets a value by performing the experiment for X and that for Y and adding the results.   It can be shown that

(7-71) $$E(X + Y) = E(X) + E(Y)$$

Similarly,

(7-72) $$E(X - Y) = E(X) - E(Y)$$

In words, we can say that the expected value of a sum (difference) is the sum (difference) of the expected values.   When we think of $E(X)$ as the long-run winnings per trial for the "payoff" X and $E(Y)$ as the long-run winnings per trial for the "payoff" Y, these results seem quite reasonable when we think of $E(X + Y)$ [or $E(X - Y)$] as the long-run winnings per trial of the game of playing both the game for X and the game for Y and adding (or subtracting) the pay-offs from these games to get the new pay-off.   Equations (7-71) and (7-72) are true whether or not X and Y are independent.

Is it true, in general, that the expected value of a product is the product of the expected values?   The answer is "no," as the following example shows.   Let X have the uniform distribution on $\{-1,1\}$, and let $Y = X$. Then $E(X) = E(Y) = -\tfrac{1}{2} + \tfrac{1}{2} = 0$, so that $E(X)E(Y) = 0$, while $E(XY) = E(X^2) = \tfrac{1}{2} + \tfrac{1}{2} = 1$.   Hence, $E(XY) \neq E(X)E(Y)$.

It can be shown, however, that

(7-73)   *If X and Y are independent, then $E(XY) = E(X)E(Y)$.*

This is an important result for some of our later discussions but will not come up directly in the next few chapters.

The expected-value notation is a handy one to use in connection with the variance. Definition (7-44) can be written as

(7-74) $$\sigma^2 = E[(X - \mu)^2]$$

Equation (7-45) becomes, in this notation,

(7-75) $$\sigma^2 = E(X^2) - \mu^2$$

or

(7-76) $$\sigma^2 = E(X^2) - [E(X)]^2$$

In words, we may say that the variance σ^2 is the difference between the expected value of the square and the square of the expected value.

PROBLEMS

7-77. If X has the uniform distribution on $\{0,1,2,3,4,5,6,7,8,9\}$ find
(a) $E(X)$ (b) $E(X - 4.5)$ (c) $E(X^2)$
(d) $E[(X - \mu)^2]$ (e) $E(X^3)$ (f) $E(X^2 + X)$

7-78. Thirteen draws with replacement are made from a standard deck of cards. What is the expected number of aces?

7-79. Fifty coins are tossed. What is the expected number of heads? Does this mean that you expect to get this number of heads in one toss of the 50 coins?

7-80. Six coins and a die are thrown together. Let Z be the sum of the number of heads and the number of spots uppermost on the die. What is the expected value of Z?

*7-81. Show that, for any random variable X, $E(X^2) \geqq [E(X)]^2$.

7-82. If X has a binomial distribution with $p = .4$ and $n = 10$, find
(a) $E(X)$ (b) $E(X - 4)$ (c) $E[(X - 4)^2]$
(d) $E\left(\dfrac{X}{10}\right)$ (e) $E\left(\dfrac{X - 4}{10}\right)$ (f) $E(X^2)$

7-83. A perfect coin is tossed until the first head is obtained. If X is the number of tosses required to obtain the first head, you are then paid 2^X dollars. What is the expected value of this game? How much would *you* be willing to pay to play it?

7-84. Let X have the uniform distribution on $\{1,2,3\}$ and Y have the uniform distribution on $\{-1,01\}$. Find the sample space and the distribution for $Z = X + Y$. Verify that $E(Z) = E(X) + E(Y)$.

7-85. Do Prob. 7-84 for $Z = X - Y$. Verify that $E(Z) = E(X) - E(Y)$.

7-86. With X and Y as in Prob. 7-84, let $Z = XY$. Find the sample space and distribution for Z. Verify that $E(Z) = E(X)E(Y)$.

*7-87. Let $A = (a_{ij})$ be a matrix of n rows and m columns with a_{ij} the number in the ith row and the jth column (see Prob. 3-68). Suppose that two players called I and II play the following game. I chooses a row of the matrix by selecting one of the numbers $1, 2, \ldots, n$. Then II, in ignorance of I's choice, chooses a column by selecting one of the numbers $1, 2, \ldots, m$. If i is the choice of player I and j is the choice of player II, then II pays I the amount a_{ij}. For instance, suppose that

$$A = \begin{pmatrix} 3 & 2 & -1 \\ 4 & 3 & 4 \end{pmatrix}$$

and I chooses 2 while II chooses 3, then II pays I 4. If I chooses 1 while II chooses 3, then II pays I the amount -1, which we interpret to mean that I pays II the amount $+1$. Such a game is called a *matrix game*. One reasonable way for I to play a matrix game is (1) to look in each row and find the worst that can happen to him if he chooses that row and then (2) choose that row which makes this worst as good as possible. (By such a rule I would choose 2 for the matrix above.) By this procedure I is certain to get at least max min a_{ij} (see Prob. 3-68), and he assures himself of this
$\quad\quad\quad\quad\quad\quad\quad\quad\quad\quad\quad\quad\quad\quad\quad\quad\quad\;\; i\;\;\; j$
amount by choosing a row whose smallest element is equal to max min a_{ij}. Similarly,
$\quad\quad\quad\quad\quad\quad\quad\quad\quad\quad\quad\quad\quad\quad\quad\quad\quad\quad\quad\quad\quad\quad\quad\quad\quad\; i\;\;\; j$
II can be certain that he will lose no more than min max a_{ij} by choosing the column
$\quad\quad\quad\quad\quad\quad\quad\quad\quad\quad\quad\quad\quad\quad\quad\quad\quad\quad\quad\quad\quad\quad\quad\; j\;\;\; i$
whose largest element is equal to min max a_{ij}. For each of the following matrices
$\quad\quad\quad\quad\quad\quad\quad\quad\quad\quad\quad\quad\quad\quad\quad\quad\quad\quad\quad\;\; j\;\;\; i$
find the possible choices for the players if they use these rules to make a choice. Also find the amount that each player assures himself.

$(a)\;\begin{pmatrix} -4 & -2 \\ -1 & 5 \end{pmatrix}$ $\quad\quad\quad\quad\quad\quad\quad\quad (b)\;\begin{pmatrix} 4 & -2 \\ -1 & 2 \end{pmatrix}$

$(c)\;\begin{pmatrix} 3 & 2 & 0 \\ 0 & 1 & -2 \\ -5 & 7 & -1 \end{pmatrix}$ $\quad\quad\quad\quad (d)\;\begin{pmatrix} 0 & 1 & -1 \\ -1 & 0 & 1 \end{pmatrix}$

*7-88 (Continuation of Prob. 7-87). Show that if the matrix for a game has a saddle point (see Prob. 3-69), then I can always choose the row i_0 and be certain of winning at least $a_{i_0 j_0}$ while II by choosing j_0 can be certain of losing no more than $a_{i_0 j_0}$. A matrix game whose matrix has a saddle point is said to be a *strictly determined game*. If $a_{i_0 j_0}$ is a saddle point in a game matrix, then i_0 and j_0 are said to be (pure) *optimal strategies* for the players, the pair (i_0,j_0) is said to be a *solution* of the game, and $a_{i_0 j_0}$ is called the *value* of the game (to player I). Argue that for a strictly determined game there is a certain stability in the sense that, if a player is going to use an optimal strategy, it does the other player no good to find it out ahead of time. (Contrast the games with matrices a and b above.)

*7-89. In the game of part a of Prob. 7-87 player I flips a coin and chooses 1 if he gets a head and otherwise chooses 2. Meanwhile, player II rolls a die and chooses 1 if he gets a 1 or a 6 and chooses 2 otherwise. Find the expected value of the game for player I.

*7-90. In the game with matrix

$$\begin{pmatrix} 1 & -1 \\ -1 & 1 \end{pmatrix}$$

let I choose 1 with probability x and II choose 1 with probability y. Find the expected value of the game for player I.

*7-91 (Continuation of Prob. 7-87). In a matrix game we may allow the players to make their choices using some chance device. If I chooses i with probability p_i and II independently chooses j with probability q_j, show that the expected value of the game for player I is

$$\sum_{i=1}^{n} \sum_{j=1}^{m} a_{ij} p_i q_j$$

An assignment of probabilities to the possible choices for a player is called a *mixed strategy* for the player.

*7-92. Show that in the game of Prob. 7-90 player I can guarantee an expected value to himself of at least zero by choosing $x = \frac{1}{2}$ and that II can guarantee that his expected loss will be no more than zero by choosing $y = \frac{1}{2}$. Show that this situation is the game of matching pennies as it is usually played. Argue further that if I chooses $x \neq \frac{1}{2}$, then there is a possible choice of y for II which makes the expected value for I negative. Similarly, show that if II chooses $y \neq \frac{1}{2}$, then there is a possible choice for I which makes the expected value for I positive. (*Hint:* Factor the expression giving the expected value of the game to I.)

7-6. Further properties of discrete distributions

If X is a random variable and f is a function defined on the sample space for X, we can consider $Y = f(X)$ to define a new random variable which gets its value by performing the experiment for X and then finding the value of f at the result obtained. Y will have a certain probability distribution which will depend on that for X.

If, as an example, we let X have the uniform distribution on $\{-2, -1, 0, 1, 2\}$ and let $Y = X^2$, we see that Y has the sample space $\{0, 1, 4\}$ and the distribution given by the following calculations:

$$P(Y = 0) = P(X = 0) = \frac{1}{5}$$
$$P(Y = 1) = P(X = 1 \text{ or } X = -1) = \frac{1}{5} + \frac{1}{5} = \frac{2}{5}$$
$$P(Y = 4) = P(X = 2 \text{ or } X = -2) = \frac{1}{5} + \frac{1}{5} = \frac{2}{5}$$

Then the mean of Y is $\mu_Y = 0 \times \frac{1}{5} + 1 \times \frac{2}{5} + 4 \times \frac{2}{5} = 2$. If, on the other hand, we simply ask for the expected value of Y thought of as a function of X, we have

$$E(Y) = E(X^2) = 4 \times \frac{1}{5} + 1 \times \frac{1}{5} + 0 \times \frac{1}{5} + 1 \times \frac{1}{5} + 4 \times \frac{1}{5} = 2$$

We note that $E(Y) = \mu_Y$.

This result is true in the general case where Y is any function of any random variable X. That is, when $Y = f(X)$,

(7-93) $$\mu_Y = E(Y) = E(f(X))$$

A proof of this will not be given here. One can be constructed fairly easily by following the above example. Having defined $E(f(X))$ as our long-run winnings per trial when we are paid $f(X)$ for the outcome X, we now see that $E(f(X))$ can also be thought of as the mean of the distribution for the random variable $Y = f(X)$. We shall often use (7-93) to compute μ_Y without going to the trouble of finding the distribution for Y.

Some of the results for expected values can now be restated in terms of mean values for random variables.   In case $Y = aX + b$, we get, from (7-70),

$$(7\text{-}94) \qquad\qquad \mu_{aX+b} = a\mu_X + b$$

[See Eq. (4-32) for the analogue of this for sample means.]   If X and Y are random variables, we have, from (7-71) and (7-72),

$$(7\text{-}95) \qquad\qquad \mu_{X+Y} = \mu_X + \mu_Y$$

and

$$(7\text{-}96) \qquad\qquad \mu_{X-Y} = \mu_X - \mu_Y$$

These results can be thought of as the analogues of (4-28) and (4-29) for samples.   From (7-95) it follows more generally that for the k random variables X_i

$$(7\text{-}97) \quad \text{If } Y = \sum_{i=1}^{k} X_i, \text{ then } \mu_Y = \sum_{i=1}^{k} \mu_{X_i}.$$

Equation (7-94) enables us to express the mean of $aX + b$ in terms of the mean for X.   If we attempt to express the standard deviation for the former in terms of that for the latter, we find that for a positive

$$(7\text{-}98) \qquad\qquad \sigma_{aX+b} = a\sigma_X$$

a result analogous to Eq. (5-23) for sample standard deviations.   The proof of (7-98) will be left as an excercise, but the result should seem reasonable when we think of Y as arising from X by a linear change of scale (see Sec. 5-3) and σ_X as a measure of dispersion for the probability distribution of X.

If X and Y are independent random variables, it can be shown that the variance of their sum is the sum of their variances.   That is,

$$(7\text{-}99) \quad \textit{If } X \textit{ and } Y \textit{ are independent, } \sigma^2_{X+Y} = \sigma_X^2 + \sigma_Y^2.$$

Similarly,

$$(7\text{-}100) \quad \textit{If } X \textit{ and } Y \textit{ are independent, } \sigma^2_{X-Y} = \sigma_X^2 + \sigma_Y^2.$$

[Compare (7-99) with (5-35) for sample variances.]   The proofs for these two results will not be given here.   Equation (7-99) is a very important result.   It is largely because of the fact that the variances for independent variables are "additive" that the variance is a "natural" measure of dispersion.   In the general case of k *independent* variables $X_1, X_2, \ldots,$ X_k, we have from (7-99)[1]

(7-101)   *If X_i and X_j are independent $(i \neq j)$ and $Y = \sum\limits_{i=1}^{k} X_i$, then*

$$\sigma_Y{}^2 = \sum_{i=1}^{k} \sigma_{X_i}{}^2.$$

From the above theorems about means and variances, it is now easy to give a derivation of the mean and standard deviation for the binomial distribution as given in (7-46).   Suppose that Y is $B(n,p)$.   Then we can think of Y as the sum of n values $X_1, X_2, \ldots, X_n$, where X_i is either 0 (failure) or 1 (success) and $P(X_i = 1) = p$.   That is, $(X_1, X_2, \ldots, X_n)$ is a random sample of n values for a random variable X with sample space $\{0,1\}$ and $Y = \sum\limits_{i=1}^{n} X_i$ [see (7-5)].

From Table 7-1, $\mu_{X_i} = p$ and $\sigma_{X_i}{}^2 = pq$.   Then, by (7-97)

$$\mu_Y = \Sigma \mu_{X_i} = np$$

By (7-101), since $(X_1, X_2, \ldots, X_n)$ is a random sample, so that X_i and X_j are independent $(i \neq j)$,

$$\sigma_Y{}^2 = \Sigma \sigma_{X_i}{}^2 = npq$$

This completes the proof of (7-46).

More generally, suppose that X is any random variable and that $(X_1, X_2, \ldots, X_n)$ is a random sample of size n for X. $\bar{X} = (1/n) \Sigma X_i$ is a random variable, and we can ask for $\mu_{\bar{X}}$ and $\sigma_{\bar{X}}$ in terms of μ_X and σ_X. We find that

(7-102) $$\mu_{\bar{X}} = \mu_X$$

and

(7-103) $$\sigma_{\bar{X}} = \frac{\sigma_X}{\sqrt{n}}$$

[1] See also Prob. 7-126.

The proofs of these results follow.

$$\mu_{\bar{X}} = \mu_{(1/n)\Sigma X_i}$$

$$= \frac{1}{n}\mu_{\Sigma X_i} \qquad \text{by (7-94)}$$

$$= \frac{1}{n}\sum \mu_{X_i} \qquad \text{by (7-97)}$$

$$= \frac{1}{n}(n\mu_X)$$

$$= \mu_X$$

$$\sigma_{\bar{X}}^2 = \sigma_{(1/n)\Sigma X_i}^2$$

$$= \frac{1}{n^2}\sigma_{\Sigma X_i}^2 \qquad \text{by (7-98)}$$

$$= \frac{1}{n^2}\sum \sigma_{X_i}^2 \qquad \text{by (7-101)}$$

$$= \frac{1}{n^2}(n\sigma_X^2)$$

$$= \frac{\sigma_X^2}{n}$$

The randomness of the sample is crucial in the derivation for $\sigma_{\bar{X}}^2$. Without it we would not have the independence of the trials which gave us the additivity of the variances.

The above results enable us to find the mean and variance for $\bar{X}$ from the values of those parameters for X without actually finding the distribution for $\bar{X}$.

We asserted earlier that we can think of μ_X as being the "long-run mean value" of a sample of values of X. We now make this notion more precise. We first state the probability analogue of Chebyshev's theorem for samples. See (5-33).

(7-104) *The probability that X will fall within K standard deviations of its mean is at least as large as $1 - 1/K^2$.*

The proof of this can be carried through by following the pattern of the proof of Chebyshev's theorem (Prob. 5-36). More formally, (7-104) asserts that

(7-105) $$P(|X - \mu_X| \leqq K\sigma_X) \geqq 1 - \frac{1}{K^2}$$

Now let us apply this result to $\bar{X}$, the mean of a random sample of size n for X. We have from (7-102) and (7-103),

(7-106) $$P\left(|\bar{X} - \mu_X| \leqq \frac{K\sigma_X}{\sqrt{n}}\right) \geqq 1 - \frac{1}{K^2}$$

As n gets large, we expect $\bar{X}$ to approach μ_X and (7-106) tells us that $\bar{X}$ *does approach* μ_X in a probability sense. That is, by taking n large enough we can make the probability as close to 1 as we please, so that $\bar{X}$ will be within any preassigned distance of μ_X; for suppose that we wish $\bar{X}$ to be within d of μ_X with a probability of at least .99. Then we can choose $K = 10$ (so that $1 - 1/K^2 = .99$) and then choose n so large that $10\sigma_X/\sqrt{n} \leq d$. As a consequence, we would have

$$P(|\bar{X} - \mu_X| \leq d) \geq P\left(|\bar{X} - \mu_X| \leq \frac{10\sigma_X}{\sqrt{n}}\right) \geq .99$$

Thus, while we cannot be certain that $\bar{X}$ will be close to μ_X for large n, we can be certain that the probability that it will be close to μ_X is very high.

Equation (7-106) can also be interpreted as saying that a large random sample is representative of the population in the sense that its mean will be close (in a probability sense) to the population mean (see Sec. 7-1).

If in (7-106) we let $K\sigma_X/\sqrt{n} = e$, then we have

(7-107) $$P(|\bar{X} - \mu_X| \leq e) \geq 1 - \frac{\sigma_X^2}{e^2 n}$$

and in this form the above argument is perhaps clearer. Let e be any positive number (no matter how small). By choosing n large enough we can make the probability that $\bar{X}$ will be within e of μ_X as close as we please to 1. This result is called the *law of large numbers*.

If, for example, $\mu_X = 5$, $\sigma_X = 1$, and $e = .001$, we have

$$P(|\bar{X} - 5| \leq .001) \geq 1 - \frac{1}{(.001)^2 n} = 1 - \frac{10^6}{n}$$

Hence, if we take a sample of size 10^8, we can be sure that the probability that $\bar{X}$ will differ from 5 by no more than .001 is at least .99.

PROBLEMS

7-108. Let X have the uniform distribution on $\{-1,0,1\}$, and find $E(X^2)$. Let $Y = X^2$, find the distribution for Y, and from this distribution find μ_Y to verify that $E(X^2) = \mu_Y$.

7-109. Let X have the uniform distribution on $\{0,1,2\}$ and Y have the uniform distribution on $\{1,2,3\}$. Find the distribution for $Z = X + Y$. Compute σ_X^2, σ_Y^2, and σ_Z^2 and verify that $\sigma_X^2 + \sigma_Y^2 = \sigma_Z^2$.

7-110. Let X be $B(3,\frac{1}{3})$ and Y be uniform on $\{0,1,2,3\}$. Find the distribution for $Z = X + Y$. Verify that $\mu_Z = \mu_X + \mu_Y$ and $\sigma_Z^2 = \sigma_X^2 + \sigma_Y^2$.

7-111. Let X and Y both have a uniform distribution on $\{1,2,3,4\}$. Find the distribution for $Z_1 = X + Y$ and that for $Z_2 = 2X$. Explain why Z_1 and Z_2 are not the same random variables even though $Z_2 = 2X$ and $Z_1 = X + Y$, where Y has the same distribution as X.

7-112. If X is $B(k,p)$ and $(X_1, X_2, \ldots, X_n)$ is a random sample of n values of X, let $Y = \sum_{i=1}^{n} X_i$. Find the mean and variance for Y. What distribution does Y have?

7-113. If X is $B(n_1, p)$ and Y is $B(n_2, p)$, what is the distribution for $Z = X + Y$? Find the mean and variance for Z.

7-114. If X and Y both have the uniform distribution on a set S, does it follow that $Z = X + Y$ has a uniform distribution? Explain.

7-115. Let X be uniform on $\{-1, 0, 1\}$, and let $\bar{X}$ be the mean for a random sample of three values of X. Find the distribution for $\bar{X}$. Verify by computations from the distributions that $\mu_{\bar{X}} = \mu_X$ and $\sigma_{\bar{X}} = \sigma_X/\sqrt{3}$.

7-116. If $\mu_X = 100$ and $\sigma_X = 10$, how large a sample must one take to have $P(|\bar{X} - 100| \leq .1) \geq .99$?

7-117. If $\mu_X = 1$ and $\sigma_X = .01$, how large a sample must one take to have $P(|\bar{X} - 1| \leq .01) \geq .9$?

7-118. If X is $B(100, .5)$, how many trials for X must be made if we wish their mean to be within .1 of 50 with a probability of at least .95?

7-119. If X has the indicated distribution, find $\mu_{\bar{X}}$ and $\sigma_{\bar{X}}$ when $\bar{X}$ is the mean of a random sample of size n.

(a) $B(20, .1)$, $n = 10$
(b) Uniform on $\{0,1,2,3,4,5,6,7,8,9\}$, $n = 25$
(c) $B(30, .3)$, $n = 100$
(d) $B(30, .3)$, $n = 10,000$
(e) $B(100, .5)$, $n = 100$

7-120. If X has the sample space $\{0,1\}$ and $P(X = 1) = p$, how large a sample of values of X must be taken in order that

$$P(|\bar{X} - p| < .01) \geq .99$$

Interpret this result in terms of binomial variables. *Hint:* For all possible values of p, $pq \leq \frac{1}{4}$.

7-121. Prove (7-98). [*Hint:* Start from (7-74).]

*7-122. Prove (7-93).

7-123. Prove (7-104).

*7-124. Show that if X and Y are independent random variables and c and d are any constants, then $X + c$ and $Y + d$ are independent.

*7-125. Assuming that it has been proved that, if X and Y are independent, then $E(XY) = E(X)E(Y)$, prove (7-99). *Hint:* Start by expressing σ^2_{X+Y} as an expected value, and after simplifying, use the result in Prob. 7-124.

7-126. To derive (7-101) from (7-99) we need the fact that, if X, Y, and Z are independent, then $X + Y$ and Z are independent.

(a) Verify that this is so for the special case where X, Y, and Z all have the sample space $\{0,1\}$ and $P(X = 1) = P(Y = 1) = P(Z = 1) = p$.

*(b) Prove that this is so when X, Y, and Z have any finite sample spaces.

***7-7. The nature of probability**

The notion of probability seems to be a basic one in most of the sciences. A theory or model that a science develops to explain certain phenomena is *deterministic* to the extent that the model enables the scientist to say that, given certain conditions of a system, certain states are *bound* to follow. The scientist in such a situation may then say that the conditions *cause* the subsequent states. But it seems that more and more often in the various sciences the investigator must be satisfied with a model that enables him to say only that, given such and such conditions, certain states will *probably* follow. Or, more precisely, in view of certain given conditions, the model enables one to deduce a probability distribution for the possible subsequent states.

A classic example of this situation is the case of radioactivity in physics. To date, it seems that the physicist must be content with stating the probability that a given radioactive atom will decay in the next minute. The attempt to find a model that will predict exactly which of a given group of atoms will decay in the next minute has failed.

As in this example from physics, many of the basic questions in the physical sciences, as well as in the social sciences, seem to require an answer given in probabilistic terms. It is not surprising, then, to discover that the nature of probability is a major problem in the philosophy of science and that there have been several different answers proposed to the problem.

The so-called classical approach to probability usually connected with Laplace and Jacob Bernoulli was to define probability as a ratio of the number of favorable cases to the total number of equally likely cases [see (6-16)]. But this interpretation seems to have the weakness that we cannot discover the probability of an event until we are certain that the underlying cases are equally likely, and what do we mean by "equally likely" if not simply "equally probable"? Thus, the proposed definition appears to be caught in a vicious circle.

The approach that we have taken in this book is that probability is to be thought of as a long-run relative frequency. Some philosophers such as von Mises and Reichenbach have contended that this interpretation of probability is sufficient unto the needs of those who use the term "probability."

On the other hand, some philosophers of science, such as Rudolph Carnap, contend that, in the light of the way that the term "probability" is used, there must be two different interpretations of the notion. One of these interpretations is as a relative frequency, but the other is as a degree of confirmation. That is, in this second case, probability is to be thought of as the degree to which a certain hypothesis is confirmed by the evidence. In this sense, probability is to be taken as a property of two statements (or propositions). A great deal has been written on probability as a degree of confirmation.

To illustrate the type of example that has been given to point up the need for some alternative to the relative-frequency interpretation, suppose that an expert on foreign affairs says "There will probably not be a war between the major powers next year." It is difficult to see how we could interpret the term "probably" here in any relative-frequency sense. Yet somehow the statement has meaning for us, and thus we may well wish to consider certain probability statements as assertions about the degree of confirmation of a certain hypothesis (there will not be a war next year between the big powers) in view of certain evidence (current world conditions).

In *Readings in the Philosophy of Sciences*, edited by Herbert Feigl and May Brodbeck (Appleton-Century-Crofts, Inc., New York, 1953), the interested reader will find quite readable discussions of the problem of the nature of probability along with a bibliography on the subject. Other articles (such as C. G. Hempel's On the Nature of Mathematical Truth) in this same book may assist the reader in achieving a deeper understanding of the nature of mathematical models which we have discussed (rather superficially) in connection with probability.

7-8. Review

Having now discussed the most important topics connected with discrete distributions, we pull the main results together in an outline. The reader will find it helpful to compare this outline with that given in Sec. 5-6. We let X be a random variable with sample space

$$S = \{x_1, x_2, \ldots, x_N\}$$

DEFINITION 1

If P is a real function defined on S with the properties that $P(x_i) \geq 0$ for all $x_i \in S$ and $\sum_{i=1}^{N} P(x_i) = 1$, then P is called a *probability function* on S. [(6-1) and (6-2)] To give a *probability distribution* for X is to give a probability function on S. Intuitively, $P(x_i)$ is the long-run relative frequency with which X takes on the value x_i.

DEFINITION 2

An *event* is a subset of S.

DEFINITION 3

The *probability of an event* A is given by

$$P(A) = \sum_{x_i \in A} P(x_i) \qquad P(\phi) = 0 \qquad (6\text{-}6)$$

THEOREM 1
$$P(S) = 1 \qquad (6\text{-}7)$$

THEOREM 2
$$\text{If } A \subseteq B, \text{ then } P(A) \leqq P(B) \qquad (6\text{-}8)$$

THEOREM 3
$$0 \leqq P(A) \leqq 1 \qquad (6\text{-}9)$$

THEOREM 4
$$\text{If } A \cap B = \phi, \text{ then } \quad P(A \cup B) = P(A) + P(B) \qquad (6\text{-}10)$$

THEOREM 5
$$P(A) = 1 - P(A') \qquad (6\text{-}11)$$

THEOREM 6
$$P(A \cup B) = P(A) + P(B) - P(A \cap B) \qquad (6\text{-}12)$$

DEFINITION 4

If P assigns the same probability to each point in S, then X is said to have a *uniform distribution*.

THEOREM 7

If X has a uniform distribution, then $P(x_i) = 1/N$ for all $x_i \in S$ and

$$P(A) = \frac{No\ (A)}{N}$$

DEFINITION 5

X and Y are said to be *independent* random variables if

$$P(X = a \text{ and } Y = b) = P(X = a)P(Y = b)$$

for all values of a and b (6-17).   Events A and B are said to be *independent* if $P(A \cap B) = P(A)P(B)$.   (6-18)

DEFINITION 6

The *conditional probability for B, given A*, is given by

$$P(B|A) = \frac{P(A \cap B)}{P(A)} \qquad (6\text{-}30)$$

THEOREM 8

If an act A_1 can be performed in n_1 ways, and if, after A_1 has been performed, another act A_2 can be performed in n_2 ways, then the act A_1 followed by A_2 can be performed in $n_1 n_2$ ways.   (6-44)

DEFINITION 7

A *permutation* of objects is an ordered arrangement of those objects.

THEOREM 9

If $No\ (A) = n$, there are

$$\frac{n!}{(n-k)!} = n(n-1)\ \cdots\ (n-k+1)$$

permutations of the elements of A taken k at a time.   [(6-47) and (6-49)]

THEOREM 10

If $No\ (A) = n$, there are

$$\binom{n}{k} = \frac{n!}{k!(n-k)!}$$

different subsets of A that contain k elements.   [(6-67), (6-68), and (6-69)]

DEFINITION 8

The results $X_1,\ X_2,\ \ldots\ ,\ X_n$ of n trials for X constitute a *random sample of size n for X* if

$$P(X_1 = a_1 \text{ and } X_2 = a_2 \text{ and } \cdots \text{ and } X_n = a_n)$$
$$= P(X_1 = a_1) \cdot P(X_2 = a_2)\ \cdots\ P(X_n = a_n)$$

for all values of the a's.

THEOREM 11

If $S = \{0,1\}$, $P(X = 1) = p$, and $Y = \displaystyle\sum_{i=1}^{n} X_i$, where $X_1,\ X_2,\ \ldots\ ,$ X_n is a random sample for X, then $P(Y = y) = \binom{n}{y} p^y q^{n-y}$ for $y = 0, 1,$ $2,\ \ldots\ ,\ n$ and $q = 1 - p$.   (7-5)

DEFINITION 9

If Y has the probability function $P(y) = \binom{n}{y} p^y q^{n-y}$, then Y is said to have the *binomial distribution* with parameters n and p.   This distribution is denoted by $B(n,p)$.

DEFINITION 10

A table of random digits is intended to be a random sample for a variable having the uniform distribution on the decimal digits.

DEFINITION 11

The *mean* of $X = \mu = \displaystyle\sum_{i=1}^{N} x_i P(x_i)$.   (7-43)

DEFINITION 12

The *standard deviation* of X is

$$\sigma = \left[\sum_{i=1}^{N} (x_i - \mu)^2 P(x_i) \right]^{1/2} \qquad (7\text{-}44)$$

The *variance* of X is σ^2.

DEFINITION 13

A *parameter* is a numerical property of a distribution. A *statistic* is a numerical property of a sample.

THEOREM 12

$$\sigma^2 = \sum_{i=1}^{N} x_i^2 P(x_i) - \mu^2 \qquad (7\text{-}45)$$

THEOREM 13

If $S = \{0,1\}$ and $P(X = 1) = p$, then $\mu = p$ and $\sigma = \sqrt{pq}$. (Table 7-1)

THEOREM 14

If X is $B(n,p)$, then $\mu = np$ and $\sigma = \sqrt{npq}$.

DEFINITION 14

The *cumulative probability function* for X is $CP(x) = P(X \leq x)$. x_0 is a *median* for X if x_0 is the smallest value for which $CP(x_0) \geq .5$. x_k is the *mode* for X if

$$P(x_k) = \max \{P(x_1), P(x_2), \ldots, P(x_N)\}$$

and only one such x_k exists. The *range* of X is $\max (S) - \min (S)$.

DEFINITION 15

If f is defined on S, the *expected value* of $f(x)$ is given by

$$E(f(X)) = \sum_{i=1}^{N} f(x_i) P(x_i) \qquad (7\text{-}67)$$

THEOREM 15

If $Y = f(X)$, then

$$\mu_Y = E(Y) = E(f(X)) \qquad (7\text{-}93)$$

THEOREM 16

(a) $\qquad\qquad E(aX + b) = aE(X) + b \qquad (7\text{-}70)$

(b) $\qquad\qquad \mu_{aX+b} = a\mu_X + b \qquad (7\text{-}94)$

THEOREM 17

(a)
$$E(X + Y) = E(X + Y) \qquad \text{(7-71)}$$
(b)
$$\mu_{X+Y} = \mu_X + \mu_Y \qquad \text{(7-95)}$$

THEOREM 18

(a)
$$E(X - Y) = E(X) - E(Y) \qquad \text{(7-72)}$$
(b)
$$\mu_{X-Y} = \mu_X - \mu_Y \qquad \text{(7-96)}$$

THEOREM 19

$$\sigma^2 = E(X^2) - \mu^2 \qquad \text{(7-75)}$$

THEOREM 20

$$\sigma_{aX+b} = a\sigma_X \qquad \text{(7-98)}$$

THEOREM 21

If X and Y are independent, then

$$\sigma^2_{X+Y} = \sigma_X{}^2 + \sigma_Y{}^2 \text{ and } \sigma^2_{X-Y} = \sigma_X{}^2 + \sigma_Y{}^2 \qquad \text{(7-99) and (7-100)}$$

THEOREM 22

If $\bar{X}$ is the mean of a random sample of size n for X, then $\mu_{\bar{X}} = \mu_X$ and $\sigma_{\bar{X}} = \sigma_X/\sqrt{n}$.

THEOREM 23

The probability that X will fall within K standard deviations of its mean is at least as great as $1 - 1/K^2$.

THEOREM 24   (Law of large numbers)

If $\bar{X}$ is the mean of a random sample of size n, then for any positive number e, no matter how small,

$$P(|\bar{X} - \mu_X| \leqq e) \geqq 1 - \frac{\sigma_X{}^2}{e^2 n}$$

Hence, by taking n sufficiently large we can make the probability that $\bar{X}$ will be within e of μ_X as close to 1 as we please.   (7-107)

CHAPTER 8

Applications of Discrete Distributions

8-1. Estimation and likelihood functions

Do you approve of capital punishment? Suppose that we were to ask this question of each student in your school. A certain proportion p of them would answer "yes." Suppose that we should like to know the value of p but we do not have the time to survey the whole school and do not have the money to pay people to do it. We still might be able to estimate p by taking a random sample of, say, n students in the school and asking the question of each student in the sample. If X represents the number of "yes" answers in the sample, then X will have a binomial distribution with the parameters n and p. We know n, the number of people in the sample, and we wish to estimate the unknown parameter p.

This problem is typical of a large class of problems in statistics where we wish to make an estimate of a parameter on the basis of information about a sample. In other words, we wish to estimate a characteristic of the population in view of certain characteristics of the sample.

Let us suppose that in the above example we take a random sample of size 10 and 6 people answer "yes." That is, suppose that in one trial, with $n = 10$, we find $X = 6$. We could now ask the following question: If the true proportion of people in the population who would answer "yes" is .10 (i.e., if $p = .10$), what is the probability of getting the result we observed (i.e., $X = 6$)? Since X has a binomial distribution, we can answer this. If $p = .10$ then $P(X = 6) = \binom{10}{6} (.1)^6 (.9)^4 = .0001$.

Similarly, we can answer the questions: If $p = .2$ what is $P(X = 6)$? If $p = .3$, what is $P(X = 6)$? etc. We collect the results in a table:

(8-1)

p	0	.1	.2	.3	.4	.5	.6	.7	.8	.9	1.0
$P(X = 6)$	0	.0001	.0055	.0368	.1115	.2051	.2508	.2001	.0881	.0112	0

The lower row gives in each case the probability of getting the result that was actually observed. It is also the case that, given any other value of p (such as $p = .4712$), we could find $P(X = 6)$. Then we can think of the function $L(y) = P(X = 6|p = y)$ which is defined for all y's satisfying the inequality $0 \leqq y \leqq 1$. $[P(X = 6|p = y)$ is the conditional probability that $X = 6$, given that $p = y$.]   This function is called the *likelihood function* for p and the observed result $X = 6$.   We can graph the likelihood function by plotting the values given in (8-1) and connecting them with a smooth curve.   Doing this, we obtain Fig. 8-1 for the *likelihood curve* for p, given $n = 10$ and $X = 6$.

What value of p seems to make the observed outcome most likely?   In other words, what value of p makes the probability $P(X = 6)$ as large as possible?   Inspection of the curve in Fig. 8-1 indicates that this value is

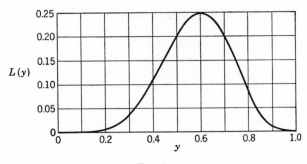

FIG. 8-1

$p = .6$.   We might then reason as follows: In our sample of 10 we found 6 people who answered "yes."   Among all the possible values of p the value $p = .6$ seems to make this observed outcome most likely.   Therefore, we shall estimate p to be .6.

When we have done this, we have made a *maximum likelihood estimate* for p.   In general, a value of a parameter which makes the probability of obtaining the observed outcome as high as possible is called a *maximum likelihood estimate* for that parameter.

To formalize the above discussion, suppose that X is a random variable with probability function $P(x;\theta)$ which depends on an unknown parameter θ (pronounced "theta").   Even though θ is unknown, we may well know a set A of numbers to which θ must belong. A, then, is the collection of possible values of the parameter θ.   In the above case of the survey, the unknown parameter was p and the set of possible values of p was $A = \{x : 0 \leqq x \leqq 1\}$.   Also the probability function in the above case was $P(x;p) = \binom{10}{x} p^x (1 - p)^{10-x}$.   In the general case, if x_0 is an observed value of the variable, we can consider the function

$$L(y) = P(X = x_0|\theta = y)$$

This function is called the *likelihood function for* θ, *given* $X = x_0$. If $\hat{\theta} \in A$ is a number with the property that

(8-2) $$L(\hat{\theta}) = \max \{L(y) : y \in A\}$$

then we say that $\hat{\theta}$ is a *maximum likelihood estimate* of (or for) θ. We read "$\hat{\theta}$" as "theta hat."

A more general kind of likelihood function is often useful. If E is any fixed event, we can consider the function defined by

$$L(y) = P(X \in E | \theta = y)$$

This function is called the *likelihood function for* θ, *given the event* E. $L(y)$ is the probability that the event E happens when y is the true value of the parameter. When $P(x;\theta)$ is the probability function for X, then

$$L(y) = \sum_{x \in E} P(x;y)$$

The likelihood function involved in (8-2) is the case where $E = \{x_0\}$.

For the example where we found six "yes" answers in a sample of 10, we discovered that the maximum likelihood estimate for p was .6, which is the same as the proportion of "yes" answers in the sample. Even without all the discussion about likelihood functions, it would have seemed reasonable to estimate the population proportion by means of the sample proportion, perhaps. We now see that, apart from our "common sense" suggesting the sample proportion as the estimate for the population proportion, the sample proportion is the maximum likelihood estimate. This is true in general for the binomial distribution.

(8-3) *If X is a binomial variable with parameters n and p, where p is unknown and a single value x_0 of X is observed, then the maximum likelihood estimate for p is given by x_0/n.*

The graph of a likelihood function can be very helpful in deciding if a given value of p is "reasonable" in the light of the observed data. If we look at Fig. 8-1, for instance, the graph suggests that we should doubt that our population contains 10 per cent who would answer "yes" to our question about capital punishment. This is so because if only 10 per cent of the population answered "yes," then the probability of getting six "yes" answers in a random sample of 10 is .0001. That is, we should expect to get $X = 6$ only about one time in 10,000 trials if the true value of p is .1. If, however, the true value of p is .6, the graph tells us that we should expect to get $X = 6$ about once in every four trials on the average. Since we actually observed $X = 6$, the estimate of .6 for p seems much more reasonable than the estimate $p = .1$. It is, of course, *possible* to get $X = 6$ when the true value of p is .1, but the outcome $X = 6$ is a rare one when .1 is the true value of the parameter.

PROBLEMS

8-4. A bin contains a very large number of bolts of which a proportion p is defective. A random sample of 20 bolts contains two defectives. Plot the likelihood function for p, and give the maximum likelihood estimate for p.

8-5. Let p be the proportion of people in a certain town who hold driver's licenses. In a random sample of 10 people from this town, five hold driver's licenses. Graph the likelihood function for p and find a maximum likelihood estimate for p.

8-6. A box contains n balls numbered 1, 2, 3, . . . , n, where n is unknown. A single ball is drawn at random. The number on it is 3. Graph the likelihood function for n, and find the maximum likelihood estimate for n. Is this a "reasonable" estimate, or would you suggest a different one?

8-7. On the same set of axes graph the likelihood functions for p when $n = 5$ and the observed values of X are 0, 1, 2, 3, 4, and 5 (a curve for each value of X).

8-8. If X has the two-point probability model, plot the likelihood functions for p when (a) $X = 0$ and (b) $X = 1$.

8-9. A town contains a proportion p of Democrats. A random sample of 30 contains 15 Democrats. Plot the likelihood function for p.

8-10. In order to prove (8-3) we must show that, if $\hat{p} = x_0/n$, then

$$\binom{n}{x_0} \hat{p}^{x_0}\hat{q}^{n-x_0} \geqq \binom{n}{x_0} p^{x_0}q^{n-x_0}$$

for all values of p (here $q = 1 - p$). Certain techniques of the calculus make this easy to show in the general case. However, using only algebra, it is not too difficult to verify it for a special case such as $n = 10$ and $x_0 = 5$. Do so.

8-11. If X is $B(20,p)$, graph the likelihood function for p for each of the following events.

(a) $\{X: X \leqq 5\}$ (b) $\{X: X \leqq 10\}$
(c) $\{X: 5 \leqq X \leqq 15\}$ (d) $\{X: X \geqq 15\}$

8-12. If X has the uniform distribution on $\{1,2,3, . . . ,n\}$, where n is unknown, graph the likelihood function for n for each of the following events:

(a) $\{X: X \leqq 5\}$ (b) $\{X: X > 5\}$ (c) $\{X: 3 < X < 7\}$

8-13. If X is $B(10,p)$, graph the likelihood function for p for the event

(a) $\{X: X \leqq 2\}$ (b) $\{X: X \leqq 4\}$
(c) $\{X: X \leqq 6\}$ (d) $\{X: X \leqq 8\}$

8-2. Properties of estimates

We have now become familiar with some of the logical consequences for various probability models and are on our way to seeing how we can apply what we know to various problems of statistics. One of the important problems of statistics is that of estimation of parameters. In this general situation, we have some information about a sample and we wish to estimate one or more of the parameters of the underlying probability distribution.

Suppose, for example, that we know that in a certain random sample of 20 families from Northfield, Minnesota, 11 families have college-age children. We would like to estimate the proportion of all the families in Northfield that have college-age children. If p is this true proportion and Y is the number of families with college-age children in a random sample of 20 families, then Y has a binomial distribution with parameters p (which is unknown) and $n = 20$. We are told that in one particular sample $Y = 11$, and we are then asked to estimate p on the basis of this information alone. We have seen that the maximum likelihood estimate for p would be the sample proportion $11/20$. Such an estimate is called a *point estimate* for p, since it specifies a particular value as an estimate for p.

In a more general situation, suppose that θ is an unknown parameter of a distribution for a random variable X. (θ might be the mean or standard deviation of X, for instance.) Suppose further that we have a random sample of n values of X. From the observed sample values we would like to produce an estimate for θ. Since our estimate would depend on the sample values $X_1, X_2, \ldots, X_n$, we can say that the estimate will be a function of these values, say,

$$\hat{\theta} = f(X_1, X_2, \ldots, X_n)$$

where we have written $\hat{\theta}$ ("theta hat") for the estimate for θ. $\hat{\theta}$ is then a random variable which obtains a value by drawing a random sample $(X_1, X_2, \ldots, X_n)$ of n values of X and computing the value of $f(X_1, X_2, \ldots, X_n)$.

In the case above where we wish to estimate the proportion p of families with college-age children in the city, a reasonable estimate seems to be

$$\hat{p} = \frac{\Sigma X_i}{n}$$

where $X_i = 1$ or 0 according to whether the ith family in the sample has college-age children or not. In this case the function f is defined by $f(X_1, X_2, \ldots, X_n) = \Sigma X_i/n$.

$\hat{\theta}$, being a random variable in the general case, will have a certain probability distribution. The mean of this distribution is $E(\hat{\theta})$. If $E(\hat{\theta}) = \theta$, then we call $\hat{\theta}$ an *unbiased estimate* of θ. If $\hat{\theta}$ is an unbiased estimate for θ and we repeat many times the experiment which yields values of $\hat{\theta}$ and take the mean of all the values of $\hat{\theta}$ which we observe, we expect this mean to be quite close to θ, the value that we are trying to estimate. In general, an estimate, to be a "good" estimate, should be unbiased.

If an estimate is unbiased, what more can be expected of it?   Consider two different estimates $\hat{\theta}_1$ and $\hat{\theta}_2$ both of which are unbiased.   (For example, if we are trying to estimate the mean of a certain distribution, $\hat{\theta}_1$ might be the sample mean and $\hat{\theta}_2$ might be the sample median.)   Suppose that the distributions of $\hat{\theta}_1$ and $\hat{\theta}_2$ have variances $\sigma_1{}^2$ and $\sigma_2{}^2$, respectively, and suppose that $\sigma_1{}^2 < \sigma_2{}^2$.   This means that the distribution of $\hat{\theta}_1$ has less spread than the distribution of $\hat{\theta}_2$.   That is, the distribution for $\hat{\theta}_1$ is more concentrated about θ (the expected value of $\hat{\theta}_1$) than is that for $\hat{\theta}_2$. Hence, $\hat{\theta}_1$ is more likely to be close to θ in a single trial.   In this case, we say that $\hat{\theta}_1$ is a *more efficient estimate* of θ than is $\hat{\theta}_2$.   In general, if $\hat{\theta}_1$ and $\hat{\theta}_2$ are both estimates (unbiased or not) for θ, we say that $\hat{\theta}_1$ is *more efficient* than $\hat{\theta}_2$ if the variance of $\hat{\theta}_1$ is smaller than the variance of $\hat{\theta}_2$.   In some (but not all) cases, there is an estimate which, among all unbiased estimates, has the smallest possible variance.   In such a case, this estimate is said to be the *most efficient* unbiased estimate.

It can be shown that

(8-14)   *If* X *has the sample space* $\{0,1\}$ *and* $P(X = 1) = p$, *and if* $X_1, X_2, \ldots , X_n$ *is a random sample for* X, *then the most efficient unbiased estimate for* p *based on this sample is given by*

$$\hat{p} = \frac{\displaystyle\sum_{i=1}^{n} X_i}{n}$$

Since $u_X = p$ and $\Sigma\, X_i/n$ is the sample mean, this theorem simply asserts that in this case the most efficient unbiased estimate for the mean of the distribution is the sample mean.   The fact that $\hat{p}$ as given is unbiased follows immediately from (7-102).   The proof that this estimate is most efficient need not concern us (but see Prob. 8-27).

When X has a two-point distribution, $Y = \Sigma\, X_i$ has the binomial distribution $B(n,p)$ and Y is simply the number of "successes" in the n trials for X.

$\Sigma\, X_i/n = Y/n$ is then the proportion of "successes" in the sample. Theorem (8-14) tells us that, on the basis of the n results leading to the binomial variable Y, the most efficient unbiased estimate for p (which may be thought of as the population proportion) is the sample proportion.

In view of the fact that $u_{\bar{X}} = u_X$, we see that the mean of a random sample is always an unbiased estimate of the mean of the variable. Furthermore, since $\sigma_{\bar{X}} = \sigma_X/\sqrt{n}$, we see that the sample mean becomes a more and more efficient estimate as the sample size increases.   This is so because $\sigma_{\bar{X}} = \sigma_X/\sqrt{n}$ gets smaller as n increases.   In a sense, this is what we already discovered in the law of large numbers.

PROBLEMS

8-15. Suppose that X has the binomial probability function

$$P(x) = \binom{10}{x} (.2)^x(.8)^{10-x}$$

What is the sample space for the random variable $Y = X/10$?   Find the probability distribution for Y.   Directly from the definitions find the mean and variance for Y.

8-16. Do Prob. 8-15 with $P(x) = \binom{10}{x} (\tfrac{1}{2})^{10}$.

8-17. Do Prob. 8-15 with $P(x) = \binom{5}{x} (.2)^x(.8)^{5-x}$ and $Y = X/5$.

8-18. In a random sample of 20 students at a certain college, 12 are males.   Estimate the proportion of males in the entire student body on the basis of this information.

8-19. Suppose that in a random sample of 10 students at a certain elementary school five students walk at least three blocks to get to school.   Suppose that in a second random sample of 10 three students walk at least three blocks.   Estimate the proportion of students in the school who walk at least three blocks to get to school.

8-20. Suppose that investigator A finds that in a random sample of 20 students at a certain college 12 are car owners.   Investigator B finds that another random sample of 30 students from the same college contains 10 car owners.   On the basis of this information, how would you estimate the proportion of students in the population who are car owners?   Is your estimate unbiased?

8-21. Suppose that X has the binomial probability function $\binom{10}{x} p^x q^{n-x}$, where p is unknown.   Suppose that we observe two values of X, X_1, and X_2.   On the basis of this information, how would you estimate p?   Is your estimate unbiased?

8-22. If X has a binomial probability function $\binom{10}{x} p^x q^{10-x}$ with p unknown and $(X_1, X_2, \ldots, X_k)$ is a random sample of k values of X, estimate p on the basis of this sample.   Is your estimate unbiased?

8-23. In Prob. 8-22 replace "10" by "n."   Estimate p in this general case.

8-24. Prove that the maximum likelihood estimate of a parameter is not necessarily an unbiased estimate of the parameter (see Prob. 8-6).

8-25. A box contains n balls numbered 1, 2, 3, $\ldots$, n, where n is unknown.   A ball is drawn at random, and its number X noted.   We estimate n by $\hat{n} = 2X$.   Is $\hat{n}$ unbiased?   What is the variance of $\hat{n}$?

8-26. In Theorem (8-14) what is the variance for $\hat{p}$?

8-27. If X has the sample space $\{0,1\}$ and $P(X = 1) = p$ and (X_1, X_2, X_3, X_4) is a random sample for X, show that $\hat{p}_1 = (2X_1 + \tfrac{1}{2}X_2 + \tfrac{1}{2}X_3 + X_4)/4$ is an unbiased estimate for p.   Find the variance for $\hat{p}_1$, and compare it with the variance for $\hat{p}_2 = \Sigma\, X_i/4$.

8-28. In some special cases a certain biased estimate is better to use than a certain unbiased estimate.   Explain how this might be.

8-29. Suppose that we wish to estimate the mean μ of X on the basis of random sample $(X_1, X_2, \ldots, X_n)$, where $n > 2$.   The estimate $\hat{\mu}_1 = (X_1 + X_2)/2$ is an unbiased estimate of μ (prove it) but is intuitively an unsatisfactory estimate because it ignores the data $X_3, X_4, \ldots, X_n$ that we have before us.   Justify this intuitive reaction by showing that $\hat{\mu}_2 = (1/n) \sum_{i=1}^{n} X_i$ is a more efficient estimate than $\hat{\mu}_1$.

8-3. Tests of hypotheses

The scene is a pub in North Groves, California. Two characters lounge at a wooden table. The first speaks.

KEN (*as he fondles a fifty-cent piece*): Did you ever see a guy control a coin?

JEAN: Watdya mean?

KEN: I mean flip it so that he can make heads come up as often as he pleases.

JEAN: No. I never saw anybody do that.

KEN: I can do it.

JEAN: Lemme see the coin. (*He takes the coin, inspects it carefully, and flips it a couple of times.*) I don't believe it.

KEN: I can, though. I can flip it so that heads come up 80 per cent of the time.

JEAN: You mean you could start flipping right now, do it 30 times, and be sure to get exactly 24 heads?

KEN: No, of course, I don't mean that. What I mean is that in the long run I can make heads come up 80 per cent of the time. In the first 30 tosses I might not get exactly 24 heads. I might get more or less than 24.

JEAN: I still don't believe it. Show me.

KEN: O.K. I will. (*Starts to flip the coin, then stops.*) Before I start, maybe we should decide how well I have to do before you will be convinced. If I toss the coin 30 times, how many heads must I get to convince you?

JEAN: It would be pretty convincing if you tossed 30 straight heads, of course. The probability of that happening with a true coin and "no control" (*heavy sarcasm*) is $\frac{1}{2}^{30}$ or a chance of about one in a billion. But you don't claim to be that good. You only claim to be able to get heads 80 per cent of the time in the long run. Let me see. (*He pulls a book of tables out of his pocket.*) If the probability of getting a head when you toss the coin is $\frac{1}{2}$, which I believe it is, and you are going to toss the coin 30 times, 99 per cent of the time you are going to get (*runs his finger down a column in the table*) fewer than 22 heads. I'll be generous. If you can get 22 or more heads in 30 tosses, I'll agree you can control the coin. O.K.?

KEN: Let me see your table. (*Takes it and studies several pages.*) It looks as if that's not too bad. Since I really can control the coin and make heads come up 80 per cent of the time in the long run, the probability that I can convince you by this test on a single trial is about .76. The test is not quite fair, I suppose, since you are only taking a chance of 1 in 100 of being called wrong when you're actually right and I'm not doing that well. However, I'm willing to make an allowance for your stubbornness. Besides, I'm the one that is making a claim which seems to be out of the ordinary. Here we go! (*Starts to flip the coin.*)

And here we interrupt the dialogue. What was Jean's position in the above discussion? He had considerable confidence that, when the coin was flipped, the probability of getting a head would be about $\frac{1}{2}$, but he was willing to be convinced that he was wrong. He was willing (as we shall see) on the basis of empirical data to make a decision to accept one or the other of two *statistical hypotheses.* If p was the true probability of getting a head when Ken tossed the coin, Jean would be deciding whether to accept the statement "$p = .5$" as true or to accept the statement "$p = .8$" as true. If X is the number of heads obtained in 30 tosses of the coin, then X has a binomial distribution. The statements "$p = .5$" and "$p = .8$" are then statements about the probability distribution of X. Either of them may be called a *statistical hypothesis.* In general, any assertion about the probability distribution of a random variable may be called a *statistical hypothesis.* Usually, as in the above discussion, a statistical hypothesis is an assertion about the parameter or parameters of a distribution. It is convenient to give brief names to hypotheses. In the above case, let us use "H_0" to denote the assertion "$p = .5$" and "H_1" to denote the assertion "$p = .8$." That is, in the above discussion Ken and Jean were considering the hypotheses

$$H_0: p = .5 \qquad \text{and} \qquad H_1: p = .8$$

In the discussion, the two of them agreed on a test which could be run. On the basis of the outcome of this test they would decide which of the two hypotheses to accept. The test was: Flip the coin 30 times, note X (the number of heads), and if $X \geq 22$, accept H_1; otherwise accept H_0.

We refer to H_0 as the *null hypothesis* and to H_1 as the *alternative hypothesis.* In the general case, it is not always clear which of two hypotheses should be called the *null* hypothesis. But, in many cases, the null hypothesis is the one which asserts that a certain treatment or action does not have the effect claimed for it. If, for example, 40 per cent of the people contracting a certain disease recovered under treatment A and a new treatment B is developed which is reported to be more effective, we might let p be the proportion that would recover with treatment B. Then we would be interested in testing the hypothesis that $p = .40$ against the hypothesis that $p > .40$. In such a situation it is traditional to call the hypothesis "$p = .40$" the null hypothesis and label it H_0. Then the hypothesis "$p > .40$" is called the alternative hypothesis and is labeled H_1.

Returning to the problem with the coins, let us assume that one or the other of the hypotheses H_0 or H_1 must be true.   Then when the coin is flipped 30 times, X observed, and a decision made, one and only one of the following four alternatives must occur: (1) H_0 is true and the result of the test tells us to accept H_0, (2) H_1 is true and the result of the test tells us to accept H_1, (3) H_0 is true and the result of the test tells us to accept H_1, or (4) H_1 is true but the result of the test tells us to accept H_0. In the first two of these cases, correct decisions are made.   In the last two cases, errors are made.   The situation can be displayed in the form of a table.

	H_0 is true	H_1 is true
H_0 is accepted	Correct decision	Error of type II
H_1 is accepted	Error of type I	Correct decision

The error of rejecting the null hypothesis when it is true is called an *error of type* I, or an *error of the first kind*.   The error of accepting the null hypothesis when actually the alternative hypothesis is true is called an *error of type* II, or an *error of the second kind*.   The probability of committing an error of type I is called the size of the error of type I and is usually denoted by α ("alpha").   The probability of committing an error of type II is called the size of the error of type II and is usually denoted by β ("beta").   A test with a size of error of type I of α is said to be an α-*level test* or else a *test of level* α or a test *at significance level* α.

In the case of the argument over Ken's ability to control the coin, the test that was decided on was as follows: Reject H_0 if and only if $X \geqq 22$, where X is the number of heads obtained in 30 tosses.   In this case, the probability that the hypothesis H_0 is rejected when it is actually true (that is, the size of the error of type I) is given by

$$\alpha = P(X \geqq 22 | p = .5)$$

$$= \sum_{x=22}^{30} \binom{30}{x} \left(\frac{1}{2}\right)^{30} = .01$$

where the numerical value was found by using Table A-3 for the cumulative binomial distribution for $n = 30$ and $p = .5$.   When Jean agreed to use this test, he was willing to take the chance of being called wrong one time in a hundred about the value of p when actually he was right.

The size of error of type II for this test (that is, the probability of accepting H_0 when actually H_1 is true) is given by

$$\beta = P(X < 22 | p = .8)$$

$$= \sum_{x=0}^{21} \binom{30}{x} (.8)^x (.2)^{30-x}$$

$$= .24$$

where again Table A-3 was used to obtain the approximate numerical value. We see that Ken was willing to use this test even though, when H_1 was true, the test would cause you to reject it about 24 per cent of the time.

We might argue that a "more fair" test would be to reject H_0 if and only if $X \geq 20$, since 20 is close to halfway between 15 (the expected number of heads in 30 tosses if $p = .5$) and 24 (the expected number of heads if $p = .8$). If this test is used, the sizes of the errors are given by

$$\alpha = P(X \geq 20 | p = .5)$$

$$= \sum_{x=20}^{30} \binom{30}{x} \frac{1}{2^{30}} = .05$$

and
$$\beta = P(X < 20 | p = .8)$$

$$= \sum_{x=0}^{19} \binom{30}{x} (.8)^x (.2)^{30-x} = .06$$

We might, in fact, for various values of k consider this test: Reject H_0 if and only if $X \geq k$. For each proposed value of k we may compute α and β. We obtain the values given below:

k	$\alpha = p(X \geq k | p = .5)$	$\beta = p(X < k | p = .8)$
10	.97	.00
13	.82	.00
15	.57	.00
17	.29	.00
19	.10	.03
20	.05	.06
22	.01	.24
24	.00	.57
26	.00	.88
28	.00	.99

If we wish to consider how the sizes of our errors change as we change k, the above data suggest the graph shown in Fig. 8-2.

From the graph we see clearly that, as we change k in an attempt to make α small, we must thereby increase β. This is typical of trying to design a test which we wish to use to decide between a null hypothesis H_0 and an alternative hypothesis H_1. That is, changing the test to make the chance of an error of type I small will usually increase the chance of an error of type II.

In the case of the coin being considered, the graph of the two kinds of errors leads us to conclude that the test with $k = 20$ is a pretty good one, since it seems to be about "fair" and with $k = 20$ both α and β are quite small.

In the general case, where we are given two hypotheses H_0 and H_1 and wish to design a test which, on the basis of certain empirical data, will tell us whether or not to reject H_0 in favor of H_1, the above definitions of the two kinds of error apply and the usual procedure is as follows: We choose α to be .05 or .01 and then try to design a test which has α equal to that chosen value and β as small as possible. This is simply a conventional policy, but it makes considerable sense in most applications in view of the kind of null hypotheses involved. We shall see that this is so in later examples.

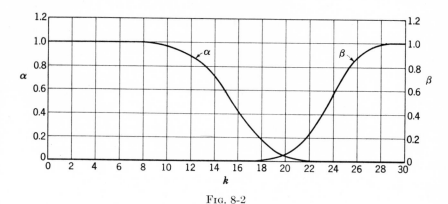

FIG. 8-2

Suppose that we have two tests T_1 and T_2 for deciding between two hypotheses. If T_1 and T_2 both have a size of the error of type I of α, T_1 has a size of the error of type II of β_1, T_2 has a size of the error of type II of β_2, and $\beta_1 < \beta_2$, then we say that T_1 is a *more powerful test at level α* than T_2. If a test T_1 is at least as powerful as any other test T_2 at level α, we say that T_1 is the *most powerful test at level α* for the given hypotheses and the given data.

In the case of flipping a coin 30 times and deciding between $H_0: p = .5$ and $H_1: p = .8$, it can be shown (by methods beyond the scope of this book) that the most powerful test at level .05 is as follows: Reject H_0 if and only if $X \geq 20$. The most powerful test at the 1 per cent level is as follows: Reject H_0 if and only if $X \geq 22$. It is fortunate that these tests which seem so reasonable to our common sense do, in fact, turn out to be most powerful at the given levels. The most powerful test could conceivably have turned out to involve some much more complicated restriction on X or perhaps even have been involved with the order in which the heads came up in our trials.

By considering likelihood functions we could arrive at the symmetric test for the above coin situation, where the sizes of the two kinds of error are approximately the same. Suppose that the coin is flipped 30 times and x_0 heads are obtained.   If we consider the likelihood function

$$L(y) = P(X = x_0|p = y)$$

we might adopt the following test: Reject H_0: $p = .5$ in favor of H_1: $p = .8$ if and only if $L(.8) > L(.5)$.   That is, reject H_0 if and only if the observed result is more likely when $p = .8$ than it is when $p = .5$.   It is not too difficult to show that $L(.8) > L(.5)$ if and only if $x_0 \geq 20$.   Thus, this approach leads to the symmetric test arrived at before.

PROBLEMS

8-30. Let X have the binomial probability function with $n = 10$, and consider the hypotheses H_0: $p = .5$, H_1: $p = .1$.   We observe a single value for X.   As a method for deciding between these hypotheses we adopt the following test: Reject H_0 if and only if $X < 2$.   Find α and β, the sizes of the type I and type II errors.

8-31. If X has a binomial distribution with $n = 20$ and a decision is made between H_0 and H_1 on the basis of a single observation of X by the indicated test, find α and β.

	H_0	H_1	*Test*
(a)	$p = .5$	$p = .8$	Reject H_0 if and only if $X > 12$
(b)	$p = .5$	$p = .9$	Reject H_0 if and only if $X > 12$
(c)	$p = .5$	$p = .2$	Reject H_0 if and only if $X \leq 6$
(d)	$p = .5$	$p = .2$	Reject H_0 if and only if $X < 6$
(e)	$p = .9$	$p = .1$	Reject H_0 if and only if $X \leq 10$
(f)	$p = .4$	$p = .6$	Reject H_0 if and only if $X \leq 10$
(g)	$p = .2$	$p = .5$	Reject H_0 if and only if $X > 6$
(h)	$p = .6$	$p = .7$	Reject H_0 if and only if $X > 13$

8-32. Let X be a binomial variable with $n = 10$.   Let H_0: $p = .4$ and H_1: $p = .8$ be decided between by the following test: Reject H_0 if and only if $X \geq y$, where X is a single observed value of the variable.   Find α and β for $y = 3, 4, 5, 6, 7, 8, 9$, and plot α and β as functions of y, putting the two curves on the same graph.

8-33. Let X have a binomial distribution, and suppose that we wish to decide between the hypotheses H_0: $p = .4$ and H_1: $p = .6$.   Suppose that we use the following test: Reject H_0 if and only if $X/n > \frac{1}{2}$.   Find α and β for the cases $n = 5, 10, 20$, and 30.

8-34. Let X have a binomial distribution with $n = 20$, and reject H_0 if and only if $X > 8$, where H_0: $p = .3$ and H_1: $p = p_1$ are the two hypotheses.   Find α and β for $p_1 = .4, .5, .6, .7, .8, .9$.

8-35. The same as Prob. 8-34 except take H_0: $p = .5$ and $p_1 = .1, .2, .3, .4, .6, .7, .8, .9$.   Graph β as a function of p_1.

8-36. Suppose that a box contains n balls numbered $1, 2, 3, 4, \ldots , n$, where n is unknown.   Consider the hypotheses H_0: $n = 10$, H_1: $n = 14$.   We draw a single ball, note its number X, and decide between H_0 and H_1 by the following test: Reject H_0 if and only if $X \geq 9$.   Find α and β, the sizes of the errors of the two kinds.

8-37. If the probability functions for X and Y are given by $P(x) = \binom{5}{x} p_1^x q_1^{5-x}$ and $P(y) = \binom{10}{y} p_2^y q_2^{10-y}$, respectively, and we decide between the hypotheses H_0: $p_1 = p_2 = .5$ and H_1: $p_1 = .3$ and $p_2 = .4$ by the following test: Reject H_0 if and only if $X + Y \leq 2$, find the sizes of the two kinds of errors.

8-38. Suppose that X is $B(10,p)$ and we wish to test $H_0: p = .5$ against $H_1: p = .6$. Suppose that we draw no value for X but instead draw a random number Y between 1 and 100, inclusive, and reject H_0 if and only if $Y \geq 90$. Find the size of each kind of error. Discuss how we can always construct a test of this kind with an error of the first kind as small as we please even though we observe no values for the original variable. Does it make any difference what the two given hypotheses are?

*8-39. For the situation discussed in the last paragraph of this section show that $L(.8) > L(.5)$ is equivalent to $x_0 \geq 20$. (*Hint:* Use logs.)

8-40. Suppose that X is $B(n,p)$, where p is unknown, and we wish to test $H_0: p = p_0$ against $H_1: p = p_1$ on the basis of a single observed value of X. If x_0 is the observed result, let $L(y) = P(X = x_0|p = y)$. Discuss the nature of the following test: Reject H_0 if and only if

$$\frac{L(p_1)}{L(p_0)} \geq 1$$

*8-41. Do Prob. 8-40 if the last inequality is replaced by

$$\frac{L(p_1)}{L(p_0)} \geq k$$

where k is chosen so that the test has level .05.

8-4. More on tests of hypotheses

A man who thought himself sane
Found decisions a terrible pain.
So he'd flip a coin
His choices to loin
But he kept his alpha the same.

In the preceding section we discussed the problem of setting up a test for deciding between the hypotheses $H_0: p = .5$ and $H_1: p = .8$ for a binomial variable X with $n = 30$. Each of these hypotheses is said to be *simple* because, with the other information we have about X, each of them completely determines the probability distribution of X. A statistical hypothesis that is not simple is said to be *composite*.

Suppose, for example, that we are faced with the problem of deciding whether or not for a certain die the probability of getting a "6" is $\frac{1}{6}$. If the problem is stated in this way, we are evidently interested in deciding between the hypotheses

$$H_0: p = \tfrac{1}{6}$$
$$H_1: p \neq \tfrac{1}{6}$$

where p is the probability of getting a "6" on a single throw of the die. Suppose that we have the time to throw the die 600 times, and let X be the number of "6's" obtained. Then X has the binomial probability function $P(x) = \binom{600}{x} p^x q^{600-x}$. H_0 is a simple hypothesis, since, if we know that H_0 is true, the probability distribution for X is completely specified.   On the other hand, H_1 is a composite hypothesis, since, even if we know H_1 is true, we do not know the exact distribution for X. With a composite alternative such as this, it is not possible to compute the size of error of type II for a given test.   However, we can still find the size of the error of type I for a given test, since H_0 is a simple hypothesis. In trying to find a good test for this situation, we can then choose among tests which give $\alpha = .05$.   If H_0 is true, we expect to get about 100 "6's" in the 600 tosses of the die.   If X is too much below 100 *or* too much above 100, we would have reason to doubt that $p = \frac{1}{6}$ (i.e., to doubt H_0). Hence, it would seem that our test might well take the following form: Accept H_0 if and only if $100 - d < X < 100 + d$ for some number d. It is possible by means of tables to find d so that the test will have $\alpha = .05$. In fact such a d is given by $d = 18$, so that our test becomes: Accept H_0 if and only if $82 < X < 118$.   That this test has an error of type I of .05 follows from the fact that, when $p = \frac{1}{6}$, $P(82 < X < 118) \cong .95$.

In general, as "reasonable" tests we have

(8-42)   *Tests for H_0: $p = p_0$ against H_1 when X is $B(n,p)$:*

H_1	Test: Reject H_0 if and only if	Where
$p \neq p_0$	$X \geq k_1$ or $X \leq k_2$	$\displaystyle\sum_{x=k_1}^{n}\binom{n}{x}p_0^x q_0^{n-x} \cong \frac{\alpha}{2}$ $\displaystyle\sum_{x=0}^{k_2}\binom{n}{x}p_0^x q_0^{n-x} \cong \frac{\alpha}{2}$
$p > p_0$	$X \geq k_3$	$\displaystyle\sum_{x=k_3}^{n}\binom{n}{x}p_0^x q_0^{n-x} \cong \alpha$
$p < p_0$	$X \leq k_4$	$\displaystyle\sum_{x=0}^{k_4}\binom{n}{x}p_0^x q_0^{n-x} \cong \alpha$

In the last column we have indicated how the k values should be chosen if the tests are to have a significance level of approximately α.

Suppose, for example, that X is $B(30,p)$ and we wish to test H_0: $p = .5$ against H_1: $p \neq .5$.   We see from Table A-3 that $p(X \leq 9) = .021$ and $P(X \geq 21) = .021$ when H_0 is true.   Then a good test for the given hypotheses is to reject H_0 if and only if $X \leq 9$ or $X \geq 21$.   This test will have a significance level of approximately 5 per cent (actually 4.2 per cent).

The cases where $n = 50$ and $n = 100$ are not covered by Table A-3. In (8-43) and (8-44) we find the "critical values" for these values of n and $\alpha = .05$.

(8-43)   *When X is B(50,p):*

p	$P(X \leq k_1) \cong .025$ k_1	$P(X \geq k_2) \cong .025$ k_2	$P(X \leq k_3) \cong .05$ k_3	$P(X \geq k_4) \cong .05$ k_4
.1	1	10	1	9
.2	4	16	5	15
.3	8	22	9	21
.4	13	27	14	26
.5	18	32	19	31
.6	23	37	24	36
.7	28	42	29	41
.8	34	46	35	45
.9	40	49	41	49

(8-44)   *When X is B(100,p):*

p	$P(X \leq k_1) \cong .025$ k_1	$P(X \geq k_2) \cong .025$ k_2	$P(X \leq k_3) \cong .05$ k_3	$P(X \geq k_4) \cong .05$ k_4
.1	4	17	5	16
.2	12	29	13	27
.3	21	40	22	38
.4	30	50	31	49
.5	40	60	41	59
.6	50	70	51	69
.7	60	79	62	78
.8	71	88	73	87
.9	83	96	84	95

In the second case given in (8-42) the test given is a *uniformly most powerful test.* By this we mean that, if we consider the simple alternative hypothesis $H_1': p = p_1$, where p_1 is any value satisfying $p_1 > p_0$, then the test given is the most powerful test at level α for deciding between H_0 and H_1'. Similarly, the test for the third case in Table (8-42) is a uniformly most powerful test. The test for the first case is not a uniformly most powerful test. There is none such when the alternative hypothesis is simply that $p \neq p_0$.

Suppose that we are testing $H_0: p = p_0$ against $H_1: p \neq p_0$ and our test has an error of the first kind of size α. When the observation causes us to reject H_0, we say that the observed value is *significant at the α level.* For example, if our test has $\alpha = .05$ and the observation leads to rejection of H_0, then we say that the observed value is significant at the 5 per cent level (for the given hypotheses).   Since we accept H_0 if the observed X is close enough to np_0, it is also true that we accept H_0 if the sample proportion X/n is close enough to p_0.   Then if X is significant at a certain level, we sometimes say that the sample proportion is *significantly different from* p_0 at that level.

Similar terminology is used for other pairs of hypotheses.

In research reports asserting the statistical significance of certain results it is customary to give approximately the smallest level α for which the results would be significant.

Consider the general case where X is a random variable with probability function $P(x;\theta)$ on some sample space S, θ is some parameter for the distribution, and we wish to decide between the hypotheses $H_0: \theta = \theta_0$ and $H_1: \theta \in A$, where A is some set of possible alternative values for θ. We are to base our decision on a single observed value of X.   A test of the two hypotheses will be some rule which tells us which values for X will cause us to reject H_0.   The collection of all these values is called the *critical region* for the test.   That is, if CR is a set and a test tells us to reject H_0 if and only if $X \in CR$, then we call CR the *critical region* for the test.

The significance level of the test (i.e., the size of the error of the first kind) is then

$$(8\text{-}45) \qquad\qquad \alpha = \sum_{x \in CR} P(x,\theta_0)$$

since this sum gives the probability of X being in CR (and, hence, the probability of rejecting H_0) when θ_0 is the true value of the parameter.

$$\text{If } \theta_1 \in A, \text{ then } \sum_{x \in CR} P(x,\theta_1)$$

is the probability of rejecting H_0 when θ_1 is the true value of the parameter.   When $\theta_1 \in A$, rejecting H_0 is a correct decision, so we would like to have this probability large.

For a given test with critical region CR the function

$$(8\text{-}46) \qquad pf(y) = P(X \in CR | \theta = y) = \sum_{x \in CR} P(x;y)$$

is called the *power function* for the test.   Thus, the power function for a test is the likelihood function for the critical region of the test.   By (8-45) $pf(\theta_0)$ is the level of significance of the test.   If $\theta_1 \in A$, then

$$1 - pf(\theta_1) = 1 - \sum_{x \in CR} P(x,\theta_1)$$

is the probability of accepting H_0 when θ_1 is the true value of the parameter. That is, $1 - pf(\theta_1)$ is the size of the error of the second kind for this test when it is used to decide between the hypotheses $H_0: \theta = \theta_0$ and $H_1': \theta = \theta_1$. This error will be small if $pf(\theta_1)$ is large. Thus, if $pf(\theta_1)$ is large, the test is a "powerful one" for deciding between $H_0: \theta = \theta_0$ and $H_1': \theta = \theta_1$. We call $pf(\theta_1)$ the *power of the test* at the alternative θ_1.

A test for deciding between $H_0: \theta = \theta_0$ and $H_1: \theta \in A$ is called a *uniformly most powerful* test at level α if $pf(\theta_0) = \alpha$ and if for any $\theta_1 \in A$ the power of the test at θ_1 is at least as large as is the power for any other α-level test at θ_1.

The above results for the binomial situation assert that for testing $H_0: p = p_0$ against $H_1: p > p_0$ the uniformly most powerful test is one which has a critical region of the form $CR = \{X: X \geq K\}$, where the constant K can be found from the condition that we must have

$$P(X \geq K) = \alpha$$

when p_0 is the true value of the parameter. Also for testing $H_0: p = p_0$ against $H_1: p < p_0$ a uniformly most powerful test will have the form $CR = \{X: X \leq K\}$.

The graph of the power function of a test is often helpful. In Fig. 8-3 we find the power functions for the following situations for a binomial variable X with $n = 30$:

Test	H_0	H_1	Reject H_0 if and only if
a	$p = .5$	$p > .5$	$X \geq 20$
b	$p = .5$	$p < .5$	$X \leq 10$
c	$p = .5$	$p \neq .5$	$X \leq 9$ or $X \geq 21$

For a composite alternative hypothesis the size of the error of type II cannot usually be computed for a given test. We can, however, find the graph of the power function for the test, and this will tell us how well the test does against various alternatives. For example, a glance at Fig. 8-3a tells us that the test at hand does not have much of a chance of detecting the fact that $p > p_0$ if $p = .6$. The power of the test at $p = .6$ is about .29. Hence, the size of the error of type II for this test for the hypotheses $H_0: p = .5$ and $H_1': p = .6$ is $1 - .29 = .71$, which is not small.

If X is $B(p,n)$, where p is unknown, and we wish to test the hypotheses $H_0: p \leq p_0$ and $H_1: p > p_0$, then we are faced with a situation where neither of the hypotheses is simple. In this case, for a given test, we usually cannot even find the size of the error of type I. Using the critical region of a proposed test, however, we can still consider the power func-

tion of the test.   As an example, suppose that X is $B(30,p)$ and the
hypotheses are $H_0: p \leq .5$ and $H_1: p > .5$.   If we use the following test:
Reject H_0 if and only if $X \geq 20$, then Fig. 8-3a is the graph of the power
function for the test.   Inspection of this graph convinces us that the test

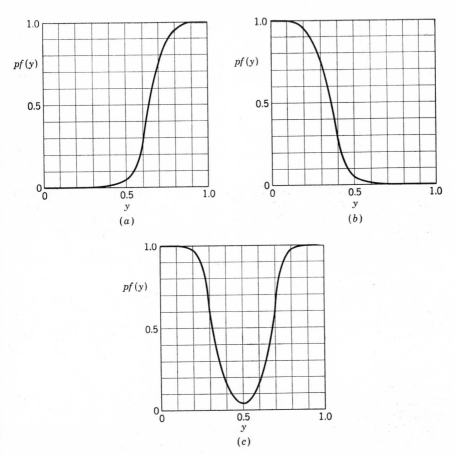

FIG. 8-3. (a) Graph of $P(X \geq 20 \,|\, p = y)$, the power function for test a.   (b). Graph of
$P(X \leq 10 \,|\, p = y)$, the power function for test b.   (c) Graph of $P(X > 20$ or $X <
10 \,|\, p = y)$, the power function for test c.

being considered is a good one for the proposed hypotheses.   For any
value of p less than .5 we see that the power function has a value less than
.05.   This means that the probability of rejecting $H_0: p \leq p_0$ when it is
true would never exceed .05, whatever value p might have which satisfies
the given condition.   In case H_0 is false, the situation is just as it was for
deciding between $H_0: p = .5$ and $H_1: p > .5$.   In this example we see,
then, that the test given in Table (8-42) for deciding between $H_0: p = .5$

and $H_1: p > .5$ is also a good test for deciding between $H_0: p \leq .5$ and $H_1: p > .5$. This is true more generally. That is, the test given in Table (8-42) for deciding between $H_0: p = p_0$ and $H_1: p > p_0$ is also a good test for deciding between $H_0: p \leq p_0$ and $H_1: p > p_0$. Similarly, the test given in (8-42) for deciding between $H_0: p = p_0$ and $H_1: p < p_0$ is also a good test for deciding between $H_0: p \geq p_0$ and $H_1: p < p_0$.

This situation is typical of several cases where the null hypothesis is composite. In these cases a good test is discovered by considering tests for a simple hypothesis which is "at the boundary" for the composite situation.

PROBLEMS

8-47. A coin is tossed 30 times and 21 heads are obtained. Test the hypothesis that the coin is perfectly balanced.

8-48. Thirty throws of a die yield 12 sixes. Is the die fair?

8-49. With a certain well-established method of teaching reading, it has been observed that 90 per cent of the students can pass a certain examination at the end of the second grade. Using a new method of teaching, a teacher discovers that 96 children in a group of 100 pass the exam. Is the new method significantly better than the old?

8-50. In a random sample of 30 voters in a town we find 18 who are Democrats. May we conclude that a majority of the voters in the town are Democrats?

8-51. Under treatment A it has been observed in the past that 40 per cent of the people who contracted a certain disease were seriously crippled. A new treatment B was used on 50 patients with the disease. Of these only 12 were seriously crippled. May we conclude that treatment B is better than treatment A?

8-52. A person claims that he can control the fall of a die by "willing" that it fall a certain way. "Willing" that the die will fall a 6, he throws the die 100 times and obtains 30 sixes. Do you believe his claim?

8-53. Consider your class to be a random sample of the student body, and let p be the proportion of people in your school who would answer "yes" to the following questions. On the basis of answers in your class, test the hypothesis $H_0: p = \frac{1}{2}$ against $H_1: p \neq \frac{1}{2}$.

(a) Would you be in favor of outlawing capital punishment?

(b) Do you think quite a few people in this school cheat on examinations?

(c) Do you think it would be wise to reschedule national and state holidays so that there were more "three-day week ends"?

(d) Do you approve of fluoridation of public drinking water?

(e) Has the advice you received from high school counselors been helpful in planning your academic career?

(f) Have you read The Communist Manifesto?

(g) Do you regularly read The Readers Digest?

(h) Make up a question or questions concerning some recent controversy at your school or some other matter of interest to you.

8-54. Two dice are tossed, and the total spots uppermost noted. Find the probability that the result is even if the dice are perfect. From the data in Table 1-2 test the hypothesis that the dice are perfect by considering the number of even results obtained.

8-55. Toss a coin 50 times, and note the number of heads obtained.   Test the hypothesis that $P(\text{heads}) = \frac{1}{2}$.

8-56. Given a pair of random digits, it should be just as likely that the first exceeds the second as that the second exceeds the first.   Test the table of random digits in the back of the book for randomness by noting in 50 successive pairs the number of cases where the first digit exceeds the second.   (Do not count pairs where the first and second digits are the same.)

8-57. A manufacturer wants to determine customer preferences for two items A and B.   He has 50 people state whether they prefer A to B or B to A (indifference is not allowed).   Thirty people say that they prefer A.   Test the hypothesis that there is no real difference in the population at large as to preference for A or B.   (*Hint:* Let p be the proportion in the population at large that would prefer A over B, and test $H_0: p = \frac{1}{2}$ against $H_1: p > \frac{1}{2}$.)

8-58. In a sample of 20 items from a large bin 3 are found to be defective.   The manufacturer of these items considers his production to be satisfactory if no more than 10 per cent of the items are defective.   Should he consider the bin from which this sample was drawn to be satisfactory?

8-59. *Quality-control charts.*   In a continuous manufacturing process one method of *quality control* is periodically to take samples of a fixed size, test the items in each sample, and note the number of defective items.   Suppose that 12 samples of size 20 have been drawn in this fashion, the number of defectives being 2, 2, 1, 0, 3, 2, 1, 3, 4, 6, 5, 6.   These results can be plotted in a so-called quality-control chart as in Fig. 8-4. On the basis of past experience the manufacturer usually knows the percentage p_0 of defectives that his process puts out when the process is "under control."   After each sample is drawn, we may then decide between $H_0: p = p_0$ and $H_1: p > p_0$ on the basis of the observed number of defectives in the sample.   (Here p is the actual proportion of defectives being produced at the time the sample is taken.)   In the above case, let us assume that $p_0 = .1$.   To test $H_0: p = .1$ against $H_1: p > .1$, we see from Table A-3 that, if we wish a 5 per cent level test, we reject H_0 when the number of defectives exceeds 4.   If in our control chart we draw a horizontal line at $X = 4$, we call this line the upper control limit (UCL).   Whenever our plotted point falls above this line, we strongly suspect that the process is "out of control" and look for the trouble on the production line.   Thus, at the tenth sample, we probably would have stopped production in the above example.   The quality-control chart is helpful in revealing trends

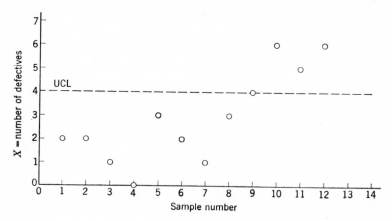

FIG. 8-4

which may indicate wear on machine parts or other cumulative factors in the manufacturing process. (In the above example p_0 was taken rather larger than would be realistic so that computations would be easier.) Construct a quality-control chart with a UCL line for taking samples of size 30 when $p_0 = .1$.

8-60. A box contains n balls numbered 1, 2, 3, . . . , n, where n is unknown. A single ball is drawn, and the number X on it noted. We decide between the hypotheses $H_0: n = 10$ and $H_1: n > 10$ by the following test: Reject H_0 if and only if $X > 8$. Graph the power function for this test.

8-61. With the box of Prob. 8-60 suppose that we decide between $H_0: n = 10$ and $H_1: n \neq 10$ by the following test: Reject H_0 if and only if $X < 6$ or $X > 15$. Graph the power function for this test.

8-62. Suppose that X is $B(10,p)$ and we decide between $H_0: p = .1$ and $H_1: p > .1$ on the basis of one observed value for X by the following test: Reject H_0 if and only if $X > 4$. Graph the power function for this test.

8-63. Suppose that X is $B(15,p)$ and we decide between $H_0: p = .5$ and $H_1: p \neq .5$ by the following test: Toss four coins, and reject H_0 if and only if we get four heads. Graph the power function for the test.

8-64. Graph the power function for the test that you used in

(a) Prob. 8-47   (b) Prob. 8-48
(c) Prob. 8-50   (d) Prob. 8-58

*8-65. Suppose that θ is a parameter for X and we wish to decide between the hypotheses $H_0: \theta \in B$ and $H_1: \theta \in A$, where B and A are certain disjoint sets. Suppose that a proposed test for these hypotheses has a critical region CR. Let $pf(y) = P(X \in CR | \theta = y)$ be the power function for the test. If $pf(y) \geq \alpha$ for all $y \in A$ and $pf(y) \leq \alpha$ for all $y \in B$, then the test is said to be *unbiased* at level α.

(a) If X is $B(30,p)$, $B = \{y: y \leq .5\}$, $A = \{y: y > .5\}$, and $CR = \{X: X \geq 22\}$, show that the test is unbiased at the 1 per cent level.

(b) Show that the test given in Fig. 8-3c is unbiased at the 5 per cent level.

8-5. Confidence intervals

> *A crusty old guy from the Transvaal*
> *Desired a confidence interval.*
> *To make it quite small*
> *Was nothing at all*
> *But the confidence then became trivial.*

Suppose that X is the number of heads obtained in 30 tosses of a bent coin. Then X is $B(30,p)$, where p is the probability of getting a head on a single toss. Suppose that we flip the coin 30 times and obtain 10 heads. On the basis of this information, we know that the $\hat{p} = {}^{10}\!/_{30} = \frac{1}{3}$ is then the most efficient unbiased estimate for p and (incidentally) that this estimate is also the maximum likelihood estimate for p. In other words, $\hat{p} = \frac{1}{3}$ is the best *point* estimate that we can give for p from the given data. But rather than give a point estimate for p, we might ask, "Within what range could we reasonably expect p to be, in view of the observed value of X?" That is, we might ask for an *interval estimate* for p.

There are several ways to arrive at such an interval estimate. Perhaps the most reasonable is as follows: We know that X is $B(30,p)$, and we have observed a single value of X, $x_0 = 10$. With these data in mind, we ask what values of p are "acceptable" in view of our discussion of tests of hypotheses. More precisely, if we use the tests of level 5 per cent given by Table (8-42), for what values of p_0 would we accept $H_0\colon p = p_0$ as opposed to $H_1\colon p \neq p_0$ when we have the observed value $x_0 = 10$? Would we accept, for instance, $H_0\colon p = .1$ as opposed to $H_1\colon p \neq .1$, given that $x_0 = 10$? We see that the answer is in the negative, since from Tables (8-42) and A-3 we would accept $H_0\colon p = .1$ as opposed to $H_1\colon p \neq .1$ only when $1 \leq X \leq 6$. Thus, .1 is not a "reasonable" value for p in view of our observations. Proceeding in this fashion, we obtain the following answers to the question, "Would we accept $H_0\colon p = p_0$ as opposed to $H_1\colon p \neq p_0$ when the value $x_0 = 10$ is observed?"

p_0	.1	.15	.16	.17	.2	.3	.4	.5	.53	.54	.6	.7	.8	.9
Accept?	No	No	No	Yes	Yes	Yes	Yes	Yes	Yes	No	No	No	No	No

We conclude that the "reasonable" values of p in view of the observed value of X are those satisfying $.17 \leq p \leq .53$. This result is called a *confidence interval* for p.

If we were to repeat the entire procedure above another time, tossing the coin 30 times, noting the number of heads obtained, and then finding the acceptable values of p based on this new number of heads, we would most probably find a different confidence interval for p (because we probably would not get 10 heads on the next trial). We see then that the limits of the interval arrived at in this way are themselves random variables. That is, we can consider the variables $L(X)$ and $U(X)$, which are the lower and upper end points of the interval obtained by observing a value of X and then finding the acceptable values of p when 5 per cent level tests are used with this observed value of X. For an observed value x_0, we call $L(x_0) < p < U(x_0)$ a 95 per cent *confidence interval* for p. We do this because

$$P(L(X) < p < U(X)) = .95$$

To see that this is so, consider what it means when we observe a value x_0 and find that p is not between $L(x_0)$ and $U(x_0)$. It means that for this observed value of X we would reject the hypothesis that p is the true value of the parameter. But p *is* the true value of the parameter, and we are using tests of level .05. Then the probability that p will not be between $L(X)$ and $U(X)$ is .05, and hence, the probability that $L(X)$ and $U(X)$ will bracket p is .95.

Let us generalize the above example. Suppose that X is $B(n,p)$, and suppose that we have a single observed value of X. For these data, a $1 - \alpha$ *confidence interval* for p is the set

(8-66) $\{p_0 :$ we would accept $H_0: p = p_0$ as opposed to $H_1: p \neq p_0$

given the observed value of $X\}$

where we assume that the tests used are at level α.   We call this set a

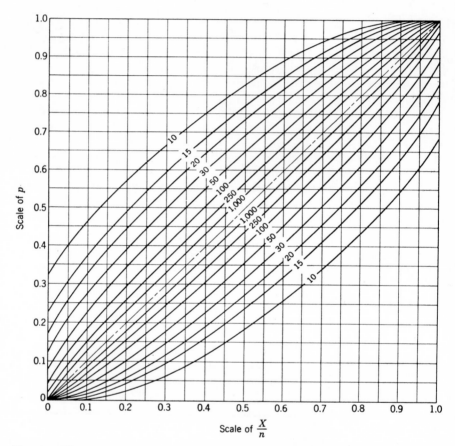

FIG. 8-5. Ninety-five per cent confidence intervals for p.   (*This graph is reproduced with the kind permission of Professor E. S. Pearson from C. J. Clopper and E. S. Pearson, The Use of Confidence or Fiducial Limits Illustrated in the Case of the Binomial, Biometrika, vol. 26, p. 404, 1934.*)

random set to emphasize that we arrive at this set by observing a value of the random variable X, and we shall get different sets as we get different values for X. The probability that this random set will contain the true value of p is $1 - \alpha$, and the set is actually an interval if we use the tests given by Table (8-42).

Fortunately, it is not necessary to go through long computations to discover such confidence intervals for p. We can instead use the graphs of Fig. 8-5 or 8-6. To use Fig. 8-5 to find a 95 per cent confidence interval, we first find the sample proportion x_0/n for the observed value x_0. Then we find the point corresponding to this number on the hori-

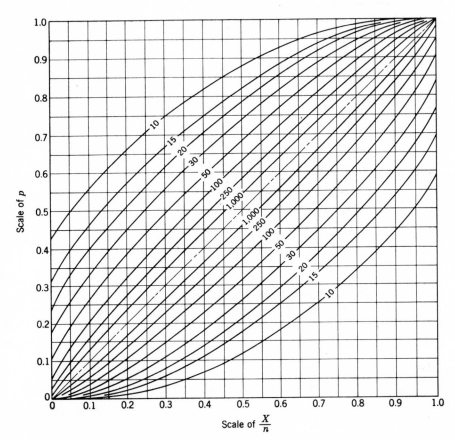

FIG. 8-6. Ninety-nine per cent confidence intervals for p. (*This graph is reproduced with the kind permission of Professor E. S. Pearson from C. J. Clopper and E. S. Pearson, The Use of Confidence or Fiducial Limits Illustrated in the Case of the Binomial, Biometrika, vol. 26, p. 404, 1934.*)

zontal axis and find the lower and upper limits of the 95 per cent confidence interval by moving up to the curves marked with the proper value of n. For values of n not shown we can interpolate between curves. If, for example, 50 throws of a (perhaps loaded) die yield 10 sixes, then a 95 per cent confidence interval for p, the probability of a 6 on a single toss, is $.10 < p < .34$.

The confidence intervals obtained so far were *two-sided* confidence intervals because they put both a lower and an upper limit on p. Often, however, we are interested in a *one-sided* confidence interval for p. In a continuous manufacturing process, for instance, where p is the proportion of defective items being put out by the process, the manufacturer will be primarily concerned with being sure that p is not too large. A one-sided confidence interval can easily be obtained by altering the alternative hypothesis used in our preceding definition. Thus, if we are primarily interested in whether or not p is too large, we would use the $1 - \alpha$ confidence interval

$\{p_0 :$ the observed value of X causes us to accept $H_0: p = p_0$ as

opposed to $H_1: p > p_0\}$

where we assume that the tests used are at level α as given in Table (8-42).

If p is the proportion of cures due to a certain medical treatment, our major concern may be in saying that p is at least so much with a certain degree of confidence. In this case the $1 - \alpha$ confidence interval to use would be the set

$\{p_0:$ the observed value of X causes us to accept

$H_0: p = p_0$ as opposed to $H_1: p < p_0\}$

From Table A-3 and the tables in Sec. 8.4 we can work out approximations to such one-sided intervals in much the same fashion as we did with the bent coin above for the two-sided case.

For the case where n is fairly large, we shall discover later a rather easy method for finding approximate confidence intervals for p with any degree of confidence and in either the one- or two-sided case.

One word of warning about confidence intervals. Suppose that $.50 < p < .75$ with 95 per cent confidence as the result of observing a value for X. The temptation is strong to say that this means that $P(.50 \leq p \leq .75) = .95$. But this is *nonsense*. p is *not* a random variable. It is a parameter and *not* a statistic. p is a fixed constant. The proper interpretation of the phrase ".$50 < p < .75$ is a 95 per cent confidence interval for p" is that the numbers .50 and .75 were arrived at by a (random) process having the property that the probability is .95 that the two numbers resulting from the process will bracket p.

We now consider the more general situation where X is a random variable (not necessarily binomial) which has a distribution that depends on a parameter θ. If we observe a value of X and, on the basis of the observation, construct a set $C(X)$, then we can call $C(X)$ a $1 - \alpha$ *confidence set* for θ if

$$P(\theta \in C(X)) = 1 - \alpha$$

If we have in mind a certain kind of α-level test for deciding between $H_0: \theta = \theta_0$ and $H_1: \theta \neq \theta_0$, then we can always obtain a $1 - \alpha$ confidence set for θ by letting

$$C(X) = \{\theta_0: \text{the observed value } X \text{ causes us to accept}$$
$$H_0: \theta = \theta_0 \text{ as opposed to } H_1: \theta \neq \theta_0\}$$

That is, a confidence set is obtained by considering the collection of all those values of θ which are acceptable by the given kind of test in view of the observed value of X.

Another way of looking at confidence intervals is the following: If X has a distribution which depends on a parameter θ, then it will, in general, be possible to find two numbers $k_1(\theta)$ and $k_2(\theta)$ depending on θ such that

$$P(k_1(\theta) < X < k_2(\theta)) = .95$$

Then it may be possible to rearrange (or "solve") the inequality involved so that $k_1(\theta) < X < k_2(\theta)$ if and only if $L(X) < \theta < U(X)$ for some functions L and U. Then, given an observed value for X, we can say that $L(X) < \theta < U(X)$ is a 95 per cent confidence interval for θ, since

$$P(L(X) < \theta < U(X)) = .95$$

The two-sided confidence interval for the binomial case can be considered to be a special case of this approach.

Using the law of large numbers, we see that we can obtain an arbitrarily small confidence interval for μ_X with confidence arbitrarily close to 1 (but less than 1) by taking a sufficiently large random sample. If $\bar{X}$ is the mean of a random sample of size n, then for any positive e

$$P(|\bar{X} - \mu_X| < e) \geqq 1 - \frac{\sigma_X^2}{e^2 n}$$

Then for a given e, the set

$$\{y: |\bar{X} - y| < e\} = \{y: \bar{X} - e < y < \bar{X} + e\}$$

is a confidence interval for μ_X of level at least $1 - \sigma_X^2/e^2 n$. If, for example, we know that $\sigma_X = 1$, let $e = .01$, and then observe a value of $\bar{X} = 100$ for a random sample of size 10^6, then $99.99 < \mu_X < 100.01$ with a confidence of at least

$$1 - \frac{1}{(.01)^2 10^6} = 99 \text{ per cent}$$

PROBLEMS

8-67. Find 95 per cent confidence intervals for the population proportion in each part of Prob. 8-53.

8-68. In a sample of 30 registered voters from a certain town, 20 say that they will vote for candidate A. Find a 95 and a 99 per cent confidence interval for p, the proportion of registered voters in the town who would say that they will vote for candidate A.

8-69. In a sample of 30 students at a certain college, 18 say that they do not approve of compulsory chapel services. Can we conclude with 95 per cent confidence that a majority of the student body is opposed to compulsory chapel?

8-70. In 1000 tosses of a coin, 490 heads are obtained. Find a 95 per cent confidence interval for the probability of getting a head on a single toss.

8-71. From the data of Table 1-2, find a 95 per cent confidence interval for the probability of

(*a*) Getting a total of 7

(*b*) Getting an even total

(*c*) Getting an odd total

8-72. It is known that $\sigma_X = 10$. A random sample of 1000 values yields $\bar{X} = 100$. From the law of large numbers, find an interval for μ_X for which we have a confidence of at least 99 per cent.

8-73. Making use of the fact that $p(1 - p) \leqq \frac{1}{4}$ for $0 \leqq p \leqq 1$, use the law of large numbers to find a 95 per cent (or more) confidence interval for P (head) if 100 tosses of a coin yield 50 heads. Compare this result with the 95 per cent confidence interval obtained from Fig. 8-5.

8-74. Assuming that your class is a random sample of the student body, make observations in your class and find 95 per cent confidence intervals for the proportion in the student body of

(*a*) Blondes   (*b*) Females

(*c*) People who wear glasses

(*d*) Girls who wore a sweater and skirt today

(*e*) Those who have taken mathematics courses in college

Do some of these results cause you to doubt the assumption of randomness?

CHAPTER 9

Continuous Probability Distributions

9-1. Continuous variables

Up to this point, we have (with the exception of Prob. 7-40 and the problems based on it) restricted our attention to experiments which had a finite number of possible outcomes. There are many problems where it is convenient to relax this restriction. If, for instance, we are interested in the heights of adult males in a certain town and we consider the experiment of choosing a person in the town and measuring his height X, it is most convenient to think of the set of possible outcomes (i.e., the sample space for X) as being an interval of real numbers (see Sec. 3-7). If we do so, we shall not be strictly realistic, since whatever measuring device we use will be limited in accuracy and it follows that there is only a finite number of different possible heights that we could record. As we shall see, however, it greatly simplifies our work with the problem to assume that any point in a certain interval is a possible outcome. Where the sample space for a random variable is taken to be an interval of real numbers or a union of such intervals, we say that the random variable is *continuous*. The random variables that we previously discussed which have finite sample spaces or sample spaces such as $\{0,1,2,3, \ldots\}$ are said to be *discrete* variables. The distinction between the two kinds of variables is very important, for the two types require probability models of different natures.

To introduce continuous random variables, we consider an experiment with a "spinner" as shown in Fig. 9-1.

On the circumference of the circle in Fig. 9-1 is a uniform scale running from 0 to 1. The "perfectly balanced" spinner is spun, and the position X of the tip of the arrow when it stops is the outcome of the experiment. We imagine that the spinner can end up at any point on the circumference. Then the outcome of the experiment will be in the set $S = \{x : 0 \leqq x < 1\}$, and evidently any real number in this set is a possible outcome. (The point $x = 1$ is not included, since it coincides with the point $x = 0$.) We call S the sample space for the random variable X. Just as was done with discrete random variables, we may refer to a subset E of S as an *event*.

An event E is said to *happen* if the result is in E.   Let

$$A = \{x\colon 0 < x < .5\}$$

Then the event A is said to happen if the outcome of the experiment is in A, that is, if $X \in A$.   Looking at the spinner we see that A happens if and only if the arrow point ends up on the right side of the circle.   Similarly, the event $B = \{x\colon .25 < x < .75\}$ happens if and only if the arrow point ends up on the bottom half of the circle.   As was the case with dis-

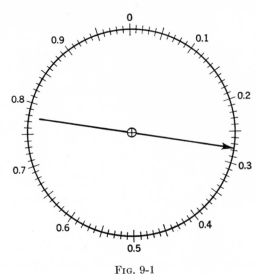

Fɪɢ. 9-1

crete variables, the events A and B both happen if and only if the outcome X is in the set $A \cap B = \{x\colon .25 < x < .5\}$.   Either A or B happens if and only if the outcome X is in the set $A \cup B = \{x\colon 0 < x < .75\}$. The event $A' = \{x\colon .5 \leqq x < 1\}$ happens if and only if A fails to happen. This terminology applies to events in general in any continuous case.

Suppose, now, that we spin the arrow 100 times, each time recording the value indicated by the arrow point.   The results will be similar to those shown in Table 9-1.

In the table we have recorded the result with only three significant digits, although with our idealized spinner we would, in theory, be able to read the result to any degree of accuracy that was desired.

Table 9-1 is very similar in form to that obtained in Chap. 1 when we threw a pair of dice 100 times (Table 1-1).   If we try to make a frequency distribution for the results with the spinner in the same way that we did with the results for the dice, we immediately run into trouble, however. With the dice, there were only 11 possible outcomes: 2, 3, 4, 5, 6, 7, 8, 9, 10, 11, 12.   With the spinner, there are, in theory, an infinite number of different possible outcomes. Even when the results are rounded off to three significant figures as in Table 9-1, there are still 1000 different possible outcomes: .000, .001, .002, . . . , .999. To make a frequency distribution with 1000 rows (one for each possible outcome) would certainly not be practical. A solution immediately suggests itself. To

Table 9-1
Results of 100 Spins
(X = number indicated by pointer)

Trial no. i	Result X_i	Trial no. i	Result X_i	Trial no. i	Result X_i	Trial no. i	Result X_i
1	.460	26	.732	51	.791	76	.989
2	.090	27	.586	52	.988	77	.251
3	.143	28	.569	53	.022	78	.356
4	.510	29	.546	54	.274	79	.780
5	.688	30	.286	55	.553	80	.075
6	.799	31	.564	56	.577	81	.305
7	.901	32	.777	57	.373	82	.398
8	.964	33	.929	58	.768	83	.922
9	.616	34	.841	59	.067	84	.644
10	.886	35	.609	60	.414	85	.604
11	.128	36	.589	61	.307	86	.620
12	.080	37	.534	62	.251	87	.496
13	.037	38	.152	63	.501	88	.773
14	.847	39	.655	64	.417	89	.036
15	.196	40	.472	65	.456	90	.662
16	.112	41	.289	66	.277	91	.991
17	.545	42	.363	67	.307	92	.636
18	.413	43	.022	68	.816	93	.490
19	.662	44	.661	69	.321	94	.598
20	.611	45	.706	70	.456	95	.311
21	.811	46	.448	71	.565	96	.448
22	.875	47	.861	72	.902	97	.632
23	.547	48	.960	73	.928	98	.793
24	.921	49	.803	74	.458	99	.756
25	.133	50	.166	75	.365	100	.889

condense the data of Table 9-1 we shall make a *grouped frequency distribution* as in Table 9-2.

In making this grouped frequency distribution we have chosen certain sets $A_1, A_2, \ldots, A_{10}$ which constitute a *partition* of the sample space S. That is, any two of the A_i's are disjoint and the union of all of them is S. In the case at hand, as in most grouped frequency distributions, the sets which constitute the partition are intervals all having the same length. The intent in Table 9-2 is that $A_1 = \{x: 0 \leqq x < .1\}$, $A_2 = \{x: .1 \leqq x < .2\}$, $A_3 = \{x: .2 \leqq x < .3\}$, etc. In the column headed $FR(A_i)$ we have entered the number of times that a result of the experiment was in A_i. [In other terminology, we could say that $FR(A_i)$ is the number of times the event A_i occurred in our 100 trials.] FR is the empirical frequency function for the subsets of S as introduced in Sec. 3-6.

Table 9-2
Grouped Frequency Distribution for the Results of 100 Spins (Table 9-1)

A_i	$FR(A_i)$	$RF(A_i)$	$CF(A_i)$	$RCF(A_i)$
.000–.099	8	.08	8	.08
.100–.199	7	.07	15	.15
.200–.299	6	.06	21	.21
.300–.399	10	.10	31	.31
.400–.499	12	.12	43	.43
.500–.599	14	.14	57	.57
.600–.699	13	.13	70	.70
.700–.799	10	.10	80	.80
.800–.899	9	.09	89	.89
.900–.999	11	.11	100	1.00
Totals.......	100	1.00		

In the construction of a grouped frequency distribution for a collection of empirical results, the choice of the partition of the sample space is quite arbitrary.   There are, however, some rules of thumb which should usually be followed to make the resulting frequency distribution of practical value.   If feasible, we should choose the partition so that the partitioning sets are intervals of equal length.   The number of partitioning sets should not be too small, for we then lose too much information.   In the extreme case of one partitioning set, for instance, we would have had for our spinner experiment A_1 designated by .000 to .999 and $FR(A_1) = 100$, which is far from illuminating.   On the other hand, there should not be too many partitioning sets, for then the table becomes bulky and hard to comprehend.   It seems that, in most cases, from 7 to 20 partitioning sets make a practical grouped distribution.   As we shall discover later, it is also desirable to choose the intervals so that their mid-points are convenient numbers to calculate with.

The notation used to designate the partitioning intervals in Table 9-2 needs a word of explanation.   In the table, the set $A_1 = \{x: 0 \leq x < .1\}$ was designated by ".000–.099."   Since the results had been rounded off to three places, .099 was the largest possible result in A_1 while .000 was the smallest possible result in A_1.   In general, we shall always attempt to designate an interval by stating the highest and lowest recorded results possible which would belong to that interval.   This is standard practice in the literature of the various fields in which statistics occur but is not always followed.

Moreover, we here adopt the convention that, when the intervals are designated as a_1-b_1, a_2-b_2, a_3-b_3, etc., the intervals intended are $\{x: a_1 \leqq x < a_2\}$, $\{x: a_2 \leqq x < a_3\}$, $\{x: a_3 \leqq x < a_4\}$, etc. That is, the first given number is taken as the left-end point of the interval and is included in the interval. For example, if the intervals are given as 100–109, 110–119, and 120–129 in a table, then the intended intervals are $\{x: 100 \leqq x < 110\}$, $\{x: 110 \leqq x < 120\}$, and $\{x: 120 \leqq x < 130\}$. This practice is not always followed by those who make up tables, but it is a convention that will help us avoid some confusion.

The column headed $RF(A_i)$ in Table 9-2 gives the relative frequency with which the result was in A_i. RF is the empirical relative frequency function for the subsets of S as introduced in Sec. 3-6.

In the column headed $CF(A_i)$ in Table 9-2, we find the cumulative frequency up to and including the interval A_i. In general, if A_1, A_2, A_3, ... , A_p are consecutive nonoverlapping intervals with A_1 the left-most interval, then $CF(A_i)$ is the number of times the result was in $A_1 \cup A_2 \cup A_2 \cup \cdots \cup A_i$. The $CF(A_i)$ column is easily obtained from the values of $FR(A_i)$, since

$$(9\text{-}1) \qquad \begin{aligned} CF(A_1) &= FR(A_1) \\ CF(A_i) &= CF(A_{i-1}) + FR(A_i) \end{aligned}$$

In the column headed $RCF(A_i)$ is found the empirical relative cumulative frequency for each A_i. In general,

$$(9\text{-}2) \qquad RCF(A_i) = \frac{CF(A_i)}{n}$$

where n is the number of trials.

Suppose that we now ask for the sample mean and the standard deviation of the 100 results found in Table 9-1. These we could compute from the definitions given in Secs. 4-1 and 5-2:

$$\bar{X} = \frac{\Sigma X_i}{n}$$

and
$$s = \sqrt{\frac{\Sigma (X_i - \bar{X})^2}{n}}$$

For the given data, there would be 100 terms in each sum and the actual evaluation of $\bar{X}$ and s would be quite tedious. Is it possible to compute $\bar{X}$ and s from the more concise Table 9-2? Strictly speaking, the answer is "no," since from the grouped frequency distribution we do not know the exact location of any of the results. It is possible, however, to get very good approximations to $\bar{X}$ and s from the grouped data. The standard procedure for doing this is to *assume for the purposes of computation that all the results in a given interval occurred at the mid-point of that interval.*

Since we expect the results in a given interval to occur in roughly equal numbers on both sides of the mid-point, the errors committed in making this assumption should come close to balancing each other. Once we make the above assumption, the data can be thought of as discrete data which can take on only the values at the mid-points of the interval. Then the methods of Sec. 5-3 can be used to compute $\bar{X}$ and s. If the data of Table 9-2 are treated in this manner, we obtain Table 9-3.

Table 9-3
Computation of the Mean and Standard Deviation
for the Data of Table 9-1

A_i	m_i	z_i	$FR(A_i)$	$z_iFR(A_i)$	$z_i^2FR(A_i)$
.000–.099	.050	−5	8	−40	200
.100–.199	.150	−4	7	−28	112
.200–.299	.250	−3	6	−18	54
.300–.399	.350	−2	10	−20	40
.400–.499	.450	−1	12	−12	12
.500–.599	.550	0	14	0	0
.600–.699	.650	1	13	13	13
.700–.799	.750	2	10	20	40
.800–.899	.850	3	9	27	81
.900–.999	.950	4	11	44	176
Totals...............		...	100	−14	728

$$\bar{X} = .550 + .1\left(\frac{-14}{100}\right) = .536 \qquad \text{by (5-25)}$$

$$s_Z = \sqrt{\frac{728 - 14^2/100}{100}} = 2.69 \qquad \text{by (5-12)}$$

$$s_X = (.1)(2.60) = .269 \qquad \text{by (5-26)}$$

It should be remembered that the values for $\bar{X}$ and s_X found in Table 9-3 are only approximations to the values that would be found if the sample mean and sample standard deviation were computed from the ungrouped data. For most purposes, however, the approximations are sufficiently close to the true values.

Notice that with the notation used to designate intervals in Table 9-3 the length of the interval can be obtained by taking the difference between any two consecutive numbers which designate the left-end points of intervals. (The length of the interval .100 to .199 is .200 − .100 = .1 and *not* .199 − .100 = .099.) The mid-point m_i of an interval A_i is obtained by adding half the interval length to the number at the left end of the interval.

In a grouped distribution in which the intervals are not of equal length, the above method can still be used to estimate the mean and standard deviation of the sample, except that the process of coding will break down and one must fall back on the methods of Secs. 4-2 and 5-2.

Having estimated the sample mean and sample standard deviation from grouped data, it is natural to ask if other statistics such as the sample range, sample median, and sample mode can also be so estimated. The range of the sample cannot be estimated with any precision from grouped data alone, but an interval can be found in which this range must lie. For example, the range for the data of Table 9-3 must be between .8 and 1.0. We cannot be more precise, since we do not know (from Table 9-3 by itself) the exact position of the results in the first and last intervals. The sample mode, if any, for the original values also cannot be obtained precisely from the grouped data. One can, however, sometimes give a modal class or a modal interval for the grouped data. In Table 9-3 the modal class is .500 to .599.

To estimate the sample median from grouped data, the placing of each result at the center of its interval (as we did in estimating the mean) does not seem very reasonable. Rather, it is more natural to assume that all the measurements in a given interval are "equally spread" throughout that interval. If we wish to estimate the median for the data of Table 9-1 from the information given in Table 9-2, we do so by first noting that there are 100 items. From Table 9-2 we see that, if the data in Table 9-1 were ranked, the fiftieth and fifty-first items would fall in the interval .500 to .599. Assuming that the 14 results in this interval are about evenly spread, we would expect half way between the fiftieth and fifty-first results to be approximately at

$$.500 + \frac{7.5}{14}\,(.1) = .554$$

since we must go $50.5 - 43 = 7.5$ "items" into this interval to reach the median. Thus, .554 would be our estimate for the sample median.

In the general case where there are n results in a grouped frequency distribution, we find the first interval (moving from small numbers to large) for which $CF(A_i) > n/2$. Call this interval A_k. Let d be the length of A_k. An estimate of the median is then given by

$$(9\text{-}3) \qquad a_k + \left[\frac{n+1}{2} - CF(A_{k-1})\right]\frac{d}{FR(A_k)}$$

where a_k is the value at the left-end point of A_k. The quantity in the brackets in (9-3) is the number remaining to be counted to reach the median after counting all the items in A_1 through A_{k-1}. If the results in A_k were equally spread through the interval, $d/FR(A_k)$ would be the space between items in that interval. In the grouped distribution, as we start counting from below to reach the "middle item," we go through all the lower classes A_1, A_2, . . . , and A_{k-1} and then must go

$$\frac{n+1}{2} - CF(A_{k-1})$$

items into A_k.   But if we assume equal spacing of the items in A_k, this should take us to the value

$$a_k + \left[\frac{n+1}{2} - CF(A_{k-1})\right]\frac{d}{FR(A_k)}$$

as given by (9-3).   The reader will perhaps notice the similarity between this method for estimating the median and the process of interpolation.

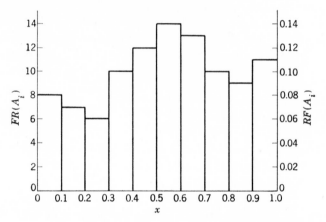

FIG. 9-2. Graph of the frequency and relative frequency distributions for Table 9-2.

In using this method we should remember that it yields only an estimate of the median of the ungrouped data.   If we wish to estimate a quartile or a percentile from a grouped distribution, it can be done in a similar manner.

We can graph grouped distributions for continuous variables in much the same way as we did the frequency distributions for discrete variables. The frequency and relative frequency distributions of Table 9-2 are graphed in Fig. 9-2.

The difference between the graph of a grouped frequency distribution and one which is ungrouped is that, in the former case, we construct a box over each interval, taking the height of the box to be the frequency (or relative frequency) associated with that interval.   For the ungrouped data, a single line of the proper length was constructed at each value which occurred as a result.   Strictly speaking, we are not thinking of Fig. 9-2 as the graph of a function of X but rather as the graph of a set function $FR(A_i)$ which assigns a certain frequency to each of the intervals

A_1, A_2, . . . , and A_{10}.   Thus, once the intervals are selected, we might think of the experiment as involving a discrete variable which "takes on the value" A_1 or A_2 or $\cdot$ $\cdot$ $\cdot$ or A_{10}, according as to where the arrow point stops.   Strictly doing this, however, we would not graph the frequency distribution as we did in Fig. 9-2.   Instead, we would simply construct a line whose length indicated the frequency at certain points marked A_1, A_2, . . . , and A_{10}.   The graph as given in Fig. 9-2 is more helpful than such a line graph would be.   It helps to emphasize the nature of the

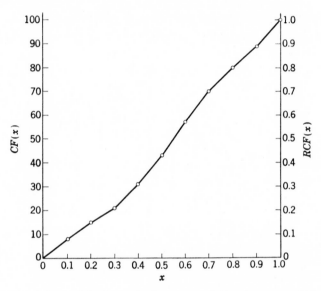

FIG. 9-3. Graph of the cumulative and relative cumulative frequency distributions for Table 9-2.

A_i intervals and gives (it is hoped) a clearer picture of the distribution. We should remember, however, that if we go to Fig. 9-2, find the point on the horizontal axis where $X = .25$, say, and then go up to the top of the rectangle over that point, we *do not* find the frequency with which the value .25 was taken on.

The graph of the cumulative frequency distributions of Table 9-2 is given in Fig. 9-3.   This graph gives an approximation to the actual cumulative frequency and relative cumulative frequency functions (for the sample of 100 values of X) that one would find by using the ungrouped data of Table 9-1.   The graph of the cumulative distributions for the ungrouped data of Table 9-1 would be a stair step similar to Fig. 1-2 but with many more steps.   The graph in Fig. 9-3 is constructed by plotting a point over the right-hand end of each interval at a height equal to the cumulative (or relative cumulative) frequency for that interval and then

connecting consecutive points with straight lines. The curve so constructed will then agree exactly at each interval end point with the stair-
step curve that is obtained from the ungrouped data. The construction
of straight lines between these points is similar to our making the assumption (as we did in estimating the median) that the results in a given
interval are equally spaced. In fact, the graph of a cumulative frequency
distribution can be used to obtain easily an estimate for the median. We
simply find the point on the vertical axis corresponding to a relative
frequency of .5 and go over on the horizontal to the curve and down to the
horizontal axis to find this estimate. From Fig. 9-3 we find the median
to be approximately .55, which agrees well with our previous computation
with these data.

In general, the graph of Fig. 9-3 can be used to obtain approximate
values for the cumulative distribution functions of the ungrouped
data of Table 9-1. For example, as estimates from the graph we get
$CF(.35) \cong 26$ and $RCF(.35) \cong .26$. Also if we wish to estimate quartiles
or percentiles from the grouped data, one of the easiest ways is to construct the graph of the relative cumulative frequency and use it to get
the estimate. Thus, from Fig. 9-3 we estimate the lower quartile and
the 65th percentile for the data of Table 9-1 to be $Q_1 = .33$ and
$P_{65} = .64$.

PROBLEMS

9-4. For each of the following sets of data construct grouped frequency, relative
frequency, cumulative frequency, and relative cumulative frequency distributions.
Find the mean, median, and standard deviation. Graph the distributions.

(*a*) The weights of students in your class.

(*b*) The weights of men students in your class.

(*c*) The weights of women students in your class.

(*d*) The heights of students in your class.

(*e*) The heights of male students in your class.

(*f*) The heights of female students in your class.

(*g*) The distance in miles from the home of each student in your class to school.

(*h*) One hundred consecutive three-digit numbers drawn from a table of random
digits where the three digits are taken to mean a number between 1 and 10 (so that,
for example, the digits 6, 7, 4 give the number 6.74).

(*i*) One hundred numbers obtained by taking the third and fourth digits in successive entries in a five-place table of logarithms and considering these digits as designating numbers between 1 and 100 (so that, for example, "01" designates 1 and "00"
designates 100).

(*j*) The results of 100 draws with replacement from the box of balls given in
Table 9-4. (The box contains 1000 balls and with each ball is associated a value.
To "draw a ball from the box," take a three-digit random number from a table of
random digits, then record the value associated with the ball having that number.
For example, with the random number 123 we get the result 14.)

(*k*) Have each student in the class draw *k* samples of size 10 from the box as described in part j, where $k \cong 100/S$ and S is the number of students in your class. Consider the distribution of the means of all the samples so obtained.

Table 9-4
A Box of 1000 Balls

Ball number	Value
1	4
2	5
3–4	6
5–7	7
8–11	8
12–18	9
19–29	10
30–45	11
46–67	12
68–97	13
98–136	14
137–184	15
185–242	16
243–308	17
309–381	18
382–460	19
461–540	20
541–619	21
620–692	22
693–758	23
759–816	24
817–864	25
865–903	26
904–933	27
934–955	28
956–971	29
972–982	30
983–989	31
990–993	32
994–996	33
997–998	34
999	35
1000	36

(l) The various mean values obtained by the students in your class in doing Prob. 1-3.

(m) The various mean values obtained by the students in your class in performing Prob. 1-4.

(n) The various mean values obtained by the students who performed Prob. 1-5.

9-5. From Fig. 9-2 estimate for the data of Table 9-1 the following percentiles: P_{15}, P_{55}, P_{97}.

9-2. Probability density functions

As in the preceding section, let X be the number indicated by the arrow point after a spin of the "perfectly balanced" spinner shown in Fig. 9-1.

The sample space for X is $S = \{x: 0 \leq x < 1\}$. With some intuitive notion of what "probability" should mean and of what "perfectly balanced" should mean, let us try to discover a "probability model" for the random variable X. Suppose that we make n spins and get the n results $X_1, X_2, \ldots, X_n$, where n is very large. About what proportion of these results would we expect to lie in $A = \{x: 0 \leq x < \frac{1}{2}\}$, i.e., on the right half of the circle? Intuitively, we would expect about half of them to do so, since, if the spinner is "perfectly balanced," we see no reason for the spinner to "prefer" the right-hand side to the left, or vice versa. Now, in our terminology, A is an event, and evidently, the "probability of A" should mean something like the relative frequency with which A occurs in a large number of trials. Then in a probability model for X we would hope to find $P(A) = \frac{1}{2}$. What probability should be associated with the event $B = \{x: 0 \leq x < \frac{1}{4}\}$? Reasoning as above, we should have $P(B) = \frac{1}{4}$. In fact, it appears that we should have $P\{x: 0 \leq x < a\} = a$ for $0 < a \leq 1$. It appears to be the case that the probabiilty associated with an interval should simply be the length of that interval. For example, it seems reasonable that $P\{x: .3 \leq x < .4\} = .1$, $P\{x: .2 \leq x < .9\} = .7$, etc. This appears to describe the situation quite well. But what about the probability that $X = .5$? Apparently the only reasonable thing to do is to have $P(X = .5) = 0$! This is so because we have $P(.499 < X < .501) = .02$, $P(.49999 < X < .50001) = .00002$,

$$P(.4999999 < X < .5000001) = .0000002, \ldots$$

and yet all these intervals contain the point $X = .5$. Thus we discover a striking fact about continuous variables: The probability of an event may be zero even though it is perfectly possible that the event may happen!

In the construction of a probability model for a discrete random variable a positive probability was assigned to each point in the sample space in such a way that the sum of all the probabilities was 1. This cannot be done in the continuous case above because it would seem that the only reasonable probability to associate with each point is zero! This is the typical situation for a continuous variable. We are forced, then, to take a new approach in constructing a model for the continuous case.

If we return to the consideration of a discrete variable and the graph of its probability function, we get a hint as to what this new approach might be. Consider the binomial variable Y with $n = 20$ and $p = .3$. In Fig. 9-4 we have graphed the probability distribution for Y. We have, however, modified the graph somewhat by constructing a box of width one unit centered at each possible value Y. The height of the box was in each case taken to be the probability associated with the value of y at the center of the base.   In terms of Fig. 9-4 we note that certain probabilities may be thought of as areas.   For example, $P(5 \leq Y < 10)$ is, as we know, the sum of the heights of the boxes centered at 5, 6, 7, 8, and 9, but since each box has a width of 1, this sum of heights is the same as the sum of the areas of the boxes.   Similarly, such probabilities as $P(0 \leq Y \leq 7)$ and $P(7 < Y \leq 15)$ may be thought of as sums of areas of certain of the boxes.   If, now, we think of the tops of the boxes as giving us the graph of a (stair-step) curve, it seems that the probability that Y fall in a

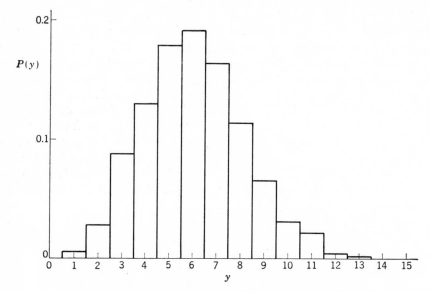

F<small>IG</small>. 9-4. Modified graph of the probability function for $B(20, .3)$.

certain interval is given roughly by the *area under this curve* which lies over the given interval.   It is this (approximate) property for discrete variables which we take as the keynote for construction of a probability model for a continuous variable.

If X again refers to the outcome of a spin for the spinner of Fig. 9-1, it is not difficult to find a "curve" which has the property that $P(a < X < b)$ is given by the area lying under that curve and over the interval from a to b.   Such a "curve" is shown in Fig. 9-5.

It is easy to check from the graph that the area under the curve which lies over the interval from 0 to .5 is $\frac{1}{2}$, as it should be, since we have determined that we should have $P(0 \leq X < .5) = \frac{1}{2}$.   Similarly, $P(0 \leq X < \frac{1}{4}) = \frac{1}{4} =$ the area under the curve which lies over the interval from 0 to $\frac{1}{4}$, and $P(0 \leq X < a) = a =$ the area under the curve which lies over the interval from 0 to a for $0 < a \leq 1$.   In fact, it seems that here the probability that X will fall in a certain interval is given exactly by the area which lies over the given interval and under the curve in Fig. 9-5.

The function whose graph is given in Fig. 9-5 can be defined by the following equations:

$$
(9\text{-}6) \qquad
\begin{aligned}
f(x) &= 0 & &\text{if } x < 0 \\
f(x) &= 1 & &\text{if } 0 \leq x \leq 1 \\
f(x) &= 0 & &\text{if } x > 1
\end{aligned}
$$

This function is called the *probability density function* for the random variable X generated by the spinner of Fig. 9-1.

In general, when X is a continuous random variable, we say that a function f is the *probability density function* for X if, for all a and b, $P(a < X < b)$ is given by the area that lies under the curve $y = f(x)$ and over the interval from a to b. We assume that the domain of a probability density function is the set of all real numbers. If the continuous variable has a sample space which is not the set of all reals, then we simply define the density function to be equal to zero at all points outside the sample space. This enables us always to treat the function as having a domain which is the entire real line. In the graph of such a function, if at a certain x value there is no point shown on the graph above the x axis, then we understand that the function is to be taken as equal to zero there. The area "under" a curve which lies along the x axis in an interval is, of course, zero over that interval.

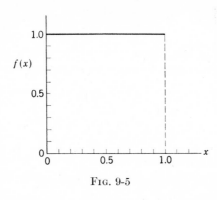

Fig. 9-5

For brevity, we sometimes speak of a probability density function as simply a *density function*.

Since we shall so often be speaking of areas under curves, we now introduce an abbreviation.

$$
(9\text{-}7) \qquad \int_a^b f(x)\, dx
$$

will stand for the area which lies under the curve $y = f(x)$ and over the interval from a to b. We read "$\int_a^b f(x)\, dx$" as "the area under (fx) from a to b," as "the *definite integral* from a to b of $f(x)$," or (more simply) as "the *integral* from a to b of $f(x)$." The sign $\int$ which occurs in (9-7) is called the *integral sign*, and a and b are called the *lower* and *upper limits* of the integral, respectively. The notion of the definite integral is a fundamental one in calculus. We have not given a rigorous definition of it here and simply rely on our intuitive understanding of area to give it meaning. We shall use the notation only when f is a nonnegative function so that the problem of areas below the x axis will not arise. We also shall write "$\int_a^b f(x)\, dx$" only in the case that a is not larger than b so that the area intended will be over the interval running from a to b with a not to the right of b. From our grasp of the meaning of "area" we see that the following hold:

$$(9\text{-}8) \qquad\qquad \int_a^a f(x)\, dx = 0$$

$$(9\text{-}9) \qquad \int_a^b f(x)\, dx + \int_b^c f(x)\, dx = \int_a^c f(x)\, dx \qquad \textit{if } a \leq b \leq c$$

In using the above integral notation, we shall also allow infinite intervals. We shall write "$\int_{-\infty}^a f(x)\, dx$" for the area which is under the curve $y = f(x)$ and over the interval $\{x: x \leq a\}$. "$\int_{-\infty}^a b(x)$" is read as "the integral from minus infinity to a of $f(x)$." Similarly, $\int_b^\infty f(x)\, dx$ stands for the area under the curve $y = f(x)$ and over the interval $\{x: x \geq b\}$. "$\int_b^\infty f(x)\, dx$" is read as "the integral from b to infinity of $f(x)$." Also $\int_{-\infty}^\infty f(x)\, dx$ stands for the total area between the curve $y = f(x)$ and the x axis. "$\int_{-\infty}^\infty f(x)$" is read as "the integral from minus infinity to infinity of $f(x)$." For example, for $f(x)$ as given by (9-6) and graphed in Fig. 9-5 we have

$$\int_{-\infty}^{1/4} f(x)\, dx = \tfrac14 \qquad \int_{1/4}^\infty f(x)\, dx = \tfrac34 \qquad \text{and} \qquad \int_{-\infty}^\infty f(x)\, dx = 1$$

For another example, consider the function

$$(9\text{-}10) \qquad\qquad \begin{aligned} g(x) &= 0 & \text{if } x < 0 \\ g(x) &= x & \text{if } x \geq 0 \end{aligned}$$

The graph of g is shown in Fig. 9-6. Here we have

$$\int_0^1 g(x)\, dx = \tfrac12 \qquad \int_1^2 g(x)\, dx = \tfrac32$$

$$\int_{-\infty}^0 g(x)\, dx = 0 \qquad \int_{-\infty}^2 g(x)\, dx = 2$$

However,

$$\int_0^\infty g(x)\, dx \qquad \text{and} \qquad \int_{-\infty}^\infty g(x)\, dx$$

are undefined, since there is no well-defined area (or else an "infinite area") over these intervals.

If X is a continuous random variable with probability density function $f(x)$, what properties must $f(x)$ have? By *definition*, we must have

(9-11) $$\int_a^b f(x)\, dx = P(a < X < b)$$

We also insist that

(9-12) $$f(x) \geq 0 \qquad \text{for all } x$$

and since the probability that X must be somewhere on the x axis is 1, we must have

(9-13) $$\int_{-\infty}^\infty f(x)\, dx = 1$$

Thus, a probability density function must be nonnegative and the total area under its graph must be 1.

Conversely, any function which satisfies (9-12) and (9-13) can be taken as a probability density function for some random variable. Given such a function, we get probabilities for X from (9-11). We shall see in Sec. 9-4 how to construct a "spinner" which will "generate" a random variable with a given density function.

For some simple probability density functions, inspection of the graph and some elementary geometry enable us to find areas over intervals (and hence probabilities). But for most of the probability density functions with which we shall deal, there is no easy way to compute these areas even if the tools of calculus are available to us. In this latter case,

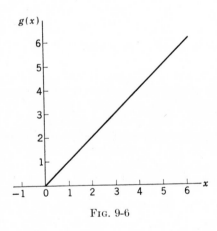

Fig. 9-6

we make use of tables which have been calculated to give us the desired areas. The various probability density functions most often encountered in statistics will be discussed in subsequent chapters.

We have, then, come to one possible answer as to how to specify a probability model for a continuous random variable. Given an experiment whose outcome can be thought of as a continuous random variable, we can specify a model for the random variable by giving a probability density function for that variable.   For an idealized experiment such as the use of our "perfectly balanced" spinner of Fig. 9-1 we are led to a specific probability density function as the suitable one.   In a "real" experimental situation the question will often be, "Which probability density function(s) seem most suitable in the face of the empirical data on hand?"

Specification of a probability density function for a random variable is essentially a means of giving the probabilities which will be associated with intervals on the real line.   In the case of a discrete variable a probability model was obtained by assigning a probability to each point in the sample space.   In the continuous case, probabilities are assigned to intervals on the real line by means of a probability density function— areas under the graph of the function being taken as probabilities.

If an event A is made up of several disjoint intervals so that

$$A = B_1 \cup B_2 \cup \cdots \cup B_k$$

then the probability that we associate with A is the sum of the probabilities for the B's.   Given a density function, the probabilities to which it gives rise have the properties that we discovered for the discrete case in Sec. 6-2.   That is, if S is the sample space for a variable X and A and B are events, then the following hold:

(9-14) $P(S) = 1$

(9-15)   If $A \cap B = \phi$, then $P(A \cup B) = P(A) + P(B)$.

(9-16) $P(A') = 1 - P(A)$

(9-17) $P(A \cup B) = P(A) + P(B) - P(A \cap B)$

These results are easy to see in terms of areas if A and B are intervals.

If $P(A) \neq 0$, we define the conditional probability for B, given A, by

(9-18) $$P(B|A) = \frac{P(A \cap B)}{P(A)}$$

In general, when X is a continuous variable, $P(X = a) = 0$ for all a. This means that, whether or not we include an end point of an interval, it makes no difference for the probabilities.   In terms of equations, we have, when X is continuous,

(9-19) $P(a < X < b) = P(a \leq X < b)$
$$= P(a < X \leq b) = P(a \leq X \leq b)$$

PROBLEMS

9-20. For $g(x)$ as given by (9-10) find

$$\int_0^{1/4} g(x)\, dx \qquad \int_{-\infty}^{1/4} g(x)\, dx \qquad \int_0^5 g(x)\, dx \qquad \int_0^{50} g(x)\, dx \qquad \int_5^6 g(x)\, dx$$

9-21. Which of the functions graphed in Fig. 9-7 could be taken as probability density functions.

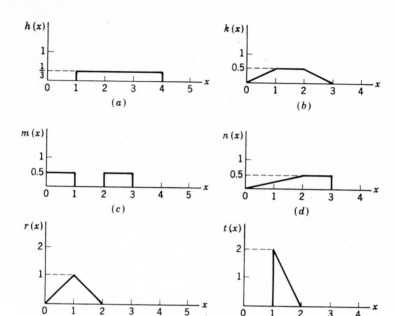

FIG. 9-7

9-22. Referring to the functions whose graphs are given in Fig. 9-7, find

(a) $\int_0^3 h(x)\, dx$ (b) $\int_2^{2.5} h(x)\, dx$ (c) $\int_3^{\infty} h(x)\, dx$

(d) $\int_0^1 k(x)\, dx$ (e) $\int_{1.5}^{2.5} k(x)\, dx$ (f) $\int_{.5}^{2.5} k(x)\, dx$

(g) $\int_{-\infty}^0 m(x)\, dx$ (h) $\int_1^2 m(x)\, dx$ (i) $\int_{.5}^{2.5} m(x)\, dx$

(j) $\int_1^2 n(x)\, dx$ (k) $\int_2^3 n(x)\, dx$ (l) $\int_{.1}^3 n(x)\, dx$

(m) $\int_0^1 r(x)\, dx$ (n) $\int_1^2 r(x)\, dx$ (o) $\int_{1.9}^{\infty} r(x)\, dx$

(p) $\int_0^1 t(x)\, dx$ (q) $\int_1^{1.5} t(x)\, dx$ (r) $\int_{1.3}^{1.4} t(x)\, dx$

9-23. For each of the functions shown in Fig. 9-7 which can be taken as probability density functions for a random variable, say X, interpret the areas of Prob. 9-22 as probabilities for X.

9-24. In the graph shown in Fig. 9-8 the total area under the curve is to be taken as one unit. Thus the function whose graph is shown can be taken as a probability density function for some random variable, say X. From the graph estimate the following roughly:

(a) $P(X < 1)$ (b) $P(1 < X < 4)$ (c) $P(X > 4)$ (d) $P(X > 2.5)$

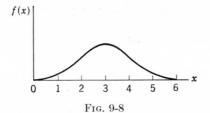

FIG. 9-8

9-25. In Fig. 9-9 assume that the given curve is the graph of the probability density function for a random variable X. Estimate the following roughly from the graph:

(a) $P(X < 10)$ (b) $P(X > 30)$ (c) $P(-10 < X < 10)$

(d) $P(0 < X < 20)$ (e) $P(X > 40)$

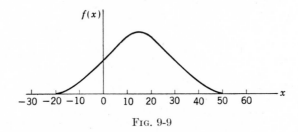

FIG. 9-9

9-26. In terms of areas it is not obvious that

$$\int_a^b [f(x) + g(x)]\, dx = \int_a^b f(x)\, dx + \int_a^b g(x)\, dx$$

Nevertheless, this is so for all functions f and g. Verify this for various a's and b's with f as given by (9-6) and g as given by (9-10).

***9-27.** To illustrate the fact that we have glossed over some logical difficulties in interpreting probabilities as areas for a continuous variable, let X be the result of a spin in Fig. 9-1 and consider the problem of finding the probabilities for the following "events":

(a) $\{X: X \text{ is a rational}^1 \text{ number}\}$

(b) $\{X: \text{in the decimal representation for } X \text{ the digit 3 does not occur}\}$

(c) $\{X: \text{the digits in the decimal representation of } X \text{ are all "even"; i.e., only the digits 0, 2, 4, 6, 8 occur}\}$

9-28. Argue for (9-16) and (9-17) when A and B are intervals.

9-29. Suppose that X has the density function

$$\begin{aligned} f(x) &= 0 && \text{if } x < 0 \text{ or } x > 2 \\ f(x) &= x && \text{if } 0 \leq x \leq 1 \\ f(x) &= \tfrac{1}{2} && \text{if } 1 < x \leq 2 \end{aligned}$$

Find

(a) $P(X < 0)$ (b) $P(X < 1)$

(c) $P(X > 1)$ (d) $P(\tfrac{1}{2} < X < \tfrac{3}{2})$

[1] A number is said to be rational if it can be written as the ratio of two whole numbers.

*9-30. If X has the density function given in Prob. 9-29, graph the function F defined by $F(x) = P(X \leq x)$.

9-31. If X has the density function f, where

$$
\begin{aligned}
f(x) &= 0 && \text{for } x < 0 \text{ or } x > 3 \\
f(x) &= x && \text{for } 0 \leq x \leq \tfrac{1}{2} \\
f(x) &= k && \text{for } \tfrac{1}{2} < x \leq 3
\end{aligned}
$$

and

determine the constant k.

9-32. If X has the density function f, where

$$
\begin{aligned}
f(x) &= 0 && \text{if } x < -1 \text{ or } x > 1 \\
f(x) &= k && \text{for } -1 \leq x \leq 1
\end{aligned}
$$

and

determine the constant k.

9-33. If X has the density function f, where

$$
\begin{aligned}
f(x) &= 0 && \text{for } x < -1 \text{ or } x > 1 \\
f(x) &= kx && \text{for } 0 \leq x \leq 1 \\
f(x) &= -kx && \text{for } -1 \leq x < 0
\end{aligned}
$$

and

determine the constant k.

9-34. In Prob. 9-31 find $P(X < 0)$, $P(X < \tfrac{1}{2})$, $P(X \leq \tfrac{1}{2})$.

9-35. In Prob. 9-33 find $P(-\tfrac{1}{2} < X < \tfrac{1}{2})$.

*9-36. If X has the density function given in Prob. 9-33, graph the function F defined by $F(x) = P(X \leq x)$.

9-37. The graph of the density function for a random variable is a semicircle with center at the origin. Determine the radius.

9-38. Argue in terms of areas for the fact that, if $f(x) \leq M$ for $a \leq x \leq b$, then $\int_a^b f(x)\,dx \leq M(b - a)$.

9-39. Show that, if $f(x) \geq g(x)$ for $a < x < b$, then

$$
\int_a^b f(x)\,dx \geq \int_a^b g(x)\,dx
$$

(Include the possibility that $a = -\infty$ or $b = \infty$.)

9-40. If $a > 0$ and $f(x) \geq 0$ for all x, show that

$$
\int_a^\infty x^2 f(x)\,dx \geq a^2 \int_a^\infty f(x)\,dx
$$

and

$$
\int_{-\infty}^{-a} x^2 f(x)\,dx \geq a^2 \int_{-\infty}^{-a} f(x)\,dx
$$

9-41. (a) Argue for the fact that, if $f(x) \geq 0$ for all x and $a > 0$, then

$$
\int_{-\infty}^{\infty} f(x)\,dx \geq \int_{-\infty}^{-a} f(x)\,dx + \int_a^{\infty} f(x)\,dx
$$

(b) Verify by carrying through at least two examples that, if C is a constant, then

$$
\int_a^b Cf(x)\,dx = C \int_a^b f(x)\,dx
$$

9-3. Properties of continuous probability distributions

A querulous gent from Fleet Street
Said, "What if it isn't discrete?"
A real estate man
Proposed a good plan.
With areas all is quite neat.[1]

Suppose that a continuous random variable X has a probability density function f.   Then for any real numbers a and b we have

$$P(a < X < b) = \int_a^b f(x)\, dx$$
$$= \text{the area which lies over the interval from } a \text{ to } b$$

and under the graph of $y = f(x)$.   Suppose that the graph of $y = f(x)$ is as shown in Fig. 9-10.   Let x_0 be a fixed number, and suppose that we ask

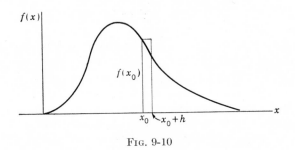

FIG. 9-10

for $P(x_0 < X < x_0 + h)$, where h is very small.   This probability is given by

$$\int_{x_0}^{x_0 + h} f(x)\, dx$$

that is, the area over the interval from x_0 to $x_0 + h$.   But since h is small, $f(x)$ does not change very much in this interval.   Then the desired area is approximately the same as the area of the rectangle with width h and height $f(x_0)$.   That is, $P(x_0 < X < x_0 + h) \cong f(x_0)h$.   It is because of this that f is called the probability density function.   Its values play a role something like "the probability per unit length" for small intervals. Putting it another way, we may think of probabilities as long-run relative frequencies and say that $f(x_0)$ is approximately the proportion of all the outcomes per unit length that we expect to find (in the long run) in a very small interval about x_0.

A physical analogy may be given as follows: Suppose that a long thin rod of uniform cross section has a density which changes as one moves along

[1] But see Prob. 9-27.

the rod. Let x be the distance measured from one end of the rod, and let d be a function with the property that $d(x_0)$ is the linear density of the rod (say in pounds per foot of length) at the distance x_0 from the end. Then the weight of the piece of rod between x_0 and $x_0 + h$ is given approximately by $d(x_0)h$, when h is small. This is so because, if h is small, in the piece from x_0 to $x_0 + h$ the density will not vary much from $d(x_0)$. A high value of d at x_0 means that the weight in a small interval about x_0 will be relatively high. Similarly, if f is a probability density function, a high value of f at x_0 means that the probability that X will fall in a small interval about x_0 is relatively high. Just as the values of the density function d for the rod are not weights, so the values of a probability density function f are not probabilities. Yet where d is large, the rod will be heavy per unit length, and where f is large, the probability will be high per unit length.

We now "explain" the strange appearance of the notation

$$``\int_a^b f(x)\ dx"$$

From whence the "dx"? Mathematicians use "dx" to stand for a small change or a small increment in x. Then $f(x)\ dx$ is approximately the area under the graph of f and over the interval from x to $x + dx$. If we break up the interval from a to b into many small pieces of length dx and consider the sum of all the resulting products $f(x)\ dx$, we find that this sum should be approximately the same as the area under f over the interval from a to b. In fact, as we take the dx's smaller and smaller, this sum must approach the desired area. The integral sign—an elongated S—suggests this summation process acting on terms in the form $f(x)\ dx$. Actually, there is much to be said for using the notation

$$``\int_a^b f"$$

where we have used $\qquad ``\int_a^b f(x)\ dx"$

and some careful modern mathematics texts use the former notation. The notation that we have chosen to use is the more common one, however.

To tie together the notion of a probability density function and the graph of an empirical grouped relative frequency distribution for a large number of trials, let $X_1, X_2, \ldots, X_n$ be the results of n trials of a random variable X with probability density function f. Let $A_1, A_2, \ldots, A_k$ be k intervals all with the same length h used in constructing a grouped relative frequency distribution for these empirical data. If n is very large, then we can take k very large (which we would not wish to do for a "practical" grouped distribution) and, hence, make h very small. With

n large, the relative frequency for A_i, $RF(A_i)$, should be approximately the probability $P(X \in A_i)$.   Then if $A_i = \{x : a_i \leqq x < a_{i+1}\}$, we have

$$RF(A_i) \cong \int_{a_i}^{a_{i+1}} f(x)\ dx \cong f(a_i)h$$

since $h = a_{i+1} - a_i$ and h is small.   Then

$$\frac{RF(A_i)}{h} \cong f(a_i)$$

Hence, we see that the value of the probability density function is approximately the relative frequency per unit length when n is large.   This agrees with the interpretation given earlier.

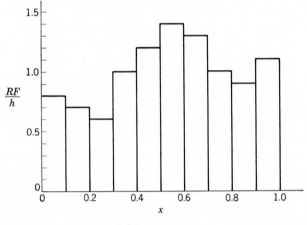

Fɪɢ. 9-11

Given a grouped (empirical) distribution for a large number of trials, we can use the graph of the grouped relative frequency distribution to estimate the graph of the underlying probability density function.   This is done by dividing the relative frequency for each interval by the length of that interval and using this result, instead of the relative frequency, as the height of the box.   When all the intervals have equal length, this amounts to a change of scale on the vertical axis, so that the total area of all the boxes is 1.

If, for instance, we take the graph of Fig. 9-1, divide the relative frequency for each interval by .1 (the interval length), and use the results as new heights, we get the graph of Fig. 9-11.   The graph is not very close to the one with a straight line across at the height of 1, which is the graph of probability density function (Fig. 9-5).   But if our spinner is "perfectly balanced," we would expect this kind of graph to look more and more like that of the probability density function as we take more and more trials.   The reader can check for himself that the total area of the boxes in Fig. 9-11 is 1.

The empirical relative cumulative frequency distribution has a direct theoretical counterpart.   If X has probability density function f, then

$$P(X \leq a) = \int_{-\infty}^{a} f(x) \, dx$$

and this last can be thought of as function of a.   In general, if X is a continuous random variable and a function $F(x)$ has the property that

(9-42) $$F(x) = P(X \leq x)$$

then we call F the *probability distribution function for X*.   We shall also often speak more briefly and call such an F simply the *distribution function* for X.   A distribution function plays the same role for a continuous variable as a cumulative probability function does for a discrete variable.

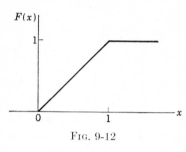

FIG. 9-12

A probability model for a continuous random variable may be given by a distribution function instead of by a probability density function.   In the experiment with the spinner in Fig. 9-1, we found that $P(X \leq x) = x$ for $0 \leq x \leq 1$. It is also easy to see that in this case $P(X \leq x) = 0$ for $x < 0$ and $P(X \leq x) = 1$ for $x > 1$.   Thus, the distribution function for this variable is

(9-43)
$$F(x) = 0 \qquad \text{if } x < 0$$
$$F(x) = x \qquad \text{if } 0 \leq x \leq 1$$
$$F(x) = 1 \qquad \text{if } x > 1$$

The graph of this function is shown in Fig. 9-12.

If we have an empirical grouped distribution with a large number of trials, we expect the graph of the relative cumulative frequency function to approximate that of the distribution function.   (In the general case we shall need also a large number of classes, so that the straight-line segments used in graphing the empirical distribution are very short and together they can approximate a smooth curve.)   Thus the graph of the empirical data in Fig. 9-3 approximates the graph in Fig. 9-12.

The intimate relationship between a distribution function F and its corresponding probability density function f is given by

(9-44) $$F(b) - F(a) = \int_{a}^{b} f(x) \, dx$$

This important relationship will be used many times in our subsequent endeavors because most of the tables for probability distributions give values for F.   In terms of area, $F(b)$ is the area under $y = f(x)$ and over the interval $\{x: x \leq b\}$. $F(a)$ is the area over $\{x: x \leq a\}$.   Then $F(b) - F(a)$ is the area which lies under $y = f(x)$ between a and b, as (9-44) asserts.

The notation that we have used for distribution functions and probability density functions is standard.   Lower-case letters are used to designate probability density functions, and the corresponding capital letters are used to designate the corresponding distribution functions. If, for example, g is a probability density function, then G is its distribution function.

In view of the discussion above and in the preceding section, it can now be said that there are six useful ways to "give the probability distribution" for a continuous random variable:

1. Give an explicit formula for the probability density function.

2. Give a graph of the probability density function.

3. Give an explicit formula for the probability distribution function.

4. Give a graph of the probability distribution function.

5. Give values for the probability distribution function in the form of a table.

6. Give a picture of a spinner (or perhaps the spinner itself) whose scale is designed so that the random variable can be thought of as gaining its value as a result of a spin.

For the purposes of a mathematical statistician, methods 1 and 3 are indispensable.   For our purposes, however, it is seldom helpful to concern ourselves with explicit functional representations.   For getting some "feel" for a distribution or making rough calculations, methods 2, 4, and 6 are very useful.   In more precise calculations, method 5 is the one most useful to us (and to all those who "apply" statistics).   As we proceed to discuss various kinds of distributions, we shall first attempt to get some intuitive understanding of each distribution in terms of a spinner and graphs, then consider the use of tables to compute probabilities, and sometimes (and then incidentally) mention explicit functional representations.

Before discussing various families of distributions and their applications, however, we must consider some aspects common to all distributions.   We would expect a probability distribution for a continuous random variable to have a mean and standard deviation and perhaps other properties similar to those for discrete distributions.   The definitions needed for the continuous case follow.

The *mean* of a continuous probability distribution is the value corresponding to the point on the horizontal axis at which the area under the graph of the probability density function can be supported on a knife-edge and be in balance.   In other words, the mean is the x coordinate of the center of gravity of the area under the graph of the probability density function.   (Here we are thinking of the area as being cut out of some thin homogeneous material.)   This is in direct analogue with the physical interpretation of the mean of a discrete distribution.   Since the graph of the probability density function is (with a scale adjustment on the vertical axis) given approximately by the graph of the empirical grouped relative frequency distribution when the number of trials is large, we can also think of the mean of the probability distribution as being the "long-run" mean of the empirical distribution.   We shall use "μ" (as we did for the discrete case) to designate the mean.   As before, we say that μ is a *parameter* of the distribution.   That is, it is a numerical property of the probability distribution (as opposed to a numerical property of an empirical distribution which could be called a statistic). The mean of a random variable is also called its *expected value*, and the previously introduced notation is used, so that $E(X) = \mu_X$.

A more formal definition of the mean need not actually concern us here, but it is included for the sake of completeness:

$$(9\text{-}45) \qquad\qquad \mu = \int_{-\infty}^{\infty} x f(x)\, dx$$

The other measures of central tendency for a continuous distribution are defined in the manner that one would expect. x_0 is called a *median* of the distribution if

$$(9\text{-}46) \qquad\qquad F(x_0) = .5$$

There may be several (in fact, infinitely many) medians for a continuous distribution.   A median is most easily obtained from the graph of $F(x)$. The *mode* for a continuous distribution is a number x_m such that

$$(9\text{-}47) \qquad\qquad f(x_m) = \max f(x)$$

if one and only one such number exists.   The mode is the x value corresponding to the highest point on the curve $y = f(x)$ if there is a single such x.   The mode is the point where the probability density is highest.

If X is the outcome of a spin for Fig. 9-1, the distribution for X (Fig. 9-5) has $\mu = .5$, a median of .5, and no mode.

The mean, median, or mode for a distribution for a random variable is also referred to as the mean, median, or mode, respectively, of the random variable.   If more than one random variable is involved in a discussion, we shall use subscripts to distinguish among the means.   Thus, μ_X will be the mean of X and μ_Y will be the mean of Y.

As measures of dispersion, we shall introduce the range, the variance, and the standard deviation. The *range* of a distribution is given by

(9-48) $\max \{x: f(x) > 0\} - \min \{x: f(x) > 0\}$

[This formulation is not completely correct, since the sets involved may be infinite. To be correct, we would interpret $\max \{x: f(x) > 0\}$ as being the smallest number x_1 such that, if $f(x_2) > 0$, then $x_2 \leq x_1$, and similarly for $\min \{x: f(x) > 0\}$. See Prob. 3-84.] There will be no range for a continuous distribution if f is positive over an infinite interval. The range of the distribution for Fig. 9-5 is 1.

The *variance* of a continuous distribution is defined to be the moment of inertia of the area under the probability density function, this moment being taken about the vertical line through the mean μ. The variance can also be thought of as the long-run sample variance, that is, as the value approached by the variance of the empirical distribution as more and more trials are made. We shall use "σ^2" to refer to the variance, attaching subscripts as needed. The *standard deviation* is defined to be the positive square root of the variance and is denoted by "σ." The formal definition for the variance is

(9-49) $$\sigma^2 = \int_{-\infty}^{\infty} (x - \mu)^2 f(x) \, dx$$

Once these notions are defined, it follows that most of the results for the discrete case carry over to the continuous case. If X and Y are continuous random variables, then

(9-50) $\mu_{aX+b} = a\mu_X + b$
(9-51) $\sigma_{aX+b} = a\sigma_X \quad (a > 0)$
(9-52) $\mu_{X+Y} = \mu_X + \mu_Y$
(9-53) $\mu_{X-Y} = \mu_X - \mu_Y$

(9-54)   *If X and Y are independent, then*

$$\sigma_{X+Y}^2 = \sigma_X^2 + \sigma_Y^2 \text{ and } \sigma_{X-Y}^2 = \sigma_X^2 + \sigma_Y^2$$

(9-55)   *If X is a continuous random variable, then the probability that X will be within k standard deviations of its mean is at least as large as $1 - 1/k^2$.*

A sequence of results $X_1, X_2, \ldots, X_n$ for a random variable X is called a *random sample* of size n for X if X_i and X_j are independent for all values of i and j with $i \neq j$. If $\bar{X}$ is the mean of a random sample, then

(9-56) $\mu_{\bar{X}} = \mu_X$

and

(9-57) $$\sigma_{\bar{X}} = \frac{\sigma_X}{\sqrt{n}}$$

These last two results follow from (9-50), (9-51), (9-52), and (9-54) just as in the discrete case.   The results (9-55), (9-56), and (9-57) yield

(9-58)   (Law of large numbers.)   *If $\bar{X}$ is the mean of a random sample of size n, then for any positive number e*

$$P(|\bar{X} - \mu_X| < e) \geqq 1 - \frac{\sigma_X^2}{e^2 n}$$

Hence, the probability that $\bar{X}$ will be within e of μ_X can be made arbitrarily close to 1 by taking n large enough.

We have not given a formal definition of what it means for two continuous variables to be independent and shall not at this stage.   We rely now on the intuitive notion that "independence" means that the outcome for one variable does not affect the probabilities for the other.

When it comes to applications connected with continuous variables, we carry over bodily the notions introduced for the discrete case.   A numerical property of a distribution (such as a distribution mean, median, or variance) is called a *parameter* of the distribution.   If $\hat{\theta}$ is a statistic (i.e., a numerical property of a sample), we call $\hat{\theta}$ an *unbiased* estimate for a parameter θ if $E(\hat{\theta}) = \theta$.   If $\hat{\theta}_1$ and $\hat{\theta}_2$ are two estimates, we say that $\hat{\theta}_1$ is more efficient than $\hat{\theta}_2$ if $\sigma_{\hat{\theta}_1}^2 < \sigma_{\hat{\theta}_2}^2$.   If $f(x,\theta)$ is a density function for X which depends on the unknown parameter θ, and if x_0 is an observed value of X, then $\hat{\theta}$ is called a *maximum likelihood estimate* for θ if $f(x_0,\hat{\theta}) = \max \{f(x_0,\theta) : \theta \in A\}$, where A is the collection of all possible values of θ.

If we are testing $H_0: \theta = \theta_0$ against $H_1: \theta = \theta_1$, then the *size of the error of type* I (or, alternatively, the *significance level of the test*) is the probability of rejecting H_0 when H_0 is true.   The *size of the error of type* II is the probability of accepting H_0 when H_1 is true.   The collection of those values of the random variable which cause us to reject the null hypothesis is called the *critical region* for a test.   If a test has critical region CR for the hypotheses $H_0: \theta = \theta_0$ and $H_1: \theta \in A$, then the function

$$pf(y) = P(X \in CR | \theta = y)$$

is called the *power function* for the test.   For $y \in A$ the value $pf(y)$ is called the *power* of the test for $\theta = y$. $1 - pf(y)$ is then the size of the error of type II when the given test is used for deciding between $H_0: \theta = \theta_0$ and $H_1': \theta = y$.   A test is *uniformly most powerful* if for each $y \in A$ its power is at least as large as is the power of any other test for the alternative $\theta = y$.

A random set $S(X)$ which is constructed on the basis of the observed value of the random variable X is called a $1 - \alpha$ *confidence set* for a parameter θ if $P(\theta \in S(X)) = 1 - \alpha$.   If $S(X)$ is an interval which is a

$1 - \alpha$ confidence set for θ, we call $S(X)$ a $1 - \alpha$ *confidence interval* for θ, and if X_0 is an observed value for X, we say that $\theta \in S(X_0)$ with confidence of $1 - \alpha$.

PROBLEMS

9-59. Graph the probability distribution function for the density function given in Fig. 9-7 as (*a*) h, (*b*) m, (*c*) r.

9-60. Estimate the mean, median, mode (if any), and range for the distributions given in Fig. 9-7.

9-61. Which of the distributions in Fig. 9-7 has the largest standard deviation? Which has the smallest? Rank all of them according to the size of their standard deviations.

9-62. Sketch a rough graph of a density function for which

(*a*) The median would be to the right of the mean.

(*b*) The median, mode, and mean all coincide.

(*c*) The mode is to the right of the mean.

9-63. Under what conditions will the median and mean of a distribution coincide?

*9-64. Conjecture a geometric relationship between the graph of a distribution function and its density function by inspecting $y = m(x)$ in Fig. 9-7 and the slope of portions of the graph of its distribution function.

*9-65. For $f(x)$ as given in Fig. 9-5, verify that $\mu = .5$ by graphing $xf(x)$ and evaluating

$$\int_{-\infty}^{\infty} xf(x)\, dx$$

*9-66. Do Prob. 9-65 for the density function $h(x)$ as given in Fig. 9-7 and $\mu = 2.5$.

*9-67. Do Prob. 9-65 for the density function $m(x)$ as given in Fig. 9-7 and $\mu = 1.5$.

9-68. If X is the outcome of a spin in Fig. 9-1 and $A = \{x: .3 < x < .5\}$, $B = \{x: .4 < x < .7\}$, find

(*a*) $P(A \cup B)$ (*b*) $P(A \cap B)$ (*c*) $P(A|B)$ (*d*) $P(B|A)$

9-69. In many mathematics and engineering tables it is possible to find formulas for the moments of inertia of various plane figures. Using such a table, find the variance and standard deviation for the distributions given in

(*a*) Fig. 9-7*a*   (*b*) Fig. 9-7*e*   *(c*) Fig. 9-7*f*
(*d*) Prob. 9-32   (*e*) Prob. 9-33   (*f*) Prob. 9-37

9-70. Derive (9-58) from (9-55), (9-56), and (9-57).

9-71. Derive (9-56) and (9-57) from (9-50) through (9-54).

*9-72. Prove (9-55) for the special case where $\mu = 0$. [See Probs. 9-40 and 9-41 and Eq. (9-49), and apply the method of Prob. 5-36.]

9-4. Rectangular distributions

The spinners shown in Fig. 9-13 all correspond to distributions which are called rectangular.

With the spinner in Fig. 9-13*a* we generate a random variable, say Y, which gains its values by spinning the arrow and noting where the point stops. Evidently the sample space Y is $\{y: 0 \leq y < 100\}$. Similarly, if Z and W are the random variables generated by the spinners in Fig. 9-13*b* and *c*, respectively, then the sample space for Z is $\{z: 6 \leq z < 9\}$

and that for W is $\{w: -2 \leq w < 2\}$.   The scales on all three of these spinners are uniform.   That is, the length of an interval (or, more precisely, an arc) on the scale is proportional to the difference between the values found at the ends of the interval.   [The reader who has inspected a slide rule is familiar with nonuniform scales.   The C and D scales on a

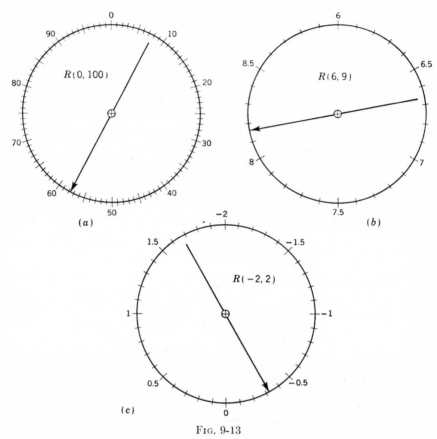

Fig. 9-13

slide rule are not uniform, while the L (log) scale is uniform.]   The situation is very similar to that with the spinner in Fig. 9-1.   It is not difficult to see that the probability density functions for Y, Z, and W, which we shall denote by f_Y, f_Z, and f_W, are given by the graphs in Fig. 9-14.   In these graphs we have used different scales on the vertical and horizontal axes so that the graphs will be legible.   This is a common practice that we shall follow, and the reader must be warned that reading areas from graphs where two different scales are used is a little tricky. In most area problems in geometry we assume that the scale is the same in all directions, and we are doing differently here.

F_Y, F_Z, and F_W, the distribution functions for Y, Z, and W, are graphed in Fig. 9-15.

In general, a *rectangular distribution* is one whose random variable is generated by a spinner with a uniform scale running from one number, say a, to another number, say b. We denote such a distribution by "$R(a,b)$." The distributions for Y, Z, and W above are $R(0,100)$, $R(6,9)$, and $R(-2,2)$, respectively. The graphs of the probability

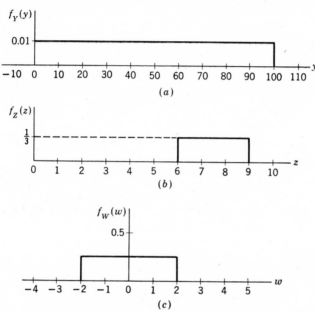

(a)

(b)

(c)

FIG. 9-14. Graphs of the density functions for (a) $R(0,100)$, (b) $R(6,9)$, and (c) $R(-2,2)$.

density function and of the distribution function for $R(a,b)$ are shown in Fig. 9-16.

The rectangular distribution is the one which corresponds to the uniform distribution for a discrete variable. With a rectangular distribution we are just as likely to end up in a given interval in the sample space as in any other such interval of equal length. If we like, we may say that such a distribution corresponds to complete symmetry among the points in the sample space. If X has the distribution $R(a,b)$, then we may write more briefly that "X is $R(a,b)$" and call X a *rectangular variable*.

To illustrate how to compute probabilities for a given rectangular variable, suppose that we find $P(-5 < X < 5)$ when X is $R(-10,20)$. We first sketch a rough picture of the density function for X, as shown in Fig. 9-17. In making the sketch it is not necessary to determine the height of the box (which is $\frac{1}{30}$). Shading the area which represents the

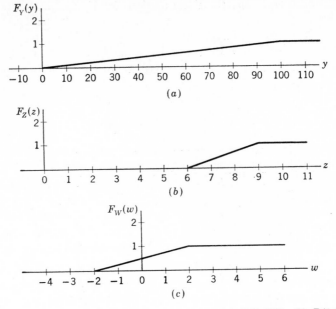

FIG. 9-15. Graphs of the distribution functions for (a) $R(0,100)$, (b) $R(6,9)$, and (c) $R(-2,2)$.

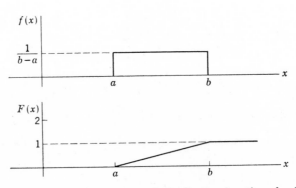

FIG. 9-16. Graphs of the density and distribution functions for $R(a,b)$.

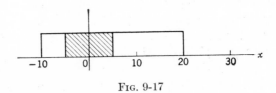

FIG. 9-17

probability we wish, we see by inspection that this area is one-third of the total area.   Therefore, $P(-5 < X < 5) = \frac{1}{3}$.

As to the parameters for the distribution $R(a,b)$, we have

(9-73) $$\mu = \frac{b + a}{2}$$

(9-74) $$\text{Median} = \frac{b + a}{2}$$

(9-75) $$\text{Range} = b - a$$

(9-76) $$\sigma = \frac{b - a}{2 \sqrt{3}}$$

$R(a,b)$ has no mode.   The probability density function and distribution function for $R(a,b)$ are relatively simple.

(9-77) $$\begin{aligned} f(x) &= 0 && \text{if } x < a \\ f(x) &= \frac{1}{b - a} && \text{if } a \leqq x \leqq b \\ f(x) &= 0 && \text{if } x > b \end{aligned}$$

(9-78) $$\begin{aligned} F(x) &= 0 && \text{if } x < a \\ F(x) &= \frac{x - a}{b - a} && \text{if } a \leqq x \leqq b \\ F(x) &= 1 && \text{if } x > b \end{aligned}$$

Before proceeding to distributions more complex than the rectangular ones, let us make some remarks about the construction of a spinner for a given random variable X which may not have a rectangular distribution. If $F(x)$ is known to be the distribution function for X, we can construct a spinner which could be used to generate X.   To indicate the method of construction, we consider the spinner shown in Fig. 9-18.   This spinner

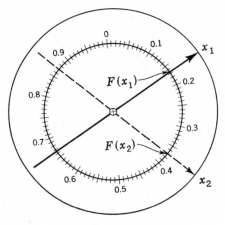

Fig. 9-18

has two circles marked on it, both with the center at the pivot point. The inner circle is marked with a uniform scale running from 0 to 1. We shall mark a scale on the outer circle as follows: Choose a number y between 0 and 1. Find a value x such that $F(x) = y$. Move the arrow so that it lies over the point marked y on the inner circle, and label as x the point indicated by the arrow point on the outer circle. Continuing in this fashion by taking various values for y, we determine the scale on the outer circle. Let us now spin the arrow and note the scale marking S at the point on the outer circle where the arrow point comes to rest. We shall show that this random variable S has the same distribution as the original X that we were given. Let x_1 and x_2 ($x_1 < x_2$) be any two values shown on the scale on the outer circle. What is $P(x_1 < S < x_2)$? Since the inner scale is uniform, between 0 and 1, this probability is equal to $y_2 - y_1$, where y_2 is the point on the inner circle corresponding to x_2 on the outer circle and similarly for y_1. But $y_2 - y_1 = F(x_2) - F(x_1)$ from the manner in which we constructed the outer scale. Then $P(x_1 < S < x_2) = F(x_2) - F(x_1) = P(x_1 < X < x_2)$. Since x_1 and x_2 were arbitrary, S and X must have the same distribution. Hence, we can consider X to be generated by the spinner that we have constructed. We expect, in general, that the scale on the outer circle will not be uniform. In fact, the outer scale will be uniform if and only if the given X is a rectangular variable.

PROBLEMS

9-79. Find the mean, median, range, and standard deviation for each of the distributions given in Fig. 9-14.

9-80. Sketch a spinner for each of the following distributions, and graph the corresponding density and distribution function. Find the mean, median, range, and standard deviation for each distribution.

    (a) $R(2,6)$ (b) $R(-\sqrt{3},\sqrt{3})$ (c) $R(0,1000)$
    (d) $R(-2,0)$ (e) $R(0,4\sqrt{3})$

9-81. Find each of the following probabilities for the indicated distributions:

    (a) $P(10 < X < 20)$, $R(0,100)$ (b) $P(20 < X < 40)$, $R(0,100)$
    (c) $P(-10 < X < 50)$, $R(0,100)$ (d) $P(.1 < X < .11)$, $R(.1,.2)$
    (e) $P(X < 5)$, $R(4,9)$ (f) $P(X = 7)$, $R(5,9)$
    (g) $P(X > 10)$, $R(6,9)$ (h) $P(-1 < X < 1)$, $R(-2,2)$
    (i) $P(\frac{1}{2} < X < 1)$, $R(-\sqrt{2},\sqrt{2})$ (j) $P(100 < X < 500)$, $R(0,1000)$
    (k) $P(X + 1 < 3)$, $R(0,4)$

9-82. For each of the distributions in Prob. 9-80 find $P(\mu - \sigma < X < \mu + \sigma)$, $P(\mu - 2\sigma < X < \mu + 2\sigma)$, and $P(\mu - 3\sigma < X < \mu + 3\sigma)$.

9-83. Verify by example or argument that (9-78) gives the distribution function for the density function (9-77).

9-84. Design a spinner for the distribution given in Fig. 9-7c.

*9-85. Consider the distribution $R(-1,1)$ with density function f. Graph $x^2 f(x)$ for this distribution, and verify approximately by estimation of an area that (9-76) is correct [see (9-49)].

9-86. If X is $R(0,1)$, find

(a) $P(X^2 < 1)$ (b) $P(X^2 < \frac{1}{4})$ (c) $P(X^2 + 1 > 0)$

(d) $P(\frac{1}{9} < X^2 < \frac{1}{4})$ (e) $P(X^2 < a)$ for $0 < a < 1$

*9-87. Let X be $R(0,1)$, and let X_1 and X_2 be the result of two consecutive (independent) trials for X. Let $Y = \max \{X_1, X_2\}$. Show that the distribution function for Y is $F_Y(y) = [F_X(y)]^2$. Graph the distribution function for Y. Find and graph the distribution function for $W = \min \{X_1, X_2\}$.

*9-88. Generalize Prob. 9-87 by considering n trials instead of two.

9-89. If X is $R(0,1)$, Y is $R(2,3)$, and X and Y are independent, find

(a) $P(X < .5 \text{ and } Y < 2.5)$ (b) $P(X < .5 \text{ or } Y < 2.5)$

(c) $P(X < .5 \text{ or } Y < 0)$ (d) $P(.2 < X \text{ and } 2.9 < Y)$

9-90. If X is $R(0,1)$, find the following conditional probabilities:

(a) $P(X < \frac{1}{4}|X < \frac{1}{2})$ (b) $P(X > \frac{1}{4}|X < .7)$

(c) $P(X \leq .2|X \leq .1)$ (d) $P(X \geq .9|X > \frac{1}{2})$

CHAPTER 10

Normal Distributions

10-1. Properties of normal distributions

One of the most important families of distributions is the family of normal distributions. The spinners in Fig. 10-1 will all yield variables with normal distributions. Before we proceed to a further discussion of this family, the reader should get some feel for these distributions by working parts of Prob. 10-5. The method of attack for this problem is illustrated by the following example: Suppose that X is the result of a spin for the spinner of Fig. 10-1A. What is $P(-1 < X < 1)$? Looking at the spinner, we think of the arrow as flying around and finally coming to rest to give us our value of X (which is read, of course, from the outer scale). X will be between -1 and 1 if and only if the arrow is between about .16 and .84 on the inner uniform scale. But the probability that the arrow will be between .16 and .84 on the uniform scale is

$$.84 - .16 = .68$$

Therefore, $P(-1 < X < 1) = .68$. Thus, by using the inner scale (and perhaps a straightedge to lay between an X value and the center to find the corresponding value on the uniform scale) we can estimate the probability that X will be between two given values. The probability density functions and distribution functions for the variables given by the spinners in Fig. 10-1 are shown in Fig. 10-2. In the construction of these graphs the scales on the various axes were chosen so that the shape of the graph would be clear. As has been done before, the vertical scale was sometimes taken to be different from the horizontal scale. The scales chosen also emphasize the similarity in form among the various distributions. If the same scale were used throughout, the curves would look quite different. In Fig. 10-3 the density functions for A, B, and D are graphed on the same set of axes to help make this fact clear.

There is a certain symmetry in each normal distribution which is obvious from the graphs of the density functions. In each of these graphs the vertical line of symmetry occurs at the mean of the distribu-

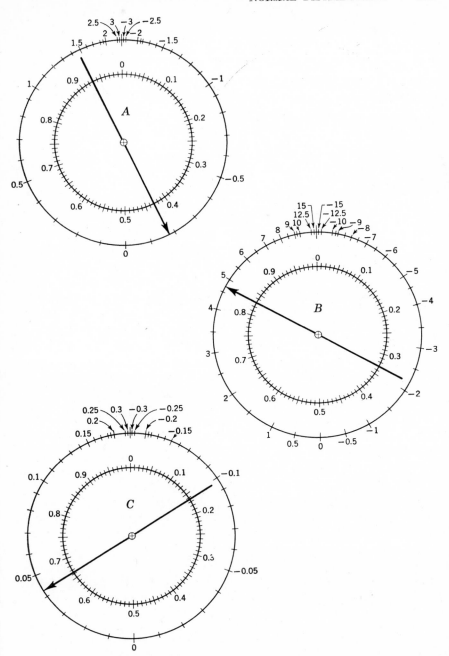

FIG. 10-1. Spinners for some normal distributions.

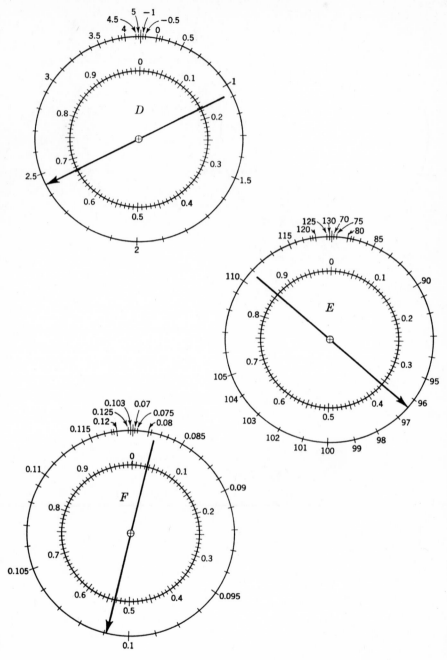

FIG. 10-1 (*Continued*)

tion, and this value is also the median and the mode. The mean values are indicated in Fig. 10-2.

Inspection of any one of the graphs of the density functions in Fig. 10-2 indicates that there is a point on each side of the mean where the curve changes its direction of curvature. In Fig. 10-2A, for example, let us start where the density curve crosses the vertical axis and move in the direction of increasing x along the curve. We must turn toward the right at first in order to stay on the curve. When we reach the point on the curve where $x = 1$, we find that we must start to turn toward the left as we proceed along the curve. Such a point at which the direction of curvature changes is called an *inflection point*. In Fig. 10-2A there is another inflection point where $x = -1$. It turns out that these inflection points always occur exactly one standard deviation away from the mean for a normal distribution. Thus, $\sigma = 1$ for the distribution of Fig. 10-2A. The σ values for the other distributions are noted in the figure.

A normal distribution is completely determined by its mean and standard deviation. Given any number a and any positive number b, there is a normal distribution with $\mu = a$ and $\sigma^2 = b$. The normal distribution with mean μ and variance σ^2 is denoted by "$N(\mu,\sigma^2)$." If a random variable X has the distribution $N(\mu,\sigma^2)$, then we shall write, more briefly, that "X is $N(\mu,\sigma^2)$," which is read as "X is normal with mean μ and variance σ^2." We shall say that "X is normal" to indicate that X has a normal distribution. ("Normal" is a technical term here, needless to say, and a variable which is not normal is not necessarily abnormal or subnormal.)

The density function for $N(\mu,\sigma^2)$ is given by

$$f(x) = \frac{1}{\sigma \sqrt{2\pi}} e^{-\frac{1}{2}[(x-\mu)/\sigma]^2}$$

There is no simple, explicit representation for the normal distribution function except to give it as the integral of the above density function.

To get more precise values for probabilities for a normal variable we make use of a table. It would be impractical to have a different table for each possible normal distribution, and fortunately, it is possible to refer all probability questions for a normal variable to a table made out for a particular normal distribution—the so-called standard normal distribution. This *standard normal distribution* (or *unit normal distribution*) is the one with mean 0 and standard deviation 1, that is, $N(0,1)$. This is the distribution given in Figs. 10-1A and 10-2A. Table A-5 in the Appendix gives values of the distribution function $F(x)$ for this variable for values of x between 0 and 4. With the use of this table and the symmetry of the distribution about $x = 0$, it is possible to find probabilities for a standard normal variable to a sufficiently high degree of accuracy to satisfy almost any practical requirements. Suppose that X is $N(0,1)$. Then, directly from Table A-5, $P(X < 1.34) = .9099$. Also, $P(-1.30 < X < 1.30)$ is, by symmetry, twice the probability that $P(0 < X < 1.30)$, and this last is

$$P(X < 1.30) - P(X < 0) = .9032 - .5000$$

Thus, $P(-1.30 < X < 1.30) = 2(.4032) = .8064$.   Perhaps the easiest

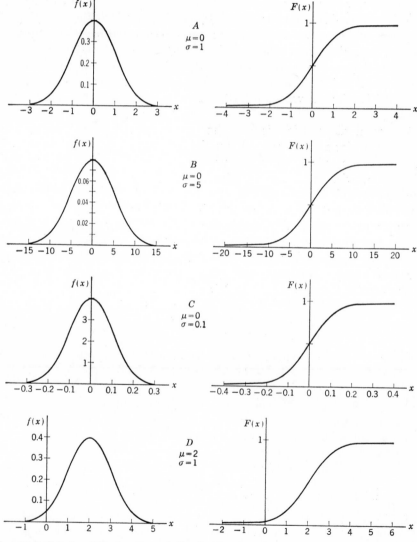

FIG. 10-2. Graphs of the density and distribution functions for the spinners of Fig. 10-1.

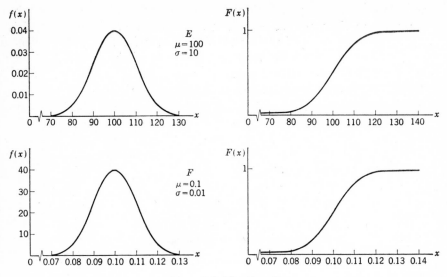

FIG. 10-2 (*Continued*)

way to make such calculations is to make a rough sketch of the graph of the density function and shade the area which represents the probability being sought. Then use is made of the symmetry of the curve and of Table A-5, which gives the area under the curve to the left of a given value.

If X is $N(\mu,\sigma^2)$ where $\mu \neq 0$ or $\sigma \neq 1$, Table A-5 still enables us to find probabilities for X. The method used depends on the following fact, which we accept without proof:

(10-1)   *If X is normal, then $Y = aX + b$ is normal ($a \neq 0$).*

That is, a linear change of scale for a normal variable results in a new variable which is normal.

If X is $N(\mu,\sigma^2)$ and $Y = (X - \mu)/\sigma$, then from (10-1), Y is normal and from (9-50) and (9-51) $\mu_Y = (\mu_X - \mu)/\sigma = 0$ and $\sigma_Y = \sigma_X/\sigma = 1$. Hence

(10-2)   *If X is $N(\mu,\sigma^2)$, then $Y = \dfrac{X - \mu}{\sigma}$ is $N(0,1)$.*

Suppose that X is $N(100,225)$ and we wish to find $P(100 < X < 130)$. When we let $Y = (X - 100)/15$, we see that we are, in effect, expressing X in different units. The Y and the X scales are shown in Fig. 10-4 with corresponding values on the same vertical. We say that Y is obtained from X by converting X to *standard units*. Given an X value, the corresponding Y value tells how far away (and in what direction) X is from its mean in units of the standard deviation for X. $Y = 2$ means that X is two standard deviations to the right of the mean; $Y = -1$ means that X is one standard deviation to the left of the mean; etc.

From Fig. 10-4 we see that $100 < X < 130$ if and only if $0 < Y < 2$. But then, Y being standard normal so that we can use Table A-5, we

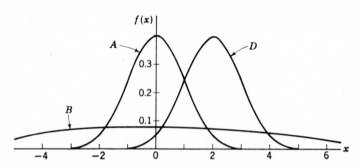

FIG. 10-3. Graphs of the density functions for (A) $N(0,1)$, (B) $N(0,25)$, and (D) $N(2,1)$.

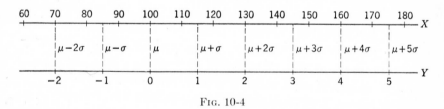

FIG. 10-4

have $P(100 < X < 130) = P(0 < Y < 2) = .4773$. Generalizing this method, we get from (10-2)

(10-3) If X is $N(\mu, \sigma^2)$, then $P(a < X < b) = P\left(\dfrac{a-\mu}{\sigma} < Y < \dfrac{b-\mu}{\sigma}\right)$,

where Y is $N(0,1)$.

This result emphasizes the previous remark that a normal distribution is characterized by its mean and standard deviation. Also we see that, in considering a certain interval for a normal variable, the crucial concern is, "How many standard deviations from the mean are we?"

Since the normal distribution arises so often, it is convenient to remember certain approximate probabilities for normal variables. If X is $N(\mu, \sigma^2)$, we have

(10-4)
$$P(\mu - \sigma < X < \mu + \sigma) \cong .68$$
$$P(\mu - 2\sigma < X < \mu + 2\sigma) \cong .95$$
$$P(\mu - 3\sigma < X < \mu + 3\sigma) \cong .997$$

Speaking less formally, we may say that for a normal variable about two-thirds of the cases lie within one standard deviation of the mean, about 95 per cent of the cases lie within two standard deviations of the mean, and almost all (99 per cent +) of the cases lie within three standard deviations of the mean.

Many observed variables seem to have approximately normal distributions. Further than that, the normal distribution would be forced on us by theoretical considerations even if it never arose "naturally." This we shall discover in the next section. Intelligence quotients (IQ's) are found to be approximately normally distributed. Thus, in a certain large group if we are told that the IQ's have mean 100 and standard deviation 15, and if we remember (10-4), we would expect about two-thirds of the group to have IQ's between 85 and 115, 95 per cent to have IQ's between 70 and 130, and almost all to have IQ's between 55 and 145. Knowing that a variable is normal and knowing (10-4), we know quite a bit about approximate values of long-run relative frequencies even if we do not have tables on hand. In the case of the above IQ's we would expect only about 2.5 per cent of the group to have IQ's above 130, for instance.

Conversely, when we are somewhat familiar with a variable and know that it is approximately normal, we can detect a gross error in a proposed value of a standard deviation. Heights of American males are, for example, approximately normally distributed. Suppose that someone tells us that the standard deviation for the heights of males in a certain city is 2 ft. Knowing that the mean height is somewhere in the neighborhood of 5 ft 10 in., this would mean that only about two-thirds of the heights would fall between about 3 ft 10 in. and 7 ft 10 in. We know from observation that a much higher percentage actually falls between these limits, so the proposed standard deviation must be too large.

PROBLEMS

10-5. Estimate directly from Fig. 10-1 the following probabilities for the variable X arising from use of the indicated spinner.

(*a*) Spinner A:

(i) $P(0 < X < 1)$ (ii) $P(X < 0)$ (iii) $P(0 < X < 2)$
(iv) $P(-3 < X < 3)$ (v) $P(-2 < X < 2)$ (vi) $P(0 < X < 5)$
(vii) $P(0 < X < .5)$ (viii) $P(-.5 < X < .5)$ (ix) $P(-.5 < X < 0)$
(x) $P(0 < X < .25)$

(*b*) Spinner B:

(i) $P(0 < X < 5)$ (ii) $P(X < 0)$
(iii) $P(0 < X < 10)$ (iv) $P(-15 < X < 15)$
(v) $P(-10 < X < 10)$ (vi) $P(0 < X < 25)$
(vii) $P(0 < X < 2.5)$ (viii) $P(-2.5 < X < 2.5)$
(ix) $P(-2.5 < X < 0)$ (x) $P(0 < X < 1.25)$

(c) Spinner C:
  (i) $P(0 < X < .1)$ (ii) $P(X < 0)$ (iii) $P(0 < X < .2)$
  (iv) $P(-.3 < X < .3)$ (v) $P(-.2 < X < .2)$ (vi) $P(.1 < X < .3)$
(d) Spinner D:
  (i) $P(2 < X < 3)$ (ii) $P(X < 2)$ (iii) $P(2 < X < 4)$
  (iv) $P(-1 < X < 5)$ (v) $P(0 < X < 4)$ (vi) $P(-1 < X < 1)$
(e) Spinner E:
  (i) $P(100 < X < 110)$ (ii) $P(X < 100)$ (iii) $P(100 < X < 120)$
  (iv) $P(70 < X < 130)$ (v) $P(80 < X < 120)$ (vi) $P(105 < X < 115)$
(f) Spinner F:
  (i) $P(.1 < X < .11)$ (ii) $P(X < .1)$ (iii) $P(.1 < X < .12)$
  (iv) $P(.07 < X < .13)$ (v) $P(.08 < X < .12)$ (vi) $P(.11 < X < 1)$

10-6. If X is standard normal, evaluate
(a) $P(X < 3)$ (b) $P(X < 1.64)$
(c) $P(X < -2)$ (d) $P(X > 2)$
(e) $P(X < 2.51)$ (f) $P(X < -2.51)$
(g) $P(0 < X < 3)$ (h) $P(0 < X < 2)$
(i) $P(-4 < X < 4)$ (j) $P(1.30 < X < 2)$
(k) $P(-1.30 < X < .99)$ (l) $P(|X| < 1)$
(m) $P(|X| > 1)$ (n) $P(X + 1 < 2)$
(o) $P(2X < 1)$ (p) $P(X^2 < 1)$
(q) $P(|X| > 3)$ (r) $P(1.51 < X < 1.52)$
(s) $P(2.67 < X < 2.68)$ (t) $P(-1.51 < X < -1.50)$

10-7. Evaluate each of the following probabilities, assuming that X has the indicated distribution:
(a) $P(0 < X < 2)$, $N(0,4)$ (b) $P(-2 < X < 2)$, $N(0,4)$
(c) $P(40 < X < 42)$, $N(40,1)$ (d) $P(38 < X < 42)$, $N(40,1)$
(e) $P(-15 < X < -10)$, $N(-10,25)$ (f) $P(300 < X < 1000)$, $N(500,400)$
(g) $P(83 < X < 95)$, $N(85,100)$ (h) $P(.1 < X)$, $N(.01,.0001)$
(i) $P(X = 4)$, $N(10,25)$ (j) $P(|X - 10| < 4)$, $N(10,4)$
(k) $P(-50 < X < 50)$, $N(100,100)$

10-8. If X is the value associated with a ball drawn at random from the "box" given in Table 9-4, then X is approximately $N(20,25)$. Verify this by finding the probabilities for several different intervals for X and for a variable which is $N(20,25)$.

10-9. Let X have the binomial distribution with $n = 30$ and $p = .5$. Let Y be $N(15, 3\%)$. Compute
  (a) $P(15 < X \leq 18)$ (b) $P(15 < Y \leq 18)$ (c) $P(13 < X \leq 18)$
  (d) $P(13 < Y \leq 18)$ (e) $P(18 < X \leq 22)$ (f) $P(18 < Y \leq 22)$
What conjecture do these results suggest?

10-10. If X is $N(\mu,\sigma^2)$ in each of the following cases, find k so that
(a) $P(X > \mu + k\sigma) = .05$ (b) $P(X < \mu - k\sigma) = .05$
(c) $P(\mu - k\sigma < X < \mu + k\sigma) = .95$ (d) $P(X > \mu + k\sigma) = .01$
(e) $P(X < \mu - k\sigma) = .01$ (f) $P(\mu - k\sigma < X < \mu + k\sigma) = .99$

10-11. If X is $N(10,25)$, what is the distribution of Y when
(a) $Y = X - 10$ (b) $Y = 10X$ (c) $Y = 10X - 50$
(d) $Y = 5X + 20$ (e) $Y = -X$ (f) $Y = -10X + 50$

10-12. Compare the results given in (10-4) with those obtained by use of (7-104). Discuss.

10-13. If X is a binomial variable and a and b are constants, does it follow that $Y = aX + b$ is a binomial variable?

*__10-14.__ If X is $R(0,1)$, does it follow that $Y = aX + b$ is a rectangular variable?

10-15. If X is a discrete variable with a uniform distribution on a set of real numbers, does it follow that $Y = aX + b$ has a uniform distribution?

10-16. Assuming approximate normality for the variables involved, use the results of your everyday experience to make rough estimates of the standard deviation for

(a) Heights of adult American males

(b) Weights of adult American males

(c) Hours of sleep for students in your school on a typical week night

(d) Pounds of food consumed by each student in your school in a week

(e) Number of different boys that American girls have kissed by the time they are 18

*10-17. Directly from the formula for the normal density function, graph the density function for

(a) $N(0,1)$ (b) $N(5,2)$ (c) $N(100,10)$

(*Hint:* Tables of powers of e can be found in almost any set of mathematical tables.)

10-2. The distribution of a sample mean

We accept without proof the fact that

(10-18)   *If X and Y are independent normal variables, then $X + Y$ is normal.*

If X is normal and $X_1, X_2, \ldots, X_n$ is a random sample for X, we know from (9-56) and (9-57) that $\mu_{\bar{X}} = \mu_X$ and $\sigma_{\bar{X}} = \sigma_X/\sqrt{n}$, where $\bar{X}$ is the sample mean. From (10-18) we know that $\sum\limits_{i=1}^{n} X_i$ is normal. Then by (10-1), $\bar{X} = \Sigma X_i/n$ is normal. Thus,

(10-19)   *If X is $N(\mu,\sigma^2)$, then $\bar{X}$ is $N(\mu,\sigma^2/n)$.*

Thus a normal variable has the very nice property that its sample mean is also normal.

When X is normal, $\bar{X}$ is normal and has the same mean as X. Hence, the density function for $\bar{X}$ has the same general shape as that for X and is centered at the same place. The density function for $\bar{X}$ is, however, more concentrated about its mean than is that for X. As n gets larger, the distribution for $\bar{X}$ becomes more and more concentrated about the mean of X. In Fig. 10-5 the graphs of the density functions for a normal X and various $\bar{X}$ are shown to illustrate this. In Fig. 10-5 X is $N(10,1)$ and n is the sample size.

Suppose that X has the rectangular distribution $R(0,1)$ and $\bar{X}$ is the mean of a random sample of n values of X. What does the distribution for $\bar{X}$ look like? In Fig. 10-6 we show the density function for $\bar{X}$ for various values of n.

The striking thing that we note about this graph is that for large n it looks very much as if the distribution of $\bar{X}$ is almost normal. This is, in fact, the case.

Moreover, the startling and immensely important fact is that, when X is any random variable that is sufficiently well behaved to have a mean

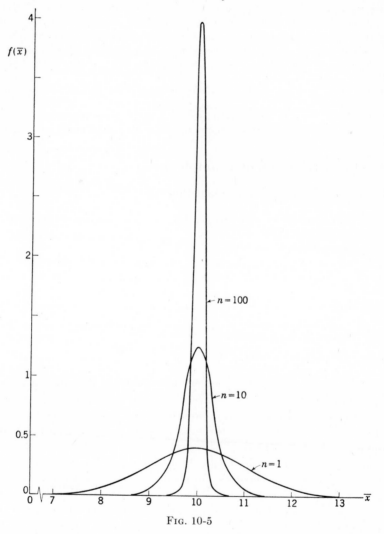

FIG. 10-5

and a variance, $\bar{X}$ will be approximately normal when n is large. This applies whether X is a continuous or a discrete variable. That is,

(10-20)   (Central limit theorem.)   *If X is any random variable which has a mean and a variance, then for n sufficiently large, $\bar{X}$, the mean of a random sample of size n, has approximately a normal distribution.*

It is because of this result that we would be forced to consider normal distributions even if they never arose "in nature." This central limit theorem is involved in a myriad of statistical problems. Wanting to refer to it often we shall abbreviate "central limit theorem" as "CLT."

The CLT would not be of great practical importance if it developed that we had to take enormous samples before $\bar{X}$ started to be normal. Fortunately, in many applications $\bar{X}$ will be approximately normal when the sample size is 30 or larger! Since 30 is a practical sample size in many instances, the CLT is of great practical importance.

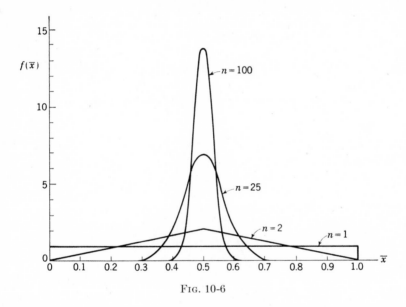

FIG. 10-6

Combining the CLT with our previous results about $\mu_{\bar{X}}$ and $\sigma_{\bar{X}}$ we get

(10-21)   *If X is a random variable, then when n is large, $\bar{X}$ has approximately the distribution $N(\mu_X, \sigma_X^2/n)$.*

If we wish to estimate μ_X or test hypotheses about μ_X and are able to take large samples, the CLT enables us to use the normal distribution in our considerations even though we may not know the form of the distribution for X.

The CLT has an immediate consequence for the binomial distribution. If the discrete variable X has sample space $\{0,1\}$ and $P(X = 1) = p$ and $X_1, X_2, \ldots, X_n$ is a random sample for X, then $Y = \Sigma X_i$ is $B(n,p)$. Also $\mu_X = p$ and $\sigma_X^2 = pq$. The mean $\bar{X}$ of the sample of X values is such that $n\bar{X} = Y$. By the CLT, when n is large $\bar{X}$ will be approximately normal with mean p and variance pq/n. Hence, $Y = n\bar{X}$ will be approximately normal [by (10-1)] with mean np and variance

$$n^2 \frac{pq}{n} = npq$$

Thus, we have proved that

(10-22)   *If Y is B(n,p) with n large, then Y is approximately N(np,npq).*

This theorem means, for example, that, if Y is $B(30,.5)$, then

$$P(15 \leqq Y \leqq 18) \cong P(15 \leqq Z \leqq 18)$$

where Z is $N(15, 3\%)$, and this last probability is easy to work out using Table A-5.

In Fig. 10-7 we have graphed the probability function for $B(30,.5)$

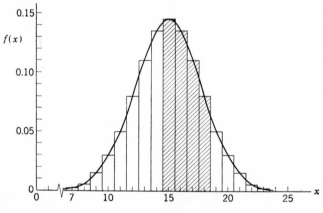

FIG. 10-7

(modified as in Sec. 9-2) and the density function for $N(15, 3\%)$. We see that the density curve fits the tops of the boxes very nicely. We also notice that we could make a slight improvement on the above approximation to $P(15 \leqq Y \leqq 18)$. The exact value of this probability is given by the sum of the areas of the boxes centered at 15, 16, 17, and 18. The probability $P(15 \leqq Z \leqq 18)$ is given by the area under the density curve for Z which lies over the interval from 15 to 18. Clearly, we get a better approximation to the sum of the areas of the boxes if we take the area lying under the curve between 14.5 and 18.5. That is, a better approximation is given by $P(15 \leqq Y \leqq 18) \cong P(14.5 \leqq Z \leqq 18.5)$. If n were a great deal larger, this so-called *continuity correction* would not matter very much, but it should be made for relatively small values of n (or for very short intervals). The easiest way to determine what continuity correction should be made is from a rough sketch of the density curve and the boxes whose areas give the binomial probabilities. If we wanted to estimate $P(15 \leq Y < 18)$ in the above case, for example, we would estimate it to be $P(14.5 \leq Z \leq 17.5)$.

If the idea of a sketch does not appeal to you, we can always make the continuity correction by noting the following: If n_1 and n_2 are integers and X is a binomial variable,

$$(10\text{-}23) \qquad \begin{aligned} P(X < n_1) &= P(X \leq n_1 - 1) \\ P(X > n_1) &= P(X \geq n_1 + 1) \\ P(n_1 < X < n_2) &= P(n_1 + 1 \leq X \leq n_2 - 1) \\ P(n_1 \leq X < n_2) &= P(n_1 \leq X \leq n_2 - 1) \\ P(n_1 < X \leq n_2) &= P(n_1 + 1 \leq X \leq n_2) \end{aligned}$$

And if Z is the corresponding normal variable, then

$$(10\text{-}24) \qquad \begin{aligned} P(n_1 \leq X \leq n_2) &\cong P(n_1 - \tfrac{1}{2} \leq Z \leq n_2 + \tfrac{1}{2}) \\ P(X \leq n_1) &\cong P(Z \leq n_1 + \tfrac{1}{2}) \\ P(X \geq n_1) &\cong P(Z \geq n_1 - \tfrac{1}{2}) \end{aligned}$$

If we wish to find an approximation to the probability that a binomial variable X will fall in a certain interval, we first find an equivalent interval which includes its end points by using (10-23), and then convert to the normal variable by (10-24).

In this fashion we can, as was suggested earlier, easily estimate probabilities for a binomial variable without lengthy computations or the use of bulky tables whenever n is large enough. How large n must be for the approximations to be good will depend on the value for p. In general, when $p \leq \tfrac{1}{2}$ and $np > 5$ or when $p > \tfrac{1}{2}$ and $nq > 5$, we find that the normal approximations are satisfactory.

PROBLEMS

10-25. Let X be $N(0,1)$ and $\bar{X}$ be the mean of a random sample of n values for X. Find

   (a) $P(\bar{X} > 0)$, $n = 17$ (b) $P(\bar{X} < 1)$, $n = 9$ (c) $P(\bar{X} < 1)$, $n = 100$
   (d) $P(|\bar{X}| < .5)$, $n = 100$ (e) $P(|\bar{X}| < .01)$, $n = 10{,}000$

10-26. Suppose that X is $N(0,1)$ and Y is $N(2,4)$ and that X and Y are independent. Find

   (a) $P(0 < X + Y < 1)$ (b) $P(-1 < X + Y < 3)$

10-27. Suppose that X is $N(10,100)$. Let $Y = X/2 + 5$. Find

   (a) $P(Y > 15)$ (b) $P(0 < Y < 10)$ (c) $P(X + Y < 10)$

10-28. If X is $N(10,100)$ and $\bar{X}$ is the mean of a random sample of 100 values for X, find
   (a) $P(\bar{X} < 0)$ (b) $P(\bar{X} > 0)$ (c) $P(\bar{X} \leq 10.5)$

10-29. If $\mu_X = 100$, $\sigma_X = 5$, and $\bar{X}$ is the mean of a random sample of size 100, find approximately
   (a) $P(\bar{X} < 101)$ (b) $P(\bar{X} > 99.5)$ (c) $P(99 < \bar{X} < 102)$
What assumption is needed in order to make your calculations?

10-30. Find approximate numerical values for the probabilities in Prob. 7-19.

10-31. Use normal approximations to estimate the probabilities in
   (a) Prob. 7-25   (b) Prob. 7-26   (c) Prob. 7-27

10-32. If $\bar{X}$ is the mean of 2500 draws from a table of random digits, find $P(\bar{X} < 4.5)$, $P(\bar{X} < 5)$, and $P(X < 4.55)$.

10-33. If a perfect die is tossed 1000 times and X sixes are obtained, find $P(X < 168)$ and $P(160 < X < 170)$. (Use normal approximations.)

10-34. In a town where 57 per cent of the families are homeowners, a random sample of 100 families includes X homeowners. Find $P(X < 60)$ and $P(54 < X < 60)$.

10-35. In a certain city the mean family income is $6500 per year. The standard deviation of these incomes is $1000. If $\bar{X}$ is the mean of the incomes of 50 families chosen at random from this city, estimate $P(6000 < \bar{X} < 7000)$, $P(\bar{X} < 6550)$, and $P(\bar{X} < 5500)$.

10-36. With μ_X, σ_X, and n as given, indicate which of the following events would be surprising if $\bar{X}$ is the mean of a random sample of size n (no tables needed here):
   (a) $\mu_X = 100$, $\sigma_X = 10$, $n = 10,000$, $\bar{X} \geq 101$
   (b) $\mu_X = 1$, $\sigma_X = 10$, $n = 10,000$, $\bar{X} \geq 2$
   (c) $\mu_X = 1$, $\sigma_X = .01$, $n = 100$, $\bar{X} \geq 1.01$
   (d) $\mu_X = 1$, $\sigma_X = .01$, $n = 100$, $\bar{X} \geq .99$
   (e) $\mu_X = 50$, $\sigma_X = 5$, $n = 100$, $\bar{X} \leq 47$
   (f) $\mu_X = 50$, $\sigma_X = 5$, $n = 100$, $\bar{X} \leq 49.5$
   (g) $\mu_X = 70$, $\sigma_X = 100$, $n = 100$, $\bar{X} \geq 0$
   (h) $\mu_X = -70$, $\sigma_X = 100$, $n = 100$, $\bar{X} \geq -40$

10-37. As a class project draw a large number of samples of 25 random digits. Find the mean for each sample drawn. Graph the grouped frequency distribution for these sample means, and compute the mean and standard deviation. Compare these statistics with the μ and σ obtained from the theory. Also compare some of the empirical relative frequencies with the probabilities obtained from the approximating normal distribution.

10-38. If X is $N(0,1)$, Y is $N(2,1)$, and X and Y are independent, let $Z = X + Y$ and find
   (a) $P(Z > 2)$ (b) $P(1 < Z < 3)$ (c) $P(0 < Z < 2)$

10-39. If $\bar{Z}$ is a random sample of 25 values of the Z in Prob. 10-38, what distribution does Z have?

10-40. If X and Y are normal independent variables and $Z = aX + bY + c$, what distribution will Z have?

****10-41.** If X and Y are independent rectangular variables, does it follow that $Z = X + Y$ is a rectangular variable?

10-42. If X is $N(0,1)$ and X_1, X_2, $\ldots$, X_n is a random sample for X, and if $Z = a_1X_1 + a_2X_2 + \cdots + a_nX_n$, where the a's are positive constants, what is the distribution of Z?

10-43. Generalize Prob. 10-42 by taking X to be $N(\mu,\sigma^2)$.

****10-44.** If X is normal, does it follow that $Y = X^2$ is normal?

****10-45.** Under what conditions would one expect a Poisson variable to be approximately normal (see Prob. 7-40)?

10-3. Testing the hypothesis $\mu = \mu_0$

In a certain suburban area we suspect that the IQ's of the residents tend to run above the national average of 100. We draw a random sample of 100 residents from the area and determine their IQ's. Let X be the IQ of a person drawn at random from the area. Then we have on hand a random sample of 100 values of X. On the basis of past experience, we assume that X is normal and that $\sigma_X = 15$. We wish to decide between the two hypotheses $H_0: \mu = 100$ and $H_1: \mu > 100$, where μ is the mean of X. From our previous considerations we know that $\bar{X}$, the mean of the sample of 100, is an unbiased estimate for μ. It seems reasonable to base our decision on the value of $\bar{X}$. Values of $\bar{X}$ which are considerably above 100 will tend to make us believe that $\mu > 100$. Hence, a reasonable kind of test seems to be as follows: Reject H_0 when $\bar{X}$ is too large. That is, reject H_0 when $\bar{X} \geq K$ for some constant K. If we choose to use a test in this form, our only problem is to choose the *critical value K*.

If we wish our test to have a significance level of 5 per cent, then we should choose K so that $P(\bar{X} \geq K) = .05$ when $\mu = 100$. But when $\mu = 100$, X is $N(100,225)$. Then, by (10-19), $\bar{X}$ is $N(100,2.25)$. From the results of Prob. 10-10 we then have

$$.05 = P(\bar{X} \geq 100 + (1.65) \sqrt{2.25}) = P(\bar{X} \geq 102.5)$$

That is, we should take $K = 102.5$ and reject H_0 if and only if $\bar{X} \geq 102.5$. Using other terminology, we say that a value of $\bar{X}$ which is greater than 102.5 differs significantly from 100 at the 5 per cent level.

If X is any normal variable with a known standard deviation and we wish to test the hypothesis $H_0: \mu = \mu_0$ against some alternative, the situation is very similar to the above. The tests arrived at by similar arguments for the various cases are collected in (10-46).

(10-46)   *Tests for $H_0: \mu = \mu_0$ against H_1 when X is $N(\mu,\sigma^2)$ with σ known:*

H_1	Reject H_0 if and only if	For .05 level tests	For .01 level tests
$\mu > \mu_0$	$\bar{X} \geq K$	$K = \mu_0 + 1.65 \dfrac{\sigma}{\sqrt{n}}$	$K = \mu_0 + 2.33 \dfrac{\sigma}{\sqrt{n}}$
$\mu < \mu_0$	$\bar{X} \leq K$	$K = \mu_0 - 1.65 \dfrac{\sigma}{\sqrt{n}}$	$K = \mu_0 - 2.33 \dfrac{\sigma}{\sqrt{n}}$
$\mu \neq \mu_0$	$\bar{X} \leq K_1$ or $\bar{X} \geq K_2$	$K_1 = \mu_0 - 1.96 \dfrac{\sigma}{\sqrt{n}}$	$K_1 = \mu_0 - 2.58 \dfrac{\sigma}{\sqrt{n}}$
		$K_2 = \mu_0 + 1.96 \dfrac{\sigma}{\sqrt{n}}$	$K_2 = \mu_0 + 2.58 \dfrac{\sigma}{\sqrt{n}}$

Alternatively, the tests can be stated as follows.

(10-47)   *Tests for H_0: $\mu = \mu_0$ against H_1 when X is $N(\mu,\sigma^2)$ and σ is known:*

H_1	Reject H_0 if and only if	
	5 per cent level test	1 per cent level test
$\mu > \mu_0$	$\dfrac{\bar{X} - \mu_0}{\sigma/\sqrt{n}} \geqq 1.65$	$\dfrac{\bar{X} - \mu_0}{\sigma/\sqrt{n}} \geqq 2.33$
$\mu < \mu_0$	$\dfrac{\bar{X} - \mu_0}{\sigma/\sqrt{n}} \leqq -1.65$	$\dfrac{\bar{X} - \mu_0}{\sigma/\sqrt{n}} \leqq -2.33$
$\mu \neq \mu_0$	$\left|\dfrac{\bar{X} - \mu_0}{\sigma/\sqrt{n}}\right| \geqq 1.96$	$\left|\dfrac{\bar{X} - \mu_0}{\sigma/\sqrt{n}}\right| \geqq 2.58$

It is in the form given in (10-47) that the tests are usually used. That is, the value of $(\bar{X} - \mu_0)/(\sigma/\sqrt{n})$ is computed and it is then noted whether or not it "differs significantly" from zero at the given significance level.

The power function for the above test with the IQ's where we rejected H_0: $\mu = 100$ when $\bar{X} > 102.5$ is given by

$$pf(y) = P(\bar{X} \geqq 102.5 | \mu = y)$$

This function is graphed in Fig. 10-8. Given $\mu_1 > 100$, the value $pf(\mu_1)$

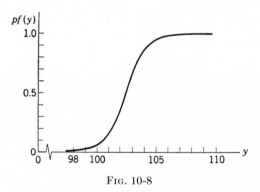

FIG. 10-8

is the probability that $\bar{X} > 102.5$ when the true mean of X is μ_1. That is, $pf(\mu_1)$ is the probability of rejecting H_0 when $\mu = \mu_1$. This probability is then equal to 1 minus the probability of committing an error of type II when we use the given test for deciding between H_0: $\mu = 100$ and H_1': $\mu = \mu_1$. Thus, as before with power functions, the graph tells at a glance how well our test will do at detecting a value of μ above 100.

It turns out that the test that we have "dreamed up" is the uniformly most powerful test for the situation at hand.   That is, for each $\mu_1 > 100$, the power of this test is at least as large as the power for any other test for deciding between $H_0: \mu = 100$ and $H_1': \mu = \mu_1$ at the 5 per cent level.

So that the reader may get some feel for the situation in terms of areas, Fig. 10-9 shows the density functions for $\bar{X}$ in the two cases $\mu = 100$ and $\mu = 105$.   The shaded area which lies under the curve on the left and over the critical region $\{\bar{X}: \bar{X} \geq 102.5\}$ is the size of the error of type I, i.e., .05.   The area which lies under the curve on the right and over the critical region is $pf(105)$.   The area under the curve on the right which does not lie over the critical region is the size of the error of type II when this test is used to decide between $H_0: \mu = 100$ and $H_1': \mu = 105$.   If we

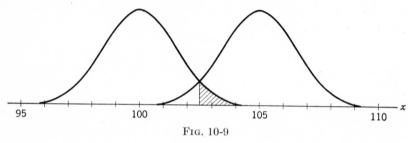

FIG. 10-9

were allowed to increase the sample size and used this same test for deciding between $H_0: \mu = 100$ and $H_1: \mu = 105$, what would happen? For a larger sample, both of the density curves for $\bar{X}$ would become narrower as $\sigma_{\bar{x}}$ decreased and we would have smaller errors of both kinds, as we might expect.

In general the tests given in the first two cases in (10-46) are uniformly most powerful tests.   There is no uniformly most powerful test for the case $H_0: \mu = \mu_0$ and $H_1: \mu \neq \mu_0$, but the test given for this case in (10-46) is a reasonable one on many counts.

As was the case when we considered a similar situation for the binomial variable, it turns out that the test given in the first line of (10-46) is also an excellent test for the hypotheses $H_0: \mu \leq \mu_0$ and $H_1: \mu > \mu_0$.   Similarly the test on the second line of (10-46) is a good one for the hypotheses $H_0: \mu \geq \mu_0$ and $H_1: \mu < \mu_0$.

What kind of a position do we find ourselves in if we wish to test $H_0: \mu = \mu_0$ and do not know that X is normal?   The CLT tells us that, if we can take a large sample, all the above argument goes through.   The only place where we made use of the normality of X was in deducing the normality of $\bar{X}$.   But if n is large, $\bar{X}$ is approximately normal even when X is not normal.   Thus,

(10-48)   *When n is large and σ is known, the tests given in (10-46) can be used even though X is not normal.*

In many practical applications a value of $n \geq 30$ is large enough to make the tests given in (10-46) have approximately the correct significance level.

What is the situation for testing $H_0: \mu = \mu_0$ against some alternative when σ^2 is not known? If the reader goes over the above example with IQ's, he will note that we made no use of the value of σ^2 until we tried to find K. In order to find K we needed to know the distribution of $\bar{X}$, and for this we needed σ^2. If we do not know σ^2, how can we find what K to use? If the sample is large, perhaps we can use the sample data to estimate σ^2 and then use this estimate for σ^2 to find K.

The "natural" estimate for σ^2 would seem to be s^2, the variance of the sample. However, it turns out that s^2 is not an unbiased estimate for σ^2. As we shall discuss in more detail in the next chapter, it is actually the case that, when s^2 is the variance of a random sample of size n, we have

$$(10\text{-}49) \qquad\qquad E(s^2) = \frac{n-1}{n} \sigma^2$$

This means that, if we were to draw many random samples of size n and compute s^2 for each, then the mean of these many values for s^2 would be close to $\sigma^2(n-1)/n$. That is, the mean of the distribution for the statistic s^2 is $\sigma^2(n-1)/n$. This does not violate our previous interpretation of σ^2 as being the value approached by s^2 as we take n larger and larger, since $(n-1)/n$ approaches 1 as n gets large.

In the light of (10-49) it seems that we should perhaps use $s^2 n/(n-1)$ as our estimate for σ^2 and, hence, $\sqrt{n/(n-1)}\, s$ as an estimate of σ. When X is normal and n is 30 or larger, this turns out to be an entirely satisfactory estimate.

But once we have a satisfactory estimate for σ, we can use the tests given in (10-46). Since the $\sigma/\sqrt{n}$ involved in the tests becomes $s/\sqrt{n-1}$ when we put $\sqrt{n/(n-1)}\, s$ in place of σ, we have

$(10\text{-}50)$ *If σ is unknown but n is large, the tests of (10-46) can still be used if we replace $\sigma/\sqrt{n}$ by $s/\sqrt{n-1}$, where s is the sample standard deviation.*

This procedure will be entirely satisfactory and yield tests with the desired significance level if X is normal and n is 30 or larger. If X is not normal, a larger n may be required. But in many practical applications $n \geq 30$ will be sufficient even when X is not normal.

Roughly speaking, (10-50) says that we may use s in place of σ for our tests with large samples. But to be more precise we should also replace n by $n-1$.

As a numerical example, let us consider the data of Table 9-2. If the spinner used to generate the data was perfectly balanced, then the results in the table constitute a random sample of 100 values of X, where X has the distribution $R(0,1)$. This distribution has mean 0.5. Let us test whether or not it is reasonable to suppose that the data of Table 9-2 came from a population with $\mu = .5$. That is, let us test the hypothesis $H_0: \mu = .5$ against $H_1: \mu \neq .5$. From Table 9-3 we have for the random sample $\bar{X} = .536$ and $s = .269$. From (10-50) and (10-46) we see that we would reject H_0 if and only if

$$\bar{X} \leq .5 - (2.58)\frac{.269}{\sqrt{99}} = .430$$

or

$$\bar{X} \geq .5 - (2.58)\frac{.269}{\sqrt{99}} = .570$$

where we have chosen to use a 1 per cent level test. Since the observed value of $\bar{X}$ satisfies neither of these inequalities, we accept $H_0: \mu = .5$. With a 5 per cent level test we would reject H_0 if and only if $\bar{X} \geq .553$ or $\bar{X} \leq .447$. Thus, at this significance level also, we would accept H_0 in view of the observed value of $\bar{X}$.

We now apply the above results about tests to the case of a binomial variable. Let X have the two-point distribution on $\{0,1\}$, and let $X_1, X_2, \ldots, X_n$ be a random sample for X. Let $P(X = 1) = p$, where p is unknown. $Y = \Sigma X_i$ has the distribution $B(n,p)$. If we wish to test $H_0: p = p_0$ against $H_1: p > p_c$, we see that this is equivalent to testing $H_0: \mu_X = p_0$ against $H_1: \mu_X > p_0$, since $\mu_X = p$. When H_0 is true, then σ_X is known, since $\sigma_X = p_0 q_0$. Writing $\hat{p}$ for the sample proportion $\bar{X} = Y/n$, we get the following from (10-48):

(10-51)   *Tests for $H_0: p = p_0$ against H_1 when Y is $B(n,p)$, n is large, and $\hat{p} = Y/n$:*

H_1	Reject H_0 if and only if	For 5 per cent tests	For 1 per cent tests
$p > p_0$	$\hat{p} \geq K$	$K = p_0 + 1.65\sqrt{\dfrac{p_0 q_0}{n}}$	$K = p_0 + 2.33\sqrt{\dfrac{p_0 q_0}{n}}$
$p < p_0$	$\hat{p} \leq K$	$K = p_0 - 1.65\sqrt{\dfrac{p_0 q_0}{n}}$	$K = p_0 - 2.33\sqrt{\dfrac{p_0 q_0}{n}}$
$p \neq p_0$	$\hat{p} \leq K_1$ or $\hat{p} \geq K_2$	$K_1 = p_0 - 1.96\sqrt{\dfrac{p_0 q_0}{n}}$	$K_1 = p_0 - 2.58\sqrt{\dfrac{p_0 q_0}{n}}$
		$K_2 = p_0 + 1.96\sqrt{\dfrac{p_0 q_0}{n}}$	$K_2 = p_0 + 2.58\sqrt{\dfrac{p_0 q_0}{n}}$

Alternatively, if we wish to state the tests in terms of the value of Y, we have the following:

(10-52)   *Tests for $H_0: p = p_0$ against H_1 when Y is $B(n,p)$ and n is large:*

H_1	Reject H_0 if and only if	
	For 5 per cent tests	For 1 per cent tests
$p > p_0$	$\dfrac{Y - np_0}{\sqrt{np_0q_0}} \geq 1.65$	$\dfrac{Y - np_0}{\sqrt{np_0q_0}} \geq 2.33$
$p < p_0$	$\dfrac{Y - np_0}{\sqrt{np_0q_0}} \leq -1.65$	$\dfrac{Y - np_0}{\sqrt{np_0q_0}} \leq -2.33$
$p \neq p_0$	$\left\| \dfrac{Y - np_0}{\sqrt{np_0q_0}} \right\| \geq 1.96$	$\left\| \dfrac{Y - np_0}{\sqrt{np_0q_0}} \right\| \geq 2.58$

Since, when n is large, we know that Y is approximately $N(np,npq)$, we see that (10-52) is a direct application of (10-47) for the case of a sample of size 1. That (10-52) is equivalent to (10-51) follows from the equivalence of the inequalities involved. For example,

$$\hat{p} = \frac{Y}{n} \geq p_0 + 1.65 \sqrt{\frac{p_0q_0}{n}}$$

is easily seen to be equivalent to

$$\frac{Y - np_0}{\sqrt{np_0q_0}} \geq 1.65$$

Suppose, for example, that a coin is tossed 10,000 times and 4800 heads are obtained. Is the coin perfectly balanced? We test $H_0: p = .5$ against $H_1: p < .5$, where p is the probability of getting a head on a single toss. From (10-51) we would reject H_0 if and only if

$$\hat{p} \leq .500 - 2.33 \sqrt{\frac{(.5)(.5)}{10,000}} = .488$$

for a test at the 1 per cent level. Since the observed value of $\hat{p}$ is .480, which is less than .488, we reject H_0 and conclude that the coin is not "fair."

In general, we may apply (10-52) with assurance that the approximations involved are good ones when $np_0 > 5$ for $p_0 \leq \frac{1}{2}$ or when $nq_0 > 5$ for $p_0 > \frac{1}{2}$. Thus, when n is large, we have arrived at a simple method for designing tests for $H_0: p = p_0$ for a binomial variable without the use of extensive tables for the binomial distribution.

PROBLEMS

10-53. Suppose that X is normal with unknown mean μ and $\sigma^2 = 100$. If $\bar{X}$ is the mean of a random sample of size 9, design .01 level tests for the hypotheses H_0 and H_1 given by

(a) $\mu = 5, \mu < 5$ (b) $\mu = -10, \mu > -10$ (c) $\mu = 0, \mu \neq 0$

(d) $\mu = 0, \mu > 0$ (e) $\mu = 1000, \mu < 1000$

10-54. Suppose that X is normal with unknown mean and unknown variance. Let $\bar{X}$ and s^2 be the mean and variance of a random sample of size 50. Design .05-level tests for the following hypotheses:

	H_0	H_1
(a)	$\mu = 5$	$\mu < 5$
(b)	$\mu = -10$	$\mu > -10$
(c)	$\mu = 0$	$\mu \neq 0$
(d)	$\mu = 0$	$\mu > 0$
(e)	$\mu = 1000$	$\mu < 1000$

10-55. Suppose that X has an unknown distribution with mean μ and variance $\sigma^2 = 100$. If $\bar{X}$ is the mean of a random sample of size 100, design .01-level tests for the following hypotheses:

	H_0	H_1
(a)	$\mu = 0$	$\mu \neq 0$
(b)	$\mu = 50$	$\mu < 50$
(c)	$\mu = -5$	$\mu > -5$

10-56. From the data of Table 1-2 test the hypothesis that the expected number of spots for the dice used there is 7.

10-57. In view of the discussion in this section, what is the most powerful test at the 5 per cent level for deciding between $H_0: \mu = \mu_0$ and $H_1: \mu = \mu_1$, where $\mu_0 < \mu_1$ and X is normal with a known variance?

10-58. Graph the power functions for the tests derived in Prob. 10-53.

10-59. Use the data in Table 9-3 to test $H_0: \mu = .5$ against $H_1: \mu > .5$.

10-60. In a random sample of 25 students at a certain college, the mean IQ is 105. Does this sample mean differ significantly from 100 at the 5 per cent level? At the 1 per cent level? (Assume that the IQ's of the population have a standard deviation of 15 and are normally distributed.)

10-61. In view of the data in Prob. 9-4, test the hypothesis that

(a) The average weight in the student body at your school is at least 145 lb.

(b) The average weight of the men students at your school is at least 160 lb.

(c) The average weight of the female students in your school does not exceed 120 lb.

(d) The average height of the students in your school is 66 in.

(e) The average height of the male students in your school is at least 5 ft 11 in.

(f) The average height of the female students in your school is no more than 5 ft 4 in.

(g) The average distance from home to school for the students at your school is at least 100 miles.

(h) The 100 draws in Prob. 9-4h came from a distribution in which all the three digit numbers from 1 to 10 were equally likely.

(i) The 100 draws in Prob. 9-4i came from a distribution in which all the whole numbers between 1 and 100 were equally likely.

(j) The mean of X is 20 if X is the result of one draw in Prob. 9-4j.

(k) Same as part j above for Prob. 9-4k.

(l) $\mu = 7$ against $\mu \neq 7$ for Prob. 9-4l.

10-62. A die was thrown 1000 times and 120 sixes were obtained. Test the hypothesis that the probability of getting a 6 is $\frac{1}{6}$.

10-63. For the data of Table 1-2, test the hypothesis that the probability of getting a 7 on a single toss is $\frac{1}{6}$.

10-64. Check the critical values given in (8-43) by using normal approximations.

10-65. Check the critical values given in (8-44) by using normal approximations.

*10-66. Suppose that x is a quantity which can be controlled in an experiment and that the random variable Y depends on x through the equation $Y = 2x - 5 + E$, where E is a random (variable) error which is normally distributed. Discuss the problem of testing $H_0: \mu_E = 0$ on the basis of n observations $(x_1, Y_1), (x_2, Y_2), \cdots ,$ (x_n, Y_n).

10-67. Was the coin that was used in the experiment reported in Table 6-1 a "true" coin?

10-68. Compare the UCL found for the quality-control chart in Prob. 8-57 with the UCL that would be found using (10-51).

10-4. Estimating μ

As we have already seen, the mean of a random sample is always an unbiased estimate of the mean of the distribution. In the case of a normal variable, moreover, it can be shown that the sample mean is the most efficient unbiased estimate for μ. Therefore, when X is normal, the best *point estimate* for μ is $\bar{X}$.

If we wish confidence intervals for μ, we can get them from the tests considered in the preceding section. The method is illustrated in the following example.

From a large freshman class at a certain university we draw a random sample of 50 students. To each of these students we give a certain examination. The mean of their scores turns out to be 600, and the standard deviation of their scores is 25. We wish to find a 95 per cent confidence interval for the mean that we would obtain if every member of the class took the exam. Since it is evidently a two-sided confidence interval that is desired, we first consider the related problem of testing the hypothesis $H_0: \mu = \mu_0$ against $H_1: \mu \neq \mu_0$. Since the sample size is large, we get from the preceding section that our 5 per cent level test should be as follows: Reject H_0 if and only if

$$\bar{X} \leq \mu_0 - 1.96 \frac{25}{7} = \mu_0 - 7.0$$

or

$$\bar{X} \geq \mu_0 + 1.96 \frac{25}{7} = \mu_0 + 7.0$$

In other words, the acceptable values for μ_0 are those within 7 of $\bar{X}$. Since we actually observed the value $\bar{X} = 600$, we may say that $600 - 7 < \mu < 600 + 7$ or $593 < \mu < 607$ with 95 per cent confidence.

Putting the results of (10-46) through the same kind of argument we get the following:

(10-69)   *If X is $N(\mu,\sigma^2)$, σ is known, and $\bar{X}$ is the mean of a random sample of size n, then confidence intervals for μ are given by:*

95 *per cent confidence*   99 *per cent confidence*

$$\mu < \bar{X} + 1.65\,\frac{\sigma}{\sqrt{n}} \qquad\qquad \mu < \bar{X} + 2.33\,\frac{\sigma}{\sqrt{n}}$$

$$\mu > \bar{X} - 1.65\,\frac{\sigma}{\sqrt{n}} \qquad\qquad \mu > \bar{X} - 2.33\,\frac{\sigma}{\sqrt{n}}$$

$$\bar{X} - 1.96\,\frac{\sigma}{\sqrt{n}} < \mu < \bar{X} + 1.96\,\frac{\sigma}{\sqrt{n}} \qquad \bar{X} - 2.58\,\frac{\sigma}{\sqrt{n}} < \mu < \bar{X} + 2.58\,\frac{\sigma}{\sqrt{n}}$$

In case X is not normal but n is large, we can apply the CLT and get

(10-70)   *The confidence intervals of (10-69) also apply approximately when X is not normal but n is large.*

In case σ is not known, $\sqrt{n/n-1}\ s$ can be used as an estimate for σ as before.   The estimate will be a good one when n is large.   That is,

(10-71)   *When σ is unknown and n is large, the confidence intervals of (10-69) also apply approximately if $\sigma/\sqrt{n}$ is replaced by $s/\sqrt{n-1}$, where s is the sample standard deviation.*

As before, if X is normal, a sample size of 30 or more will suffice to make the approximations excellent ones.

Normal methods (i.e., the normal distribution) can also be used to obtain an interval estimate for p for a binomial variable.   Suppose that we toss a die 500 times and get 90 sixes.   We wish to find a 99 per cent confidence interval for p, the probability of getting a 6 on a single toss. If X is the number of 6's obtained in 500 tosses, then X is $B(500,p)$. But by (10-22) X is approximately $N(500p,500pq)$.   A 1 per cent level test for the hypotheses $H_0\colon p = p_0$ and $H_1\colon p \neq p_0$ is as follows: Reject H_0 if and only if

$$\frac{X}{500} < p_0 - 2.58\sqrt{\frac{p_0 q_0}{500}} \quad \text{or} \quad \frac{X}{500} > p_0 + 2.58\sqrt{\frac{p_0 q_0}{500}}$$

Then with our observed value of $X = 90$, a 99 per cent confidence interval for p (i.e., the set of values acceptable for p in the face of these data) is

$$\left\{ p_0\colon p_0 - 2.58\sqrt{\frac{p_0 q_0}{500}} < \frac{90}{500} < p_0 + 2.58\sqrt{\frac{p_0 q_0}{500}} \right\}$$

$$= \left\{ p_0\colon .18 - 2.58\sqrt{\frac{p_0 q_0}{500}} < p_0 < .18 + 2.58\sqrt{\frac{p_0 q_0}{500}} \right\}$$

We still have not expressed this set as an interval for p_0, but it turns out that we can estimate the p_0 under the radicals by $X/n = .18$ and get a satisfactory confidence interval for p.   This seems downright dishonest, since we are trying to get bounds for p_0 and in doing so estimate p_0 to be .18.   Nevertheless, it is justifiable because we expect X/n to be fairly close to p and we find that $\sqrt{pq} = \sqrt{p(1 - p)}$ changes very, very little for a relatively small change in p (see Prob. 3-102).   Thus, in a way, we can estimate the variance from the sample values as before.   Taking $p_0 = .18$ and $q_0 = .84$ under the radicals we get as the (approximate) 99 per cent confidence interval

$$.18 - 2.58 \sqrt{\frac{(.18)(.82)}{500}} < p < .18 + (2.58) \sqrt{\frac{(.18)(.82)}{500}}$$

or

$$.136 < p < .224$$

This agrees well with the values found using Fig. 8-6.

Similar considerations in the general case lead to the following result:

(10-72)   *When X is $B(n,p)$ and $\hat{p} = X/n$ and n is large, approximate confidence intervals for p are*

95 *per cent confidence*	99 *per cent confidence*
$p < \hat{p} + 1.65 \sqrt{\dfrac{\hat{p}\hat{q}}{n}}$	$p < \hat{p} + 2.33 \sqrt{\dfrac{\hat{p}\hat{q}}{n}}$
$p > \hat{p} - 1.65 \sqrt{\dfrac{\hat{p}\hat{q}}{n}}$	$p > \hat{p} - 2.33 \sqrt{\dfrac{\hat{p}\hat{q}}{n}}$
$\hat{p} - 1.96 \sqrt{\dfrac{\hat{p}\hat{q}}{n}} < p < \hat{p} + 1.96 \sqrt{\dfrac{\hat{p}\hat{q}}{n}}$	$\hat{p} - 2.58 \sqrt{\dfrac{\hat{p}\hat{q}}{n}} < p < \hat{p} + 2.58 \sqrt{\dfrac{\hat{p}\hat{q}}{n}}$

Thus, in the case of large values of n, we have discovered a very easy method for finding either one-sided or two-sided confidence intervals for p without the use of extensive tables of the binomial distribution.

PROBLEMS

10-73. Find two-sided 95 and 99 per cent confidence intervals for the mean of X when X is normal with variance σ^2 and $\bar{X}$ is the mean of a random sample of size n and

(a) $\bar{X} = 50$, $n = 10$, $\sigma^2 = 25$ (b) $\bar{X} = 50$, $n = 1$, $\sigma^2 = 25$
(c) $\bar{X} = 50$, $n = 1000$, $\sigma^2 = 25$ (d) $\bar{X} = .001$, $n = 10$, $\sigma^2 = 25$
(e) $\bar{X} = 50$, $n = 10$, $\sigma^2 = 100$ (f) $\bar{X} = 32$, $n = 60$, $\sigma^2 = 40$
(g) $\bar{X} = 20$, $n = 2$, $\sigma^2 = 1$

10-74. Find two-sided 95 and 99 per cent confidence intervals for the mean of X when X is normal and a random sample of size n yields

(a) $\bar{X} = 50$, $n = 100$, $s^2 = 25$ (b) $\bar{X} = 50$, $n = 1000$, $s^2 = 25$
(c) $\bar{X} = 50$, $n = 7$, $s^2 = 25$ (d) $\bar{X} = 100$, $n = 100$, $s^2 = 100$
(e) $\bar{X} = 1$, $n = 100$, $s^2 = 1$ (f) $\bar{X} = 4.6$, $n = 35$, $s^2 = 7$

10-75. Using methods of this section, find two-sided 95 and 99 per cent confidence intervals for p when X is $B(n,p)$ and one observation for X yields

(a) $X = 50$, $n = 100$ (b) $X = 25$, $n = 100$ (c) $X = 10$, $n = 100$
(d) $X = 50$, $n = 1000$ (e) $X = 500$, $n = 1000$ (f) $X = 900$, $n = 1000$
(g) $X = 40$, $n = 50$ (h) $X = 20$, $n = 30$

10-76. Check the results for 95 per cent intervals in the preceding problem by means of the graphs of Sec. 8-5.

10-77. Find two one-sided confidence intervals for each case in (a) Prob. 10-73, (b) Prob. 10-74, (c) Prob. 10-75.

10-78. Find a 95 per cent confidence interval for the mean of the distribution for which a random sample is given by (a) Table 5-2, (b) Table 5-3, (c) Table 9-3.

10-79. Find 95 per cent confidence intervals for the means of the distributions from which you drew samples in Probs. 1-3 through 1-17.

10-80. Let X have the distribution $R(0,\theta)$, where θ is unknown. To test $H_0: \theta = \theta_0$ against $H_1: \theta > \theta_0$, suppose that we observe one value of X and reject H_0 if $X > K$. Find K in terms of θ_0 so that the test has the significance level .05. Use the result to find a 95 per cent confidence set for θ when the observed value of X is 10.

10-81. Find a 95 per cent confidence interval for the probability of getting a head with the coin used to obtain Table 6-1.

10-5. Testing the hypothesis $\mu_X = \mu_Y$

When two treatments or two results are compared under different conditions, it is often of interest to test the hypothesis that two distribution means are the same. Various facts may be known about the distributions being considered in a given instance. We shall start by considering the quite restrictive case where the given variables X and Y are independent and normal with known variances. Let $X_1, X_2, \ldots, X_n$ be a random sample of n values for X and $Y_1, Y_2, \ldots, Y_m$ be a random sample of m values for Y. Since the sample means $\bar{X}$ and $\bar{Y}$ are unbiased estimates of μ_X and μ_Y, respectively, it perhaps seems reasonable to base a decision about the sizes of μ_X and μ_Y on the values $\bar{X}$ and $\bar{Y}$. Suppose that we wish to test $H_0: \mu_X = \mu_Y$ against $H_1: \mu_X > \mu_Y$. A natural kind of test would be to reject H_0 in favor of H_1 when $\bar{X}$ is "significantly" larger than $\bar{Y}$. That is, reject when $\bar{X} - \bar{Y}$ is sufficiently large, say when $\bar{X} - \bar{Y} \geqq K$ for some appropriately chosen K.

To choose the appropriate K, we must consider the distribution of the quantity $\bar{X} - \bar{Y}$. When X is $N(\mu_X, \sigma_X^2)$ and Y is $N(\mu_Y, \sigma_Y^2)$ we know that $\bar{X}$ is $N(\mu_X, \sigma_X^2/n)$ and $\bar{Y}$ is $N(\mu_Y, \sigma_Y^2/m)$ by (10-19). $-\bar{Y}$ is normal by (10-1) so that $\bar{X} - \bar{Y} = \bar{X} + (-\bar{Y})$ is normal by (10-18). In fact, $\bar{X} - \bar{Y}$ is $N(\mu_X - \mu_Y, \ \sigma_X^2/n + \sigma_Y^2/m)$ by (9-53) and (9-54).[1] The hypothesis $H_0: \mu_X = \mu_Y$ we now see to be equivalent to the hypothesis $H_0': \mu_{\bar{X}-\bar{Y}} = 0$, and $H_1: \mu_X > \mu_Y$ we see to be equivalent to $H_1': \mu_{\bar{X}-\bar{Y}} > 0$. But deciding between H_0' and H_1' is a problem that we have faced before. We see that we should reject H_0' in favor of H_1' in case

$$\bar{X} - \bar{Y} \geqq 1.65 \sqrt{\frac{\sigma_X^2}{n} + \frac{\sigma_Y^2}{m}}$$

[1] We must also know that the variance for $-\bar{Y}$ is the same as the variance of $\bar{Y}$, but this is not difficult to see, since changing the sign on $\bar{Y}$ does not affect its dispersion but merely reverses the direction for $\bar{Y}$.

for a 5 per cent level test.   This is so because when H'_0 is true,

$$P\left(\bar{X} - \bar{Y} \geq 1.65\sqrt{\frac{\sigma_X{}^2}{n} + \frac{\sigma_Y{}^2}{m}}\right) = .05$$

A similar argument for the alternative hypothesis H_1: $\mu_X \neq \mu_Y$ yields the following:

(10-82)   *Tests for H_0: $\mu_X = \mu_Y$ against H_1 when X and Y are independent and normal with known variances and $\bar{X}$ and $\bar{Y}$ are the means of random samples of size n and m, respectively:*

H_1	Reject H_0 if and only if	Where K is	
		For 5 per cent level	For 1 per cent level
$\mu_X > \mu_Y$	$\dfrac{\bar{X} - \bar{Y}}{\sqrt{\sigma_X{}^2/n + \sigma_Y{}^2/m}} \geq K$	1.65	2.33
$\mu_X \neq \mu_Y$	$\left\lvert\dfrac{\bar{X} - \bar{Y}}{\sqrt{\sigma_X{}^2/n + \sigma_Y{}^2/m}}\right\rvert \geq K$	1.96	2.58

The case where we wish to consider the alternative hypothesis H_1: $\mu_X < \mu_Y$ is taken care of by simply interchanging the roles of X and Y.

The test given for the alternative hypothesis $\mu_X > \mu_Y$ is uniformly most powerful.   That given for the alternative $\mu_X = \mu_Y$ is not uniformly most powerful but does have many desirable properties.   There is no uniformly most powerful test for this latter situation.

If X and Y are not known to be normal but their variances are known, and if n and m are large, the tests of (10-82) are still good tests with approximately the desired significance levels.   This is so because the CLT tells us that $\bar{X}$ and $\bar{Y}$ are approximately normal when n and m are large.

When $\sigma_X{}^2$ and $\sigma_Y{}^2$ are unknown but sufficiently large samples are available, it may be possible to use sample variances as estimates for the population variances and still apply the tests of (10-82).   This is often a satisfactory procedure when n and m are both larger than 50.   The case where the standard deviations are unknown and the samples are small will be discussed in a later section.

In the case of two binomial variables, say X, which is $B(n,p_1)$, and Y, which is $B(m,p_2)$, it is often of interest to test the hypothesis that $p_1 = p_2$.   Normal methods can be used if n and m are large.   An example follows.

To investigate the change in mutation frequency due to treatment with a certain antibiotic, a group of fruit flies of a certain strain was divided into two groups.   The first group was treated with the antibiotic.   The second was not.   Both groups were then irradiated with X rays to cause mutations.   Among 952 treated cases 31 lethal mutations were observed. Among 1168 untreated cases 67 were lethal mutations.[1]   Does the treatment significantly lower the mutation rate?   Let X be $B(952, p_1)$ and Y be $B(1168, p_2)$.   We have one observed value for X and one for Y and wish to test $H_0: p_1 = p_2$ against $H_1: p_1 < p_2$.   We know that X is approximately $N(952 p_1, 952 p_1 q_1)$ and Y is approximately $N(1168 p_2, 1168 p_2 q_2)$.   Then $\hat{p}_1 = X/952$ is approximately

$$N\left(p_1, \frac{p_1 q_1}{952}\right)$$

and $\hat{p}_2 = Y/1168$ is approximately

$$N\left(p_2, \frac{p_2 q_2}{1168}\right)$$

When H_0 is true, we have $p_1 = p_2 = p$, and hence, $\hat{p}_1 - \hat{p}_2$ is approximately

$$N\left(0, \frac{pq}{952} + \frac{pq}{1168}\right)$$

If we could estimate p, we would then know the approximate variance for $\hat{p}_1 - \hat{p}_2$.   But when H_0 is true, the treated and untreated groups can be combined and considered as one large sample from a single population.   Then the best estimate for p is the ratio of the total number of mutations to the total number of trials; that is, $\hat{p} = {}^{98}\!/_{2120}$.   Then the estimated variance for $\hat{p}_1 - \hat{p}_2$ is

$$\frac{\hat{p}\hat{q}}{952} + \frac{\hat{p}\hat{q}}{1168} = \hat{p}\hat{q}\left(\frac{1}{952} + \frac{1}{1168}\right) = 8.35 \times 10^{-5}$$

By taking the square root we find the estimated standard deviation for $\hat{p}_1 - \hat{p}_2$ to be .0091.   If H_0 is true, the observed value of

$$\hat{p}_1 - \hat{p}_2 = \frac{31}{952} - \frac{67}{1168} = -.0248$$

differs from its expected mean of 0 by $-.0248/.0091 = -2.73$ standard deviations.   Since $-2.73 < -2.33$, we reject H_0 and conclude that the treatment significantly (at the 1 per cent level) reduces the number of mutations.

[1] Data from W. J. Burdette, Alteration of Mutation Frequency by Treatment with Actinomycin D, *Science*, vol. 133, p. 40, January, 1961.

The same type of reasoning in the general case leads to the following result:

(10-83)   *Tests for $H_0: p_1 = p_2$ against H_1 when X is $B(n,p_1)$, Y is $B(m,p_2)$, n and m are large, and $\hat{p} = (X + Y)/(n + m)$:*

H_1	Reject H_0 if and only if:	Where K is	
		For 5 per cent level	For 1 per cent level
$p_1 > p_2$	$\dfrac{X/n - Y/m}{\sqrt{\hat{p}\hat{q}\,(1/n + 1/m)}} \geq K$	1.65	2.33
$p_1 \neq p_2$	$\left\| \dfrac{X/n - Y/m}{\sqrt{\hat{p}\hat{q}\,(1/n + 1/m)}} \right\| \geq K$	1.96	2.58

PROBLEMS

10-84. If X and Y are independent and normal and $\sigma_X^2 = 8$ and $\sigma_Y^2 = 12$, test the hypothesis that $H_0: \mu_X = \mu_Y$ against $H_1: \mu_X \neq \mu_Y$ when random samples of size n and m have sample means $\bar{X}$ and $\bar{Y}$ and
(a) $\bar{X} = 5$, $\bar{Y} = 5$ (b) $\bar{X} = 6$, $\bar{Y} = 5$, $n = m = 10$
(c) $\bar{X} = 6$, $\bar{Y} = 5$, $n = m = 1000$ (d) $\bar{X} = 9$, $\bar{Y} = 5$, $n = m = 10$
(e) $\bar{X} = 14$, $\bar{Y} = 20$, $n = 7$, $m = 25$ (f) $\bar{X} = 14$, $\bar{Y} = 20$, $m = 25$, $n = 7$
10-85. Use the data in the preceding problem to test $H_0: \mu_X = \mu_Y$ against $H_1: \mu_X > \mu_Y$ in each case.
10-86. Test $H_0: p_1 = p_2$ against $H_1: p_1 \neq p_2$ when X is $B(n,p_1)$, Y is $B(m,p_2)$, and a single trial for each yields
(a) $X = 60$, $n = 120$, $Y = 30$, $m = 60$
(b) $X = 90$, $n = 120$, $Y = 30$, $m = 60$
(c) $X = 90$, $n = 120$, $Y = 35$, $m = 60$
(d) $X = 40$, $Y = 60$, $n = m = 100$ (e) $X = 40$, $Y = 60$, $n = m = 1000$
(f) $X = 4$, $Y = 6$, $n = m = 100$ (g) $X = 10$, $Y = 15$, $n = m = 30$
(h) $X = 96$, $Y = 94$, $n = m = 100$ (i) $X = 46$, $Y = 46$, $n = 60$, $m = 70$
(j) $X = 10$, $Y = 10$, $n = 30$, $m = 35$
10-87. For each set of data in the preceding problem, test $H_0: p_1 = p_2$ against $H_1: p_1 > p_2$.
10-88. Design a test at the 5 per cent level for $H_0: \mu_X = \mu_Y$ against $H_1: \mu_X \neq \mu_Y$ when X and Y are independent and normal, $\sigma_X^2 = 9$, $\sigma_Y^2 = 25$, and we must base our decision on $\bar{X}$ and $\bar{Y}$ the means of random samples of size 25 and 100, respectively. Find, for various values of C, the size of the type II error if this test is used with H_0 as given and the alternative hypothesis $H_1': \mu_X = \mu_Y + C$. Plot the size of this error as a function of C.
10-89. Do the preceding problem with H_1 taken to be $\mu_X > \mu_Y$.
10-90. At what point in the derivation of (10-82) was use made of the fact that X and Y were independent?
10-91. In many instances where measured results for X and Y occur in pairs, the tests in (10-82) are not the best to use or are not applicable. Consider, for example, the problem of testing whether a person's right foot tends to be longer than his left. Design a test based on foot measurements of 50 people.

10-92. Collect data in your class or in your class and another group so that you have data for more than 20 male and 20 female students.   Use the data to test whether in your school the proportions are the same among the male students and among the female students who

(*a*) Own automobiles

(*b*) Know how to play poker

(*c*) Know how to play chess

(*d*) Know how to crochet

(*e*) Oppose capital punishment

(*f*) Read the comic pages regularly

10-93. If X is $N(\mu_X, 9)$, Y is $N(\mu_Y, 16)$, and $\bar{X}$ and $\bar{Y}$ are means of random samples of size 10 and 20, respectively, design a test at the 1 per cent level for deciding between $H_0: \mu_X = \mu_Y$ and $H_1: \mu_X > \mu_Y$.   Graph the critical region for your test in a plane with $\bar{X}$ on the vertical axis and $\bar{Y}$ on the horizontal.

10-94. Do the preceding problem for the alternative hypothesis $H_1: \mu_X \neq \mu_Y$.

CHAPTER 11

Chi-square Distributions

11-1. Properties of chi-square distributions

Suppose that X is a variable with the standard normal distribution. Will the variable X^2 also be normal? The answer is in the negative. What will be the distribution of X^2? This question leads us to consider the family of distributions which are called *chi-square distributions*. There are infinitely many chi-square distributions, one corresponding to each positive integer n. The chi-square distribution corresponding to the number n will be denoted by "$\chi^2(n)$." We write "X is $\chi^2(n)$" to mean that X has the distribution $\chi^2(n)$. The number n is called the *number of degrees of freedom* for the distribution $\chi^2(n)$.

The spinners in Fig. 11-1 will generate variables with the chi-square distributions indicated there. The probability density functions and distribution functions for these spinners are shown in Fig. 11-2.

We shall accept without proof two fundamental facts about chi-square distributions.

(11-1) *If X is $N(0,1)$, then X^2 is $\chi^2(1)$.*

(11-2) *If Y_1 is $\chi^2(n)$ and Y_2 is $\chi^2(m)$ and Y_1 and Y_2 are independent, then $Y_1 + Y_2$ is $\chi^2(n + m)$.*

From these two results we can derive other important properties of chi-square distributions. Suppose that X is $N(0,1)$ and X_1, X_2, . . . , X_n is a random sample of n values for X. $X_1{}^2$ has the distribution $\chi^2(1)$ by (11-1). Also $X_2{}^2$ has the distribution $\chi^2(1)$. X_1 and X_2 are independent, since the sample is random, and it seems reasonable then (and can be proved rigorously) that $X_1{}^2$ and $X_2{}^2$ are independent. Then, by (11-2), $X_1{}^2 + X_2{}^2$ is $\chi^2(2)$. Continuing in this fashion we get

(11-3) *If X is $N(0,1)$ and X_1, X_2, . . . , X_n is a random sample then $\sum_{i=1}^{n} X_i{}^2$ has the distribution $\chi^2(n)$.*

As an example, suppose that we have a sample of size 3 and wish to find $P\left(\sum_{i=1}^{3} X_i^2 < 1\right)$ when X is $N(0,1)$. The sum of squares has the distribution $\chi^2(3)$ which is generated by the spinner in Fig. 11-1B. From this spinner we see that $P\left(\sum_{i=1}^{3} X_i^2 < 1\right) = .198$.

If Y is normal but not standard normal, we know that $(Y - \mu)/\sigma$ is standard normal. It follows from (11-3) that

(11-4)   *If Y is $N(\mu,\sigma^2)$ and Y_1, Y_2, . . . , Y_n is a random sample, then*

$$\sum_{i=1}^{n} \left(\frac{Y_i - \mu}{\sigma}\right)^2$$

       has the distribution $\chi^2(n)$.

As an application, suppose that Y is the IQ of a person chosen at random from a certain population and that Y is $N(100,225)$. In a random sample of 20 values of Y what is the probability that the sum of squares of the deviations from 100 exceeds 450? We have

$$P\left(\sum_{i=1}^{20} (Y_i - 100)^2 < 450\right) = P\left(\sum_{i=1}^{20} \left(\frac{Y_i - 100}{15}\right)^2 < 2\right)$$

But by (11-4),

$$\sum_{i=1}^{20} \left(\frac{Y_i - 100}{15}\right)^2$$

has the distribution $\chi^2(20)$ which is generated by the spinner in Fig. 11-1E. From this spinner we see that

$$P\left(\sum_{i=1}^{20} (Y_i - 100)^2 < 450\right) = .003$$

If X is $\chi^2(n)$, then the mean and variance for X are

(11-5) $\mu = n$
(11-6) $\sigma^2 = 2n$

Table A-6 in the Appendix gives various percentile points for $\chi^2(n)$ for $1 \leqq n \leqq 30$. We find from Table A-6, for instance, that, when X is $\chi^2(11)$,

$$P(X > 5.578) = .90 \quad \text{and} \quad P(X > 17.275) = .10$$

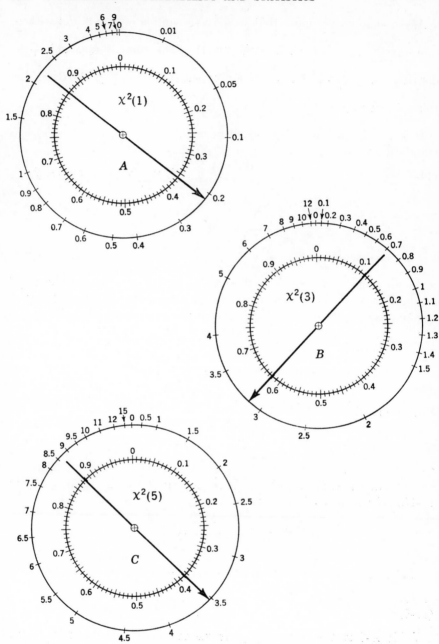

FIG. 11-1. Spinners for some χ^2 distributions.

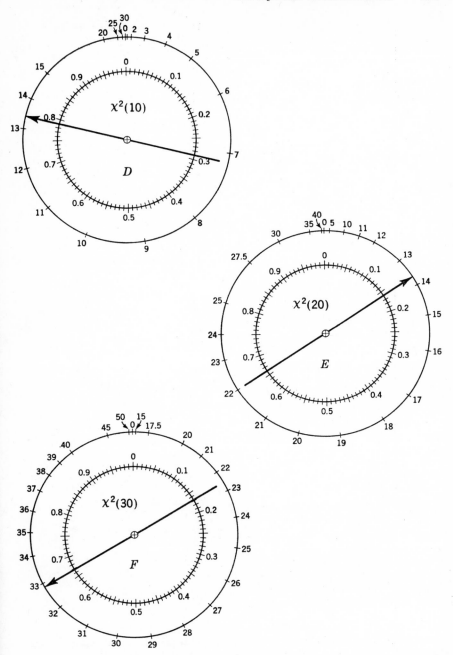

Fig. 11-1 (*Continued*)

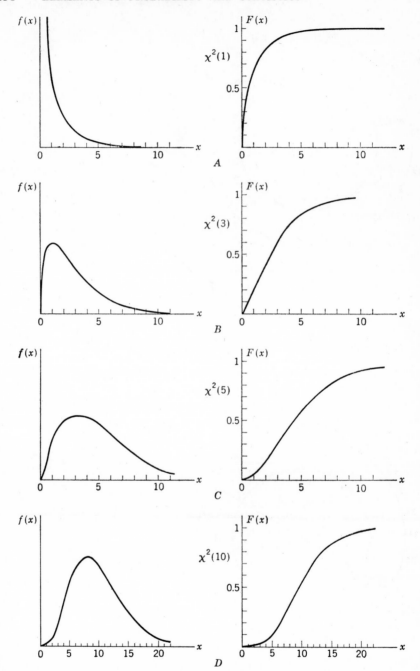

FIG. 11-2. Graphs of the density and distribution functions for $\chi^2(1)$, $\chi^2(3)$, $\chi^2(5)$, $\chi^2(10)$, $\chi^2(20)$, and $\chi^2(30)$.

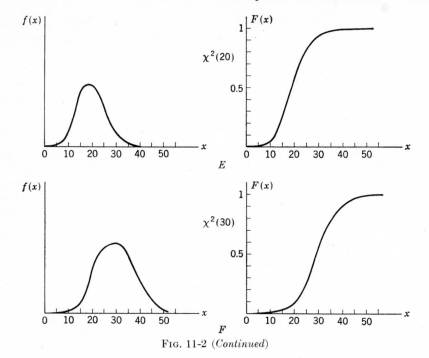

Fig. 11-2 (*Continued*)

The table shows values corresponding to various-sized right tails for the distribution.

As n gets large, the distribution $\chi^2(n)$ approaches the normal distribution with mean n and variance $2n$. $\chi^2(50)$ is, for example, roughly normal with mean 50 and variance 100. For $\chi^2(50)$ we would expect to find about 95 per cent of the area between $\mu - 2\sigma$ and $\mu + 2\sigma$, which is to say between 30 and 70. From tabulated values for $\chi^2(50)$ we find that $P(X < 32.4) = .025$ and $P(X > 71.4) = .025$, so that $P(32.4 \leq X \leq 71.4) = .95$, which agrees well with our expectations.

A better way to estimate probabilities for $\chi^2(n)$ when n is large (>30) is to make use of the fact that, when X is $\chi^2(n)$, then

$$Y = \sqrt{2X} - \sqrt{2n - 1}$$

has approximately a standard normal distribution. This approximation is closer than the above simpler one when n is of medium size. As an application, suppose that X is $\chi^2(40)$ and we wish to find $P(X < 30)$. We have

$$P(X < 30) = P(2X < 60) = P(\sqrt{2X} < \sqrt{60} = 7.73)$$
$$= P(\sqrt{2X} - \sqrt{79} < 7.73 - \sqrt{79})$$
$$\cong P(Y < -1.17) = .121$$

where Y is $N(0,1)$ and for the last equality use was made of Table A-5.

In much statistical writing, "χ^2" is used to denote a random variable with a chi-square distribution. In this notation, we would have written the last equality as "$P(\chi^2 < 30) \cong .121$ for 40 degrees of freedom."

PROBLEMS

11-7. If X is $\chi^2(1)$, use Fig. 11-1 to estimate the following probabilities:
(a) $P(X > 1)$ (b) $P(1 < X < 2)$
(c) $P(2 < X < 20)$ (d) $P(20 < X < 70)$

11-8. Find the probabilities of Prob. 11-7 for $\chi^2(n)$ when n is (a) 3, (b) 5, (c) 10, (d) 20, (e) 30.

11-9. Use Table A-5 to find $P(X^2 \leq K) = P(-\sqrt{K} \leq X \leq \sqrt{K})$ for various values of K when X is $N(0,1)$. Use your results to graph the distribution function for $Y = X^2$. Verify (11-1) by comparing your result with the distribution function graphed for $\chi^2(1)$ in Fig. 11-2.

11-10. Suppose that it has already been shown that the mean for $\chi^2(1)$ is 1. Prove (11-5) by using the basic property (11-2).

11-11. Suppose that it has already been shown that the variance for $\chi^2(1)$ is 2. Prove (11-6).

11-12. If X is $\chi^2(n)$, estimate the following:
(a) $P(X < 1000), n = 1000$ (b) $P(X < 65), n = 75$
(c) $P(X < 180), n = 200$ (d) $P(X < 100), n = 500$

11-13. If X is $N(5,2)$ and $X_1, X_2, \ldots, X_{10}$ is a random sample for X, find

$$E\left[\sum_{i=1}^{10} (X_i - 5)^2\right]$$

11-14. If $\bar{X}_1, \bar{X}_2, \ldots, \bar{X}_K$ are the means of K random samples of size n for X, what can be said about the distribution of

$$Y = \sum_{i=1}^{K} \left(\frac{\bar{X}_i - \mu}{\sigma}\right)^2$$

where μ and σ are the mean and standard deviation for X and n is large?

11-15. Show that, if X is $\chi^2(n)$, then $E(X^2) = 2n + n^2$.

11-16. As a class project, draw about 100 values for the variable

$$Y = \sum_{i=1}^{3} \left(\frac{X_i - 20}{5}\right)^2$$

where (X_1, X_2, X_3) is a random sample of three draws from the box of Table 9-4. Graph the relative frequency distribution for these results. Find the sample mean and variance for the values of Y obtained. Compare the graph and the statistics with the results expected by theory for a very large number of trials (see Prob. 10-8).

11-17. Show that, when n is large and X is $B(n,p)$, then

$$\frac{(X - np)^2}{npq}$$

is approximately $\chi^2(1)$.

11-18. If Y is a χ^2 variable with n degrees of freedom, find approximate values for the following probabilities:

(a) $P(Y \leq 5)$, $n = 5$ (b) $P(Y \geq 5)$, $n = 5$
(c) $P(1 \leq Y \leq 5)$, $n = 5$ (d) $P(Y \geq 9.24)$, $n = 5$
(e) $P(Y \leq 15.99)$, $n = 10$ (f) $P(4.11 \leq Y \leq 19.81)$, $n = 13$
(g) $P(Y \geq 26.30)$, $n = 16$ (h) $P(Y \geq 16.81)$, $n = 6$
(i) $P(Y \geq 38.89)$, $n = 26$ (j) $P(33.20 < Y < 42.90)$, $n = 24$

*11-19.** Assume that X and Y are discrete random variables. Prove that, if X and Y are independent, then X^2 and Y^2 are independent.

11-20. The probability density function f for the distribution $\chi^2(n)$ is given by

$$\begin{aligned}
f(x) &= C_n x^{n/2-1} e^{-(x/2)} &&\text{for } x > 0 \\
f(x) &= 0 &&\text{for } x \leq 0
\end{aligned}$$

Here C_n is a constant (depending on n) chosen so that the total area under the curve is equal to 1.

(a) Express C_n in terms of an integral.
(b) Use the above equation to graph f for $\chi^2(2)$.
(c) Graph f for $\chi^2(3)$. (Use C_n as a unit on the vertical scale.)

11-2. Testing the hypothesis $\sigma^2 = \sigma_0^2$

The variance of a sample of size n for X was defined to be

$$s^2 = \frac{1}{n} \sum_{i=1}^{n} (X_i - \bar{X})^2$$

Dividing both sides of this equality by the population variance σ^2 we get

$$\frac{s^2}{\sigma^2} = \frac{1}{n} \sum_{i=1}^{n} \left(\frac{X_i - \bar{X}}{\sigma}\right)^2$$

Hence,

$$\frac{ns^2}{\sigma^2} = \sum_{i=1}^{n} \left(\frac{X_i - \bar{X}}{\sigma}\right)^2$$

This last equation has on its right an expression very much like the

$$\sum \left(\frac{X_i - \mu}{\sigma}\right)^2$$

obtained in (11-4) (if Y_i is written in place of X_i). In fact, these two expressions differ only in that, where one involves the distribution mean

μ, the other has the sample mean $\bar{X}$. We might hope then that ns^2/σ^2 will have a distribution similar to that for

$$\sum \left(\frac{X_i - \mu}{\sigma} \right)^2$$

This hope is not in vain when X is normal. We state without proof:

(11-21)   *If X is $N(\mu,\sigma^2)$ and s^2 is the variance of a random sample of size n for X, then ns^2/σ^2 is $\chi^2(n-1)$.*

Thus, replacement of μ by $\bar{X}$ in (11-4) reduced the number of degrees of freedom of the distribution by 1. This is a pattern that we shall observe again. In an expression which yields a χ^2 variable with n degrees of freedom, a parameter was replaced by a statistic which estimates the parameter, and the result was an expression which yields a χ^2 variable with $n - 1$ degrees of freedom. That is, replacing a parameter by a statistic which estimates it, we found that the number of degrees of freedom was reduced by 1.

To illustrate the application of (11-21), suppose that X is $N(\mu,4)$ and s^2 is the variance of a random sample of 11 values of X. Then $11s^2/\sigma^2 = 11s^2/4$ has the distribution $\chi^2(10)$. This distribution is the one corresponding to the spinner shown in Fig. 11-1D. If we wish to find $P(3 < s^2 < 5)$, we have from this spinner that

$$P(3 < s^2 < 5) = P \left(3\tfrac{3}{4} < \frac{11s^2}{4} < 5\tfrac{5}{4} \right)$$
$$= P \left(8.25 < \frac{11s^2}{4} < 13.75 \right) \cong .39$$

Since the mean of $\chi^2(n-1)$ is $n - 1$, we may use (11-21) to derive a result mentioned in an earlier section. ns^2/σ^2 has the $\chi^2(n-1)$ distribution, so that $E(ns^2/\sigma^2) = n - 1$. From this it follows that

(11-22) $$E(s^2) = \frac{n-1}{n} \sigma^2$$

[See (10-49).] While our derivation applies only for normal X, (11-22) actually holds in general for the variance of a random sample for any variable with variance σ^2 (see Prob. 11-36). We see then that s^2 is a biased estimate of σ^2. Nevertheless, the expected value of s^2 is simply a constant times σ^2, so that we expect a large value of σ^2 to be reflected in large values for s^2 and a small value for σ^2 to be reflected in small values for s^2.

Imagine that we are interested in studying a new method of teaching long division. We use the new method with a class of 31 students and at the end of the trial period give them a certain standard test. In the past, scores on this test have been approximately normal with standard deviation 10. It is suggested about the new method that it favors the bright student and penalizes the dull ones, so that the good students tend to do better and the poor students tend to do worse. If this actually happens, we would expect the scores obtained after using the new method to have a wider spread than before. That is, we would expect the variance to be larger than the 100 found using the old method. Suppose that we consider our class of 31 students to be a random sample and that, after the new method has been used, the variance of the 31 scores is 150. Is this "significant" evidence that the new method does cause a larger spread?

We let X be the score obtained by a student chosen at random and taught by the new method. We assume that X is $N(\mu,\sigma^2)$. We have a random sample of 31 values of X for which $s^2 = 150$. We wish to test the hypothesis $H_0: \sigma^2 = 100$ against the alternative $H_1: \sigma^2 > 100$.

Since we expect a large value of σ^2 to be reflected in large values of s^2, a reasonable kind of test would be to reject H_0 when s^2 is too large. That is, reject H_0 when $s^2 \geq K$ for some appropriately chosen K. If we wish our test to have a significance level of, say, 5 per cent, then we should choose K so that $P(s^2 \geq K) = .05$ when H_0 is true. But when H_0 is true, we know that $31s^2/100$ has the distribution $\chi^2(30)$. Then from Table A-6 (using 30 degrees of freedom) we see that

$$P\left(\frac{31s^2}{100} \leq 43.8\right) = .95$$

In other words,

$$P(s^2 \leq {}^{4380}\!/_{31} = 141) = .95$$

Then $K = 141$ will make our test have a significance level of 5 per cent. Since our observed sample variance of 150 exceeds $K = 141$, we reject H_0 and say that 150 differs significantly from 100 at the 5 per cent level.

A slightly different way to do the arithmetic involved is to compute $31s^2/100$ for $s^2 = 150$ and compare this value with 43.8, rejecting H_0 if and only if $31s^2/100$ exceeds 43.8. This is an equivalent test, since $s^2 \leq (43.8)(100)/31$ if and only if $31s^2/100 \leq 43.8$. The latter method is the more common one.

At the 1 per cent level we see that we cannot reject H_0, since $31s^2/100 = 46.9 \leq 50.9$ and $P(Y \leq 50.9) = .99$ when Y is $\chi^2(30)$.

Generalizing the above example and using the same kind of argument we arrive at the following:

(11-23) *Tests for $H_0: \sigma^2 = \sigma_0^2$ against H_1 when X is normal and s^2 is the variance of a random sample of size n:*

H_1	Reject H_0 if and only if	Where Y is $\chi^2(n-1)$ and for an α-level test
$\sigma^2 > \sigma_0^2$	$\dfrac{ns^2}{\sigma_0^2} \geqq K$	$P(Y \geqq K) = \alpha$
$\sigma^2 < \sigma_0^2$	$\dfrac{ns^2}{\sigma_0^2} \leqq K$	$P(Y \leqq K) = \alpha$
$\sigma^2 \neq \sigma_0^2$	$\dfrac{ns^2}{\sigma_0^2} \leqq K_1$ or $\dfrac{ns^2}{\sigma_0^2} \geqq K_2$	$P(Y \leqq K_1) = \dfrac{\alpha}{2}$ $P(Y \geqq K_2) = \dfrac{\alpha}{2}$

In setting up these tests, we have assumed that the mean of X is unknown. This is usually the situation in most applications where we wish to test $H_0: \sigma^2 = \sigma_0^2$. The test given for the alternative hypothesis $\sigma^2 > \sigma_0^2$ in (11-23) is a uniformly most powerful test. The other tests given there are not uniformly most powerful but do possess several desirable properties besides appealing to our intuitive grasp of the situation. Uniformly most powerful tests do not exist for the alternative hypotheses $H_1: \sigma^2 < \sigma_0^2$ and $H_1: \sigma^2 \neq \sigma_0^2$ in (11-23).

The test in the first case in (11-23) is also a good test in the event that we wish to test $H_0: \sigma^2 \leqq \sigma_0^2$ against $H_1: \sigma^2 > \sigma_0^2$. Similarly, the test in the second case may be used for deciding between $H_0: \sigma^2 \geqq \sigma_0^2$ and $H_1: \sigma^2 < \sigma_0^2$.

When the above results are applied, it is well to remember that we can be sure that they have the desired significance level only when it is safe to assume that the underlying random variable is normal or, at least, approximately normal.

PROBLEMS

11-24. If X is $N(\mu, 25)$ and s^2 is the variance for a random sample of 21 values for X, find (see Fig. 11-1)

(a) $P(23 < s^2 < 26)$ (b) $P(s^2 > 25)$
(c) $P(s^2 < 50)$ (d) $P(40 < s^2 < 50)$

11-25. Suppose that X is normal with a *known* mean and we wish to test $H_0: \sigma^2 = \sigma_0^2$ against $H_0: \sigma^2 > \sigma_0^2$. Design a test for these hypotheses which is an improvement on the test given by (11-23). Assume that the test is to be based on an observed sample $X_1, X_2, \ldots, X_n$.

11-26. In a random group of 20 students at a certain school the standard deviation of their IQ's is 10. Does this indicate that the IQ's at this school are more homogeneous than in the population at large, where the standard deviation of IQ's is 15?

11-27. In a certain production process it is permissible to have a variance of no more than .01 sq in. in the length of a certain part. If a sample of 15 of these parts yields lengths with a variance of s^2, how large may we allow s^2 to be before stopping production?

11-28. Express the tests given in (11-23) in terms of conditions on the sample standard deviation.

11-29. Construct a quality-control chart for the variability of a product (see Prob. 11-27) if it is known that, when production is under control, the measured quantity is normal with $\sigma^2 = 20$. Assume that samples of size 6 are to be taken periodically.

11-30. A sample of 13 values of a normal variable has variance $s^2 = 1$. Test the hypothesis that $\sigma^2 = .5$.

11-31. A sample of 15 values of a normal variable has variance $s^2 = 50$. Test the hypothesis that $\sigma^2 \geq 75$.

11-32. If s^2 is the variance of a random sample of 11 values of a normal variable with variance 100, graph the distribution function for s^2 (see Fig. 11-1).

11-33. As a class project, draw about 100 random samples of size 4 from Table 9-4. Compute s^2 for each sample. Plot the cumulative frequency function for the values of s^2. Compare this result with the theoretical distribution function for s^2 (see Prob. 10-8).

11-34. Graph the power function for the test given by (11-23) for $H_0: \sigma^2 = 50$ against $H_1: \sigma^2 > 50$ when (a) $n = 11$, (b) $n = 21$. Let $pf(y) = P(ns^2/50 \geq K | \sigma^2 = y) = P(X \geq (50/y)K | X$ is $\chi^2(10))$ for (a).

11-35. Graph the power function for the test given by (11-23) for $H_0: \sigma^2 = 50$ against $H_1: \sigma^2 < 50$ for (a) $n = 11$ and (b) $n = 21$.

11-36. Show that, when X is any random variable and s^2 is the variance of a random sample of size n for X, then $E(s^2) = (n - 1/n)\sigma^2$. [*Hint:* $E(X^2) = \sigma^2 + \mu^2$.]

11-37. Graph the power function for Prob. 11-34 when H_1 is taken to be $H_1: \sigma^2 \neq 50$.

11-38. Let X_1, X_2 be a sample of size 2 for a normal variable. Design a test for $H_0: \sigma^2 = 9$ against $H_1: \sigma^2 > 9$. Express the critical region for the test in terms of X_1 and X_2. Graph the critical region in the $X_1 X_2$ plane. Make the test have a 5 per cent significance level.

11-39. Do the preceding problem with the alternative hypothesis taken to be (a) $H_1: \sigma^2 < 9$ and (b) $H_1: \sigma^2 \neq 9$.

11-40. In connection with (11-21) show that

$$\sum_{i=1}^{n} \left(\frac{X_i - \mu}{\sigma}\right)^2 = \sum_{i=1}^{n} \left(\frac{X_i - \bar{X}}{\sigma}\right)^2 + \left(\frac{\bar{X} - \mu}{\sigma/\sqrt{n}}\right)^2$$

Hint: Add and subtract $\bar{X}$ inside the parentheses on the left.

11-41. Show that in the equation in Prob. 11-40, when X is normal, the left member is $\chi^2(n)$ and that the second term on the right is $\chi^2(1)$.

11-3. Estimation of σ^2

When s^2 is the sample variance for n independent values of a random variable X, we know that $E(s^2) = (n - 1)\sigma^2/n$, where σ^2 is the variance of X.   Thus, s^2 is a biased estimate of σ^2.   However, $ns^2/(n-1)$ is an unbiased estimate of σ^2, since we have

$$E\left(\frac{n}{n-1}\,s^2\right) = \frac{n}{n-1}\,E(s^2) = \frac{n}{n-1}\left(\frac{n-1}{n}\right)\sigma^2 = \sigma^2$$

In terms of the original X values $X_1,\,X_2,\,\ldots,\,X_n$ we have

$$(11\text{-}42)\quad \frac{n}{n-1}\,s^2 = \frac{n}{n-1}\left[\frac{1}{n}\sum_{i=1}^{n}(X_i-\bar X)^2\right] = \frac{1}{n-1}\sum_{i=1}^{n}(X_i-\bar X)^2$$

As a consequence of this, some authors use the last expression in (11-42) to define the sample variance.   The reader is, therefore, warned that in some statistics books "s^2" is used as we have used it while in others it is defined to be equal to the last expression in (11-42).

If, instead of a point estimate for σ^2, we wish to find a confidence interval, we can derive one from the tests of the previous section.   As an example, suppose that a random sample of 18 values of a normal random variable has a variance of 30.   Let us find a two-sided 95 per cent confidence interval for σ^2.   The related hypothesis-testing problem is to decide between $H_0: \sigma^2 = \sigma_0^2$ and $H_1: \sigma \neq \sigma_0^2$.   From (11-23) and Table A-6 we see that we should accept H_0 whenever $7.3 < 18s^2/\sigma_0^2 < 31.0$. Then the set of values for σ^2 which are acceptable is the set

$$\left\{\sigma_0^2: 7.3 < \frac{18s^2}{\sigma_0^2} < 31.0\right\} = \left\{\sigma_0^2: \frac{18s^2}{31.0} < \sigma_0^2 < \frac{18s^2}{7.3}\right\}$$

This (random) set is then a 95 per cent confidence set for σ^2.   For our observed value of $s^2 = 30$, we get $17.4 < \sigma^2 < 74.0$ as a 95 per cent confidence interval for σ^2.   Taking square roots we get $4.18 < \sigma < 8.60$ as a 95 per cent confidence interval for σ.

Carrying through the general cases as we did the above example we get the following from (11-23):

(11-43)   *If X is $N(\mu,\sigma^2)$ and s^2 is the variance of a random sample of size n, then the following are good $1-\alpha$ confidence intervals for σ^2:*

Where Y is $\chi^2(n-1)$ and

$$\sigma^2 > \frac{ns^2}{K} \qquad\qquad P(Y \geq K) = \alpha$$

$$\sigma^2 < \frac{ns^2}{K} \qquad\qquad P(Y \leq K) = \alpha$$

$$\frac{ns^2}{K_2} < \sigma^2 < \frac{ns^2}{K_1} \qquad\qquad P(Y \leq K_1) = \frac{\alpha}{2}$$

$$P(Y \geq K_2) = \frac{\alpha}{2}$$

It is of interest to note that, contrary to what we might at first expect, we get a confidence interval in the form $\{\sigma^2: \sigma^2 > C\}$ by considering the hypotheses $H_0: \sigma^2 = \sigma_0{}^2$ and $H_1: \sigma^2 > \sigma_0{}^2$. This is so because, when n is given and s^2 is observed, the acceptable values of $\sigma_0{}^2$ are those which make $ns^2/\sigma_0{}^2 < K$. But we make $ns^2/\sigma_0{}^2$ small by making $\sigma_0{}^2$ large. Hence, the acceptable values for $\sigma_0{}^2$ are those which are sufficiently big, i.e., greater than some constant C.

Which one of the three confidence intervals given in (11-43) we may wish to use in a given case will depend on the nature of the particular application. We obtain confidence intervals for σ from the results of (11-43) by simply taking square roots, since, when the numbers involved are positive, $a < b$ if and only if $\sqrt{a} < \sqrt{b}$.

PROBLEMS

11-44. Find 95 and 99 per cent confidence intervals for the variance of the scores obtained using the new method of teaching discussed in Sec. 11-2. What kind of a confidence interval would be best to use in this case in your opinion?

11-45. Find a two-sided 98 per cent confidence interval for σ if X is $N(\mu,\sigma^2)$ and a random sample of n values of X has a variance of $s^2 = 100$ where (a) $n = 20$, (b) $n = 10$, (c) $n = 4$, (d) $n = 2$.

11-46. Graph the length of the confidence interval found in Prob. 11-45 as a function of n.

11-47. A certain method of selecting a sample may well select a more homogeneous sample than one would expect if the sample were random. Suppose that it is known that X is $N(\mu,200)$ and that a sample of 10 values of X is chosen by a certain procedure. If the variance of the sample is 100, should we doubt the randomness of the sample?

11-48. Discuss the problem of finding a $1 - \alpha$ confidence interval for σ^2 when X is $N(\mu,\sigma^2)$, μ is *known*, and the interval is based on n random values of X (see Prob. 11-25).

11-49. When X is $N(\mu,\sigma^2)$ and a random sample of 13 values has a variance of s^2, let $L(s^2)$ be the length of a two-sided 95 per cent confidence interval for σ^2 based on the observed value s^2. Graph $L(s^2)$ as a function of s^2.

11-50. The same as the preceding problem except let $L(s^2)$ be the length of a confidence interval for σ (instead of for σ^2).

11-51. Find the variance of s^2 when s^2 is the sample variance of a random sample of size n for a normal variable with mean μ and variance σ^2.

11-52. Find $E[(s^2)^2]$ for s^2 as given in Prob. 11-51.

11-53. Find a two-sided 95 per cent confidence interval for σ^2 when X is $N(\mu,\sigma^2)$ and a random sample of size n has variance s^2, where

(a) $s^2 = .001$, $n = 10$ (b) $s^2 = 1000$, $n = 10$
(c) $s^2 = 50$, $n = 30$ (d) $s^2 = 100$, $n = 1000$
(e) $s^2 = 47$, $n = 24$

11-54. For each case in the preceding problem find a two-sided 95 per cent confidence interval for σ.

11-55. Consider the scores on the last hour exam to be a sample from a large population, and find a 95 per cent confidence interval for the population variance.

11-4. Testing goodness of fit

Suppose that $A_1, A_2, \ldots, A_k$ are sets which constitute a partition of the sample space S for a random variable X. Then the A_i's are disjoint and their union is S. Suppose that n observations for X lead to the empirical frequency function FR, so that $FR(A_i)$ is the number of observed values which belong to A_i. If we know the probability distribution for X, then we can find $p_i = P(X \in A_i)$ for $i = 1, 2, \ldots, k$. Then $FR(A_i)$ is the number of successes in n trials where the probability of success in a single trial is p_i (when we think of ending up in A_i as being a success). Then the random variable $FR(A_i)$ has the binomial distribution $B(n,p_i)$. The expected value of $FR(A_i)$ is np_i. We may then speak of np_i as the expected frequency for A_i. The quantity $[FR(A_i) - np_i]^2$ is a measure of how far the observed frequency is from the expected frequency. The quantity

$$\frac{[FR(A_i) - np_i]^2}{np_i}$$

is a measure of this deviation as a fraction of the expected frequency. The total

$$\sum_{i=1}^{k} \frac{[FR(A_i) - np_i]^2}{np_i}$$

is then a measure of how well the observed frequencies fit the theoretical expected frequencies. It turns out that, when n is large, this sum has approximately a $\chi^2(k - 1)$ distribution.

(11-56)   *If A_1, A_2, $\ldots$, A_k are the classes in an empirical frequency distribution for n observations and if $P(X \in A_i) = p_i$ for $i = 1, 2, \ldots, k$, then*

$$\sum_{i=1}^{k} \frac{[FR(A_i) - np_i]^2}{np_i}$$

has approximately the distribution $\chi^2(k - 1)$ when n is large.

More precisely, the approximation will be sufficiently close for most practical purposes when n is large enough so that $np_i \geqq 5$ for each p_i.

We can make the above theorem reasonable, perhaps, by proving it for the special case of $k = 2$. When $k = 2$, let us denote $FR(A_1)$ by Y. Then Y is $B(n,p_1)$, where $P(X \in A_1) = p_1$. Now

$$FR(A_2) = n - FR(A_1) = n - Y$$

and $P(X \in A_2) = p_2 = 1 - p_1$. Denoting p_2 by q_1 we have

$$\sum_{i=1}^{2} \frac{[FR(A_i) - np_i]^2}{np_i} = \frac{(Y - np_i)^2}{np_i} + \frac{[n - Y - n(1 - p_1)]^2}{nq_1}$$

$$= \frac{(Y - np_1)^2}{np_1} + \frac{(np_1 - Y)^2}{nq_1}$$

$$= \frac{(Y - np_1)^2 q_1}{np_1q_1} + \frac{(Y - np_1)^2 p_1}{np_1q_1}$$

$$= \frac{(Y - np_1)^2}{np_1q_1}$$

$$= \left(\frac{Y - np_1}{\sqrt{np_1q_1}}\right)^2$$

But Y is $B(n,p_1)$, and when both np_1 and nq_1 exceed 5, Y is approximately normal with mean np_1 and standard deviation $\sqrt{np_1q_1}$. Then $(Y - np_1)/\sqrt{np_1q_1}$ is approximately normal with mean 0 and variance 1. But then the square of this quantity has approximately the distribution $\chi^2(1)$. This completes the proof for the case $k = 2$, since in this case $k - 1 = 1$.

In view of the result (11-56), the χ^2 distributions are useful for testing the hypothesis that a variable has a certain probability distribution when we have an empirical distribution for a sample for that variable. If we let O_i be the frequency observed for the ith class in an empirical distribution and let e_i be the expected frequency for that class, then we may write the sum involved in (11-56) more concisely as

(11-57)
$$Z = \sum_{i=1}^{k} \frac{(O_i - e_i)^2}{e_i}$$

Here k is the number of classes in the distribution. When n is large so that $e_i \geqq 5$ for each i, then Z is approximately $\chi^2(k - 1)$.

Suppose, for example, that we wish to test the hypothesis that the dice used to obtain the results in Table 1-2 were perfectly balanced. For each of the classes in Table 1-2 we know the corresponding probability if the dice were perfect (see Prob. 6-27). These are shown in the column headed p_i in Table 11-1. In this case each A_i is a one-element set. Table 11-1 shows the computation of Z for our data.

Thus, for this sample of 100 throws of the dice, $Z = 9.42$. In the table the calculations were made by slide rule, which gives sufficient accuracy for the problem. (The difference between 100 and the total of the e_i column is due to round-off error.) As is customary, in making such computations we combined the two classes at each end of the distribution so that all expected frequencies exceed 5. If the dice used were perfect, we have, then, one value (9.42) of a statistic Z which will have the distribution $\chi^2(7)$, since there are now eight classes in the frequency distribution. If, on the other hand, the value observed for Z is larger than one would usually expect from the distribution $\chi^2(7)$, we shall reject the hypothesis that the dice were perfect. From Table A-6 we see that, when Z is $\chi^2(7)$, then $P(Z < 9.8) = .8$, so that 20 per cent of the values of Z will have values greater than 9.8 when the dice are perfect. Our observed result of 9.42 consequently gives us little cause to doubt that the dice are well balanced. That is, we can accept the hypothesis that the dice are perfect at the usual significance levels.

Table 11-1
Computation of Z for the Data of Table 1-2

x	O_i	p_i	$e_i = 100p_i$	$O_i - e_i$	$\dfrac{(O_i - e_i)^2}{e_i}$
2	$\left.\begin{array}{c}2\\4\end{array}\right\}6$	$\frac{1}{36}$	$\left.\begin{array}{c}2.77\\5.55\end{array}\right\}8.32$	-2.32	.65
3		$\frac{1}{18}$			
4	5	$\frac{1}{12}$	8.33	-3.33	1.33
5	5	$\frac{1}{9}$	11.11	-6.11	3.36
6	14	$\frac{5}{36}$	13.89	.11	.00
7	18	$\frac{1}{6}$	16.67	1.33	.11
8	14	$\frac{5}{36}$	13.89	.11	.00
9	14	$\frac{1}{9}$	11.11	2.89	.75
10	12	$\frac{1}{12}$	8.33	3.67	1.61
11	$\left.\begin{array}{c}8\\4\end{array}\right\}12$	$\frac{1}{18}$	$\left.\begin{array}{c}5.55\\2.77\end{array}\right\}8.32$	3.68	1.61
12		$\frac{1}{36}$			
Totals......	100	1	99.97	......	$Z = 9.42$

Generalizing the above argument, suppose that $A_1, A_2, \ldots, A_k$ is a partition of the sample space. We have the following:

(11-58)   *To test at level α the hypothesis that $P(X \in A_i) = p_i$ for $i = 1, 2,$* *$\ldots, k$ on the basis of n observations which yield $FR(A_i) = O_i$, let $e_i = np_i$ and reject the hypothesis when*

$$\sum_{i=1}^{k} \frac{(O_i - e_i)^2}{e_i} > C$$

where C is chosen so that $P(Z \geq C) = \alpha$ when Z is $\chi^2(k - 1)$. To apply the test, each of the e_i's should not be less than 5.

Fortunately, the χ^2 test for goodness of fit is even more broadly applicable than indicated by (11-58). Suppose that we have the observed frequencies $O_1, O_2, \ldots, O_k$ and wish to test the hypothesis that the sample came from a normal distribution—without specifying *which* normal distribution. This can be done by computing the statistics $\bar{X}$ and s_X for the data and then computing the expected frequencies e_i by assuming that X is normally distributed with mean $\bar{X}$ and standard deviation s_X. The Z value computed from these e_i values will have approximately the distribution $\chi^2(k-3)$. That is, when the two parameters μ and σ are replaced by the estimates suggested for them, the random variable Z is still a χ^2 variable but with its degrees of freedom reduced by 2. The same restriction on the size of the e_i values still applies. That is, the approximation is good if $e_i \geqq 5$ for each i. It should be clear how this leads to a test for normality. We simply apply (11-58) with the e_i computed as indicated and with $k-1$ replaced by $k-3$.

In general, when the e_i's are computed by estimating l parameters by means of their maximum likelihood estimates, then Z will have approximately the distribution $\chi^2(k-l-1)$. Hence, the so-called χ^2 test for goodness of fit is quite broadly applicable when large enough samples are available.[1]

PROBLEMS

11-59. Test whether the dice you used in Prob. 1-3 were "perfectly balanced."

11-60. Test whether the coins used in Prob. 1-4 were perfectly balanced.

11-61. Use the data of Prob. 1-6 to test whether the number of tacks that fall point up has the distribution $B(12,.1)$.

11-62. Use the data of Prob. 1-7 to test whether the "fourth digits" are uniformly distributed in the table.

11-63. Use the data of Prob. 1-8 to test the hypothesis that sentence length for the author has a uniform distribution on $\{1,2, \ldots ,100\}$.

11-64. Use the data of Prob. 1-9 to test whether the number of odd digits has the appropriate binomial distribution with $p = .5$.

11-65. Use the data of Prob. 1-13 to test the hypothesis that the dates are uniformly distributed on $\{1900,1901, \ldots ,d\}$, where d is the current year.

11-66. Use the data of Prob. 1-15 or of Prob. 1-16 to test whether the dice used were perfect.

11-67. Use the data of Prob. 1-17 to test the hypothesis that the dice used were perfect.

11-68. Use the data of Prob. 1-13 to test the hypothesis that the dates are normally distributed.

11-69. Use the data of Prob. 1-8 to test the hypothesis that the sentence lengths are normally distributed.

11-70. Use the data of Prob. 1-14 to test the hypothesis that the number of runs has (*a*) the uniform distribution on $\{1,2,3, \ldots ,25\}$ and (*b*) a normal distribution.

11-71. Use the data of Prob. 1-23*b* to test the hypothesis that the number of living grandparents has a uniform distribution on $\{0,1,2,3,4\}$.

[1] For a more complete discussion of χ^2 tests and, in particular, a discussion of so-called contingency tables, the reader is referred to P. G. Hoel, *Introduction to Mathematical Statistics*, 2d ed., chap. 9, John Wiley & Sons, Inc., New York, 1954.

11-72. Use the data of Prob. 1-23a to test the hypothesis that the number of siblings X has the distribution given by $P(X = x) = \frac{1}{2}^{x+1}$ on the set $\{0,1,2,3, \ldots \}$.

*11-73. Use the data of Prob. 1-11 to test the hypothesis that the correct guesses occur "purely by chance."

*11-74. Use the data of Prob. 1-12 to test the hypothesis that the correct guesses occur "purely by chance."

11-75. For the data of Prob. 1-22 test the hypothesis that the value came from a uniform distribution on $\{1,2,3,4,5,6\}$.

11-76. From the data of Prob. 1-23d test the hypothesis that "name length" is uniformly distributed on $\{10,11, \ldots ,35\}$.

11-77. Find the month of birth for each student in your class.   Test the hypothesis that births are uniformly distributed over the 12 months.

11-78. Use the data of Prob. 7-36 to test the hypothesis that your class "produces random digits."

11-79. Test Table A-4 for randomness by using a χ^2 test on the data of Prob. 7-35.

CHAPTER 12

F Distributions

12-1. Properties of F distributions

The ratio of two χ^2 variables will have a distribution which is called an F *distribution*. More precisely,

(12-1) *If* Y_1 *is* $\chi^2(n)$, Y_2 *is* $\chi^2(m)$, *and* Y_1 *and* Y_2 *are independent, then* $(Y_1/n)/(Y_2/m)$ *has the distribution denoted by* $F(n,m)$.[1]

The distributions $F(2,2)$, $F(2,3)$, $F(2,5)$, $F(2,8)$, $F(2,24)$, $F(3,2)$, $F(5,2)$, $F(12,12)$, $F(12,24)$, and $F(24,24)$ are generated by the spinners shown in Fig. 12-1. The density functions and distribution functions for these distributions are shown in Fig. 12-2.

There is a distribution $F(n,m)$ for each pair of positive integers n and m. Each such distribution is called an F distribution. If X has the distribution $F(n,m)$, we can say more briefly that "X is $F(n,m)$." n and m are said to be the *degrees of freedom* for the distribution $F(n,m)$.

The mean and variance of $F(n,m)$ are given by

(12-2) $$\mu = \frac{m}{m-2}$$

when $m > 2$ and

(12-3) $$\sigma^2 = \frac{2m^2(n+m-2)}{n(m-2)^2(m-4)}$$

when $m > 4$. $F(n,m)$ has no mean for $m \leq 2$ and no variance for $m \leq 4$.

From (12-1) we obtain the following useful fact:

(12-4) *If* X *is* $F(n,m)$, *then* $Y = 1/X$ *is* $F(m,n)$.

We can, for example, use the spinner in Fig. 12-1 for $F(2,8)$ to find approximate probabilities for a variable with the distribution $F(8,2)$. Suppose that X is $F(8,2)$ and we wish to evaluate $P(X < 10)$. Let Y

---

[1] The notation F_{nm} is also used to denote the distribution $F(n,m)$.

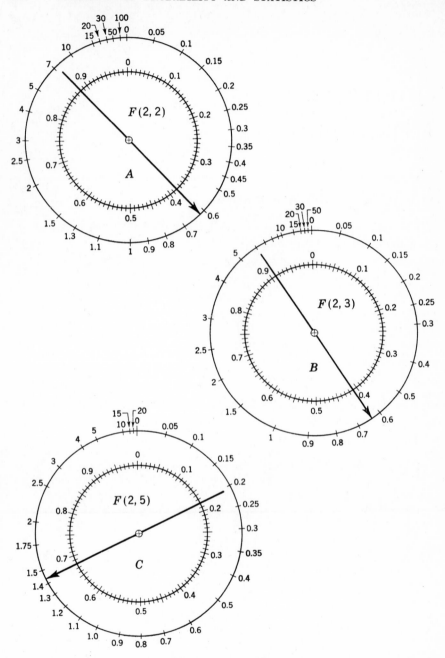

Fig. 12-1. Spinners for some F distributions.

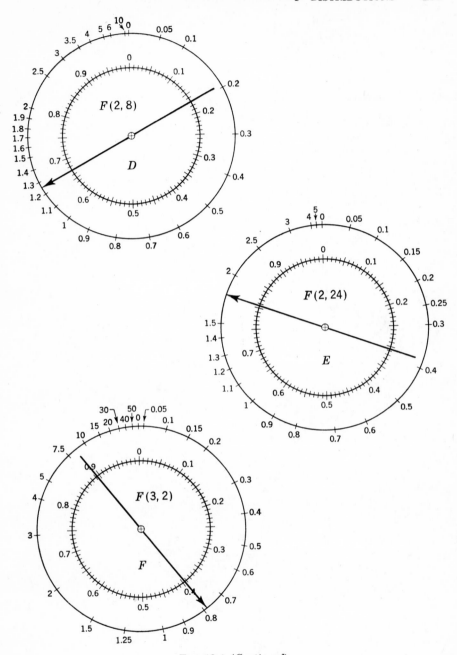

FIG. 12-1 (*Continued*)

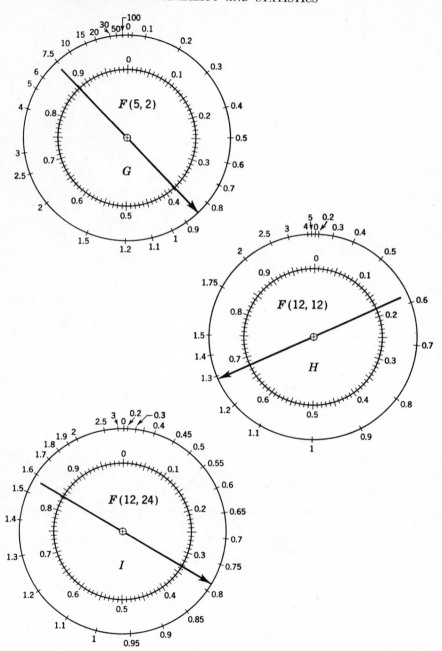

FIG. 12-1 (*Continued*)

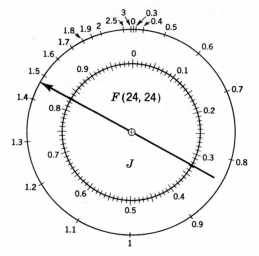

F (24, 24)

J

FIG. 12-1 (*Continued*)

be $F(2,8)$. Then Y is generated by the spinner in Fig. 12-1D. By (12-4) and this figure we have $P(X < 10) = P(1/X > .1) = P(Y > .1) = .91$.

Critical values for the right tail of the F distribution are given in Table A-7. When X is $F(4,5)$, we see from Table A-7 that $P(X > 5.19) = .05$ and $P(X > 11.39) = .01$. Left-tail critical values can also be obtained from this table. To find C so that $P(X < C) = .01$ when X is $F(10,25)$, we let Y have the distribution $F(25,10)$. From Table A-7,

$$P(Y > 4.32) = .01$$

Then

$$P\left(\frac{1}{Y} < \frac{1}{4.32}\right) = .01$$

By (12-4) $1/Y$ has the same distribution as X. Hence

$$P\left(X < \frac{1}{4.32}\right) = P(X < .231) = .01$$

Therefore, $C = .231$.

PROBLEMS

12-5. Use the spinners of Fig. 12-1 to find the following probabilities when X has the indicated distribution:

(*a*) $P(X < 10)$, $F(2,2)$

(*b*) $P(X < 20)$, $F(2,2)$

(*c*) $P(X < 3)$, $F(2,3)$

(*d*) $P(1 < X < 5)$, $F(2,3)$

(*e*) $P(.1 < X < 1.5)$, $F(2,5)$

(*f*) $P(1 < X < 4)$, $F(2,8)$

(*g*) $P(X < 1)$, $F(2,8)$

(*h*) $P(X < 4)$, $F(2,24)$

(*i*) $P(X < .2)$, $F(3,2)$

(*j*) $P(X < .1)$, $F(3,2)$

(*k*) $P(.5 < X < 5)$, $F(5,2)$

(*l*) $P(1 < X < 10)$, $F(5,2)$

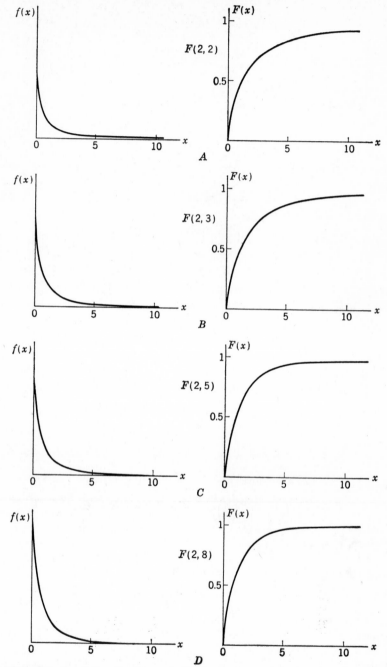

Fig. 12-2. Graphs of the density and distribution functions for the F distributions of Fig. 12-1.

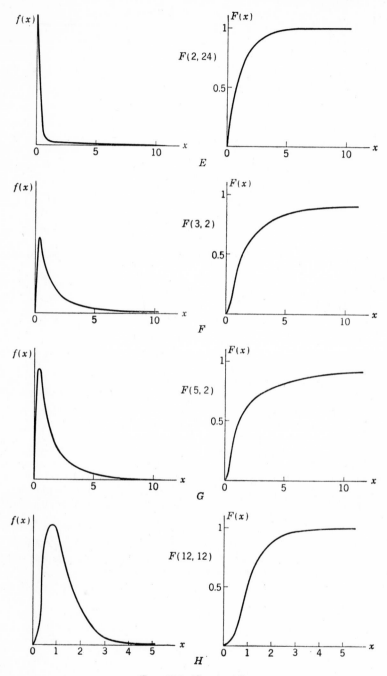

FIG. 12-2 (*Continued*)

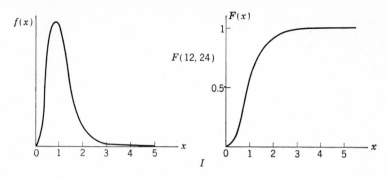

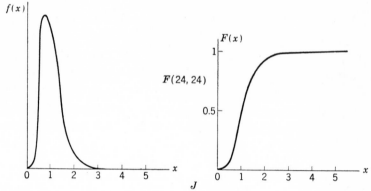

FIG. 12-2 (*Continued*)

(*m*) $P(1 < X < 2)$, $F(12,12)$ (*n*) $P(.5 < X < 2)$, $F(12,12)$
(*o*) $P(X < 5)$, $F(12,24)$ (*p*) $P(X > 1)$, $F(12,24)$
(*q*) $P(.5 < X < 1.5)$, $F(24,24)$ (*r*) $P(.5 < X < 2)$, $F(24,24)$

12-6. Find the following probabilities when Y has the indicated distribution:
(*a*) $P(Y > 1)$, $F(8,2)$ (*b*) $P(Y > .5)$, $F(8,2)$
(*c*) $P(.2 < Y < 2)$, $F(8,2)$ (*d*) $P(Y > .2)$, $F(24,12)$
(*e*) $P(Y < 1)$, $F(24,12)$ (*f*) $P(.1 < Y < 2)$, $F(24,12)$
(*g*) $P(1 < Y < 1.5)$, $F(24,12)$ (*h*) $P(.3 < Y < 3)$, $F(24,12)$

12-7. Justify (12-4) by reference to (12-1).

12-8. Find the mean and variance for each distribution in Fig. 12-1 to which the formulas (12-2) and (12-3) apply.

12-9. Let $X_1, X_2, \ldots, X_n$ and $Y_1, Y_2, \ldots, Y_m$ be random samples, and let X and Y be independent standard normal variables. Show that

$$\frac{m \sum_{i=1}^{n} X_i^2}{n \sum_{k=1}^{m} Y_k^2}$$

has the distribution $F(n,m)$.

12-10. Use Table A-7 to find C if

(a) X is $F(9,100)$ and $P(X > C) = .05$

(b) X is $F(7,5)$ and $P(X < C) = .95$

(c) X is $F(100,10)$ and $P(X < C) = .99$

(d) X is $F(9,25)$ and $P(X < C) = .01$ (e) X is $F(10,50)$ and $P(X < C) = .05$

(f) X is $F(50,50)$ and $P(X < C) = .01$ (g) X is $F(10,10)$ and $P(X < C) = .05$

12-11. When X has the indicated distribution, find values C_1 and C_2 so that

(a) $P(C_1 < X < C_2) = .90$, $F(5,8)$ (b) $P(C_1 < X < C_2) = .90$, $F(2,8)$

(c) $P(C_1 < X < C_2) = .98$, $F(6,10)$ (d) $P(C_1 < X < C_2) = .98$, $F(10,5)$

(e) $P(C_1 < X < C_2) = .90$, $F(25,50)$ (f) $P(C_1 < X < C_2) = .90$, $F(8,8)$

(g) $P(C_1 < X < C_2) = .98$, $F(25,25)$ (h) $P(C_1 < X < C_2) = .98$, $F(50,50)$

12-12. Let X be $N(\mu_X, \sigma_X{}^2)$ and Y be $N(\mu_Y, \sigma_Y{}^2)$. Let $X_1, X_2, \ldots, X_n$ and $Y_1, Y_2, \ldots, Y_m$ be random samples. Show that

$$\frac{\dfrac{1}{n} \sum_{i=1}^{n} \left(\dfrac{X_i - \mu_X}{\sigma_X}\right)^2}{\dfrac{1}{m} \sum_{i=1}^{m} \left(\dfrac{Y_i - \mu_Y}{\sigma_Y}\right)^2}$$

has the distribution $F(n,m)$.

12-13. Draw four balls from the box in Table 9-4. Let the values on them be X_1, X_2, Y_1, Y_2. Compute

$$Z = \frac{\dfrac{1}{2} \sum_{i=1}^{2} \left(\dfrac{X_i - 20}{5}\right)^2}{\dfrac{1}{2} \sum_{i=1}^{2} \left(\dfrac{Y_i - 20}{5}\right)^2} = \frac{\sum_{i=1}^{2} (X_i - 20)^2}{\sum_{i=1}^{2} (Y_i - 20)^2}$$

Obtain 50 or more values of Z by repeating the experiment. Graph the resulting grouped frequency distribution, and compare with the density function for $F(2,2)$ (see Probs. 12-12 and 10-8).

12-14. If X is $F(n,m)$, then the density function for X is

$$f(x) = C x^{(n/2)-1} (nx + m)^{-(n+m)/2}$$

for $x > 0$ and $f(x) = 0$ otherwise. Here C is an appropriately chosen constant which depends on n and m.

(a) Express C in terms of an integral.   (b) Graph f for $n = 1$ and $m = 1$.

(c) Graph f for $n = 2$ and $m = 2$.

(d) Graph f for $n = 2$ and $m = 4$. (Use C as a unit on the vertical scale.)

12-15. Show that, as m gets large, the mean of $F(n,m)$ approaches 1.

12-16. Find the variance of $F(n,n)$. What happens to this variance as n gets very large?

12-2. Testing the hypothesis $\sigma_X{}^2 = \sigma_Y{}^2$

Familiarity with F distributions enables us to test the hypothesis $H_0: \sigma_X{}^2 = \sigma_Y{}^2$ against various alternatives when X and Y are normal variables. Suppose that s_X^2 is the variance of a random sample of size n for X and s_Y^2 is the variance of a random sample of size m for Y. From (11-21), ns_X^2/σ_X^2 has the distribution $\chi^2(n-1)$ while ms_Y^2/σ_Y^2 is $\chi^2(m-1)$. Then we may apply (12-1) and discover that

$$Z = \frac{[n/(n-1)](s_X^2/\sigma_X^2)}{[m/(m-1)](s_Y^2/\sigma_Y^2)}$$

has the distribution $F(n-1, m-1)$.

If we let

(12-17)
$$T = \frac{\dfrac{n}{n-1}s_X^2}{\dfrac{m}{m-1}s_Y^2} = \frac{\displaystyle\sum_{i=1}^{n}(X_i - \bar{X})^2/(n-1)}{\displaystyle\sum_{j=1}^{m}(Y_j - \bar{Y})^2/(m-1)}$$

then T is a statistic which does not depend on any parameters. Also we know that

$$Z = \frac{\sigma_Y^2}{\sigma_X^2}T$$

has the distribution $F(n-1, m-1)$. In other words,

$$T = \frac{\sigma_X^2}{\sigma_Y^2}Z$$

where Z has the distribution $F(n-1, m-1)$.

When $\sigma_X^2 = \sigma_Y^2$, then $T = Z$ and T has the distribution $F(n-1, m-1)$. When $\sigma_X^2 > \sigma_Y^2$, then T will tend to be larger than a variable with the distribution $F(n-1, m-1)$, since, in this case, $\sigma_X^2/\sigma_Y^2 > 1$. If, on the other hand, $\sigma_X^2 < \sigma_Y^2$, then T will tend to be smaller than a variable with the distribution $F(n-1, m-1)$. Hence, if we wish to test $H_0: \sigma_X^2 = \sigma_Y^2$ against $H_1: \sigma_X^2 \neq \sigma_Y^2$, it would be reasonable to base our decision on the size of T. When T is larger or smaller than we would expect for a variable with the distribution $F(n-1, m-1)$, we have reason to doubt H_0. Thus, we could agree to accept H_0 when and only when $C_1 < T < C_2$ for some appropriately chosen C_1 and C_2. When H_0 is true, T is $F(n-1, m-1)$, so that our test will have significance level α if we choose C_1 and C_2 so that $P(C_1 < T < C_2) = 1 - \alpha$ when T is $F(n-1, m-1)$. There are various ways of choosing C_1 and C_2 so that this is true, but the sensible thing to do seems to be to choose C_1 and C_2 so that they cut off equal tails for the distribution. Such a choice will evidently treat symmetrically the alternatives where $\sigma_X^2 > \sigma_Y^2$ and those where $\sigma_Y^2 > \sigma_X^2$. We wish to choose C_1 and C_2 so that $P(T > C_2) = \alpha/2$ and $P(T < C_1) = \alpha/2$ when T is $F(n-1, m-1)$.

Since Table A-7 gives only critical values for the upper tail of the F distribution, the test is usually set up so that C_1 need not actually be found. This can be done as follows: T is computed from (12-17). For the distribution $F(n - 1, m - 1)$, C_2 can be read directly from Table A-7 for $\alpha = .10$ or $\alpha = .02$. If the observed value of T exceeds C_2, then H_0 is rejected. If T is less than 1, then we consider $1/T$. This variable will [by (12-2)] have the distribution $F(m - 1, n - 1)$ when H_0 is true. Directly from Table A-7 we can find K so that $P(1/T > K) = \alpha/2$ for $\alpha = .10$ or $\alpha = .02$. Then H_0 is rejected when $1/T$ exceeds K. The value C_1, which we might compute, would be $C_1 = 1/K$.

In practice, this test comes down to considering only values for T which are greater than 1. That is, the variables are labeled "X" and "Y" so that T turns out to be bigger than 1. Then only one critical value need be determined from Table A-7. In summary, we have

(12-18)   *To test $H_0 : \sigma_X{}^2 = \sigma_Y{}^2$ against $H_1 : \sigma_X{}^2 \neq \sigma_Y{}^2$ at level α when X and Y are normal and independent, reject H_0 when T [as given by (12-17)] exceeds C and C is chosen so that $P(Z > C) = \alpha/2$ when Z is $F(n - 1, m - 1)$.*

If H_0 is not rejected by this test, then X and Y can be interchanged and the test tried again. But the total effect of this procedure is to choose X and Y so that $T \geq 1$ and then to apply (12-18) just once.

Using Table A-7, we can then construct tests at significance levels of 10 and 2 per cent for the hypotheses we are discussing. These rather strange significance levels will be satisfactory to use in most instances. In one very important application of (12-18) which we shall discuss in Sec. 13-3, it is natural to be very wary of any indication that $\sigma_X{}^2 \neq \sigma_Y{}^2$ and, hence, to use a rather large significance level such as 10 per cent.

The test given by (12-18) is not uniformly most powerful against all alternatives, but it is a good test in several respects.

As a numerical example suppose that we have one sample of size 10 with a variance of 40 and another sample of size 15 with a variance of 35. For the first sample the quantity needed in (12-17) is

$$\frac{10}{10 - 1}(40) = 44.4$$

For the second sample we have

$$\frac{15}{15 - 1}(35) = 37.5$$

Putting the larger of these in the numerator we have

$$T = \frac{44.4}{37.5} = 1.18$$

When Z is $F(9,14)$, we have, from Table A-7, $P(Z > 2.7) \cong .05$. The observed value for T is certainly not significant, so we accept $H_0: \sigma_X^2 = \sigma_Y^2$ even at a significance level of 10 per cent.

PROBLEMS

12-19. Let X and Y be normal and independent with unknown variances. Let s_X^2 and s_Y^2 be variances of samples of size n and m, respectively. Test the hypothesis $H_0: \sigma_X^2 = \sigma_Y^2$ for each of the following cases:

	s_X^2	s_Y^2	n	m
(a)	90	9	11	11
(b)	90	9	11	21
(c)	50	30	11	9
(d)	45	100	7	6
(e)	90	80	100	100
(f)	.051	.672	10	6
(g)	70	30	11	5
(h)	150	15	4	3
(i)	70	30	4	3
(j)	100	80	100	500

12-20. If X and Y are independent and normal and s_X^2 and s_Y^2 are both variances for samples of size 13, design a test at the 10 per cent level for deciding between $H_0: \sigma_X^2 = \sigma_Y^2$ and $H_1: \sigma_X^2 \neq \sigma_Y^2$. For various values of K find the size of the type II error when this test is used to decide between H_0 and $H_1': \sigma_X^2 = K\sigma_Y^2$. Graph the size of this error as a function of K (see Fig. 12-1).

12-21. In the derivation (12-18) it was implicitly assumed that μ_X and μ_Y were unknown. Design a test for the hypotheses in (12-18) assuming that μ_X and μ_Y are known. Your test should be an improvement on the test given in (12-18) for the case of unknown mean values (see Prob. 12-12).

12-22. Test for the equality of the population variances for each pair of variables involved in the data collected for Prob. 5-55 in parts c, n, q, and s. Discuss the assumptions that must be made.

12-23. Do Prob. 12-20 with both samples taken to be of size 25.

12-24. Tell how to find a 98 per cent confidence interval for σ_X^2/σ_Y^2 when X and Y are normal and sample variances for X and Y are available.

12-25. Let X and Y be normal and s_X^2 and s_Y^2 be sample variances for samples of size 9 and 6, respectively. Design a 10 per cent level test for deciding between $H_0: \sigma_X^2 = \sigma_Y^2$ and $H_1: \sigma_X^2 \neq \sigma_Y^2$. Graph the critical region for the test in the plane with s_X^2 on the horizontal and s_Y^2 on the vertical axes.

12-26. Do the preceding problem with the sample sizes taken to be (a) 5 and 50, (b) 10 and 100, (c) 100 and 500.

12-27. Considering the class exam scores to be samples from large normal populations, test the hypothesis that the underlying variances for the first- and second-hour exams in this course were the same.

12-28. When X and Y are normal and samples of size n and m are available for them, design a test of the hypothesis $H_0: \sigma_X^2 = \sigma_Y^2$ against (a) $H_1: \sigma_X^2 > \sigma_Y^2$ and (b) $H_1: \sigma_X^2 < \sigma_Y^2$. What significance levels are convenient to use with Table A-7?

12-29. To see the importance of the independence of X and Y in (12-18), suppose that $n = m$ and $Y_i = 2X_i$ for $i = 1, 2, \ldots, n$, where X is normal. What is the distribution of T for this situation?

12-3. Analysis of variance

Is there any significant difference among the IQ's in the freshman, sophomore, junior, and senior classes in your school? Is there a significant difference among the amounts of school missed because of illness in the four classes? Is there a significant difference among average grades received by each of the four classes last semester?

Each of these questions suggests the problem of testing the hypothesis that each of several population means is the same. More generally, whenever we have several groups which can be distinguished from one another by different backgrounds or by different treatments, we may be interested in testing the hypothesis that the groups do not differ with regard to some observed random variable. It is reasonable to expect that we can base our test of this hypothesis on samples drawn from each of the groups. Let us assume that in each group the variable of interest is normally distributed (or approximately so). We then can attack the problem as follows.

Let $X_1, X_2, \ldots, X_k$ be normal variables. Let $E(X_i) = \mu_i$ for $i = 1, 2, \ldots, k$, and suppose that we wish to test the hypothesis that all these mean values are the same. That is, suppose we wish to test $H_0: \mu_1 = \mu_2 = \cdots = \mu_k$. We make two assumptions to simplify the problem. First, we assume that all the variables have the same variance. That is, if σ_i^2 is the variance for X_i, we assume that

$$\sigma_1^2 = \sigma_2^2 = \cdots = \sigma_k^2 = \sigma^2$$

where we have written σ^2 for the common (but unknown) variance. Second, we assume that we shall base our decision about H_0 on a random sample of n values for X_1, a random sample of n values for $X_2, \ldots,$ and a random sample of n values for X_k. That is, we assume that the same size sample is available for each of the k variables.

Let us use double subscripts (see Prob. 3-6) and designate the sample for X_1 by $(X_{11}, X_{12}, \ldots, X_{1n})$. The sample for X_2 will be $(X_{21}, X_{22}, \ldots, X_{2n})$ . . . . The sample for X_k will be $(X_{k1}, X_{k2}, \ldots, X_{kn})$. In general, X_{ij} will be the jth result in the sample for X_i.

The mean of the sample of n values for X_i is (for $i = 1, 2, \ldots, k$)

$$(12\text{-}30) \qquad \bar{X}_i = \frac{1}{n} \sum_{j=1}^{n} X_{ij}$$

Since X_i is $N(\mu_i, \sigma^2)$ we see that $\bar{X}_i$ is $N(\mu_i, \sigma^2/n)$ for $i = 1, 2, \ldots, k$.

If H_0 is true, then the X_i's all have the same distribution. In this case we may think of all the samples as making up one large random sample of nk values from the common distribution. The mean of this large sample is

$$\bar{X} = \frac{1}{nk} \sum_{i=1}^{k} \sum_{j=1}^{n} X_{ij}$$

(12-31)
$$= \frac{1}{k} \sum_{i=1}^{k} \bar{X}_i$$

The over-all sum of the squares of the deviations from this mean is

(12-32)
$$S_0 = \sum_{i=1}^{k} \sum_{j=1}^{n} (X_{ij} - \bar{X})^2$$

Now it can be shown that this sum of squares may be expressed as a sum of two other sums of squares, each of which has an important intuitive interpretation; namely,

(12-33)
$$S_0 = S_1 + S_2$$

where

(12-34)
$$S_1 = n \sum_{i=1}^{k} (\bar{X}_i - \bar{X})^2$$

and

(12-35)
$$S_2 = \sum_{i=1}^{k} \sum_{j=1}^{n} (X_{ij} - \bar{X}_i)^2$$

The proof of (12-33) is given in Prob. 12-48. $\bar{X}_i - \bar{X}$ is the deviation of the mean for the ith sample from the over-all mean. S_1 is n times the sum of squares of these deviations. Whether H_0 is true or not, $\bar{X}_i$ is an estimate of μ_i. When H_0 is true, both $\bar{X}_i$ and $\bar{X}$ are estimates for the common mean which we call μ. Hence, when H_0 is true, we expect $(\bar{X}_i - \bar{X})^2$ to tend to be small. When H_0 is not true, then $E(\bar{X}_i) \neq E(\bar{X})$ for at least one value of i. But then for this i we find that $(\bar{X}_i - \bar{X})^2$ tends to be larger than we would expect when H_0 is true. Thus, when H_0 is false, S_1 tends to be larger than when H_0 is true.

When H_0 is true, we may consider $(\bar{X}_1, \bar{X}_2, \ldots, \bar{X}_k)$ to be a random sample of k values from the distribution $N(\mu, \sigma^2/n)$. Then the variance of this sample is $\sum_{i=1}^{k} (\bar{X}_i - \bar{X})^2/k$, which is S_1/nk. According to (11-21), this variance, multiplied by the sample size and divided by its population variance, will have the distribution $\chi^2(k-1)$.   That is,

$$\frac{k(S_1/nk)}{\sigma^2/n} = \frac{S_1}{\sigma^2}$$

has the distribution $\chi^2(k-1)$.

To investigate the second sum of squares S_2, first consider

$$\sum_{j=1}^{n} (X_{ij} - \bar{X}_i)^2$$

This is the same as ns_i^2, where s_i^2 is the variance of the sample of n values for X_i.   Since X_i is normal with variance σ^2, we see that

$$\frac{ns_i^2}{\sigma^2} = \frac{\displaystyle\sum_{j=1}^{n} (X_{ij} - \bar{X}_i)^2}{\sigma^2}$$

has the distribution $\chi^2(n-1)$.   This is so whether or not H_0 is true. Since the samples for the X_i's are independent, the s_i^2 values are independent.   Hence, by the additivity property of χ^2 distributions, (11-2),

$$\frac{S_2}{\sigma^2} = \sum_{i=1}^{k} \frac{ns_i^2}{\sigma^2}$$

has the distribution $\chi^2[k(n-1)]$, that is, $\chi^2(kn-k)$.

What we need in order to test H_0 is a statistic which does not depend on the unknown parameters and yet is sensitive to differences between the μ_i's.

Fortunately, it can be shown that S_1 and S_2 are independent.   It then follows from (12-1) that

$$Z = \frac{S_1/\sigma^2(k-1)}{S_2/\sigma^2(kn-k)} = \frac{S_1(kn-k)}{S_2(k-1)}$$

has the distribution $F(k-1, kn-k)$. Z can be computed without knowing the μ_i or σ.   Furthermore, we expect large values of S_1 to indicate the falsity of H_0 while the size of S_2 is not affected by the truth or falsity of H_0.   Hence, large values of Z will tend to make us doubt that H_0 is true.   Since we know the probability distribution for Z when H_0 is true, we can now state a test for H_0.

(12-36)   *To test H_0: $\mu_1 = \mu_2 = \cdots = \mu_k$ at level α when X_i is $N(\mu_i, \sigma^2)$ with σ unknown for $i = 1, 2, \ldots, k$, reject H_0 if and only if $Z = S_1(kn-k)/S_2(k-1) > C$, where we have $P(Z > C) = \alpha$ when Z is $F(k-1, kn-k)$.*

Here, S_1 and S_2 are defined by (12-34) and (12-35) and n is the size of the sample for each X_i.

The above is a simple example of a broad method of attack on certain statistical problems which is called *analysis of variance*. The test given exemplifies the "analysis of variance techniques" because the total variation S_0 of the data is broken down (i.e., analyzed) into other variations having certain intuitive interpretations. In our case, $S_0 = S_1 + S_2$, where S_1 is the variation *between* samples and S_2 is the sum of the variations *within* samples. This technique is an important one in statistics and has many interesting applications. Our single example only suggests the kind of problem to which the technique is applicable.[1] The basic discoveries about analysis of variance were made by R. A. Fisher, who has been a major figure in the development of modern statistics.

We now consider an application of (12-36). Part of our purpose in doing so is to illustrate practical computational schemes.

Suppose that X_1, X_2, and X_3 are known to be approximately normal with a common variance and a sample of size 6 for each variable yields the following data:

(12-37)

i j	1	2	3
1	15	25	13
2	17	20	19
3	24	29	19
4	19	21	18
5	28	31	15
6	19	23	25

Table (12-37) shows the values for X_{ij}, the jth result in the sample for X_i. Let us test the hypothesis H_0: $\mu_1 = \mu_2 = \mu_3$, where $E(X_i) = \mu_i$. To apply (12-36) we must compute S_1 and S_2. The easiest way to do so is to compute S_0 and S_1 and then obtain S_2 from (12-33) as $S_0 - S_1$. As a convenient formula for finding S_0 we have

(12-38)
$$S_0 = \sum_{i=1}^{k} \sum_{j=1}^{n} X_{ij}^2 - nk\bar{X}^2$$

$$= \sum_{i=1}^{k} \sum_{j=1}^{n} X_{ij}^2 - \frac{\left(\sum_{i=1}^{k} \sum_{j=1}^{n} X_{ij} \right)^2}{nk}$$

[1] For an elementary discussion of other applications of analysis of variance see W. J. Dixon and F. J. Massey, Jr., *Introduction to Statistical Analysis*, chap. 10, McGraw-Hill Book Company, Inc., New York, 1957.

This is obtained as a direct application of Eq. (5-8) when we consider the X_{ij}'s as constituting one large sample of nk values. To compute S_0 for our data (where $k = 3$, $n = 6$, and $nk = 18$) we need the sum of all the X_{ij}'s and the sum of all the $X_{ij}{}^2$'s. These are obtained in Table 12-1. In this table each entry in parentheses is the square of the immediately preceding entry. The sums needed, then, appear as grand totals at the right. Using these,

$$S_0 = 8458 - \frac{(380)^2}{18} = 434$$

Table 12-1
Analysis of Variance Computation for the Data of (12-37)

15 (225)	25 (625)	13 (169)
17 (289)	20 (400)	19 (361)
24 (576)	29 (841)	19 (361)
19 (361)	21 (441)	18 (324)
28 (784)	31 (961)	15 (225)
19 (361)	23 (529)	25 (625)

$\displaystyle\sum_{j=1}^{6} X_{ij}$ 122 (14,884) 149 (22,201) 109 (11,881)

$$\sum_{i=1}^{3}\sum_{j=1}^{6} X_{ij} = 380$$

$$\sum_{i=1}^{3}\left(\sum_{j=1}^{6} X_{ij}\right)^2 = 48{,}966$$

$$\sum_{i=1}^{3}\sum_{j=1}^{6} X_{ij}{}^2 = 8458$$

To find S_1 we use

$$S_1 = n\left(\sum_{i=1}^{k} \bar{X}_i{}^2 - k\bar{X}^2\right)$$

This is again a result of (5-8) when we think of the $\bar{X}_i$'s as making up a sample with mean $\bar{X}$. By noting the definitions of the means involved we may rewrite the above as

(12-39)
$$S_1 = n\sum_{i=1}^{k} \bar{X}_i{}^2 - \frac{\left(\sum_{i=1}^{k}\sum_{j=1}^{n} X_{ij}\right)^2}{nk}$$

$$= \frac{\sum_{i=1}^{k}\left(\sum_{j=1}^{n} X_{ij}\right)^2}{n} - \frac{\left(\sum_{i=1}^{k}\sum_{j=1}^{n} X_{ij}\right)^2}{nk}$$

In Table 12-1 we find the square of each column total and then the sum of these squares.   Then

$$S_1 = \frac{48,966}{6} - \frac{(380)^2}{18} = 137$$

Then $S_2 = S_0 - S_1 = 297$ and

$$Z = \frac{(137)(15)}{(297)(2)} = 3.46$$

When Z has the distribution $F(2,15)$, then $P(Z > 3.68) = .05$.   Hence, by the test of (12-36) we would not reject H_0 at the 5 per cent level and may not assert that there is a significant difference among the sample means.

The data of (12-37) were actually obtained by drawing three random samples of size 6 from the box of Table 9-4 and increasing each result in the middle sample by 5.   Since the distribution for the box of Table 9-4 is approximately $N(20,25)$, we see that the X_1 and X_3 for our data had approximately the distribution $N(20,25)$ while the distribution for X_2 was approximately $N(25,25)$.   Our test was not quite sensitive enough to detect this difference at the 5 per cent level for these quite small samples.

PROBLEMS

12-40. Draw three random samples of size 7 from the box of Table 9-4.   Increase each result in the last sample by 5, and see whether the test of (12-36) will detect this tampering with the data.

12-41. Test the hypothesis that the last three exams in this course were all of equal difficulty (i.e., all had the same "underlying mean").   Ignore any scores for students who did not take all three exams.

12-42. If there are representatives of more than one class (i.e., freshmen, sophomores, etc.) taking this course, test the hypothesis that each class represented did equally well on the last exam.   (Here it will be clear that our assumption of equal sample sizes is quite restrictive.   Suggest a reasonable way to handle the raw data so that our method applies.)

12-43. For some practice with summations over double subscripts, work Prob. 14-19.

12-44. Consider the three groups of students $A_1 = \{x : x$ had only two years of mathematics in high school and no college mathematics prior to this course$\}$, $A_2 = \{x : x$ had four years of high school math but no college math prior to the course$\}$, and $A_3 = (A_1 \cup A_2)'$.   Let $N = \min \{No\,(A_1), No\,(A_2), No\,(A_3)\}$.   Draw a random sample of size N from each group, and test the hypothesis that each group did equally well on the last exam.

12-45. In a book such as *Introduction to Probability and Random Variables* by G. A. Wadsworth and J. G. Bryan (McGraw-Hill Book Company, Inc., New York, 1960), look up the procedure for testing the H_0 of this section when the sample sizes are unequal.   Use the more general approach in (*a*) Prob. 12-42 and (*b*) Prob. 12-44.

12-46. Draw 10 random samples of size 2 from the box in Table 9-4. In the even-numbered samples increase each result by 3.   Test for equality of the population means by applying (12-36).

12-47. For the data of the preceding problem combine all the even-numbered samples and all the odd-numbered samples so that you have two samples of size 10. Test for equality of the means.

12-48. To prove that $S_0 = S_1 + S_2$, we have

$$S_0 = \sum_{i=1}^{k} \sum_{j=1}^{n} (X_{ij} - \bar{X})^2$$

$$= \sum_{i=1}^{k} \sum_{j=1}^{n} (X_{ij} - \bar{X}_i + \bar{X}_i - \bar{X})^2$$

$$= \sum_{i=1}^{k} \sum_{j=1}^{n} (X_{ij} - \bar{X}_i)^2 + \sum_{i=1}^{k} \sum_{j=1}^{n} (\bar{X}_i - \bar{X})^2 + 2 \sum_{i=1}^{k} \sum_{j=1}^{n} (X_{ij} - \bar{X}_i)(\bar{X}_i - \bar{X})$$

$$= S_2 + S_1 + 2 \sum_{i=1}^{k} \sum_{j=1}^{n} (X_{ij} - \bar{X}_i)(\bar{X}_i - \bar{X})$$

Hence, the proof is complete if the last sum on the right is zero.   Show that this is so.

12-49. Design a test for the hypothesis of (12-36) when σ^2 is known.

12-50. In the notation of (12-36), show that $S_1(n-1)/s_1^2(k-1)$ has the distribution $F(k-1, n-1)$.   Why not base our test on this statistic instead of on Z as given in (12-36)?

CHAPTER 13

Student's Distributions

13-1. Properties of Student's distributions

In Chap. 10 we found that we could test hypotheses about the mean of a normal distribution whenever the standard deviation is known or whenever the sample is large. In the case of a known standard deviation the tests are based on the fact that $(\bar{X} - \mu)/(\sigma/\sqrt{n})$ has a standard normal distribution when X is $N(\mu,\sigma^2)$ and $\bar{X}$ is the mean of a random sample of size n. When σ is unknown but the sample is large, we found that $s/\sqrt{n-1}$ is a good estimate for $\sigma/\sqrt{n}$ when s is the sample standard deviation.

Consequently, for large samples

$$T = \frac{\bar{X} - \mu}{s/\sqrt{n-1}}$$

will have approximately a standard normal distribution.

How will the statistic T be distributed in the case of small samples? This question was posed and answered by W. S. Gossett in 1908. Gossett wrote under the pseudonym "Student," and the distributions which arise in answering the question are called *Student's distributions* or, sometimes, *Student's t distributions* or simply *t distributions*.

There is a Student's distribution corresponding to each positive integer. The one corresponding to the integer n is denoted by $t(n)$.[1] The spinners in Fig. 13-1 generate variables with the distribution $t(1)$, $t(3)$, $t(5)$, and $t(10)$. The corresponding density and distribution functions are shown in Fig. 13-2. As we might expect, the distribution $t(n)$ is said to have n *degrees of freedom*. Each Student's distribution is symmetric about the origin and has its mean, median, and mode all equal to zero, except that $t(1)$ has no mean. The variance of the distribution $t(n)$ is $n/(n-2)$ for $n > 2$. For $n \leq 2$, $t(n)$ has no variance.

The graph of a density function for a Student's distribution has much the same bell shape as the density function for a standard normal vari-

---

[1] The notation t_n is often used in other texts to denote the distribution $t(n)$.

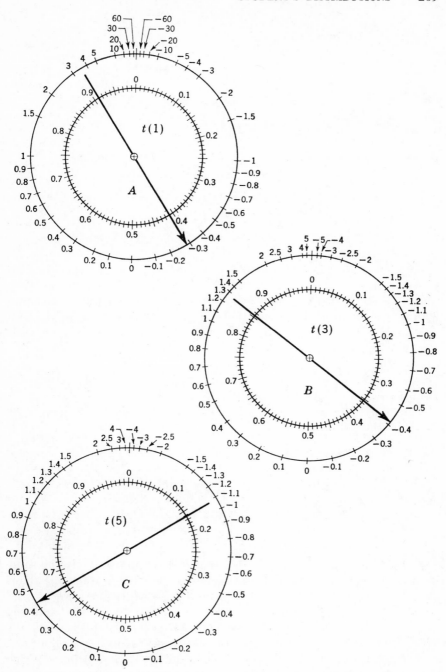

FIG. 13-1. Spinners for some Students' distributions.

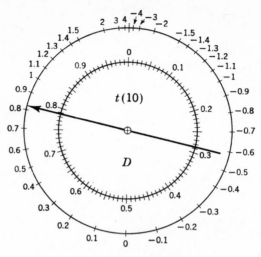

FIG. 13-1 (*Continued*)

able. In the former case, however, the distribution is more spread out. This is evident from the fact that the standard deviation for $t(n)$, which is $\sqrt{n/(n-2)}$, is always greater than 1. As n gets large, however, this standard deviation approaches 1 and, as can be proved, the Student's distribution becomes approximately normal. For most practical purposes, the distribution $t(n)$ is identical with the standard normal distribution when n is greater than 30.

The precise answer to the question about the distribution of T is given by the following:

(13-1)   *If X is normal with mean μ and $\bar{X}$ and s are the mean and standard deviation of a random sample of size n, then*

$$T = \frac{\bar{X} - \mu}{s/\sqrt{n-1}}$$

has the Student's distribution $t(n-1)$.

This result, coupled with the fact that $t(n)$ is approximately the same as $N(0,1)$ when $n \geq 30$, justifies some of our remarks in Chap. 10 about the use of the normal distribution in connection with large samples.

We may now use Student's distributions to test hypotheses and find confidence intervals for the mean of a normal distribution when the standard deviation is unknown and large samples are not available.

Various percentile points are given in Table A-8 for Student's distributions with no more than 30 degrees of freedom. The table shows the values corresponding to various size right tails on the probability

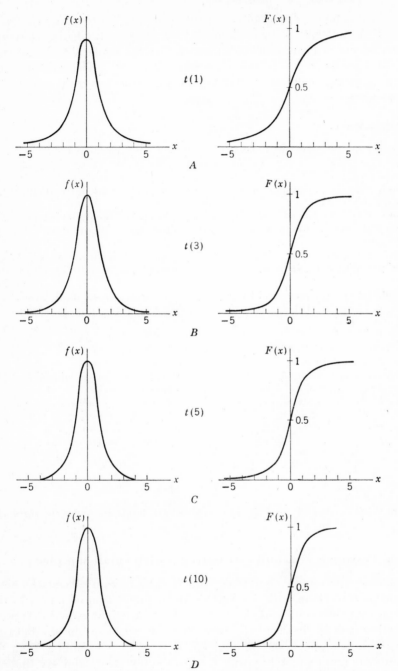

$t(1)$

A

$t(3)$

B

$t(5)$

C

$t(10)$

D

FIG. 13-2. Graphs of the density and distribution functions for $t(1)$, $t(3)$, $t(5)$, and $t(10)$.

density function. For example, when X is $t(9)$, we see from the table that $P(X > 2.262) = .025$ while $P(X > .261) = .4$. Using the symmetry of the Student's distributions we can use Table A-8 to find such probabilities as $P(|X| < .883) = .6$ when X is $t(9)$. The critical values in the first four columns of Table A-8 constitute the most useful part of the table.

PROBLEMS

13-2. Find the following probabilities when X has the distribution $t(1)$:

(a) $P(X < 5)$ (b) $P(-1 < X < 1)$ (c) $P(-2 < X < 2)$

(d) $P(-3 < X < 0)$ (e) $P(0 < X < 4)$ (f) $P(-5 < X < 5)$

13-3. Find the probabilities in the preceding problem for the distribution (a) $t(3)$, (b) $t(5)$, and (c) $t(10)$.

13-4. From the data of Prob. 11-33 obtain a sample of about 100 values of $T = (\bar{X} - 20)/(s/\sqrt{3})$. Compare the empirical distribution obtained with the distribution $t(3)$.

13-5. When X is $N(0,1)$, Y is $\chi^2(n)$, and X and Y are independent, then $\sqrt{n}\, X/\sqrt{Y}$ has the distribution $t(n)$. Use this result and the fact that $\bar{X}$ and s^2 are independent to prove (13-1).

13-6. Let X be $N(0,\sigma^2)$, and let $\bar{X}$ and s be the mean and standard deviation for a sample of size n. Let $Z = \bar{X}/s$. Find the following probabilities when n has the indicated value:

(a) $P(Z = 5)$, $n = 1$ (b) $P(Z < .3)$, $n = 11$

(c) $P(-3 < Z < 3)$, $n = 11$ (d) $P(|Z| < \sqrt{3})$, $n = 4$

(e) $P(|Z| < 2)$, $n = 4$ (f) $P(|Z| < 2)$, $n = 6$

13-7. If T has the distribution $t(k)$, find C so that for the given value of k

(a) $P(T > C) = .05$, $k = 10$ (b) $P(T < C) = .05$, $k = 10$

(c) $P(|T| < C) = .90$, $k = 7$ (d) $P(|T| < C) = .90$, $k = 20$

(e) $P(|T| < C) = .70$, $k = 50$ (f) $P(0 < T < C) = .45$, $k = 9$

(g) $P(C < T < 0) = .45$, $k = 4$ (h) $P(C < |T|) = .90$, $k = 3$

(i) $P(T > C) = .65$, $k = 100$ (j) $P(T > C) = .60$, $k = 40$

13-8. The density function for the distribution $t(n)$ is given by

$$f(x) = C \left(1 + \frac{x^2}{n}\right)^{-(n+1)/2}$$

where C (which depends on n) is chosen so that the total area under the curve is 1. Using C as unit, graph f for (a) $n = 1$ and (b) $n = 2$.

13-2. Testing $\mu = \mu_0$ and estimating μ with small samples

In a random sample of 10 male students at a certain college, the mean height is 5 ft 11 in. with a sample standard deviation of 1 in. Is this significant evidence that at this college the mean height exceeds 5 ft 9 in.? In other words, in view of these data we wish to decide between $H_0: \mu = 5$ ft 9 in. $= 69$ in. and $H_1: \mu > 69$ in. Assuming that the heights are approximately normal, we can apply (13-1) and say that

$$T = \frac{\bar{X} - \mu}{s/\sqrt{9}}$$

will have approximately the distribution $t(9)$ when μ is the true mean for X. When H_0 is true,

$$T = \frac{\bar{X} - 69}{s/3}$$

has approximately the distribution $t(9)$. Since a large value of μ (i.e., one exceeding 69 in.) will tend to be reflected in large values of X and hence a large value of $\bar{X}$, large values of $T = (\bar{X} - 69)/(s/3)$ would tend to make us doubt H_0 and favor H_1. If our test is to have a significance level of 5 per cent, we see that we would reject H_0 if and only if $T > 1.83$ (from Table A-8). For the given data we have

$$T = \frac{71 - 69}{\frac{1}{3}} = 6$$

Hence, the sample mean of 71 in. certainly differs significantly from 69 in. and we reject H_0. In fact, we see that we may also reject H_0 at the 1 per cent level, since our T value even exceeds 2.82 (as obtained from Table A-8).

Following the above pattern for the general case we have

(13-9)   *To test H_0: $\mu = \mu_0$ against H_1 when X is normal, σ is unknown, and $T = (\bar{X} - \mu_0)/(s/\sqrt{n-1})$:*

H_1	Reject H_0 if and only if	Where Y is $t(n-1)$ and for an α-level test
$\mu > \mu_0$	$T > K$	$P(Y > K) = \alpha$
$\mu < \mu_0$	$T < K$	$P(Y < K) = \alpha$
$\mu \neq \mu_0$	$|T| > K$	$P(|Y| > K) = \alpha$

These tests are not uniformly most powerful against all possible alternatives, but they are good tests on several counts. As we would expect, the test given for deciding between H_0: $\mu = \mu_0$ and H_1: $\mu > \mu_0$ is also a good test for deciding between H_0: $\mu \leq \mu_0$ and H_1: $\mu > \mu_0$. Similarly, the test given for H_0: $\mu = \mu_0$ against H_1: $\mu < \mu_0$ is also effective for H_0: $\mu \geq \mu_0$ and H_1: $\mu < \mu_0$.

The reader should by now be somewhat accustomed to deriving confidence sets from tests for hypotheses. Following the procedure we have used before produces the following result:

(13-10)   *When X is normal the following are $1 - \alpha$ confidence intervals for μ:*

(a) $\mu \geq \bar{X} - \dfrac{Ks}{\sqrt{n-1}}$ *where* $P(Y > K) = \alpha$

(b) $\mu \leq \bar{X} + \dfrac{Ks}{\sqrt{n-1}}$ *where* $P(Y > K) = \alpha$

(c) $\bar{X} - \dfrac{Ks}{\sqrt{n-1}} \leqq \mu \leqq \bar{X} + \dfrac{Ks}{\sqrt{n-1}}$ *where* $P(|Y| > K) = \alpha$

and Y has the distribution $t(n-1)$.

For example, with our sample of 10 heights, where $\bar{X} = 71$ in. and $s = 1$, a 95 per cent confidence interval for μ is

$$\mu \geqq 71 - \frac{(1.83)(1)}{\sqrt{9}}$$

or $\mu \geqq 70.39$.

PROBLEMS

13-11. Consider your class (or a small subset thereof in case your class is large) to be a random sample, collect the necessary data, and test the following hypotheses about the population of students at your school.
(a) The mean height of the male students is at least 5 ft 11 in.
(b) The mean height of the female students is no more than 5 ft 2 in.
(c) The mean weight of the men students is no more than 150 lb.
(d) The mean weight of the female students is at least 120 lb.

13-12. Use the data of the preceding problem to find two-sided 95 per cent confidence intervals for (a) the mean height of male students, (b) the mean height of female students, (c) the mean weight of the male students, (d) the mean weight of the female students.

13-13. Let X be normal, and let (X_1, X_2) be a random sample of size 2 for X. Design a 5 per cent level test for $H_0: \mu = 10$ against $H_1: \mu > 10$. Express the critical region for the test as a condition on X_1 and X_2. Graph the critical region in the $X_1 X_2$ plane.

13-14. Derive the first case of (13-10) from the result (13-9).

13-15. When X is normal, test $H_0: \mu = \mu_0$ against $H_1: \mu \neq \mu_0$ in each of the following cases:

Case	$\bar{X}$	s	n	μ_0
a	10	72	13	10
b	30	20	2	10
c	30	20	5	10
d	30	50	2	10
e	30	50	5	10
f	30	50	10	10
g	30	50	26	10
h	150	30	3	100
i	150	30	20	100
j	400	100	9	500
k	-.1	.3	15	0
l	3	4	5	6
m	10	20	50	20
n	1	2	5	2

13-16. In each case in the preceding problem decide between $H_0: \mu = \mu_0$ and $H_1: \mu > \mu_0$.

13-17. In each case in Prob. 13-15 find (a) a two-sided 95 per cent confidence interval for μ, (b) a two-sided 99 per cent confidence interval for μ, (c) a 95 per cent confidence interval for μ in the form $\mu > C$, (d) a 99 per cent confidence interval for μ in the form $\mu < C$.

13-18. In order to graph the power function for the test given by (13-9) for H_0: $\mu = \mu_0$ against $H_1: \mu \neq \mu_0$, what else would one have to know besides the results in Sec. 13-1?

13-3. Testing $\mu_X = \mu_Y$ with small samples

The general problem of testing the hypothesis $H_0: \mu_X = \mu_Y$ is a difficult one if only small samples are available. Even if we assume that both X and Y are normally distributed, the general problem is far from simple. There is one case, however, where an excellent test can be given which relies on Student's distributions. This is the case where X and Y are normal and can be assumed to have the same variance.[1]

When X and Y are independent and normal and $\bar{X}$ and $\bar{Y}$ are means of random samples of size n and m, respectively, we know that

$$Z = \frac{\bar{X} - \bar{Y} - (\mu_X - \mu_Y)}{[(\sigma_{\bar{X}}^2/n) + (\sigma_Y^2/m)]^{1/2}}$$

has the standard normal distribution. This is so because $\bar{X} - \bar{Y}$ is normal, $\mu_X - \mu_Y$ is the expected value of $\bar{X} - \bar{Y}$, and

$$\frac{\sigma_X^2}{n} + \frac{\sigma_Y^2}{m}$$

is the variance of $\bar{X} - \bar{Y}$. When $\sigma_X = \sigma_Y = \sigma$, we see that the statistic Z which has the distribution $N(0,1)$ becomes

$$Z = \frac{\bar{X} - \bar{Y} - (\mu_X - \mu_Y)}{\sigma[(1/n) + (1/m)]^{1/2}}$$

In analogy with (13-1), we might hope that

(13-19) $$T = \frac{\bar{X} - \bar{Y} - (\mu_X - \mu_Y)}{\hat{\sigma}[(1/n) + (1/m)]^{1/2}}$$

would have a Student's distribution if $\hat{\sigma}$ is some properly chosen estimate for σ. It turns out that this is the case. Specifically, it is so when

(13-20) $$(\hat{\sigma})^2 = \frac{ns_X^2 + ms_Y^2}{n + m - 2}$$

---

[1] Two variables which have the same variance are said to be *homoscedastic*. Unfortunately, in this book we shall have little call to use this wonderful word and its even more wonderful derivative *homoscedasticity*.

We may think of $(\hat{\sigma})^2$ as a kind of weighted mean of the two sample variances. In terms of the original sample values,

$$(13\text{-}21) \qquad (\hat{\sigma})^2 = \frac{\displaystyle\sum_{i=1}^{n}(X_i - \bar{X})^2 + \sum_{j=1}^{m}(Y_j - \bar{Y})^2}{n + m - 2}$$

(13-22) *If X and Y are normal and independent and $\sigma_X = \sigma_Y$, then T [as given by (13-19) where $\hat{\sigma}$ is defined by (13-20)] has the distribution $t(n + m - 2)$.*

If we wish to test the hypothesis $H_0: \mu_X = \mu_Y$ against some alternative, we see that, when H_0 is true, (13-19) simplifies to

$$(13\text{-}23) \qquad T = \frac{\bar{X} - \bar{Y}}{\hat{\sigma}[(1/n) + (1/m)]^{1/2}}$$

It seems natural to base our decision between H_0 and some alternative on the size of T. Large values of $|T|$ will tend to make us doubt that zero is the expected value of $\bar{X} - \bar{Y}$. Hence,

(13-24) *To test $H_0: \mu_X = \mu_Y$ against H_1 when X and Y are independent and normal, $\sigma_X = \sigma_Y$, and T is given by (13-23):*

H_1	Reject H_0 if and only if	Where Z is $t(n + m - 2)$ and for an α-level test
$\mu_X > \mu_Y$	$T > C$	$P(Z > C) = \alpha$
$\mu_X \neq \mu_Y$	$|T| > C$	$P(|Z| > C) = \alpha$

To test against the alternative $H_1: \mu_X < \mu_Y$, the roles of X and Y are interchanged and the first case of (13-24) is applied.

These tests are not uniformly most powerful, but they are excellent tests for the rather restrictive situation to which they apply.

Suppose, for example, that five girls taken as a random sample from a certain high school make scores on a college entrance exam which have a mean of 590 and a variance of 400. Suppose also that eight boys taken as a random sample from the same school make scores with a mean of 560 and a variance of 650 on the same exam. May we conclude that the girls from this high school will do better on this exam (on the average) than the boys? We have [from (13-20)]

$$(\hat{\sigma})^2 = \frac{(5)(400) + (8)(650)}{5 + 8 - 2} = 654$$

and $\hat{\sigma} = 25.6$. Hence,

$$T = \frac{590 - 560}{\sqrt{\tfrac{1}{5} + \tfrac{1}{8}}\,(25.6)} = 2.06$$

[from (13-23)]. But when Z has the distribution $t(11)$, we see from Table A-8 that $P(Z > 1.80) = .05$. Since $2.06 > 1.80$, we may reject H_0 at the 5 per cent level and conclude that the girls will do better on the average on this exam. On the other hand, we see that the value of T is not significant at the 1 per cent level, and this may be taken to suggest that further observations should be made before a decision is reached.

In order for the above test to make sense we must be sure of two facts. First, we must know that the boys' and girls' scores are approximately normal. Let us assume that, on the basis of past experience with the test, this is a reasonable assumption. Second, we must be able to assume that the boys' and girls' scores have the same underlying variance. With the data on hand, we may test this assumption by the method of (12-18). Let X be the score made by a boy chosen at random from the population, and let Y be the score of a girl chosen at random from the population. To test $H_0: \sigma_X^2 = \sigma_Y^2$ against $H_1: \sigma_X^2 \neq \sigma_Y^2$ we compute [from (12-17)]

$$Z = \frac{\frac{8}{7}(650)}{\frac{5}{4}(400)} = 1.48$$

This value falls far below the critical 5 per cent right-tail value of 6.09 for $F(7,4)$ as given by Table A-7. Hence, we accept H_0 (at the 10 per cent level) and our assumption of equality of the variances seems justified.

One of the important uses of the results of Sec. 12-2 is in just such examples as the above where we wish to apply (13-24) and, hence, must check on the equality of the variances.

It can be shown that the test of (13-24) is equivalent to the analysis of variance test of (12-36) when there are only two samples, they are of equal size, and the variables have the same variance.

PROBLEMS

13-25. When X and Y are independent and normal with a common variance, test $H_0: \mu_X = \mu_Y$ against $H_1: \mu_X \neq \mu_Y$ for each of the following cases:

Case	$\bar{X}$	s_X^2	n	$\bar{Y}$	s_Y^2	m
a	10	50	2	20	30	3
b	10	50	7	20	30	5
c	10	50	15	20	30	5
d	10	10	15	20	7	10
e	100	100	15	200	70	10
f	100	100	3	200	70	10
g	1	2	5	2	2	5
h	1	50	5	2	2	5
i	1	50	10	2	2	5
j	70	25	3	75	20	7

13-26. In each case in the preceding problem test H_0 against H_1: $\mu_X < \mu_Y$.

13-27. In each case in the preceding problem test whether the assumption of a common variance is reasonable in the face of the data.

13-28. Use the data of Prob. 13-11 to test the hypothesis that (*a*) the girls in your school weigh, on the average, the same as the boys and (*b*) the boys and girls have the same average height in your school.

13-29. Use the data of Prob. 5-55c to test the hypothesis that the first and second hour exams in this course were of equal difficulty.

13-30. Test the hypothesis that, on the last hour exam in this course, male and female students would do equally well on the average.

13-31. Did the students in your class who had 4 years of high school mathematics do significantly better than the others on the last hour exam in this course?

13-32. Are the students who wear glasses in your class significantly taller than the rest of the class?

13-33. Are the students who made either an A or a B on the last hour exam significantly taller than the others in your class?

13-34. Did the students who had another hour exam on the same day as the last hour exam in this course or on the preceding day do significantly worse than the others in the class on the last hour exam?

13-35. Did the students in your class who got at least 8 hours sleep the night before the exam do significantly better than the others on the last hour exam?

13-36. Use the method of this section for Prob. 12-46.

13-37. Draw a random sample X_1, X_2, X_3 from the box of Table 9-4. Obtain a sample Y_1, Y_2, Y_3, Y_4, Y_5 by making five draws from the box of Table 9-4 and then increasing each result by 7. Determine whether the test of (13-24) detects the difference in the underlying mean values.

CHAPTER 14

Bivariate Distributions

14-1. Marginal and conditional distributions—discrete case

If the sample space for an experiment is a set of ordered pairs of real numbers, a probability distribution for the experiment is called a *bivariate distribution*. Such experiments were considered in Sec. 5-5 and in the examples using Figs. 6-3 and 6-4. The reader should now review those sections.

Throughout this section we assume that we are considering an experiment which has the discrete sample space

$$S = \{(x_i, y_j) : 1 \leq i \leq n, \ 1 \leq j \leq m\}$$

where the x_i and y_j are real numbers. Then S consists of nm points in the xy plane. A probability distribution for this sample space is an assignment of a probability to each point in the space. If an outcome of a trial of the experiment is denoted by (X,Y), then the probability assigned to the point (x_i, y_j) is to be taken as $P(X = x_i \text{ and } Y = y_j)$. If f is a function defined on S which has the property that

$$f(x,y) = P(X = x \text{ and } Y = y)$$

then we call f the *joint probability function* for the variables X and Y. If we wish to emphasize the variables involved, we may designate the joint probability function for X and Y by "$f_{X,Y}$."

If A is any event so that $A \subseteq S$, then

$$P(A) = \sum_{(x,y) \in A} f(x,y)$$

In particular, considering the event $\{(X,Y) : X = x\}$ we have

$$P(X = x) = \sum_{j=1}^{m} f(x,y_j)$$

for the probability that $X = x$, disregarding the value taken on by Y. But when X is considered as a random variable in its own right, $P(X = x)$

is the value of the probability function for X. In the bivariate context, this function is called the *marginal probability function* for X and is denoted by f_X. That is,

(14-1)
$$f_X(x) = \sum_{j=1}^{m} f_{X,Y}(x,y_j)$$

Similarly, the *marginal probability function* for Y is given by

(14-2)
$$f_Y(y) = \sum_{i=1}^{n} f_{X,Y}(x_i,y)$$

As a simple example, suppose that
$$S = \{(1,1),(1,2),(1,3),(2,1),(2,2),(2,3)\}$$
and that we assign the probabilities shown below.

(14-3)

		x	
		1	2
	1	$\frac{1}{12}$	$\frac{1}{3}$
y	2	$\frac{1}{12}$	$\frac{1}{4}$
	3	$\frac{1}{6}$	$\frac{1}{12}$

Then f_X is given by $f_X(1) = \frac{1}{12} + \frac{1}{12} + \frac{1}{6} = \frac{1}{3}$ and
$$f_X(2) = \frac{1}{3} + \frac{1}{4} + \frac{1}{12} = \frac{2}{3}$$

Similarly, $f_Y(1) = \frac{5}{12}$, $f_Y(2) = \frac{1}{3}$, $f_Y(3) = \frac{1}{4}$. Notice that, when the values of $f_{X,Y}$ are displayed in a table, then the values of f_X and f_Y are given by the appropriate column and row totals.

In the above example, what is $P(X = 2|Y = 1)$? From our earlier discussion of conditional probabilities we have

$$P(X = 2|Y = 1) = \frac{P(X = 2 \text{ and } Y = 1)}{P(Y = 1)}$$
$$= \frac{\frac{1}{3}}{\frac{5}{12}} = \frac{4}{5}$$

Similarly,
$$P(X = 1|Y = 1) = \frac{\frac{1}{12}}{\frac{5}{12}} = \frac{1}{5}$$

Thus, for $x = 1, 2$, $P(X = x|Y = 1)$ is determined, and we may think of this determination as defining a function of x. We call this function the *conditional probability function* for X, given $Y = 1$. We denote this function by "$f_{X|Y=1}$."

More generally, when X and Y are discrete variables with joint probability function $f_{X,Y}$, we define the *conditional probability function* for X

given $Y = y$ to be

(14-4)
$$f_{X|Y=y}(x) = \frac{f_{X,Y}(x,y)}{f_Y(y)}$$

Similarly, we define the *conditional probability function* for Y given $X = x$ by

(14-5)
$$f_{Y|X=x}(y) = \frac{f_{X,Y}(x,y)}{f_X(x)}$$

Then $f_{X|Y=y}(x) = P(X = x|Y = y)$ and $f_{Y|X=x}(y) = P(Y = y|X = x)$.

The probability distribution given by $f_{X|Y=y}$ will have a certain mean. We denote it by $\mu_{X|Y=y}$.   Then

(14-6)
$$\mu_{X|Y=y} = \sum_{i=1}^{n} x_i f_{X|Y=y}(x_i)$$

For the distribution given by (14-3) we have

$$\mu_{X|Y=1} = 1(\tfrac{1}{5}) + 2(\tfrac{4}{5}) = \tfrac{9}{5}$$

Similarly, the mean of the distribution given by $f_{Y|X=x}$ is given by

(14-7)
$$\mu_{Y|X=x} = \sum_{j=1}^{m} y_j f_{y|X=x}(y_j)$$

The mean $\mu_{Y|X=x}$ depends on x and hence may be thought of as a function of x.   If $g(x) = \mu_{Y|X=x}$, then $y = g(x)$ is called the *regression equation* for Y on X.   This equation tells us how the mean of the conditional distribution for Y depends on x.

Let us now interpret marginal and conditional distributions geometrically.   In Fig. 14-1 we have graphed the distribution given in (14-3). Over each point in S we erected a solid line whose length is the probability assigned to that point.   (A different scale was used on the z axis so that the graph would be legible.)   We may think of the marginal distribution for X as being obtained by "collapsing" this graph into the xz plane.   That is, we push all the lines which represent probabilities back into the xz plane, where we pile them on one another at the same x coordinates as they originally had.   The resulting marginal distribution for X is shown by dotted lines in the xz plane.

In a corresponding manner, the marginal distribution for Y is obtained by collapsing the graph for the joint probabilities into the yz plane. The marginal distribution for Y is shown by the dotted lines in the yz plane.

Consider now $f_{Y|X=1}$ in the light of Fig. 14-1.   We know that

$$f_{Y|X=1}(y) = \frac{f_{X,Y}(1,y)}{f_X(1)}$$

That is, the values of $f_{Y|X=1}(y)$ are simply the values of $f_{X,Y}(1,y)$ multiplied by the constant factor $1/f_X(1)$. Then the distribution $f_{Y|X=1}(y)$ would have a graph very similar to that obtained by "slicing" the graph in Fig. 14-1 by a vertical plane along $x = 1$. In fact, the verticals along the line $x = 1$ are in the correct proportions to give the values of $f_{Y|X=1}(y)$, and all that is required is that they all be multiplied by the proper constant which would make their total lengths equal 1. Such a constant is the reciprocal of the total of their lengths, that is, $1/f_X(1)$. Hence, except for a multiplicative factor which makes all the probabilities add

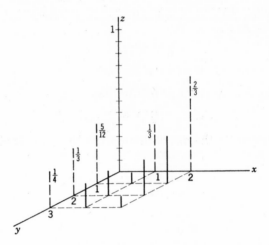

FIG. 14-1

to 1, we may think of the conditional distribution $f_{Y|X=x}$ as being obtained by taking a cross section of the joint distribution along the vertical plane where $X = x$.

These geometrical interpretations will be helpful when we consider the case of continuous variables.

In view of our definition of independence of random variables, (6-17), and our definitions of marginal distributions we now see that X and Y are independent if and only if

$$f_{X,Y}(x,y) = f_X(x)f_Y(y)$$

for all values of x and y for which $(x,y) \in S$.

When g is a function defined on S, the expected value notation is used just as it was before:

$$E[g(X,Y)] = \sum_{i=1}^{n} \sum_{j=1}^{m} g(x_i,y_j)f_{X,Y}(x_i,y_j)$$

In particular, as one would expect, we have $\mu_X = E(X)$ and $\mu_Y = E(Y)$, where μ_X and μ_Y are the means of the marginal distributions for X and Y, respectively.

PROBLEMS

14-8. Find the marginal and conditional distributions for X and Y for the uniform distribution on the set shown in Fig. 6-3.   Find $\mu_{Y|X=1}$.

14-9. Find the marginal and conditional distributions for X and Y for the uniform distribution on the set shown in Fig. 6-4.   Find $\mu_{Y|X=1}$.

14-10. Show that, if X and Y are independent, then $f_{Y|X=x}(y) = f_Y(y)$ for all values of y and x.

14-11. Three coins and a die are thrown together.   Let X be the number of heads obtained and Y be the number of spots decreased by the number of heads.   Find the joint distribution for X and Y, the marginal distribution for Y, and the conditional distribution for X given $Y = 3$.

14-12. Three pennies and three dimes are tossed together.   Let X be the number of pennies that land "heads," and let Y be the total number of heads obtained.   Find and graph the joint distribution for X and Y.   Find the marginal distribution for each variable.   Find the conditional distribution for Y, given $X = x$, and find $\mu_{Y|X=x}$ for (a) $x = 1$ and (b) $x = 3$.

14-13. Show that, if X and Y are independent, then $\mu_{Y|X=x} = \mu_Y$ for all values of x.

14-14. When X and Y are independent, then $E(XY) = E(X)E(Y)$.   In the following proof of this fact justify the various steps:

$$E(XY) = \sum_{i=1}^{n} \sum_{j=1}^{m} x_i y_j f_{X,Y}(x_i, y_j)$$

$$= \sum_{i=1}^{n} \sum_{j=1}^{m} x_i y_j f_X(x_i) f_Y(y_j)$$

$$= \left[\sum_{i=1}^{n} x_i f_X(x_i) \right] \left[\sum_{j=1}^{m} y_j f_Y(y_j) \right]$$

$$= E(X)E(Y)$$

14-15. The *covariance* of X and Y is denoted by μ_{11} and defined by

$$\mu_{11} = E\{[X - E(X)][Y - E(Y)]\}$$

Show that, if X and Y are independent, then $\mu_{11} = 0$.   (Once μ_{11} is defined, we refer to the "covariance" defined in Sec. 5.5 as the *sample covariance*.)   (*Hint:* See the preceding problem.)

14-16. Find the covariance for the distribution in

(a) Prob. 14-11   (b) Prob. 14-12   (c) Prob. 14-9

14-17. Find $\mu_{Y|X=x}$ for $x = 1$ and $x = 2$ for the distribution given in (14-3).

14-18. Find the covariance for the distribution of (14-3).

14-19. Expand each of the following double sums and simplify if possible:

(a) $\displaystyle\sum_{i=1}^{2} \sum_{j=1}^{3} (i + j)$ (b) $\displaystyle\sum_{i=1}^{3} \sum_{j=1}^{2} (x_i y_j)$

(c) $\displaystyle\sum_{i=0}^{4} \sum_{j=1}^{2} ij$ (d) $\displaystyle\sum_{i=1}^{3} \sum_{j=1}^{2} f(x_i, y_j)$

14-20. Show that, if $Z = X + Y$, then

$$\sigma_Z{}^2 = \sigma_X{}^2 + \sigma_Y{}^2 + 2\mu_{11}$$

where μ_{11} is the covariance for X and Y [see Prob. 14-15 and Eq. (5-35)].

14-21. The *correlation coefficient* ρ for X and Y can be defined by

$$\rho = \frac{\mu_{11}}{\sigma_X \sigma_Y}$$

Find ρ for the distribution of (*a*) Prob. 14-11, (*b*) Prob. 14-12, *(c)* Prob. 14-9, (*d*) (14-3). (Once ρ is defined, we refer to the "correlation coefficient" of Sec. 5.5 as the *sample correlation coefficient*.)

14-22. Prove that, if X and Y are independent, then $\rho = 0$ (see Probs. 14-21 and 14-15).

14-23. Prove that, if X and Y are independent, then $\sigma_{X+Y}^2 = \sigma_X{}^2 + \sigma_Y{}^2$ (see Probs. 14-15 and 14-20).

14-2. Marginal and conditional distributions—continuous case

An experiment which requires a bivariate distribution may have for its sample space an entire region of the xy plane and not simply a finite collection of disconnected points. A probability distribution for such an experiment is called a *continuous bivariate distribution.*

Let (X,Y) be the outcome of a certain experiment, and suppose that the sample space S for the experiment is a region in the xy plane. As was the case for a single continuous random variable, it is not feasible to assign a (nonzero) probability to each point in S in order to define a probability distribution on S. Rather a probability distribution is given for S by a function of two variables f which is called the *joint probability density function.* The graph of this function will, in general, be a surface. If R is a subset of S (that is, R is an event), the probability that we assign to R is given by the volume which lies under the surface $z = f(x,y)$ and over R. We introduce the following abbreviation for this volume:

$$\iint\limits_{R} f(x,y) \, dA$$

This notation may be read as "the volume over R which lies under f" or as "the double integral over R of f."

In order for f to be a probability density function we insist that

$$(14\text{-}24) \qquad\qquad f(x,y) \geqq 0$$

at all points (x,y) in the plane. Since the probability of ending up in the sample space must be 1, we also must have

$$(14\text{-}25) \qquad\qquad \iint\limits_{S} f(x,y) \, dA = 1$$

It is customary to consider a probability density function to be defined at all points in the xy plane, having it take on the value zero at points outside the sample space S.

In Fig. 14-2 we find the graph of the function f defined by $f(x,y) = 1$ for $0 \leq x \leq 1$ and $0 \leq y \leq 1$ and $f(x,y) = 0$ elsewhere. We may think of this function as being the probability density function for the experiment of choosing a point "at random" from $S = \{(x,y): 0 \leq x \leq 1$ and

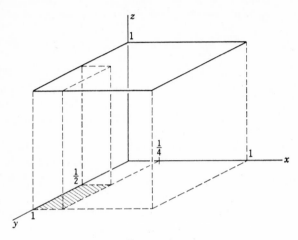

FIG. 14-2

$0 \leq y \leq 1\}$. For this function, if $R_1 = \{(x,y): 0 \leq x \leq \frac{1}{4}$ and $\frac{1}{2} \leq y \leq 1\}$, we have

$$\iint\limits_{R_1} f(x,y)\, dA = \frac{1}{8}$$

The volume sought is that over the shaded area in the figure. Using notation similar to that used before, we would say that $P(0 \leq X \leq \frac{1}{4}$ and $\frac{1}{2} \leq Y \leq 1) = \frac{1}{8}$ for this experiment.

In Fig. 14-3 we have graphed the function defined by $f(x,y) = 2y$ when $0 \leq x \leq 1$ and $0 \leq y \leq 1$ and $f(x,y) = 0$ otherwise. For the same R_1 as above we have

$$\iint\limits_{R_1} f(x,y)\, dA = \frac{3}{16}$$

When f is the probability density function for an experiment with sample space S, the *marginal probability function* for X is obtained (as in the discrete case) by "collapsing" the joint density function into the xz plane. That is, we think of all the density spread along the line $x = x_0$ in the xy plane as "accumulating" at $x = x_0$ on the x axis. The natural way to "accumulate" the density along this line is to take the total area of the cross section obtained when the surface is sliced with a vertical plane along the line $x = x_0$. That is, we define the *marginal probability density function* for X by

(14-26) $$f_X(x) = \int_{-\infty}^{\infty} f(x,y) \, dy$$

Analogously, we define the *marginal probability density function* for Y by

(14-27) $$f_Y(y) = \int_{-\infty}^{\infty} f(x,y) \, dx$$

Illustrating with the example in Fig. 14-2, if we slice the surface with a vertical plane along the line $x = \frac{1}{2}$, say, we get as a cross section a square

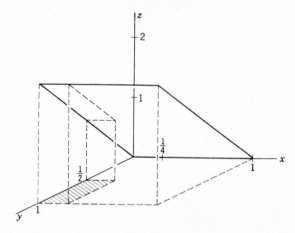

Fig. 14-3

whose area is 1. Thus, $f_X(\frac{1}{2}) = 1$. In fact, the cross section at any x between 0 and 1 gives this same square. Hence, in this case $f_X(x) = 1$ when $0 \leqq x \leqq 1$ and $f_X(x) = 0$ otherwise. That is, the marginal distribution for X is the rectangular distribution $R(0,1)$. In this case, it is easy to see that the marginal distribution for Y is also $R(0,1)$.

For the example of Fig. 14-3, let us find $f_X(\frac{1}{2})$. The vertical cross section along $x = \frac{1}{2}$ gives a triangle of area 1. Hence, $f_X(\frac{1}{2}) = 1$. We get the same result for each x between 0 and 1. Again the marginal distribution for X is $R(0,1)$. To find $f_Y(\frac{1}{3})$ we take a vertical cross section along $y = \frac{1}{3}$. We obtain a rectangle of length 1 and altitude $\frac{2}{3}$, i.e., a rectangle of area $\frac{2}{3}$. Then $f_Y(\frac{1}{3}) = \frac{2}{3}$. More generally, when y is between 0 and 1, the vertical section gives a rectangle of length 1 and of altitude $2y$.   Hence, the area is $2y$ and $f_Y(y) = 2y$ when $0 \leq y \leq 1$ and $f_Y(y) = 0$ otherwise.

In Fig. 14-4 we have graphed the function f defined by $f(x,y) = x + y$ when $0 \leq x \leq 1$ and $0 \leq y \leq 1$ and $f(x,y) = 0$ otherwise.   Taking S to be the unit square shown it is not difficult to verify that

$$\iint\limits_{S} f(x,y) \, dA = 1$$

so that this function can be taken as a density function.   It is also not

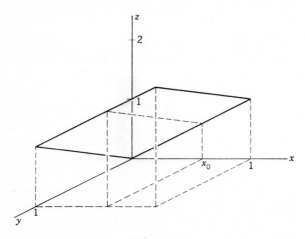

FIG. 14-4

difficult to show that, if we take a vertical cross section along the line $x = x_0$, we obtain a trapezoid whose area is $x_0 + \frac{1}{2}$.   Then for any x between 0 and 1, $f_X(x) = x + \frac{1}{2}$.   Similarly, for y between 0 and 1, $f_Y(y) = y + \frac{1}{2}$.

To obtain conditional distributions in the discrete case for a bivariate situation, we found that geometrically we could obtain the conditional distribution by simply taking a cross section of the joint distribution and then multiplying by the appropriate constant, so that the sum of the adjusted lines was 1.   In the continuous case, we follow this lead and obtain the graph of a conditional distribution by simply taking the appropriate cross section of the joint distribution except that we must make an adjustment so that the area under the curve so obtained will be 1.   Specifically, the *conditional probability density function* for Y given $X = x$ is given by

(14-28) $$f_{Y|X=x}(y) = \frac{f(x,y)}{f_X(x)}$$

Because of (14-26) we have

$$\int_{-\infty}^{\infty} f_{Y|X=x}(y) \, dy = \int_{-\infty}^{\infty} \frac{f(x,y)}{f_X(x)} \, dy$$
$$= \frac{1}{f_X(x)} \int_{-\infty}^{\infty} f(x,y) \, dy$$
$$= 1$$

as we should (see Prob. 9-41b). The conditional density function for X, given Y, may be defined in a similar manner.

As examples, we have the following: in Fig. 14-2

$$f_{Y|X=x}(y) = 1 \qquad \text{for } 0 \leqq y \leqq 1 \text{ and } 0 \leqq x \leqq 1$$

in Fig. 14-3

$$f_{Y|X=x}(y) = 2y \qquad \text{for } 0 \leqq x \leqq 1 \text{ and } 0 \leqq y \leqq 1$$

in Fig. 14-4

$$f_{Y|X=x}(y) = \frac{x + y}{x + \frac{1}{2}} \qquad \text{for } 0 \leqq x \leqq 1 \text{ and } 0 \leqq y \leqq 1$$

In the first two cases, the conditional distribution for Y does not seem to depend on which x between 0 and 1 we are given. In the last case, the conditional distribution clearly depends on x.

With our previous intuitive notion of independent variables we would expect the conditional distribution for Y not to depend on the value attained by X when X and Y are independent. That is, when X and Y are independent, we expect that $f_{Y|X=x}(y) = f_Y(y)$ for all values of x and y. But when this equality holds, we have from (14-28) that

$$f_Y(y) = \frac{f(x,y)}{f_X(x)}$$

In other words when X and Y are independent in our intuitive sense, we expect to have

(14-29) $$f(x,y) = f_X(x)f_Y(y)$$

In a rigorous treatment we would take this condition as the definition of independence. That is, we say by definition that X and Y are *independent* continuous variables when (14-29) holds.

In Figs. 14-2 and 14-3, X and Y are independent. In Fig. 14-4, X and Y are not independent.

The mean of the distribution whose density function is $f_{Y|X=x}$ is called the *conditional mean value* for Y, given $X = x$, and is denoted by $\mu_{Y|X=x}$. Formally

(14-30) $$\mu_{Y|X=x} = \int_{-\infty}^{\infty} y f_{Y|X=x}(y) \, dy$$

This conditional mean will, in general, depend on x. If g is a function of x for which $\mu_{Y|X=x} = g(x)$, then the equation $y = g(x)$ is called the *regression equation* for the distribution and a graph of $y = g(x)$ is called a *regression curve* for the distribution. (More precisely, it is called a *regression curve for Y on X*.) A regression curve is a graph showing the location of the means of the conditional distributions for various given values of X. Of particular interest is the case when the regression curve is a straight line.

In Fig. 14-2, $\qquad \mu_{Y|X=x} = \frac{1}{2}$ $\qquad$ for $0 \leqq x \leqq 1$

In Fig. 14-3, $\qquad \mu_{Y|X=x} = \frac{2}{3}$ $\qquad$ for $0 \leqq x \leqq 1$

In Fig. 14-4, $\qquad \mu_{Y|X=x} = \dfrac{3x + 2}{6x + 3}$ $\qquad$ for $0 \leq x \leq 1$

The regression curve for this last case would be a graph of

$$y = \frac{3x + 2}{6x + 3}$$

When X and Y have a joint distribution, we shall use μ_X to refer to the mean of the marginal distribution for X. μ_Y will be the mean of the marginal distribution for Y. The point (μ_X, μ_Y) may be thought of as being directly beneath the center of gravity of the entire volume lying under the graph of the density function. σ_X and σ_Y will be the standard deviations of the marginal distributions for X and Y, respectively.

A sample of n values for a random variable results in an n-tuple of values. If we were to treat rigorously the general case where the outcome of an experiment is an n-tuple of real numbers, it would be necessary to introduce a density function as a function of n variables. Geometric intuition would begin to fail but would, nonetheless, sometimes be helpful as we considered probabilities to be given by volumes in $n + 1$ dimensional space which lie "under" the graph of the density function. In actual practice, the mathematical statistician accomplishes the desired generalization by generalizing the notion of the integral. The study of the needed generalized integration is called *measure theory*. The probabilities we have considered in this book have been intimately involved with such things as the number of elements in a set, the area of a set, and the volume of a set. All these are *measures* of the sets involved. We could begin a generalization of the process of integration by asking what properties are characteristic of all such measures. We shall not pursue the matter further here.[1]

---

[1] The courageous and interested reader may consult *Measure Theory*, by P. R. Halmos, D. Van Nostrand Company, Inc., Princeton, N.J., 1950.

PROBLEMS

14-31. For the distribution given by the density function in Fig. 14-2 find

(a) $P(X \leq \frac{1}{2})$

(b) $P(Y \leq \frac{1}{2})$

(c) $P(\frac{1}{4} \leq X < \frac{1}{2})$

(d) $P(0 \leq X \leq \frac{1}{4}$ and $\frac{1}{4} \leq Y \leq \frac{1}{2})$

(e) $P(0 \leq X \leq \frac{1}{4}$ or $\frac{1}{4} \leq Y \leq \frac{1}{2})$

(f) $P(X < Y)$

(g) $P(X = Y)$

(h) $P(X = 1$ and $0 \leq Y \leq \frac{1}{4})$

14-32. For the distribution given by the density function in Fig. 14-3 find

(a) $P(X \geq \frac{1}{2})$

(b) $P(X > \frac{1}{2})$

(c) $P(\frac{1}{2} < X$ and $\frac{1}{2} < Y)$

*(d) $P(X < Y)$

14-33. Let f be defined by

$$f(x,y) = \frac{1}{4} \quad \text{for } 0 \leq x \leq 1 \text{ and } 0 \leq y \leq 1$$
$$f(x,y) = K \quad \text{for } 1 < x \leq 2 \text{ and } 0 \leq y \leq 1$$
$$f(x,y) = 0 \quad \text{otherwise}$$

Find K if f is to be a probability density function.

14-34. For the density function given in the preceding problem find f_X, f_Y, and $f_{Y|X=x}$. Are X and Y independent here?

14-35. Find $\mu_{Y|X=x}$ for the distribution in the preceding problem.

14-36. Let $f(x,y)$ be defined by

$$f(x,y) = k \quad \text{if } 0 \leq x \leq 1 \text{ and } 0 \leq y \leq x$$
$$f(x,y) = 0 \quad \text{otherwise}$$

Find K if f is to be a density function.

14-37. Find f_X and f_Y for the preceding problem. Are X and Y independent here?

14-38. Find $f_{Y|X=x}$ for the preceding problem. What is $\mu_{Y|X=x}$?

14-39. Let $f(x,y) = 2 - x - y$ for $0 \leq x \leq 1$ and $0 \leq y \leq 1$ and $f(x,y) = 0$ elsewhere. Graph the function. Find f_X, f_Y, and $f_{Y|X=x}$.

14-40. Suppose that g is a nonnegative function for which

$$\int_{-\infty}^{\infty} g(x)\,dx = 1$$

Define f by $f(x,y) = g(x)$ when $0 \leq y \leq 1$ and $f(x,y) = 0$ otherwise. Argue that f can be taken as a joint probability density function. What are f_X and f_Y for this distribution? Are X and Y independent?

14-41. Let X have the distribution $R(0,1)$ and Y have the distribution $R(1,2)$, and let X and Y be independent. Find and graph the joint probability density function for the experiment with outcome (X,Y).

14-42. Suppose that X and Y are independent, X is $R(0,1)$, and Y is $N(0,1)$. Sketch the joint density function for the experiment with outcome (X,Y).

*14-43.** Let $f(x,y) = K$ when $x^2 + y^2 \leq 1$ and $f(x,y) = 0$ elsewhere. Find K so that f can be taken as a density function. Find f_X, f_Y, and $f_{Y|X=x}$.

14-44. Let $f(x,y) = K$ when $a \leq x \leq b$ and $c \leq y \leq d$ and $f(x,y) = 0$ otherwise. Find K if f is a density function. Find f_X, f_Y, and $f_{Y|X=x}$.

*14-45.** Suppose that X and Y are independent and that each has the distribution $N(0,1)$. Sketch the joint distribution for X and Y.

*14-46.** The graph of $z = f(x,y)$ is the upper half of a sphere of radius K resting on the xy plane with center at the origin. Find K if f is a density function. Find f_X, f_Y, and $f_{Y|X=x}$. Are X and Y independent? (The volume of a sphere of radius R is $4\pi R^3/3$.)

14-3. Bivariate normal distributions

A bivariate distribution which arises often is one in which both marginal distributions are normal, every conditional distribution for each variable is normal, and the regression curve is a straight line.   Such a distribution is called a *bivariate normal distribution* or a *joint normal distribution*.   The density function for such a distribution is sketched in Fig. 14-5.

It develops that a bivariate normal distribution is determined by five parameters: μ_X, μ_Y, σ_X, σ_Y, and the slope of the regression line which we

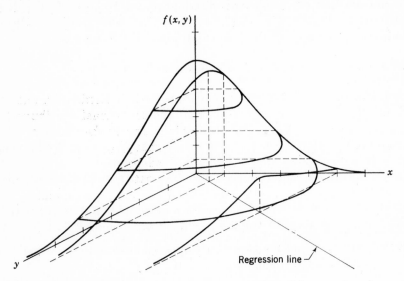

FIG. 14-5. Graph of a bivariate normal density function with $\mu_X = 0$ and $\mu_Y = 0$. (The part of the surface behind the coordinate planes is not shown.)

denote by β.   When X and Y have a joint normal distribution, the regression line is given by

$$(14\text{-}47) \qquad\qquad y = \mu_Y + \beta(x - \mu_X)$$

Thus, the regression line passes through the point (μ_X, μ_Y) in the xy plane. The highest point on the graph of the density function lies directly over the point (μ_X, μ_Y).   Another way to state (14-47) is to say that the mean of the conditional distribution for Y, given $X = x$, is given by

$$(14\text{-}48) \qquad\qquad \mu_{Y|X=x} = \mu_Y + \beta(x - \mu_X)$$

In terms of β we define a quantity called the *correlation coefficient* for a bivariate normal distribution.   The correlation coefficient is denoted by

ρ (pronounced "row") and defined by

$$(14\text{-}49) \qquad \rho = \frac{\sigma_X}{\sigma_Y}\beta$$

The standard deviation of the conditional distribution for Y given $X = x$ is easily expressed in terms of ρ:

$$(14\text{-}50) \qquad \sigma_{Y|X=x} = \sigma_Y \sqrt{1 - \rho^2}$$

Then each conditional distribution for Y has the same standard deviation. We now see that the conditional distribution for Y, given $X = x$, is the distribution $N[\mu_Y + \beta(x - \mu_X), \ \sigma_Y^2(1 - \rho^2)]$. Or, using (14-49) to eliminate β, we may say that the conditional distribution is

$$(14\text{-}51) \qquad N\left[\mu_Y + \frac{\sigma_Y}{\sigma_X}\rho(x - \mu_X), \ \sigma_Y^2(1 - \rho^2)\right]$$

Suppose that X and Y have a bivariate normal distribution and that $\rho = 0$. Then we see from (14-51) that the conditional distribution for Y, given $X = x$, is $N(\mu_Y, \sigma_Y^2)$. But this is simply the marginal distribution for Y. Hence, when $\rho = 0$, we see that $f_{Y|X=x} = f_Y$ for all values of x. But then we see that X and Y are independent.

If, on the other hand, X and Y have a bivariate normal distribution and X and Y are independent, then we must have $f_{Y|X=x} = f_Y$ for all x. But f_Y is the density function for $N(\mu_Y, \sigma_Y^2)$, and from (14-51) we see that the independence of X and Y implies $\rho = 0$. Consequently,

(14-52)   *When X and Y have a bivariate normal distribution, X and Y are independent if and only if $\rho = 0$.*

In (14-50) the quantity under the radical cannot be negative. Consequently, $-1 \leqq \rho \leqq 1$. When $\rho = \pm 1$, the conditional distributions are degenerate normal distributions with zero variance. Hence, in any bivariate normal distribution in which we have nondegenerate conditional distributions, we must have

$$(14\text{-}53) \qquad -1 < \rho < 1$$

Let X and Y have a bivariate normal distribution and let (X_1, Y_1), (X_2, Y_2), . . . , (X_n, Y_n) be the results of n trials of the experiment yielding a value for (X, Y). In Sec. 5.5 we defined the correlation coefficient r for this sample of values. We shall now call r the *sample correlation coefficient* in order to distinguish between it and ρ, the correlation coefficient of the probability distribution (or, alternatively, the *population correlation coefficient*). As we would expect from the terminology, r is a good estimate for ρ. In fact, when X and Y have the bivariate normal distribution and we have a sample of n pairs on hand, the maximum likelihood estimates for μ_X, σ_X, μ_Y, σ_Y, and ρ are the statistics $\bar{X}$, s_X, $\bar{Y}$, s_Y, and r, respectively.

In view of the results of Sec. 5-5 we would then expect the least squares regression line for the sample to be a good estimate of the regression line for the distribution. Such is the case, and we may think of the line given by (5-43) and (5-44) as an estimate for the regression line given in (14-47). We shall not go into the problems of finding a confidence region for the regression line and a confidence interval for the slope. Instead, we restrict our attention to one single hypothesis-testing problem for the bivariate normal distribution—the problem of testing H_0: $\rho = 0$ against various alternative hypotheses. Because of (14-52), testing the hypothesis H_0: $\rho = 0$ is equivalent to testing the hypothesis that X and Y are independent.

Since r is a good estimate of ρ, we might expect to base our decision on the size of r. In order to do this, it would help to know the distribution for r when H_0 is true. We accept without proof that

(14-54) *When r is the sample correlation coefficient for a random sample of size n from a bivariate normal distribution with $\rho = 0$, then*

$$T = \frac{r\sqrt{n-2}}{\sqrt{1-r^2}}$$

has the Student's distribution $t(n-2)$.

This result leads us to the following α-level tests which are not uniformly most powerful but are very good tests.

(14-55) *To test H_0: $\rho = 0$ against H_1 when ρ is the correlation coefficient for a bivariate normal distribution, r is the sample correlation coefficient for a random sample of size n, and*

$$T = \frac{r\sqrt{n-2}}{\sqrt{1-r^2}}$$

H_1	Reject H_0 if and only if	Where Z is $t(n-2)$ and for an α-level test
$\rho > 0$	$T > C_1$	$P(Z > C_1) = \alpha$
$\rho < 0$	$T < C_2$	$P(Z < C_2) = \alpha$
$\rho \neq 0$	$|T| > C_3$	$P(|Z| > C_3) = \alpha$

As an example consider the data of Table 5-5. This sample of five pairs (X,Y), where X is a height in inches and Y is a weight in pounds, has $r = .97$. If it is reasonable to assume that (X,Y) has a bivariate normal distribution, we can test $H_0: \rho = 0$ against, say, $H_1: \rho > 0$ as follows. From (14-55) we compute

$$T = \frac{.97 \sqrt{3}}{\sqrt{1 - (.97)^2}} = 6.85$$

But when Z has the distribution $t(3)$, we see from Table A-8 that $P(Z > 2.35) = .05$. Hence, we reject H_0 at the 5 per cent level. We can even reject H_0 at the 1 per cent level. In fact, we would be very much surprised if weight and height were independent.

PROBLEMS

14-56. For each set of data obtained in Prob. 5-55, discuss the applicability of (14-55) for testing $H_0: \rho = 0$ against an appropriately chosen alternative. Where (14-55) applies, carry out the test.

14-57. Test $H_0: \rho = 0$ against $H_1: \rho \neq 0$ for each of the following cases:

Case	a	b	c	d	e	f	g	h
r	0	.7	.7	.7	.5	.3	$-.5$	$-.7$
n	10	7	15	50	100	100	7	15

14-58. What would be the smallest value of r which would cause us to reject $H_0: \rho = 0$ in favor of $H_1: \rho > 0$ at the 5 per cent level when n is (a) 3, (b) 5, (c) 10, (d) 20, (e) 100, (f) 1000?

14-59. Graph the critical value of r found in the preceding problem as a function of n.

14-60. Use the preceding problem to determine the minimum sample size for which $r = .5$ is convincing evidence at the 5 per cent level that $\rho > 0$.

14-61. The density function for the bivariate normal distribution with parameters μ_X, μ_Y, σ_X, σ_Y, and ρ is given by

$$f(x,y) = \frac{\exp\left\{-\dfrac{1}{2(1 - \rho^2)}\left[\left(\dfrac{x - \mu_X}{\sigma_X}\right)^2 - 2\rho\left(\dfrac{x - \mu_X}{\sigma_X}\right)\left(\dfrac{y - \mu_Y}{\sigma_Y}\right) + \left(\dfrac{y - \mu_Y}{\sigma_Y}\right)^2\right]\right\}}{2\pi\sigma_X\sigma_Y\sqrt{1 - \rho^2}}$$

Show that, when $\rho = 0$, $f(x,y) = f_X(x)f_Y(y)$, where f_X is the density function for $N(\mu_X, \sigma_X{}^2)$ and f_Y is the density function for $N(\mu_Y, \sigma_Y{}^2)$. [Here we have used the convention that exp $(A) = e^A$.]

Appendix

Table A-1
Table of Square Roots*

	0	1	2	3	4	5	6	7	8	9
1.0	1.0000	1.0050	1.0100	1.0149	1.0198	1.0247	1.0296	1.0344	1.0392	1.0440
10.	3.1623	3.1780	3.1937	3.2094	3.2249	3.2404	3.2558	3.2711	3.2863	3.3015
1.1	1.0488	1.0536	1.0583	1.0630	1.0677	1.0724	1.0770	1.0817	1.0863	1.0909
11.	3.3166	3.3317	3.3466	3.3615	3.3764	3.3912	3.4059	3.4205	3.4351	3.4496
1.2	1.0954	1.1000	1.1045	1.1091	1.1136	1.1180	1.1225	1.1269	1.1314	1.1358
12.	3.4641	3.4785	3.4928	3.5071	3.5214	3.5355	3.5496	3.5637	3.5777	3.5917
1.3	1.1402	1.1446	1.1489	1.1533	1.1576	1.1619	1.1662	1.1705	1.1747	1.1790
13.	3.6056	3.6194	3.6332	3.6469	3.6606	3.6742	3.6878	3.7014	3.7148	3.7283
1.4	1.1832	1.1874	1.1916	1.1958	1.2000	1.2042	1.2083	1.2124	1.2166	1.2207
14.	3.7417	3.7550	3.7683	3.7815	3.7947	3.8079	3.8210	3.8341	3.8471	3.8601
1.5	1.2247	1.2288	1.2329	1.2369	1.2410	1.2450	1.2490	1.2530	1.2570	1.2610
15.	3.8730	3.8859	3.8987	3.9115	3.9243	3.9370	3.9497	3.9623	3.9749	3.9875
1.6	1.2649	1.2689	1.2728	1.2767	1.2806	1.2845	1.2884	1.2923	1.2961	1.3000
16.	4.0000	4.0125	4.0249	4.0373	4.0497	4.0620	4.0743	4.0866	4.0988	4.1110
1.7	1.3038	1.3077	1.3115	1.3153	1.3191	1.3229	1.3266	1.3304	1.3342	1.3379
17.	4.1231	4.1352	4.1473	4.1593	4.1713	4.1833	4.1952	4.2071	4.2190	4.2308
1.8	1.3416	1.3454	1.3491	1.3528	1.3565	1.3601	1.3638	1.3675	1.3711	1.3748
18.	4.2426	4.2544	4.2661	4.2778	4.2895	4.3012	4.3128	4.3243	4.3359	4.3474
1.9	1.3784	1.3820	1.3856	1.3892	1.3928	1.3964	1.4000	1.4036	1.4071	1.4107
19.	4.3589	4.3704	4.3818	4.3932	4.4045	4.4159	4.4272	4.4385	4.4497	4.4609
2.0	1.4142	1.4177	1.4213	1.4248	1.4283	1.4318	1.4353	1.4387	1.4422	1.4457
20.	4.4721	4.4833	4.4944	4.5056	4.5166	4.5277	4.5387	4.5497	4.5607	4.5717
2.1	1.4491	1.4526	1.4560	1.4595	1.4629	1.4663	1.4697	1.4731	1.4765	1.4799
21.	4.5826	4.5935	4.6043	4.6152	4.6260	4.6368	4.6476	4.6583	4.6690	4.6797
2.2	1.4832	1.4866	1.4900	1.4933	1.4967	1.5000	1.5033	1.5067	1.5100	1.5133
22.	4.6904	4.7011	4.7117	4.7223	4.7329	4.7434	4.7539	4.7645	4.7749	4.7854
2.3	1.5166	1.5199	1.5232	1.5264	1.5297	1.5330	1.5362	1.5395	1.5427	1.5460
23.	4.7958	4.8062	4.8166	4.8270	4.8374	4.8477	4.8580	4.8683	4.8785	4.8888
2.4	1.5492	1.5524	1.5556	1.5588	1.5620	1.5652	1.5684	1.5716	1.5748	1.5780
24.	4.8990	4.9092	4.9193	4.9295	4.9396	4.9497	4.9598	4.9699	4.9800	4.9900

* By permission from W. J. Dixon and F. J. Massey, Jr., *Introduction to Statistical Analysis*, 2d ed., McGraw-Hill Book Company, Inc., New York, 1957.

Table A-1 (*Continued*)

	0	1	2	3	4	5	6	7	8	9
2.5	1.5811	1.5843	1.5875	1.5906	1.5937	1.5969	1.6000	1.6031	1.6062	1.6093
25.	5.0000	5.0100	5.0200	5.0299	5.0398	5.0498	5.0596	5.0695	5.0794	5.0892
2.6	1.6125	1.6155	1.6186	1.6217	1.6248	1.6279	1.6310	1.6340	1.6371	1.6401
26.	5.0990	5.1088	5.1186	5.1284	5.1381	5.1478	5.1575	5.1672	5.1769	5.1865
2.7	1.6432	1.6462	1.6492	1.6523	1.6553	1.6583	1.6613	1.6643	1.6673	1.6703
27.	5.1962	5.2058	5.2154	5.2249	5.2345	5.2440	5.2536	5.2631	5.2726	5.2820
2.8	1.6733	1.6763	1.6793	1.6823	1.6852	1.6882	1.6912	1.6941	1.6971	1.7000
28.	5.2915	5.3009	5.3104	5.3198	5.3292	5.3385	5.3479	5.3572	5.3666	5.3759
2.9	1.7029	1.7059	1.7088	1.7117	1.7146	1.7176	1.7205	1.7234	1.7263	1.7292
29.	5.3852	5.3944	5.4037	5.4129	5.4222	5.4314	5.4406	5.4498	5.4589	5.4681
3.0	1.7321	1.7349	1.7378	1.7407	1.7436	1.7464	1.7493	1.7521	1.7550	1.7578
30.	5.4772	5.4863	5.4955	5.5045	5.5136	5.5227	5.5317	5.5408	5.5498	5.5588
3.1	1.7607	1.7635	1.7664	1.7692	1.7720	1.7748	1.7776	1.7804	1.7833	1.7861
31.	5.5678	5.5767	5.5857	5.5946	5.6036	5.6125	5.6214	5.6303	5.6391	5.6480
3.2	1.7889	1.7916	1.7944	1.7972	1.8000	1.8028	1.8055	1.8083	1.8111	1.8138
32.	5.6569	5.6657	5.6745	5.6833	5.6921	5.7009	5.7096	5.7184	5.7271	5.7359
3.3	1.8166	1.8193	1.9221	1.8248	1.8276	1.8303	1.8330	1.8358	1.8385	1.8412
33.	5.7446	5.7533	5.7619	5.7706	5.7793	5.7879	5.7966	5.8052	5.8138	5.8224
3.4	1.8439	1.8466	1.8493	1.8520	1.8547	1.8574	1.8601	1.8628	1.8655	1.8682
34.	5.8310	5.8395	5.8481	5.8566	5.8652	5.8737	5.8822	5.8907	5.8992	5.9076
3.5	1.8708	1.8735	1.8762	1.8788	1.8815	1.8841	1.8868	1.8894	1.8921	1.8947
35.	5.9161	5.9245	5.9330	5.9414	5.9498	5.9582	5.9666	5.9749	5.9833	5.9917
3.6	1.8974	1.9000	1.9026	1.9053	1.9079	1.9105	1.9131	1.9157	1.9183	1.9209
36.	6.0000	6.0083	6.0166	6.0249	6.0332	6.0415	6.0498	6.0581	6.0663	6.0745
3.7	1.9235	1.9261	1.9287	1.9313	1.9339	1.9365	1.9391	1.9416	1.9442	1.9468
37.	6.0828	6.0910	6.0992	6.1074	6.1156	6.1237	6.1319	6.1400	6.1482	6.1563
3.8	1.9494	1.9519	1.9545	1.9570	1.9596	1.9621	1.9647	1.9672	1.9698	1.9723
38.	6.1644	6.1725	6.1806	6.1887	6.1968	6.2048	6.2129	6.2209	6.2290	6.2370
3.9	1.9748	1.9774	1.9799	1.9824	1.9849	1.9875	1.9900	1.9925	1.9950	1.9975
39.	6.2450	6.2530	6.2610	6.2690	6.2769	6.2849	6.2929	6.3008	6.3087	6.3166

Table A-1 (*Continued*)

	0	1	2	3	4	5	6	7	8	9
4.0	2.0000	2.0025	2.0050	2.0075	2.0100	2.0125	2.0149	2.0174	2.0199	2.0224
40.	6.3246	6.3325	6.3403	6.3482	6.3561	6.3640	6.3718	6.3797	6.3875	6.3953
4.1	2.0248	2.0273	2.0298	2.0322	2.0347	2.0372	2.0396	2.0421	2.0445	2.0469
41.	6.4031	6.4109	6.4187	6.4265	6.4343	6.4420	6.4498	6.4576	6.4653	6.4730
4.2	2.0494	2.0518	2.0543	2.0567	2.0591	2.0616	2.0640	2.0664	2.0688	2.0712
42.	6.4807	6.4885	6.4962	6.5038	6.5115	6.5192	6.5269	6.5345	6.5422	6.5498
4.3	2.0736	2.0761	2.0785	2.0809	2.0833	2.0857	2.0881	2.0905	2.0928	2.0952
43.	6.5574	6.5651	6.5727	6.5803	6.5879	6.5955	6.6030	6.6106	6.6182	6.6257
4.4	2.0976	2.1000	2.1024	2.1048	2.1071	2.1095	2.1119	2.1142	2.1166	2.1190
44.	6.6332	6.6408	6.6483	6.6558	6.6633	6.6708	6.6783	6.6858	6.6933	6.7007
4.5	2.1213	2.1237	2.1260	2.1284	2.1307	2.1331	2.1354	2.1378	2.1401	2.1424
45.	6.7082	6.7157	6.7231	6.7305	6.7380	6.7454	6.7528	6.7602	6.7676	6.7750
4.6	2.1448	2.1471	2.1494	2.1517	2.1541	2.1564	2.1587	2.1610	2.1633	2.1656
46.	6.7823	6.7897	6.7971	6.8044	6.8118	6.8191	6.8264	6.8337	6.8411	6.8484
4.7	2.1679	2.1703	2.1726	2.1749	2.1772	2.1794	2.1817	2.1840	2.1863	2.1886
47.	6.8557	6.8629	6.8702	6.8775	6.8848	6.8920	6.8993	6.9065	6.9138	6.9210
4.8	2.1909	2.1932	2.1954	2.1977	2.2000	2.2023	2.2045	2.2068	2.2091	2.2113
48.	6.9282	6.9354	6.9426	6.9498	6.9570	6.9642	6.9714	6.9785	6.9857	6.9929
4.9	2.2136	2.2159	2.2181	2.2204	2.2226	2.2249	2.2271	2.2293	2.2316	2.2338
49.	7.0000	7.0071	7.0143	7.0214	7.0285	7.0356	7.0427	7.0498	7.0569	7.0640
5.0	2.2361	2.2383	2.2405	2.2428	2.2450	2.2472	2.2494	2.2517	2.2539	2.2561
50.	7.0711	7.0781	7.0852	7.0922	7.0993	7.1063	7.1134	7.1204	7.1274	7.1344
5.1	2.2583	2.2605	2.2627	2.2650	2.2672	2.2694	2.2716	2.2738	2.2760	2.2782
51.	7.1414	7.1484	7.1554	7.1624	7.1694	7.1764	7.1833	7.1903	7.1972	7.2042
5.2	2.2804	2.2825	2.2847	2.2869	2.2891	2.2913	2.2935	2.2956	2.2978	2.3000
52.	7.2111	7.2180	7.2250	7.2319	7.2388	7.2457	7.2526	7.2595	7.2664	7.2732
5.3	2.3022	2.3043	2.3065	2.3087	2.3108	2.3130	2.3152	2.3173	2.3195	2.3216
53.	7.2801	7.2870	7.2938	7.3007	7.3075	7.3144	7.3212	7.3280	7.3348	7.3417
5.4	2.3238	2.3259	2.3281	2.3302	2.3324	2.3345	2.3367	2.3388	2.3409	2.3431
54.	7.3485	7.3553	7.3621	7.3689	7.3756	7.3824	7.3892	7.3959	7.4027	7.4095

Table A-1 (*Continued*)

	0	1	2	3	4	5	6	7	8	9
5.5	2.3452	2.3473	2.3495	2.3516	2.3537	2.3558	2.3580	2.3601	2.3622	2.3643
55.	7.4162	7.4229	7.4297	7.4364	7.4431	7.4498	7.4565	7.4632	7.4699	7.4766
5.6	2.3664	2.3685	2.3707	2.3728	2.3749	2.3770	2.3791	2.3812	2.3833	2.3854
56.	7.4833	7.4900	7.4967	7.5033	7.5100	7.5166	7.5233	7.5299	7.5366	7.5432
5.7	2.3875	2.3896	2.3917	2.3937	2.3958	2.3979	2.4000	2.4021	2.4042	2.4062
57.	7.5498	7.5565	7.5631	7.5697	7.5763	7.5829	7.5895	7.5961	7.6026	7.6092
5.8	2.4083	2.4104	2.4125	2.4145	2.4166	2.4187	2.4207	2.4228	2.4249	2.4269
58.	7.6158	7.6223	7.6289	7.6354	7.6420	7.6485	7.6551	7.6616	7.6681	7.6746
5.9	2.4290	2.4310	2.4331	2.4352	2.4372	2.4393	2.4413	2.4434	2.4454	2.4474
59.	7.6811	7.6877	7.6942	7.7006	7.7071	7.7136	7.7201	7.7266	7.7330	7.7395
6.0	2.4495	2.4515	2.4536	2.4556	2.4576	2.4597	2.4617	2.4637	2.4658	2.4678
60.	7.7460	7.7524	7.7589	7.7653	7.7717	7.7782	7.7846	7.7910	7.7974	7.8038
6.1	2.4698	2.4718	2.4739	2.4759	2.4779	2.4799	2.4819	2.4839	2.4860	2.4880
61.	7.8102	7.8166	7.8230	7.8294	7.8358	7.8422	7.8486	7.8549	7.8613	7.8677
6.2	2.4900	2.4920	2.4940	2.4960	2.4980	2.5000	2.5020	2.5040	2.5060	2.5080
62.	7.8740	7.8804	7.8867	7.8930	7.8994	7.9057	7.9120	7.9183	7.9246	7.9310
6.3	2.5100	2.5120	2.5140	2.5159	2.5179	2.5199	2.5219	2.5239	2.5259	2.5278
63.	7.9373	7.9436	7.9498	7.9561	7.9624	7.9687	7.9750	7.9812	7.9875	7.9937
6.4	2.5298	2.5318	2.5338	2.5357	2.5377	2.5397	2.5417	2.5436	2.5456	2.5475
64.	8.0000	8.0062	8.0125	8.0187	8.0250	8.0312	8.0374	8.0436	8.0498	8.0561
6.5	2.5495	2.5515	2.5534	2.5554	2.5573	2.5593	2.5612	2.5632	2.5652	2.5671
65.	8.0623	8.0685	8.0747	8.0808	8.0870	8.0932	8.0994	8.1056	8.1117	8.1179
6.6	2.5690	2.5710	2.5729	2.5749	2.5768	2.5788	2.5807	2.5826	2.5846	2.5865
66.	8.1240	8.1302	8.1363	8.1425	8.1486	8.1548	8.1609	8.1670	8.1731	8.1792
6.7	2.5884	2.5904	2.5923	2.5942	2.5962	2.5981	2.6000	2.6019	2.6038	2.6058
67.	8.1854	8.1915	8.1976	8.2037	8.2098	8.2158	8.2219	8.2280	8.2341	8.2401
6.8	2.6077	2.6096	2.6115	2.6134	2.6153	2.6173	2.6192	2.6211	2.6230	2.6249
68.	8.2462	8.2523	8.2583	8.2644	8.2704	8.2765	8.2825	8.2885	8.2946	8.3006
6.9	2.6268	2.6287	2.6306	2.6325	2.6344	2.6363	2.6382	2.6401	2.6420	2.6439
69.	8.3066	8.3126	8.3187	8.3247	8.3307	8.3367	8.3427	8.3487	8.3546	8.3606

Table A-1 *(Continued)*

	0	1	2	3	4	5	6	7	8	9
7.0	2.6458	2.6476	2.6495	2.6514	2.6533	2.6552	2.6571	2.6589	2.6608	2.6627
70.	8.3666	8.3726	8.3785	8.3845	8.3905	8.3964	8.4024	8.4083	8.4143	8.4202
7.1	2.6646	2.6665	2.6683	2.6702	2.6721	2.6739	2.6758	2.6777	2.6796	2.6814
71.	8.4261	8.4321	8.4380	8.4439	8.4499	8.4558	8.4617	8.4676	8.4735	8.4794
7.2	2.6833	2.6851	2.6870	2.6889	2.6907	2.6926	2.6944	2.6963	2.6981	2.7000
72.	8.4853	8.4912	8.4971	8.5029	8.5088	8.5147	8.5206	8.5264	8.5323	8.5381
7.3	2.7019	2.7037	2.7055	2.7074	2.7092	2.7111	2.7129	2.7148	2.7166	2.7185
73.	8.5440	8.5499	8.5557	8.5615	8.5674	8.5732	8.5790	8.5849	8.5907	8.5965
7.4	2.7203	2.7221	2.7240	2.7258	2.7276	2.7295	2.7313	2.7331	2.7350	2.7368
74.	8.6023	8.6081	8.6139	8.6197	8.6255	8.6313	8.6371	8.6429	8.6487	8.6545
7.5	2.7386	2.7404	2.7423	2.7441	2.7459	2.7477	2.7495	2.7514	2.7532	2.7550
75.	8.6603	8.6660	8.6718	8.6776	8.6833	8.6891	8.6948	8.7006	8.7063	8.7121
7.6	2.7568	2.7586	2.7604	2.7622	2.7641	2.7659	2.7677	2.7695	2.7713	2.7731
76.	8.7178	8.7235	8.7293	8.7350	8.7407	8.7464	8.7521	8.7579	8.7636	8.7693
7.7	2.7749	2.7767	2.7785	2.7803	2.7821	2.7839	2.7857	2.7875	2.7893	2.7911
77.	8.7750	8.7807	8.7864	8.7920	8.7977	8.8034	8.8091	8.8148	8.8204	8.8261
7.8	2.7928	2.7946	2.7964	2.7982	2.8000	2.8018	2.8036	2.8054	2.8071	2.8089
78.	8.8318	8.8374	8.8431	8.8487	8.8544	8.8600	8.8657	8.8713	8.8769	8.8826
7.9	2.8107	2.8125	2.8142	2.8160	2.8178	2.8196	2.8213	2.8231	2.8249	2.8267
79.	8.8882	8.8938	8.8994	8.9051	8.9107	8.9163	8.9219	8.9275	8.9331	8.9387
8.0	2.8284	2.8302	2.8320	2.8337	2.8355	2.8373	2.8390	2.8408	2.8425	2.8443
80.	8.9443	8.9499	8.9554	8.9610	8.9666	8.9722	8.9778	8.9833	8.9889	8.9944
8.1	2.8460	2.8478	2.8496	2.8513	2.8531	2.8548	2.8566	2.8583	2.8601	2.8618
81.	9.0000	9.0056	9.0111	9.0167	9.0222	9.0277	9.0333	9.0388	9.0443	9.0499
8.2	2.8636	2.8653	2.8671	2.8688	2.8705	2.8723	2.8740	2.8758	2.8775	2.8792
82.	9.0554	9.0609	9.0664	9.0719	9.0774	9.0830	9.0885	9.0940	9.0995	9.1049
8.3	2.8810	2.8827	2.8844	2.8862	2.8879	2.8896	2.8914	2.8931	2.8948	2.8965
83.	9.1104	9.1159	9.1214	9.1269	9.1324	9.1378	9.1433	9.1488	9.1542	9.1597
8.4	2.8983	2.9000	2.9017	2.9034	2.9052	2.9069	2.9086	2.9103	2.9120	2.9138
84.	9.1652	9.1706	9.1761	9.1815	9.1869	9.1924	9.1978	9.2033	9.2087	9.2141

Table A-1 (*Continued*)

	0	1	2	3	4	5	6	7	8	9
8.5	2.9155	2.9172	2.9189	2.9206	2.9223	2.9240	2.9257	2.9275	2.9292	2.9309
85.	9.2195	9.2250	9.2304	9.2358	9.2412	9.2466	9.2520	9.2574	9.2628	9.2682
8.6	2.9326	2.9343	2.9360	2.9377	2.9394	2.9411	2.9428	2.9445	2.9462	2.9479
86.	9.2736	9.2790	9.2844	9.2898	9.2952	9.3005	9.3059	9.3113	9.3167	9.3220
8.7	2.9496	2.9513	2.9530	2.9547	2.9563	2.9580	2.9597	2.9614	2.9631	2.9648
87.	9.3274	9.3327	9.3381	9.3434	9.3488	9.3541	9.3595	9.3648	9.3702	9.3755
8.8	2.9665	2.9682	2.9698	2.9715	2.9732	2.9749	2.9766	2.9783	2.9799	2.9816
88.	9.3808	9.3862	9.3915	9.3968	9.4021	9.4074	9.4128	9.4181	9.4234	9.4287
8.9	2.9833	2.9850	2.9866	2.9883	2.9900	2.9917	2.9933	2.9950	2.9967	2.9983
89.	9.4340	9.4393	9.4446	9.4499	9.4552	9.4604	9.4657	9.4710	9.4763	9.4816
9.0	3.0000	3.0017	3.0033	3.0050	3.0067	3.0083	3.0100	3.0116	3.0133	3.0150
90.	9.4868	9.4921	9.4974	9.5026	9.5079	9.5131	9.5184	9.5237	9.5289	9.5341
9.1	3.0166	3.0183	3.0199	3.0216	3.0232	3.0249	3.0265	3.0282	3.0299	3.0315
91.	9.5394	9.5446	9.5499	9.5551	9.5603	9.5656	9.5708	9.5760	9.5812	9.5864
9.2	3.0332	3.0348	3.0364	3.0381	3.0397	3.0414	3.0430	3.0447	3.0463	3.0480
92.	9.5917	9.5969	9.6021	9.6073	9.6125	9.6177	9.6229	9.6281	9.6333	9.6385
9.3	3.0496	3.0512	3.0529	3.0545	3.0561	3.0578	3.0594	3.0610	3.0627	3.0643
93.	9.6437	9.6488	9.6540	9.6592	9.6644	9.6695	9.6747	9.6799	9.6850	9.6902
9.4	3.0659	3.0676	3.0692	3.0708	3.0725	3.0741	3.0757	3.0773	3.0790	3.0806
94.	9.6954	9.7005	9.7057	9.7108	9.7160	9.7211	9.7263	9.7314	9.7365	9.7417
9.5	3.0822	3.0838	3.0854	3.0871	3.0887	3.0903	3.0919	3.0935	3.0952	3.0968
95.	9.7468	9.7519	9.7570	9.7622	9.7673	9.7724	9.7775	9.7826	9.7877	9.7929
9.6	3.0984	3.1000	3.1016	3.1032	3.1048	3.1064	3.1081	3.1097	3.1113	3.1129
96.	9.7980	9.8031	9.8082	9.8133	9.8184	9.8234	9.8285	9.8336	9.8387	9.8438
9.7	3.1145	3.1161	3.1177	3.1193	3.1209	3.1225	3.1241	3.1257	3.1273	3.1289
97.	9.8489	9.8539	9.8590	9.8641	9.8691	9.8742	9.8793	9.8843	9.8894	9.8944
9.8	3.1305	3.1321	3.1337	3.1353	3.1369	3.1385	3.1401	3.1417	3.1432	3.1448
98.	9.8995	9.9045	9.9096	9.9146	9.9197	9.9247	9.9298	9.9348	9.9398	9.9448
9.9	3.1464	3.1480	3.1496	3.1512	3.1528	3.1544	3.1559	3.1575	3.1591	3.1607
99.	9.9499	9.9549	9.9599	9.9649	9.9700	9.9750	9.9800	9.9850	9.9900	9.9950

Table A-2
Binomial Distributions*

Table entries are values of $\binom{n}{y} p^y q^{n-y}$. For $p \leqq .5$ use the left and top scales. For $p > .5$ use the right and bottom scales. Items omitted are less than .00005.

n = 5	p					
y	.1	.2	.3	.4	.5	
0	.5905	.3277	.1681	.0778	.0312	5
1	.3280	.4096	.3602	.2592	.1562	4
2	.0729	.2048	.3087	.3456	.3125	3
3	.0081	.0512	.1323	.2304	.3125	2
4	.0004	.0064	.0284	.0768	.1562	1
5	.0000	.0003	.0024	.0102	.0312	0
	.9	.8	.7	.6	.5	y

n = 10	p					
y	.1	.2	.3	.4	.5	
0	.3487	.1074	.0282	.0060	.0010	10
1	.3874	.2684	.1211	.0403	.0098	9
2	.1937	.3020	.2335	.1209	.0439	8
3	.0574	.2013	.2668	.2150	.1172	7
4	.0112	.0881	.2001	.2508	.2051	6
5	.0015	.0264	.1029	.2007	.2461	5
6	.0001	.0055	.0368	.1115	.2051	4
7	.0000	.0008	.0090	.0425	.1172	3
8	.0000	.0001	.0014	.0106	.0439	2
9	.0000	.0000	.0001	.0016	.0098	1
10	.0000	.0000	.0000	.0001	.0010	0
	.9	.8	.7	.6	.5	y

n = 15	p					
y	.1	.2	.3	.4	.5	
0	.2059	.0352	.0047	.0005	.0000	15
1	.3432	.2319	.0305	.0047	.0005	14
2	.2669	.2309	.0916	.0219	.0032	13
3	.1285	.2501	.1700	.0634	.0139	12
4	.0428	.1876	.2186	.1268	.0417	11
5	.0105	.1032	.2061	.1859	.0916	10
6	.0019	.0430	.1472	.2066	.1527	9
7	.0003	.0138	.0811	.1771	.1964	8
	.9	.8	.7	.6	.5	y
	p					

* Condensed with permission from National Bureau of Standards, *Tables of the Binomial Distribution*, Applied Mathematics Series, vol. 6, 1950.

Table A-2 (*Continued*)

$n = 15$	p					
y	.1	.2	.3	.4	.5	
8	.0000	.0035	.0348	.1181	.1964	7
9	. . . . .	.0007	.0116	.0612	.1527	6
10	. . . . .	.0001	.0030	.0245	.0916	5
11	. . . . .	.0000	.0006	.0074	.0417	4
12	. . . . .	. . . . .	.0001	.0016	.0139	3
13	. . . . .	. . . . .	.0000	.0003	.0032	2
14	. . . . .	. . . . .	. . . . .	.0000	.0005	1
15	. . . . .	. . . . .	. . . . .	.0000	.0000	0
	.9	.8	.7	.6	.5	y

$n = 20$	p					
y	.1	.2	.3	.4	.5	
0	.1216	.0115	.0008	.0000	.0000	20
1	.2702	.0576	.0068	.0005	.0000	19
2	.2852	.1369	.0278	.0031	.0002	18
3	.1901	.2054	.0716	.0123	.0011	17
4	.0898	.2182	.1304	.0350	.0046	16
5	.0319	.1746	.1789	.0746	.0148	15
6	.0089	.1091	.1916	.1244	.0370	14
7	.0020	.0545	.1643	.1659	.0739	13
8	.0004	.0222	.1144	.1797	.1201	12
9	.0001	.0074	.0654	.1597	.1602	11
10	.0000	.0020	.0308	.1171	.1762	10
11	. . . . .	.0005	.0120	.0710	.1602	9
12	. . . . .	.0001	.0039	.0355	.1201	8
13	. . . . .	.0000	.0010	.0146	.0739	7
14	. . . . .	. . . . .	.0002	.0049	.0370	6
15	. . . . .	. . . . .	.0000	.0013	.0148	5
16	. . . . .	. . . . .	. . . . .	.0003	.0046	4
17	. . . . .	. . . . .	. . . . .	.0000	.0011	3
18	. . . . .	. . . . .	. . . . .	. . . . .	.0002	2
19	. . . . .	. . . . .	. . . . .	. . . . .	.0000	1
20	. . . . .	. . . . .	. . . . .	. . . . .	.0000	0
	.9	.8	.7	.6	.5	y
	p					

Table A-2 (*Continued*)

n = 30 y	.1	.2	.3	.4	.5	
0	.0424	.0012	.0000	.0000	.0000	30
1	.1413	.0093	.0003	.0000	.0000	29
2	.2277	.0337	.0018	.0000	.0000	28
3	.2361	.0785	.0072	.0003	.0000	27
4	.1771	.1325	.0208	.0012	.0000	26
5	.1023	.1723	.0464	.0041	.0001	25
6	.0474	.1795	.0829	.0115	.0006	24
7	.0180	.1538	.1219	.0263	.0019	23
8	.0058	.1106	.1501	.0505	.0055	22
9	.0016	.0676	.1573	.0823	.0133	21
10	.0004	.0355	.1416	.1152	.0280	20
11	.0001	.0161	.1103	.1396	.0509	19
12	.0000	.0064	.0749	.1474	.0805	18
13	. . . . .	.0022	.0444	.1360	.1115	17
14	. . . . .	.0007	.0231	.1101	.1354	16
15	. . . . .	.0002	.0106	.0783	.1445	15
16	. . . . .	.0000	.0042	.0489	.1354	14
17	. . . . .	. . . . .	.0015	.0269	.1115	13
18	. . . . .	. . . . .	.0005	.0129	.0805	12
19	. . . . .	. . . . .	.0001	.0054	.0509	11
20	. . . . .	. . . . .	.0000	.0020	.0280	10
21	. . . . .	. . . . .	. . . . .	.0006	.0133	9
22	. . . . .	. . . . .	. . . . .	.0001	.0055	8
23	. . . . .	. . . . .	. . . . .	.0000	.0019	7
24	. . . . .	. . . . .	. . . . .	. . . . .	.0006	6
25	. . . . .	. . . . .	. . . . .	. . . . .	.0001	5
26	. . . . .	. . . . .	. . . . .	. . . . .	.0000	4
27	. . . . .	. . . . .	. . . . .	. . . . .	. . . . .	3
28	. . . . .	. . . . .	. . . . .	. . . . .	. . . . .	2
29	. . . . .	. . . . .	. . . . .	. . . . .	. . . . .	1
30	. . . . .	. . . . .	. . . . .	. . . . .	. . . . .	0
	.9	.8	.7	.6	.5	y
			p			

Table A-3
Cumulative Probabilities for Binomial Distributions*

$$\text{To obtain } CP(x) = \sum_{k=0}^{x} \binom{n}{k} p^k q^{n-k}$$

1. For $p \leqq .5$ use left and top scales and subtract the table entry from 1.
2. For $p > .5$ use right and bottom scales and take the table entry.
Items omitted are less than .00005.

$n = 5$ x	p					
	.1	.2	.3	.4	.5	
0	.4095	.6723	.8319	.9222	.9688	4
1	.0815	.2627	.4718	.6630	.8125	3
2	.0086	.0579	.1631	.3174	.5000	2
3	.0005	.0067	.0308	.0870	.1875	1
4	.0000	.0003	.0024	.0102	.0312	0
	.9	.8	.7	.6	.5	x

$n = 10$ x	p					
	.1	.2	.3	.4	.5	
0	.6513	.8926	.9717	.9939	.9990	9
1	.2639	.6242	.8507	.9536	.9893	8
2	.0702	.3222	.6172	.8327	.9453	7
3	.0128	.1209	.3504	.6177	.8281	6
4	.0016	.0328	.1503	.3669	.6230	5
5	.0001	.0064	.0473	.1662	.3770	4
6	.0000	.0009	.0106	.0548	.1719	3
7	.0000	.0001	.0016	.0123	.0547	2
8	.0000	.0000	.0001	.0017	.0107	1
9	.0000	.0000	.0000	.0001	.0010	0
	.9	.8	.7	.6	.5	x

$n = 15$ x	p					
	.1	.2	.3	.4	.5	
0	.7941	.9648	.9953	.9995	1.0000	14
1	.4510	.8329	.9647	.9948	.9995	13
2	.1841	.6020	.8732	.9729	.9963	12
3	.0556	.3518	.7031	.9095	.9824	11
4	.0127	.1642	.4845	.7827	.9408	10
5	.0022	.0611	.2784	.5968	.8491	9
	.9	.8	.7	.6	.5	x
			p			

* Condensed with permission from National Bureau of Standards, *Tables of the Binomial Distribution*, Applied Mathematics Series, vol. 6, 1950.

Table A-3 (*Continued*)

$n = 15$ x	.1	.2	.3	.4	.5	
6	.0003	.0181	.1311	.3902	.6964	8
7	.0000	.0042	.0500	.2131	.5000	7
8	. . . . .	.0008	.0152	.0950	.3036	6
9	. . . . .	.0001	.0037	.0338	.1509	5
10	. . . . .	.0000	.0007	.0093	.0592	4
11	. . . . .	. . . . .	.0001	.0019	.0176	3
12	. . . . .	. . . . .	.0000	.0003	.0037	2
13	. . . . .	. . . . .	. . . . .	.0000	.0005	1
14	. . . . .	. . . . .	. . . . .	.0000	.0000	0
	.9	.8	.7	.6	.5	x

$n = 20$ x	.1	.2	.3	.4	.5	
0	.8784	.9885	.9992	1.0000	1.0000	19
1	.6083	.9308	.9924	.9995	1.0000	18
2	.3231	.7939	.9645	.9964	.9998	17
3	.1330	.5886	.8929	.9840	.9987	16
4	.0432	.3704	.7625	.9490	.9941	15
5	.0113	.1958	.5836	.8744	.9793	14
6	.0024	.0867	.3920	.7500	.9423	13
7	.0004	.0321	.2277	.5841	.8684	12
8	.0001	.0100	.1133	.4044	.7483	11
9	.0000	.0026	.0480	.2447	.5881	10
10	. . . . .	.0006	.0171	.1275	.4119	9
11	. . . . .	.0001	.0051	.0565	.2517	8
12	. . . . .	.0000	.0013	.0210	.1316	7
13	. . . . .	. . . . .	.0003	.0065	.0577	6
14	. . . . .	. . . . .	.0000	.0016	.0207	5
15	. . . . .	. . . . .	. . . . .	.0003	.0059	4
16	. . . . .	. . . . .	. . . . .	.0000	.0013	3
17	. . . . .	. . . . .	. . . . .	. . . . .	.0002	2
18	. . . . .	. . . . .	. . . . .	. . . . .	.0000	1
19	. . . . .	. . . . .	. . . . .	. . . . .	.0000	0
	.9	.8	.7	.6	.5	x

p

Table A-3 (*Continued*)

n = 30 x	.1	.2	.3	.4	.5	
0	.9576	.9988	1.0000	1.0000	1.0000	29
1	.8163	.9895	.9997	1.0000	1.0000	28
2	.5886	.9558	.9979	1.0000	1.0000	27
3	.3526	.8773	.9907	.9997	1.0000	26
4	.1755	.7448	.9698	.9985	1.0000	25
5	.0732	.5725	.9234	.9943	.9998	24
6	.0258	.3930	.8405	.9828	.9993	23
7	.0078	.2392	.7186	.9565	.9974	22
8	.0020	.1287	.5685	.9060	.9919	21
9	.0005	.0611	.4112	.8237	.9786	20
10	.0001	.0256	.2696	.7085	.9506	19
11	.0000	.0095	.1593	.5689	.8998	18
12	. . . . .	.0031	.0845	.4215	.8192	17
13	. . . . .	.0009	.0401	.2855	.7077	16
14	. . . . .	.0002	.0169	.1754	.5722	15
15	. . . . .	.0001	.0064	.0971	.4278	14
16	. . . . .	.0000	.0021	.0481	.2923	13
17	. . . . .	. . . . .	.0006	.0212	.1808	12
18	. . . . .	. . . . .	.0002	.0083	.1002	11
19	. . . . .	. . . . .	.0000	.0029	.0494	10
20	. . . . .	. . . . .	. . . . .	.0009	.0214	9
21	. . . . .	. . . . .	. . . . .	.0002	.0081	8
22	. . . . .	. . . . .	. . . . .	.0000	.0026	7
23	. . . . .	. . . . .	. . . . .	. . . . .	.0007	6
24	. . . . .	. . . . .	. . . . .	. . . . .	.0001	5
25	. . . . .	. . . . .	. . . . .	. . . . .	.0000	4
26	. . . . .	. . . . .	. . . . .	. . . . .	. . . . .	3
27	. . . . .	. . . . .	. . . . .	. . . . .	. . . . .	2
28	. . . . .	. . . . .	. . . . .	. . . . .	. . . . .	1
29	. . . . .	. . . . .	. . . . .	. . . . .	. . . . .	0
	.9	.8	.7	.6	.5	x
			p			

Table A-4. Random Digits*

Col. / Line	(1)	(2)	(3)	(4)	(5)	(6)	(7)	(8)	(9)	(10)	(11)	(12)	(13)	(14)
1	10480	15011	01536	02011	81647	91646	69179	14194	62590	36207	20969	99570	91291	90700
2	22368	46573	25595	85393	30995	89198	27982	53402	93965	34095	52666	19174	39615	99505
3	24130	48360	22527	97265	76393	64809	15179	24830	49340	32081	30680	19655	63348	58629
4	42167	93093	06243	61680	07856	16376	39440	53537	71341	57004	00849	74917	97758	16379
5	37570	39975	81837	16656	06121	91782	60468	81305	49684	60672	14110	06927	01263	54613
6	77921	06907	11008	42751	27756	53498	18602	70659	90655	15053	21916	81825	44394	42880
7	99562	72905	56420	69994	98872	31016	71194	18738	44013	48840	63213	21069	10634	12952
8	96301	91977	05463	07972	18876	20922	94595	56869	69014	60045	18425	84903	42508	32307
9	89579	14342	63661	10281	17453	18103	57740	84378	25331	12566	58678	44947	05585	56941
10	85475	36857	53342	53988	53060	59533	38867	62300	08158	17983	16439	11458	18593	64952
11	28918	69578	88231	33276	70997	79936	56865	05859	90106	31595	01547	85590	91610	78188
12	63553	40961	48235	03427	49626	69445	18663	72695	52180	20847	12234	90511	33703	90322
13	09429	93969	52636	92737	88974	33488	36320	17617	30015	08272	84115	27156	30613	74952
14	10365	61129	87529	85689	48237	52267	67689	93394	01511	26358	85104	20285	29975	89868
15	07119	97336	71048	08178	77233	13916	47564	81056	97735	85977	29372	74461	28551	90707
16	51085	12765	51821	51259	77452	16308	60756	92144	49442	53900	70960	63990	75601	40719
17	02368	21382	52404	60268	89368	19885	55322	44819	01188	65255	64835	44919	05944	55157
18	01011	54092	33362	94904	31273	04146	18594	29852	71585	85030	51132	01915	92747	64951
19	52162	53916	46369	58586	23216	14513	83149	98736	23495	64350	94738	17752	35156	35749
20	07056	97628	33787	09998	42698	06691	76988	13602	51851	46104	88916	19509	25625	58104
21	48663	91245	85828	14346	09172	30168	90229	04734	59193	22178	30421	61666	99904	32812
22	54164	58492	22421	74103	47070	25306	76468	26384	58151	06646	21524	15227	96909	44592
23	32639	32363	05597	24200	13363	28305	94342	28728	35806	06912	17012	64161	18296	22851
24	29334	27001	87637	87308	58731	00256	45834	15398	46557	41135	10367	07684	36188	18510
25	02488	33062	28834	07351	19731	92420	60952	61280	50001	67118	32586	86679	50720	94953

Table A-4 (*Continued*)

Col. / Line	(1)	(2)	(3)	(4)	(5)	(6)	(7)	(8)	(9)	(10)	(11)	(12)	(13)	(14)
26	81525	72295	04839	96423	24878	82651	61566	14778	76797	14780	13300	87074	79666	95725
27	29676	20591	68086	26432	46901	20849	84268	81536	86645	12659	92259	57102	80428	25280
28	00742	57392	39064	66432	84673	40027	32832	61362	98947	96067	64760	64584	96096	98253
29	05366	04213	25669	26422	44407	44048	37937	63904	45766	66134	75470	66520	34693	90449
30	91921	26418	64117	94305	26766	25940	39972	22209	71500	64568	91402	42416	07844	69618
31	00582	04711	87917	77341	42206	35126	74087	99547	81817	42607	43808	76655	62028	76630
32	00725	69884	62797	56170	86324	88072	76222	36086	84637	93161	76038	65855	77919	88006
33	69011	65795	95876	55293	18988	27354	26575	08625	40801	59920	29841	80150	12777	48501
34	25976	57948	29888	88604	67917	48708	18912	82271	65424	69774	33611	54262	85963	03547
35	09763	83473	73577	12908	30883	18317	28290	35797	05998	41688	34952	37888	38917	88050
36	91567	42595	27958	30134	04024	86385	29880	99730	55536	84855	29080	09250	79656	73211
37	17955	56349	90099	49127	20044	59931	06115	20542	18059	02008	73708	83517	36103	42791
38	46503	18584	18845	49618	02304	51038	20655	58727	28168	15175	56942	53389	20562	87338
39	92157	89634	94824	78171	84610	82834	09922	25417	44137	48413	25555	21246	35509	20468
40	14577	62765	35605	81263	39667	47358	56873	56307	61607	49518	89656	20103	77490	18062
41	98427	07523	33362	64270	01638	92477	66969	98320	04880	45585	46565	04102	46880	45709
42	34914	63976	88720	82765	34476	17032	87589	40836	32427	70002	70663	88863	77775	69348
43	70060	28277	39475	46473	23219	53416	94970	25832	69975	94884	19661	72828	00102	66794
44	53976	54914	06990	67245	68350	82948	11398	42878	80287	88267	47363	46634	06541	97809
45	76072	29515	40980	07391	58745	25774	22987	80059	39911	96198	41151	14222	60697	59583
46	90725	52210	83974	29992	65831	38857	50490	83765	55657	14361	31720	57375	56228	41546
47	64364	67412	33339	31926	14883	24413	59744	92351	97473	89286	35931	04110	23726	51900
48	08962	00358	31662	25388	61642	34072	81249	35648	56891	69352	48373	45578	78547	81788
49	95012	68379	93526	70765	10592	04542	76463	53328	02349	17247	28865	14777	62730	92277
50	15664	10493	20492	38391	91132	21999	59516	81652	27195	48223	46751	22923	32261	85653

51	16408	81899	04153	53381	79401	21438	83035	92350	36693	31238	59649	91754	72772	02338
52	18629	81953	05520	91962	04739	13092	97662	24822	94730	06496	35090	04822	86774	98289
53	73115	35101	47498	87637	99016	71060	88824	71013	18735	20286	23153	72924	35165	43040
54	57491	16703	23167	49323	45021	33132	12544	41035	80780	45393	44812	12515	98931	91202
55	30405	83946	23792	14422	15059	45799	22716	19792	09983	74353	68668	30429	70735	25499
56	16631	35006	85900	98275	32388	52390	16815	69298	82732	38480	73817	32523	41961	44437
57	96773	20206	42559	78985	05300	22164	24369	54224	35083	19687	11052	91491	60383	19746
58	38935	64202	14349	82674	66523	44133	00697	35552	35970	19124	63318	29686	03387	59846
59	31624	76384	17403	53363	44167	64486	64758	75366	76554	31601	12614	33072	60332	92325
60	78919	19474	23632	27889	47914	02584	37680	20801	72152	39339	34806	08930	85001	87820
61	03931	33309	57047	74211	63445	17361	62825	39908	05607	91284	68833	25570	38818	46920
62	74426	33278	43972	10119	89917	15665	52872	73823	73144	88662	88970	74492	51805	99378
63	09066	00903	20795	95452	92648	45454	09552	88815	16553	51125	79375	97596	16296	66092
64	42238	12426	87025	14267	20979	04508	64535	31355	86064	29472	47689	05974	52468	16834
65	16153	08002	26504	41744	81959	65642	74240	56302	00033	67107	77510	70625	28725	34191
66	21457	40742	29820	96783	29400	21840	15035	34537	33310	06116	95240	15957	16572	06004
67	21581	57802	02050	89728	17937	37621	47075	42080	97403	48626	68995	43805	33386	21597
68	55612	78095	83197	33732	05810	24813	86902	60397	16489	03264	88525	42786	05269	92532
69	44657	66999	99324	51281	84463	60563	79312	93454	68876	25471	93911	25650	12682	73572
70	91340	84979	46949	81973	37949	61023	43997	15263	80644	43942	89203	71795	99533	50501
71	91227	21199	31935	27022	84067	05462	35216	14486	29891	68607	41867	14951	91696	85065
72	50001	38140	66321	19924	72163	09538	12151	06878	91903	18749	34405	56087	82790	70925
73	65390	05224	72958	28609	81406	39147	25549	48542	42627	45233	57202	94617	23772	07896
74	27504	96131	83944	41575	10573	08619	64482	73923	36152	05184	94142	25299	84387	34925
75	37169	94851	39117	89632	00959	16487	65536	49071	39782	17095	02330	74301	00275	48280
76	11508	70225	51111	38351	19444	66499	71945	05422	13442	78675	84081	66938	93654	59894
77	37449	30362	06694	54690	04052	53115	62757	95348	78662	11163	81651	50245	34971	52924

Table A-4 (Continued)

Col. / Line	(1)	(2)	(3)	(4)	(5)	(6)	(7)	(8)	(9)	(10)	(11)	(12)	(13)	(14)
78	46515	70331	85922	38329	57015	15765	97161	17869	45349	61796	66345	81073	49106	79860
79	30986	81223	42416	58353	21532	30502	32305	86482	05174	07901	54339	58861	74818	46942
80	63798	64995	46583	09785	44160	78128	83991	42865	92520	83531	80377	35909	81250	54238
81	82486	84846	99254	67632	43218	50076	21361	64816	51202	88124	41870	52689	51275	83556
82	21885	32906	92431	09060	64297	51674	64126	62570	26123	05155	59194	52799	28225	85762
83	60336	98782	07408	53458	13564	59089	26445	29789	85205	41001	12535	12133	14645	23541
84	43937	46891	24010	25560	86355	33941	25786	54990	71899	15475	95434	98227	21824	19585
85	97656	63175	89303	16275	07100	92063	21942	18611	47348	20203	18534	03862	78095	50136
86	03299	01221	05418	38982	55758	92237	26759	86367	21216	98442	08303	56613	91511	75928
87	79626	06486	03574	17668	07785	76020	79924	25651	83325	88428	85076	72811	22717	50585
88	85636	68335	47539	03129	65651	11977	02510	26113	99447	68645	34327	15152	55230	93448
89	18039	14367	61337	06177	12143	46609	32989	74014	64708	00533	35398	58408	13261	47908
90	08362	15656	60627	36478	65648	16764	53412	09013	07832	41574	17639	82163	60859	75567
91	79556	29068	04142	16268	15387	12856	66227	38358	22478	73373	88732	09443	82558	05250
92	92608	82674	27072	32534	17075	27698	98204	63863	11951	34648	88022	56148	34925	57031
93	23982	25835	40055	67006	12293	02753	14827	23235	35071	99704	37543	11601	35503	85171
94	09915	96306	05908	97901	28395	14186	00821	80703	70426	75647	76310	88717	37890	40129
95	59037	33300	26695	62247	69927	76123	50842	43834	86654	70959	79725	93872	28117	19233
96	42488	78077	69882	61657	34136	79180	95726	43092	04098	73571	80799	76536	71255	64239
97	46764	86273	63003	93017	31204	36692	40202	35275	57306	55543	53203	18098	47625	88684
98	03237	45430	55417	63282	90816	17349	88298	90183	36600	78406	06216	95787	42579	90730
99	86591	81482	52667	61582	14972	90053	89534	76036	49199	43716	97548	04379	46370	28672
100	38534	01715	94964	87288	65680	43772	39560	12918	86537	62738	19636	51132	25739	56947

* By permission from *Table of 105,000 Random Decimal Digits*, Interstate Commerce Commission, U.S. Bureau of Transport Economics and Statistics, 1949.

Table A-5
Cumulative Normal Distribution*

The entries in the table are values of $F(x)$ for $N(0,1)$.

x	.00	.01	.02	.03	.04	.05	.06	.07	.08	.09
.0	.5000	.5040	.5080	.5120	.5160	.5199	.5239	.5279	.5319	.5359
.1	.5398	.5438	.5478	.5517	.5557	.5596	.5636	.5675	.5714	.5753
.2	.5793	.5832	.5871	.5910	.5948	.5987	.6026	.6064	.6103	.6141
.3	.6179	.6217	.6255	.6293	.6331	.6368	.6406	.6443	.6480	.6517
.4	.6554	.6591	.6628	.6664	.6700	.6736	.6772	.6808	.6844	.6879
.5	.6915	.6950	.6985	.7019	.7054	.7088	.7123	.7157	.7190	.7224
.6	.7257	.7291	.7324	.7357	.7389	.7422	.7454	.7486	.7517	.7549
.7	.7580	.7611	.7642	.7673	.7704	.7734	.7764	.7794	.7823	.7852
.8	.7881	.7910	.7939	.7967	.7995	.8023	.8051	.8078	.8106	.8133
.9	.8159	.8186	.8212	.8238	.8264	.8289	.8315	.8340	.8365	.8389
1.0	.8413	.8438	.8461	.8485	.8508	.8531	.8554	.8577	.8599	.8621
1.1	.8643	.8665	.8686	.8708	.8729	.8749	.8770	.8790	.8810	.8830
1.2	.8849	.8869	.8888	.8907	.8925	.8944	.8962	.8980	.8997	.9015
1.3	.9032	.9049	.9066	.9082	.9099	.9115	.9131	.9147	.9162	.9177
1.4	.9192	.9207	.9222	.9236	.9251	.9265	.9279	.9292	.9306	.9319
1.5	.9332	.9345	.9357	.9370	.9382	.9394	.9406	.9418	.9429	.9441
1.6	.9452	.9463	.9474	.9484	.9495	.9505	.9515	.9525	.9535	.9545
1.7	.9554	.9564	.9573	.9582	.9591	.9599	.9608	.9616	.9625	.9633
1.8	.9641	.9649	.9656	.9664	.9671	.9678	.9686	.9693	.9699	.9706
1.9	.9713	.9719	.9726	.9732	.9738	.9744	.9750	.9756	.9761	.9767
2.0	.9772	.9778	.9783	.9788	.9793	.9798	.9803	.9808	.9812	.9817
2.1	.9821	.9826	.9830	.9834	.9838	.9842	.9846	.9850	.9854	.9857
2.2	.9861	.9864	.9868	.9871	.9875	.9878	.9881	.9884	.9887	.9890
2.3	.9893	.9896	.9898	.9901	.9904	.9906	.9909	.9911	.9913	.9916
2.4	.9918	.9920	.9922	.9925	.9927	.9929	.9931	.9932	.9934	.9936
2.5	.9938	.9940	.9941	.9943	.9945	.9946	.9948	.9949	.9951	.9952
2.6	.9953	.9955	.9956	.9957	.9959	.9960	.9961	.9962	.9963	.9964
2.7	.9965	.9966	.9967	.9968	.9969	.9970	.9971	.9972	.9973	.9974
2.8	.9974	.9975	.9976	.9977	.9977	.9978	.9979	.9979	.9980	.9981
2.9	.9981	.9982	.9982	.9983	.9984	.9984	.9985	.9985	.9986	.9986
3.0	.9987	.9987	.9987	.9988	.9988	.9989	.9989	.9989	.9990	.9990
3.1	.9990	.9991	.9991	.9991	.9992	.9992	.9992	.9992	.9993	.9993
3.2	.9993	.9993	.9994	.9994	.9994	.9994	.9994	.9995	.9995	.9995
3.3	.9995	.9995	.9995	.9996	.9996	.9996	.9996	.9996	.9996	.9997
3.4	.9997	.9997	.9997	.9997	.9997	.9997	.9997	.9997	.9997	.9998

x	1.282	1.645	1.960	2.326	2.576	3.090	3.291	3.891	4.417
$F(x)$	.90	.95	.975	.99	.995	.999	.9995	.99995	.999995
$2[1 - F(x)]$	.20	.10	.05	.02	.01	.002	.001	.0001	.00001

* By permission from A. M. Mood, *Introduction to the Theory of Statistics*, McGraw-Hill Book Company, Inc., New York, 1950.

Table A-6
Chi-square Distribution

Degrees of freedom	P = 0.99	0.98	0.95	0.90	0.80	0.70	0.50	0.30	0.20	0.10	0.05	0.02	0.01
1	0.000157	0.000628	0.00393	0.0158	0.0642	0.148	0.455	1.074	1.642	2.706	3.841	5.412	6.635
2	0.0201	0.0404	0.103	0.211	0.446	0.713	1.386	2.408	3.219	4.605	5.991	7.824	9.210
3	0.115	0.185	0.352	0.584	1.005	1.424	2.366	3.665	4.642	6.251	7.815	9.837	11.341
4	0.297	0.429	0.711	1.064	1.649	2.195	3.357	4.878	5.989	7.779	9.488	11.668	13.277
5	0.554	0.752	1.145	1.610	2.343	3.000	4.351	6.064	7.289	9.236	11.070	13.388	15.086
6	0.872	1.134	1.635	2.204	3.070	3.828	5.348	7.231	8.558	10.645	12.592	15.033	16.812
7	1.239	1.564	2.167	2.833	3.822	4.671	6.346	8.383	9.803	12.017	14.067	16.622	18.475
8	1.646	2.032	2.733	3.490	4.594	5.527	7.344	9.524	11.030	13.362	15.507	18.168	20.090
9	2.088	2.532	3.325	4.168	5.380	6.393	8.343	10.656	12.242	14.684	16.919	19.679	21.666
10	2.558	3.059	3.940	4.865	6.179	7.267	9.342	11.781	13.442	15.987	18.307	21.161	23.209
11	3.053	3.609	4.575	5.578	6.989	8.148	10.341	12.899	14.631	17.275	19.675	22.618	24.725
12	3.571	4.178	5.226	6.304	7.807	9.034	11.340	14.011	15.812	18.549	21.026	24.054	26.217
13	4.107	4.765	5.892	7.042	8.634	9.926	12.340	15.119	16.985	19.812	22.362	25.472	27.688
14	4.660	5.368	6.571	7.790	9.467	10.821	13.339	16.222	18.151	21.064	23.685	26.873	29.141
15	5.229	5.985	7.261	8.547	10.307	11.721	14.339	17.322	19.311	22.307	24.996	28.259	30.578
16	5.812	6.614	7.962	9.312	11.152	12.624	15.338	18.418	20.465	23.542	26.296	29.633	32.000
17	6.408	7.255	8.672	10.085	12.002	13.531	16.338	19.511	21.615	24.769	27.587	30.995	33.409
18	7.015	7.906	9.390	10.865	12.857	14.440	17.338	20.601	22.760	25.989	28.869	32.346	34.805
19	7.633	8.567	10.117	11.651	13.716	15.352	18.338	21.689	23.900	27.204	30.144	33.687	36.191
20	8.260	9.237	10.851	12.443	14.578	16.266	19.337	22.775	25.038	28.412	31.410	35.020	37.566
21	8.897	9.915	11.591	13.240	15.445	17.182	20.337	23.858	26.171	29.615	32.671	36.343	38.932
22	9.542	10.600	12.338	14.041	16.314	18.101	21.337	24.939	27.301	30.813	33.924	37.659	40.289
23	10.196	11.293	13.091	14.848	17.187	19.021	22.337	26.018	28.429	32.007	35.172	38.968	41.638
24	10.856	11.992	13.848	15.659	18.062	19.943	23.337	27.096	29.553	33.196	36.415	40.270	42.980
25	11.524	12.697	14.611	16.473	18.940	20.867	24.337	28.172	30.675	34.382	37.652	41.566	44.314
26	12.198	13.409	15.379	17.292	19.820	21.792	25.336	29.246	31.795	35.563	38.885	42.856	45.642
27	12.879	14.125	16.151	18.114	20.703	22.719	26.336	30.319	32.912	36.741	40.113	44.140	46.963
28	13.565	14.847	16.928	18.939	21.588	23.647	27.336	31.391	34.027	37.916	41.337	45.419	48.278
29	14.256	15.574	17.708	19.768	22.475	24.577	28.336	32.461	35.139	39.087	42.557	46.693	49.588
30	14.953	16.306	18.493	20.599	23.364	25.508	29.336	33.530	36.250	40.256	43.773	47.962	50.892

For degrees of freedom greater than 30, the expression $\sqrt{2\chi^2} - \sqrt{2n' - 1}$ may be used as a standard normal variable, where n' is the number of degrees of freedom.

Reproduced from *Statistical Methods for Research Workers*, 6th ed., with the permission of the author, R. A. Fisher, and the publishers, Oliver & Boyd, Ltd., Edinburgh.

Table A-7

Critical Values of F with n_1 and n_2 Degrees of Freedom.* One-sided Critical Region (Right Tail) with $\alpha = .05, .01$

(Upper half, $\alpha = .05$; lower half, $\alpha = .01$)

n_2 \ n_1	1	2	3	4	5	6	7	8	9	10	15	25	50	100	∞
1	161	200	216	225	230	234	237	239	241	242	246	249	252	253	254
2	18.51	19.00	19.16	19.25	19.30	19.33	19.36	19.37	19.38	19.39	19.43	19.45	19.47	19.49	19.50
3	10.13	9.55	9.28	9.12	9.01	8.94	8.88	8.84	8.81	8.78	8.70	8.64	8.58	8.56	8.53
4	7.71	6.94	6.59	6.39	6.26	6.16	6.09	6.04	6.00	5.96	5.85	5.77	5.70	5.66	5.63
5	6.61	5.79	5.41	5.19	5.05	4.95	4.88	4.82	4.78	4.74	4.62	4.53	4.44	4.40	4.36
6	5.99	5.14	4.76	4.53	4.39	4.28	4.21	4.15	4.10	4.06	3.94	3.84	3.75	3.71	3.67
7	5.59	4.74	4.35	4.12	3.97	3.87	3.79	3.73	3.68	3.63	3.50	3.41	3.32	3.28	3.23
8	5.32	4.46	4.07	3.84	3.69	3.58	3.50	3.44	3.39	3.34	3.21	3.11	3.03	2.98	2.93
9	5.12	4.26	3.86	3.63	3.48	3.37	3.29	3.23	3.18	3.13	3.00	2.89	2.80	2.76	2.71
10	4.96	4.10	3.71	3.48	3.33	3.22	3.14	3.07	3.02	2.97	2.84	2.73	2.64	2.59	2.54
15	4.54	3.68	3.29	3.06	2.90	2.79	2.70	2.64	2.59	2.55	2.41	2.28	2.18	2.12	2.07
25	4.24	3.38	2.99	2.76	2.60	2.49	2.41	2.34	2.28	2.24	2.08	1.95	1.84	1.77	1.71
50	4.03	3.18	2.79	2.56	2.40	2.29	2.20	2.13	2.07	2.02	1.87	1.73	1.60	1.52	1.44
100	3.94	3.09	2.70	2.46	2.30	2.19	2.10	2.03	1.97	1.92	1.77	1.62	1.48	1.39	1.28
500	3.86	3.02	2.62	2.39	2.23	2.12	2.03	1.96	1.90	1.85	1.69	1.53	1.38	1.28	1.12
1,000	3.85	3.00	2.61	2.38	2.22	2.10	2.02	1.95	1.89	1.84	1.67	1.52	1.36	1.26	1.08
∞	3.84	2.99	2.60	2.37	2.21	2.09	2.01	1.94	1.88	1.83	1.66	1.51	1.35	1.24	1.00
1	4,052	4,999	5,403	5,625	5,764	5,859	5,928	5,981	6,022	6,056	6,158	6,238	6,302	6,334	6,366
2	98.49	99.01	99.17	99.25	99.30	99.33	99.34	99.36	99.38	99.40	99.43	99.46	99.48	99.49	99.50
3	34.12	30.81	29.46	28.71	28.24	27.91	27.67	27.49	27.34	27.23	26.87	26.58	26.30	26.23	26.12
4	21.20	18.00	16.69	15.98	15.52	15.21	14.98	14.80	14.66	14.54	14.19	13.91	13.69	13.57	13.46
5	16.26	13.27	12.06	11.39	10.97	10.67	10.45	10.27	10.15	10.05	9.72	9.45	9.24	9.13	9.02
6	13.74	10.92	9.78	9.15	8.75	8.47	8.26	8.10	7.98	7.87	7.56	7.30	7.09	6.99	6.88
7	12.25	9.55	8.45	7.85	7.46	7.19	7.00	6.84	6.71	6.62	6.31	6.05	5.85	5.75	5.65
8	11.26	8.65	7.59	7.01	6.63	6.37	6.19	6.03	5.91	5.82	5.52	5.27	5.06	4.96	4.86
9	10.56	8.02	6.99	6.42	6.06	5.80	5.62	5.47	5.35	5.26	4.96	4.72	4.51	4.41	4.31
10	10.04	7.56	6.55	5.99	5.64	5.39	5.21	5.06	4.95	4.85	4.56	4.32	4.12	4.01	3.91
15	8.68	6.36	5.42	4.89	4.56	4.32	4.14	4.00	3.89	3.80	3.52	3.27	3.07	2.97	2.87
25	7.77	5.57	4.68	4.18	3.86	3.63	3.46	3.32	3.21	3.13	2.85	2.61	2.40	2.29	2.17
50	7.17	5.06	4.20	3.72	3.41	3.18	3.02	2.88	2.78	2.70	2.42	2.17	1.94	1.82	1.68
100	6.90	4.82	3.98	3.51	3.20	2.99	2.82	2.69	2.59	2.51	2.22	1.96	1.73	1.59	1.43
500	6.69	4.65	3.82	3.36	3.06	2.84	2.68	2.55	2.45	2.36	2.07	1.81	1.56	1.41	1.18
1,000	6.66	4.62	3.80	3.34	3.04	2.82	2.66	2.53	2.43	2.34	2.05	1.79	1.54	1.38	1.11
∞	6.64	4.60	3.78	3.32	3.02	2.80	2.64	2.51	2.41	2.32	2.03	1.77	1.52	1.36	1.00

* By permission from G. A. Wadsworth and J. G. Bryan, *Introduction to Probability and Random Variables*, McGraw-Hill Book Company, Inc., New York, 1960.

315

Table A-8
Student's *t* Distribution*

Degrees of freedom *n*	Probability of a value greater than the table entry					
	.005	.01	.025	.05	.1	.15
1	63.657	31.821	12.706	6.314	3.078	1.963
2	9.925	6.965	4.303	2.920	1.886	1.386
3	5.841	4.541	3.182	2.353	1.638	1.250
4	4.604	3.747	2.776	2.132	1.533	1.190
5	4.032	3.365	2.571	2.015	1.476	1.156
6	3.707	3.143	2.447	1.943	1.440	1.134
7	3.499	2.998	2.365	1.895	1.415	1.119
8	3.355	2.896	2.306	1.860	1.397	1.108
9	3.250	2.821	2.262	1.833	1.383	1.100
10	3.169	2.764	2.228	1.812	1.372	1.093
11	3.106	2.718	2.201	1.796	1.363	1.088
12	3.055	2.681	2.179	1.782	1.356	1.083
13	3.012	2.650	2.160	1.771	1.350	1.079
14	2.977	2.624	2.145	1.761	1.345	1.076
15	2.947	2.602	2.131	1.753	1.341	1.074
16	2.921	2.583	2.120	1.746	1.337	1.071
17	2.898	2.567	2.110	1.740	1.333	1.069
18	2.878	2.552	2.101	1.734	1.330	1.067
19	2.861	2.539	2.093	1.729	1.328	1.066
20	2.845	2.528	2.086	1.725	1.325	1.064
21	2.831	2.518	2.080	1.721	1.323	1.063
22	2.819	2.508	2.074	1.717	1.321	1.061
23	2.807	2.500	2.069	1.714	1.319	1.060
24	2.797	2.492	2.064	1.711	1.318	1.059
25	2.787	2.485	2.060	1.708	1.316	1.058
26	2.779	2.479	2.056	1.706	1.315	1.058
27	2.771	2.473	2.052	1.703	1.314	1.057
28	2.763	2.467	2.048	1.701	1.313	1.056
29	2.756	2.462	2.045	1.699	1.311	1.055
30	2.750	2.457	2.042	1.697	1.310	1.055
∞	2.576	2.326	1.960	1.645	1.282	1.036

* This table is reproduced from *Statistical Methods for Research Workers*, 6th ed., with the generous permission of the author, Professor R. A. Fisher, and the publishers, Oliver & Boyd, Ltd., Edinburgh.

Table A-8 (*Continued*)

Degrees of freedom n	Probability of a value greater than the table entry					
	.2	.25	.3	.35	.4	.45
1	1.376	1.000	.727	.510	.325	.158
2	1.061	.816	.617	.445	.289	.142
3	.978	.765	.584	.424	.277	.137
4	.941	.741	.569	.414	.271	.134
5	.920	.727	.559	.408	.267	.132
6	.906	.718	.553	.404	.265	.131
7	.896	.711	.549	.402	.263	.130
8	.889	.706	.546	.399	.262	.130
9	.883	.703	.543	.398	.261	.129
10	.879	.700	.542	.397	.260	.129
11	.876	.697	.540	.396	.260	.129
12	.873	.695	.539	.395	.259	.128
13	.870	.694	.538	.394	.259	.128
14	.868	.692	.537	.393	.258	.128
15	.866	.691	.536	.393	.258	.128
16	.865	.690	.535	.392	.258	.128
17	.863	.689	.534	.392	.257	.128
18	.862	.688	.534	.392	.257	.127
19	.861	.688	.533	.391	.257	.127
20	.860	.687	.533	.391	.257	.127
21	.859	.686	.532	.391	.257	.127
22	.858	.686	.532	.390	.256	.127
23	.858	.685	.532	.390	.256	.127
24	.857	.685	.531	.390	.256	.127
25	.856	.684	.531	.390	.256	.127
26	.856	.684	.531	.390	.256	.127
27	.855	.684	.531	.389	.256	.127
28	.855	.683	.530	.389	.256	.127
29	.854	.683	.530	.389	.256	.127
30	.854	.683	.530	.389	.256	.127
∞	.842	.674	.524	.385	.253	.126

Index